Nile Nightshade

CALIFORNIA STUDIES IN FOOD AND CULTURE
Darra Goldstein, Editor

Nile Nightshade

AN EGYPTIAN CULINARY HISTORY
OF THE TOMATO

Anny Gaul

UNIVERSITY OF CALIFORNIA PRESS

University of California Press
Oakland, California

© 2025 by Anny Gaul

All rights reserved.

Library of Congress Cataloging-in-Publication Data

Names: Gaul, Anny, author
Title: Nile nightshade : an Egyptian culinary history of the tomato / Anny Gaul.
Other titles: California studies in food and culture 87.
Description: Oakland, California : University of California Press, [2025] | Series: California studies in food and culture ; vol 87 | Includes bibliographical references and index.
Identifiers: LCCN 2025026631 (print) | LCCN 2025026632 (ebook) | ISBN 9780520409132 cloth | ISBN 9780520409149 paperback | ISBN 9780520409156 ebook
Subjects: LCSH: Cooking (Tomatoes) | Cooking, Egyptian | Tomatoes—Social aspects—Egypt
Classification: LCC TX803.T6 G38 2025 (print) | LCC TX803.T6 (ebook) | DDC 641.6/56420962—dc23/eng/20250702
LC record available at https://lccn.loc.gov/2025026631
LC ebook record available at https://lccn.loc.gov/2025026632

Manufactured in the United States of America

GPSR Authorized Representative: Easy Access System Europe, Mustamäe tee 50, 10621 Tallinn, Estonia, gpsr.requests@easproject.com

34 33 32 31 30 29 28 27 26 25
10 9 8 7 6 5 4 3 2 1

publication supported by a grant from
The Community Foundation for Greater New Haven
as part of the *Urban Haven Project*

For those who feed us

CONTENTS

List of Illustrations x
Acknowledgments xiii
A Note on Units of Measurement xvii
Chronology xviii

Introduction 1

1 · Tomato Trajectories: From Mexico to Misr 22

2 · How Do You Say "Tomato" in Egyptian? 46

3 · *Magnuna ya Oota*: Tomato as Complaint 73

4 · Defining Egyptian Taste: Tomatoes in Domestic Cookbooks 102

5 · Creating Egyptian Flavor: Tomatoes in Home Kitchens 126

6 · Red Stew, Green Stew: Cooking Okra in the Nile Valley 155

Conclusion: How Tomatoes Became Egyptian 182

Notes 191
Bibliography 237
Index 261

ILLUSTRATIONS

MAPS

1. Egypt *xx*
2. The Mediterranean Sea *27*
3. The Indian Ocean *34*

TABLE

1. Feddans used for tomato cultivation in Egypt, 1929 *63*

FIGURES

1. African eggplant *49*
2. *Baladi* tomato *61*
3. Tomato consumption in Egypt, 1958–59, 1964–65, and 1974–75 *76*
4. Tomato production in Egypt, 1961–94 *85*
5. Feddans used for tomato cultivation by region, 1961 and 1981 *86*
6. Total feddans used for tomato cultivation in Egypt, 1961–94 *86*
7. Tomato yields in Egypt, 1961–94 *87*
8. Tomato supply and prices at Alexandria's Nuzha vegetable market, 1955–57 *91*
9. Kaha tomato sauce advertisement, 1956 *135*

10. Tomato products, Cairo supermarket, 2024 *153*
11. Wooden mifrak (hand blender) *179*
12. and 13. Tomato sculptures by Yasmine El Meleegy, from *Future Farms (Organic)*, 2023 *188*

ACKNOWLEDGMENTS

My name is on the cover of this book, but producing scholarship is a collective activity. This project was nourished by an abundance of support, knowledge, and labor generously granted by many people.

My first words of gratitude go to the families who opened their homes and kitchens to me in Egypt as well as in Jordan, Lebanon, Morocco, and Palestine. Their hospitality humbles me. I hope this book honors their generosity. Interviewees have been anonymized, but they have my deepest thanks.

I have learned from the best teachers. David Layton, Barbara Goodloe, Patricia Berini, and Robert Corbin changed the way I engage with the world. Bassam Frangieh, Belkacem Baccouche, Khaled Snobar, Sayyed Daifallah, Heba Salem, and Mohammad Alahmad nurtured my love of Arabic. I am especially thankful for the staff and faculty of the CASA program at the American University in Cairo. In graduate school I learned from many brilliant and committed scholars, including Osama Abi-Mershed, Fida Adely, Rochelle Davis, Sylvie Durmelat, Noura Erakat, and Ted Swedenburg. As members of my dissertation committee, Kathryn de Luna, Jonathan Smolin, and Judith Tucker were gracious, challenging, and supportive in equal measure. Throughout my graduate studies, Elliott Colla encouraged me to spend as much time in Egypt as I could and to think with a wide range of disciplines and influences; this book could never have happened had I not been able to do both of those things. At the University of Maryland, I have been surrounded by many wonderful colleagues and mentors, including Valerie Anishchenkova, Luka Arsenjuk, and Michele Mason. I am especially appreciative of many enriching conversations with Ahmed Hanafy about the nuances of meaning in several of the book's Arabic sources.

This project departed more significantly from my dissertation than I expected; it was therefore especially helpful to present unfinished pieces of it to a range of audiences. For their invitations and feedback, I thank Siam Bhayro, Ariana Gunderson, Sucharita Kanjilal, Golbarg Rekabtalaei, and Heather Sharkey. I am deeply grateful to Jessica Barnes for arranging a workshop at the University of South Carolina at a crucial early stage of the project's tomato turn; I relished the opportunity to think through food studies frameworks in conversation with Noha Fikry in a workshop designed by Mennat-Allah El Dorry and hosted by the Brussels Institute for Advanced Studies.

Many friends and colleagues devoted time to reading drafts of chapters. For their insights and suggestions, I thank Randa Aboubakr, Febe Armanios, Jessica Barnes, Jennifer Dueck, Amanda Erickson, Sofia Fenner, Alicia Gaul, Marya Hannun, Nour Kamel, Harry Kashdan, Nancy Linthicum, Kate O'Brien, Mounira Soliman, and Juliet Tempest. The manuscript benefited in particular from the generous feedback of Marilyn Booth, Anne Meneley, and Jayeeta Sharma.

In Cairo, support from the American Research Center in Egypt, particularly from Djodi Deutsch and Mary Sadek, was indispensable. I also thank the staffs of the Netherlands-Flemish Institute in Cairo, the Women and Memory Forum, Dar al-Kutub, and Dar al-Watha'iq. My life in Egypt was enriched by the company and conversation of Randa Aboubakr, Yousef Anwar, Hala Barakat, Mennat-Allah El Dorry, Noha Fikry, Hoda Elsadda, Hanan Hammad, Magda Hasabelnaby, Amira Howeidy, Sohila Khaled, Bassem Khalifa, William and Emana Kopycki, Samia Mehrez, Kelby Olson, Nada Ramadan, Rehaam Romero, and Mounira Soliman. I count myself especially lucky to have worked with Nour Kamel and Mariam Boctor on their "Mukawen" event series in February 2024, which provided a vital opportunity for reflection and discussion at a crucial stage of research. Humphrey Davies was a pivotal figure in my work's gradual turn toward tomatoes; his death is a loss to so many of us who remain grateful for the knowledge and encouragement he offered so liberally.

The research underpinning this book and the dissertation from which it sprouted required a lot of funding. With appreciation, I acknowledge financial support from the American Friends of the Oxford Food Symposium, the American Research Center in Egypt, the Council of American Overseas Research Centers, the Social Science Research Council's Mellon International Dissertation Research Fellowship, the American Institute for Maghrib Studies, Georgetown University's Graduate School of Arts & Sciences, the

Bibliographical Society of America, the Pine Tree Foundation, and the National Endowment for the Humanities. (Nothing expressed in this book, however, should be taken to reflect the views of any of the funders named here.) Essential support in the form of both money and time was provided by the University of Maryland's Division of Research, the College of Arts and Humanities, and School of Languages, Literatures, and Cultures. I thank Meghann Babo, Chanel Briscoe, Amanda Dykema, Charlotte Yuk Fan Tai, and Mel Scullen for making that support possible.

Nothing is "discovered" in a library or archive that was not preserved, catalogued, and made accessible through the labor and foresight of so many. I thank the workers at all the libraries and archives consulted for this book; input and advice from James Downs at the Arab World Documentation Unit at the University of Exeter, Stephen Urgola at the American University in Cairo, and the used booksellers of Cairo were particularly instrumental. I also thank the many people who pointed me to sources, gifted me used cookbooks, or otherwise provided ideas, advice, and input that I never would have found on my own: Youssef Ben Ismail, Houssem Eddine Chachia, Mennat-Allah El Dorry, Beth Godbee, Jonathan Guyer, Will Hanley, Mary Işın, Alicia Kennedy, Laleh Khalili, Yasmine El Meleegy, Taylor Moore, Nawal Nasrallah, Hussein Omar, Basma Radwan, Arafat Razzaque, Claudia Roden, Khaled El Samman, Salma Serry, Suzanne Zeidy, and Sami Zubaida. At the University of California Press, Niels Hooper has been a thoughtful, strategic, and enthusiastic supporter of this project. Nora Becker and Emily Park provided expert and patient guidance preparing the manuscript, and Amy Smith Bell's brilliant copy editing sharpened and clarified the entire text. Despite all this abundance, errors inevitably remain; I can only hope to learn from them.

Friends are to life what salt is to tomatoes; what a joy it is to share tomatoes and salt and everything else with Ruqiyyah Anbar-Shaheen, Emma Alpert, Zeina Azzam, Marley Carroll, Mary Elston, Amanda Erickson, Samia Errazzouki, Olivia Gagnon, Jonathan Guyer, Christina Hanhardt, Kelli Harris, Nour Joudah, Andrew Kadi, Rana Khoury, Mimi Kirk, Tim Loh, Jared Malsin, Grace Murray, Graham Pitts, Marcia Lynx Qualey, Claudia Setubal, and Antonio Tahhan. Particular thanks to Jyana Browne for the stationery, Sofia Fenner for always helping me find a way forward, Caroline Howe for laughter and solace, Kate O'Brien for reminding me to plan the next journey, Juliet Tempest for delivering the best meal at the eleventh hour, and Harry Kashdan for food, wine, and company. Marya Hannun is the best academic partner in the world; her friendship makes me a better writer and a better person. I am grateful to my brother Chip for short bike rides and long conversations, and to my parents, John and Alicia, for their endless and wholehearted support.

My godmother Tona died the day I defended my dissertation, but she is everywhere in the pages of this book. Her love of cooking and her conviction that there are endless ways to create "good food" have animated my work at every step.

For steadfast companionship and for reminding me that no matter how pressing the deadline there is always time for a meal, a nap, and a walk, my final words of gratitude are for Radar and Xander.

A NOTE ON UNITS OF MEASUREMENT

Land area: The common unit of measurement in Egypt is the feddan; 1 feddan is equivalent to 0.42 hectares or 1.04 acres.

Weight: 1 metric ton is equivalent to 1,000 kilograms or 10,000 hectograms. A cantar is an Egyptian unit of weight equivalent to about 99 pounds or 45 kilograms.

CHRONOLOGY

5000 BCE	A semidomesticated ancestor of the tomato is carried from South America to Mesoamerica, where it is fully domesticated
ca. 1650–1550 BCE	Increase in Nubian pottery at the Egyptian fortress of Askut indicates interaction of culinary traditions across shifting frontiers between Egypt and Nubia
1200 BCE	Black pepper used in the mummification of Ramses II
332–30 BCE	Ptolemaic period in Egypt; durum wheat and other Greek agricultural innovations introduced
7th–8th centuries CE	Following the death of the Prophet Muhammad (632), Islamic conquests incorporate territory from Southwest Asia to the western Mediterranean, including Egypt (from 639) and Iberia (from 711)
969–1171 CE	Fatimid dynasty rules Egypt, likely facilitating the incorporation of foods from elsewhere in North Africa into Egyptian cuisine
11th–15th centuries CE	Foodstuffs of Asian origin—including ginger, turmeric, cardamom, and Sichuan pepper—appear in significant quantities in Egyptian port of Qusayr, indicating increase in Indian Ocean trade
1415	Roman Catholic rulers of Portugal begin series of incursions in Africa with attack on Moroccan port of Ceuta
1492	Granada, the last Muslim-ruled stronghold in Spain, falls to Roman Catholic monarchs; Spanish Jews ordered to convert to Christianity or be expelled; departure of first Spanish voyage to reach the Americas
1497	Portuguese Jews forcibly converted to Christianity; coffee attested in Sinai

1498	Portuguese reach Calicut in India
1499–1526	Spanish Muslims expelled or forcibly converted to Christianity
1513	Portuguese besiege Aden
1517	Ottomans secure territory in Egypt and Yemen, establishing the Red Sea as a bulwark against Portuguese incursions in the Indian Ocean
1519–1521	Spanish conquest of Mexico; earliest possible departure of tomatoes from the Americas; Spanish reach the Philippines (1521)
1557	Portuguese establish colony of Macao
1565–1815	Manila Galleons regularly cross Pacific, connecting Spanish-held territories in Mexico and the Philippines
1608	Tomatoes make a fleeting appearance in the records of a hospital in Seville
1609–1614	Moriscos (Muslim converts to Christianity) and their descendants expelled from Spain
1658	Portuguese in Java described as using the term *tomatas*
1671	Tomatoes recorded as present in Moroccan gardens and diets
1692	First European recipes with tomatoes printed in Naples
1738	Reports of tomatoes in Algeria and Tunisia
1755	Attestation of Malay usage of the word *tomatte*
1798–1801	Napoleon invades Egypt, where French botanists document the tomato's presence

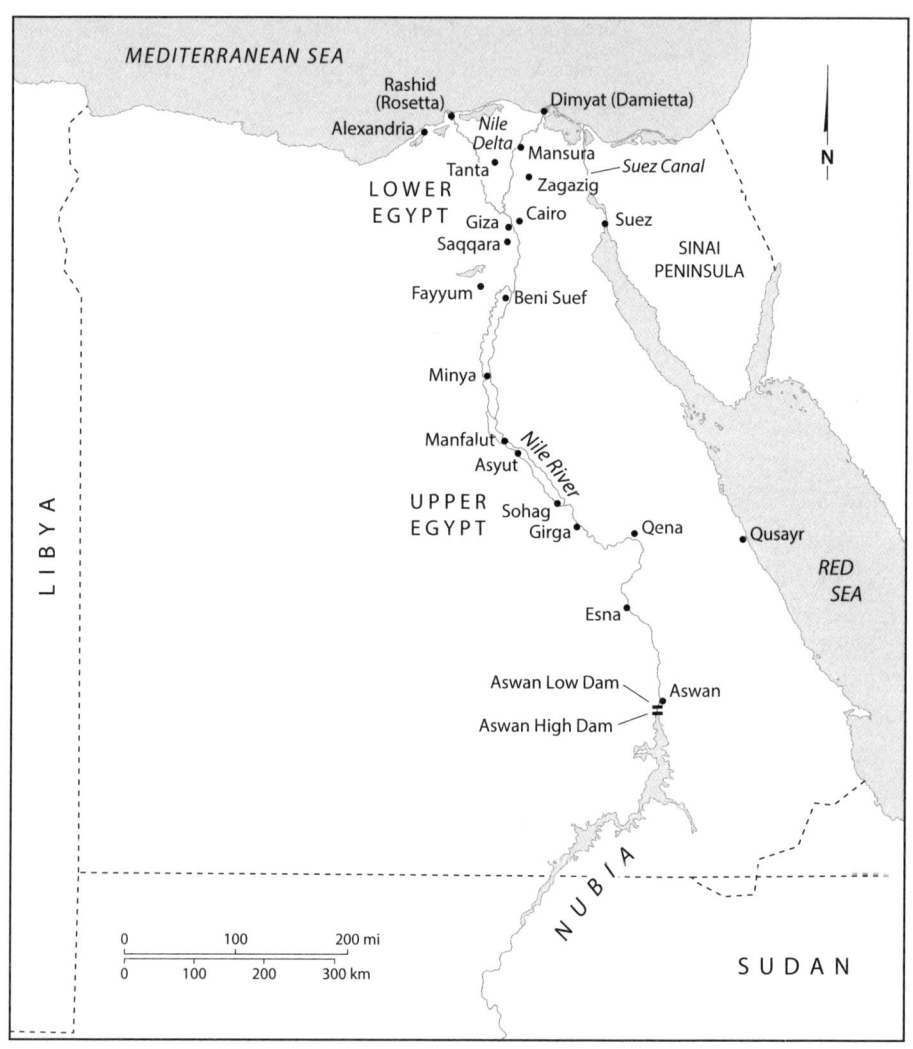

MAP 1. Egypt. Map by Bill Nelson.

Introduction

THE MORE TIME I SPENT in Egypt, the more I saw tomatoes everywhere.

When I moved to Cairo as a graduate student in 2013, they were in bowls of *koshari* from the shop down the street: rice, lentils, and pasta were topped with tomato sauce and crispy onions. When my roommate called her grandmother for instructions on how to cook the duck we'd bought from the market, she told us to add tomato paste to the basting mixture we applied as it roasted to perfection in the oven. And no matter the season, the nearby vegetable stand always had a ready supply of tomatoes.

Later, as I conducted doctoral research on (and in) Egypt's home kitchens, tomatoes were a recurring presence in my fieldwork. In a Cairo apartment above a carpenter's shop, the sounds and smells of freshly cut wood wafted through the windows as I shared a family meal that included a generous helping of noodles and tomato sauce spiked with a hint of hot pepper. In another family's apartment across town, I snacked on a dish of tiny eggplants fried then stuffed with chopped onions, parsley, and tomatoes seasoned with garlic, cumin, and salt. On a warm fall day in Alexandria, I ate fish wrapped in foil and baked with slices of tomato and onion and whole hot peppers. On a winter night in the same city a few months later, I was treated to *kamuniyya*, a cumin-heavy chicken stew made with onion and puréed tomato. Tomatoes were a perennial throughline that linked street food and home cooking, connecting Egyptian dishes of a half-dozen different origins.

Tomatoes also punctuated the political and economic discourse of postrevolutionary Egypt in the 2010s. A flurry of memes and cartoons decried the high price of tomatoes, which function as a "low-tech economic indicator of precarity" in Egypt: an essential item that frequently strains the household budgets of ordinary people.[1] When the Egyptian pound was floated in 2016, causing runaway prices and shortages of imported goods, a video of a woman lamenting the price of tomatoes went viral. The same year, a song about tomatoes by the Egyptian singer Saad El Soghayar opened with a line highlighting tomatoes' redness, sweetness, and propensity to fluctuate wildly in price.[2] Whenever I return to Egypt, I find that the cost of tomatoes is still a topic of conversation and popular complaint.

Many single-commodity histories insist on the exceptional qualities of their subject, bestowing them with the power to change the world.[3] This book is different. It tells the story of a vegetable so commonplace that its presence in dishes is often implied, not stated. The tomato is Egypt's most important horticultural crop, yet it remains overshadowed and outpaced by the powerhouse field crops that make up the vast majority of the country's agricultural production. The tomato is everywhere in Egypt, not as a star ingredient but as an ordinary staple—the scaffolding of a modern culinary culture, hiding in plain sight. It is the backdrop of this story, not its hero. I tell the history of the tomato in Egypt not to argue that it changed the world, but because its omnipresence makes it an apt lens for reexamining the relationship between food, place, and community in a modern society.

Despite its ubiquity today, the tomato's popularity in Egypt is a recent phenomenon. Native to the Americas, it was widely cultivated in the Nile Valley by the nineteenth century and became available year-round to Egyptian consumers in the twentieth. Today Egypt consistently ranks among the world's top tomato producers, and nearly all the tomatoes that Egyptian farmers grow are consumed domestically.[4] How did tomatoes become so important to Egyptian cooking and agriculture so quickly? How were they used by cookbook authors and educators to articulate visions of Egyptian taste, and what differences of geography, class, and ethnicity did their visions elide or uphold? How, alternatively, were tomatoes deployed in contestations or refusals of state power? What can tomatoes tell us about the political significance of culinary knowledge and domestic labor—particularly of subalterns and women? How can food lead us to reexamine and unsettle the ways that a collective "we" is forged and experienced in connection with a particular place? How can we conceptualize food and cuisine beyond the confines of nationalism? These are the questions at the heart of this book.

Drawing on tomatoes to provide both material context and a narrative device, I tell a history of modern Egypt that challenges the framework of the nation-state. Instead of focusing exclusively on ideologies or institutions, I consider how sensibilities and attachments associated with cooking and eating informed the way that Egyptians imagined themselves as a collectivity. I am interested in what the tomato can tell us about what it means for something to taste Egyptian, and the discourses and practices that shaped, shifted, and reproduced that "sense" of identity and belonging. While nationalism and the state play important roles in this story, the tomato invites an understanding of Egyptian-ness not just as a national category or a product of state institutions but as a structure of feeling.

Raymond Williams describes structures of feeling as a framework for looking beyond "formal and systematic beliefs" to consider "meanings and values as they are actively lived and felt" (and, in our case, cooked and tasted) as well.[5] Accordingly, this book traces tomatoes through formal expressions of food's role in the making of Egypt and Egyptians: prescriptive articulations of modern cuisine, school meals planned by state officials, and recipes included in gendered school curricula. But I also consider the practices, sensibilities, and expressive forms that implicated the tomato in Egyptians' everyday lives. I argue that these popular experiences were not merely private or personal but had social and material dimensions as well, and that their relationship to the dominant ideologies of their time—from Egyptian nationalism to pan-Arabism to modern domesticity—was never straightforward.

RELOCATING TOMATO HISTORY

In the past twenty years more than a half-dozen popular and scholarly books have been devoted to the tomato. Some fall into the category of commodity histories that follow, as Kyla Wazana Tompkins describes, "a single commodity as it is introduced to a Western consumer demographic, marketed, and disseminated through various commercial venues."[6] Her framing highlights that many such books begin with the premise that an object's history starts at the point of European "discovery." Others have critiqued the genre for promoting narratives that conveniently omit the forces of exploitation and injustice that have historically rendered certain ingredients into "accessible" commodities.[7]

These tendencies are evident in many of the "tomato books" on the market that explain the integration of the tomato into European and North American foodways. They often devote considerable space to the development of optimal varieties by US and European agronomists—with little acknowledgment of the Mesoamericans who domesticated the plant and developed a wide range of varieties that they cultivated and cooked with for thousands of years before the Spanish arrived.[8] That said, it would be a mistake to paint all tomato books with the same brush. David Gentilcore's work unsettles assumptions about tomatoes' history in Italy, highlighting the importance of local agricultural, culinary, and social factors to understanding the tomato's reception in different contexts.[9] Barry Estabrook's *Tomatoland* and Deborah Barndt's *Tangled Routes* offer essential analyses of the labor, migration, gender, and exploitation inherent to the production of the corporate tomato in North America.

This book draws from their approaches and also builds on critiques within food studies that have pushed back against "ostensibly global works" that relegate non-Western gastronomic traditions to the past, casting them as mere precursors to modern transformations of food systems and cuisines in Europe or the United States.[10] In 2021 six of the top ten tomato producers in the world were countries outside of both Western Europe and North America: China, India, Turkey, Brazil, Nigeria, and Egypt.[11] Studying the tomato in a place like Egypt reveals a familiar vegetable in a new light. For example, I situate the tomato within longer histories of edible nightshade plants in Africa and Asia. By the time novel edible nightshades like tomatoes, potatoes, and peppers were introduced to Egypt from the Americas, Egyptians had been growing and eating eggplants (*Solanum melongena*), another introduced nightshade, for centuries. The naming conventions that Egyptians applied to tomatoes, which included compound terms like "red eggplant," suggest that they recognized the botanical connection between the two. This likely facilitated the tomato's integration into Egyptian farms, gardens, and kitchens. I ground the tomato's cultural history in local dynamics of labor and capital, tracing it through Egypt's connections to regional and global trading networks and exploring how the uneven distribution of resources concentrated Egyptian tomato production in certain regions and on certain kinds of farms. I also use the tomato to examine the unpaid gendered labor of the home kitchen and the devaluing of the culinary knowledge and labor of domestic workers.[12]

Ultimately I draw on the tomato's capacious global history to question how food informs the kinds of collectivities that we tend to associate with specific spaces—most obviously, the isomorphic mapping of a given ethnicity onto the territory of a nation-state. One of the most common ways we define and categorize food cultures applies this logic to assert (or assume) the existence of "national cuisines." As one influential work on food and nationalism points out, "cuisine is a cultural product inherently linked to a common language and a specific geographical space."[13] But just like nations, national cuisines are created, not naturally occurring entities. Krishnendu Ray puts it bluntly: "There is no national cuisine without the violence of exclusion and repression."[14] A robust body of scholarship has critiqued the concept of national cuisines by examining the terms of their construction, recognizing that "food may indeed reinforce essentialized notions of national identity, yet also simultaneously contest these ideas through the assertion of heterogeneous difference."[15] Michelle King proposes "culinary nationalism" as an approach to studying food and the nation that considers "a dynamic process of creation and contestation," rather than taking for granted static canons of national foods and the territorial borders that claim to enclose them.[16] While I draw upon these insights, I aim to critically examine food, place, and collective belonging in ways that deliberately decenter the nation. To do so, I draw upon two essential concepts from food writing: terroir and mobility.

The concept of terroir was formulated in nineteenth-century France and is frequently deployed today as a riposte to the homogenizing effects of industrial food.[17] Initially defined as the soil that made French wine unique, terroir "quickly came to mean the local environment in which wine was produced" and was then extrapolated to include ingredients and meals.[18] This formulation of the relationship between food and place correlates with a very specific understanding of community—like the nation, it rests on the idea that certain people have inhabited a particular place over time. To paraphrase Rachel Laudan, this approach "makes no sense as history."[19] As Ray puts it, the notion of terroir is "structurally and inescapably anti-immigrant, because immigrants are people out of place and terroir is all about some people in place for a very long time."[20] Tompkins critiques the way that "romanticized and insufficiently theorized attachments to 'local' or organic foodways" can at times "suspiciously echo nativist ideological formations."[21] In other words, when read ahistorically or without attention to the movement of people, culture, and capital, terroir can bolster exclusion and produce or exacerbate inequalities.

As an alternative to nation and terroir as frameworks for understanding the connections between food, place, and community, I turn to the work of Claudia Roden. Born in Cairo in 1936 to a Sephardic Jewish family with roots in Istanbul and Aleppo, Roden left Egypt in 1956 for London, where she embarked upon a career as a culinary anthropologist and cookbook author amid a "diasporic network" of other "Middle Eastern expatriates."[22] The process of reassembling the recipes of her dispersed community (published in 1968 as *A Book of Middle Eastern Food*) "introduced Roden to the regional breadth of what she had considered a local, personal culture."[23]

Roden's work embraced the specificity of variations tied to particular places within a broad regional framing—the "Middle East"—unlinked from national or ethnic markers.[24] Roden's 1996 *The Book of Jewish Food* developed a more explicit framework for conceptualizing complex culinary cultures through her efforts to define Jewish food. "The main influence on the development and shaping of [Jews'] cuisine was their mobility—their propensity to move from one place to another," she writes. This approach encompassed both the Jewish diaspora's changing relationship to place and the local specificities of Jewish communities throughout the world.[25] Roden's work, which acknowledges the violent displacements that often drove the mobility she discusses, offers an alternative model for thinking through the forms of belonging and self-identification that emerge, or can be traced, through food—by embracing mobility rather than fixity and beginning from "the premise that spaces have always been hierarchically interconnected, instead of naturally disconnected."[26]

In this book that means approaching the tomato as an ingredient that connected farms to kitchens and markets to homes. It entails understanding Cairo as a place where food practices from Egypt's rural south persisted in the kitchens of migrants in northern cities. It also means using food history to reconsider how factors like human migration and environmental terrain inform the categories that order our world. Why do we associate Egypt more with the "Middle East" than with Africa? Why is Egypt affiliated more closely with the Mashriq than the Maghrib? Food's propensity to move across human-made boundaries and its myriad variations in everyday practice make it a powerful conceptual tool for unsettling what has come to appear obvious. Scholars who have traced the history and production of ordinary food items have illuminated how the most basic elements of everyday life can come to be constructed as natural, indigenous, and timeless—even though they may have been very recently introduced.[27] To frame the culinary communities connected by the tomato in Egypt, I use the concept of the public to trace forms of belonging that arose in modern Egypt with the help of the tomato.

ON CULINARY PUBLICS

In her book *Intimate Eating*, Anita Mannur argues that publics informed by practices of eating can allow us to "reimagine forms of belonging."[28] Building on her work, I propose the culinary public as a framework for narrating and interpreting the history of modern Egypt. My definition of this concept borrows from work on the public by Michael Warner and a number of other scholars: First, a public is anonymous, "a relation among strangers."[29] In this sense a public resonates with the "imagined community" of the nation, in Benedict Anderson's formulation. Both are facilitated by modern media forms, from print to television and the internet, which circulate among and link people who may never meet. Both concepts are productive of "social imaginaries" that forge connections between strangers.

But a public need not impose the claims to coherence implied by nationalism; theorists have frequently emphasized the public as a site where differences are assumed and negotiated. The public is therefore a flexible concept. It is sometimes "the people organized as the nation" or some other politically or territorially defined community; but it may also refer to a particular audience for an event or text or a transnational diaspora formed through migration.[30] A public is productive—a site of "poetic world-making."[31] That does not always mean that a public necessarily corresponds to a dominant form of community or collectivity, or that it has been formulated explicitly to counter one (although sometimes publics do these things). Publics are multiple, often overlapping, and sometimes fuzzy or ephemeral—a sense of "being connected to strangers in a kind of nebulous *communitas*."[32]

Finally, as feminist scholars have demonstrated, publics are intimate—they presume familiarity and are constituted through shared sentiments, attachments, and experiences. They can be spaces for "generating proximities and intimacies across difference."[33] This dimension of publics draws on a body of critique that has interrogated the "separate spheres" paradigm, a metaphor that refers to "a historically constituted ideology of gender relations that holds that men and women occupy distinct social, affective, and occupational realms."[34] This ideology presupposes a private sphere in opposition to a public one, with the former designated as the domain of women and the latter of men.[35]

Feminist and queer critiques have questioned understandings of the public informed by the separate spheres paradigm, pointing out how the binary construct of public and private domains fails to grasp variables of "race, sexuality, class, nation, empire, affect, region, and occupation," while ignoring—and even downplaying or discouraging—the ways that public and private realms intertwine in practice.[36] Many critical approaches to food studies have provided rich grounds for refuting the notion that public and private are mutually exclusive and demonstrating how domestic practices shape public cultures. Scholars have argued, for example, that conceptions of taste connect private experience to public identities, and have documented the role of women's unpaid domestic labor in preparing foods sold on public streets.[37]

My notion of a "culinary public" is nourished by Mannur's "eating public," which recognizes that although eating is an intimate act, "each gesture of eating is laced with multiple meanings that acquire differential public meanings."[38] It borrows too from Emiko Ohnuki-Tierney's discussion of commensality as it relates to staple foods. She describes eating together as a form of intimate interaction that establishes "a sense of community, or *we*," while the foods anchoring that commensality figure into the identification of a broader social group whose members eat the same food, even though they may never meet one another.[39] The culinary public offers a means to reframe imagined communities, polities, and social worlds through food. The term *culinary*, derived from the Latin for "kitchen," focuses centrally on the discourses and practices of cooking. But just as I seek to restore the supposedly "private" realm of the home kitchen to the formation of a "public," I also aim to use the culinary public as a framework for connecting questions of production—the farm and market that supply the kitchen as well as the industries and infrastructures that furnish it—to cultures of consumption. In summary, publics offer ways of imagining Egypt—and by extension, other categories of culture and identity that are conventionally mapped onto discrete spaces or groups—beyond the narrower frames of nation and state. Unlike the nation, with its claims to coherence and antiquity, the "we" of the public can be fickle and fragile. But it is a conceptual container for describing and making sense of historical evidence and cultural material—a framework for thinking differently about collectivities and belonging.

Culinary publics appear in different guises throughout this book. Chapter 1 speculates about the arrival of the tomato to Egypt before a modern culinary public existed on a national scale, highlighting many of the diverse influences that shaped Egypt from beyond its territorial borders. Chapter 2 considers how a shared set of words that Egyptians used to refer to tomatoes created a vernacular public sphere through a common culinary lexicon. Chapters 2 and 4 trace nationally oriented culinary publics in cookbooks that prescribed specific visions of Egyptian taste for relatively narrow readerships. Chapter 3 describes a statist public formed in relationship to the state's management of Egypt's food system, including the ambiguous standing of the tomato as a popular staple. And chapters 5 and 6 trace a culinary public defined by

Egyptian flavor: a varied and diverse collectivity informed by practices and sensibilities in which tomatoes, alongside unctuous clarified butter and pods of okra, shaped forms of identification, attachment, and belonging.

These modern culinary publics materialized alongside what Rachel Laudan defines as "middling cuisine."[40] Occupying a "middling" place between the high cuisines of elites and the humbler cuisines that most of the world's population has eaten for most of human history, middling cuisines are a modern phenomenon.[41] Laudan defines them as "rich in wheat bread or other preferred carbohydrate staples, beef and other meats, and fats and sugars," and describes how they "expanded from the bourgeoisie to two new and rapidly growing social groups: the salaried middle classes and the wage-earning working classes," chiefly in major urban areas.[42] Tomatoes were a key component of the middling cuisine that emerged in twentieth-century Egypt—which borrowed from elite culinary cultures alongside popular local practices and was sustained by state subsidies of wheat bread, meat, vegetable oil, and sugar. The various Egyptian culinary publics that this book tracks tended to cohere around this kind of cuisine, although access to it varied in practice. The contours of those publics—who could participate in them, who opted to identify with them, what kinds of foods defined them—shifted over time. They changed with the tides of subsidy policies, regional tomato cultivation patterns, urban tastes, and health discourses, among many other factors.

SOVEREIGNTY AND THE DOMESTIC

In addition to the culinary public, sovereignty is another major concept that runs throughout the book. Today it is a cliché, even a "liberal platitude," to say that food is political.[43] Food writer Alicia Kennedy pushes us to specify what we mean when we say this—"to explain precisely how and why . . . food reflects governmental policy or a clearly defined worldview," for example. Approaching sovereignty as a modern form of power associated with a particular space, I explore how it rendered tomatoes a political food in two specific settings: the nation-state and the kitchen.

The nation-state is the site of a conventional form of modern state sovereignty that in theory "is fully, flatly, and evenly operative over each square centimetre of a legally demarcated territory."[44] Of course in practice the workings of state power and even the borders of Egyptian territory unfolded incrementally and unevenly over time. But the logic of this modern form of power structured understandings of what "Egyptian" meant as it was defined variously against Ottoman suzerainty or colonial forms of occupation and control, or in relationship to the Nile, seas, or land borders. Modern modes of sovereignty transformed the physical and human landscape of Egypt by excavating the Suez Canal and damming the Nile. Nile dams were a key factor in the scaling up of tomatoes to become a major crop; they also forcibly displaced Egypt's Nubians, whose homeland straddles the Egypt-Sudan border. In the wake of the Second World War, state sovereignty informed the role of food provision in the social contract between the Egyptian state and its citizens. Articulated through nationalist political and cultural movements, modern notions of sovereignty also made legible—and sensible—a culinary style that was explicitly labeled as "Egyptian" by cookbook authors. The first half of this book concentrates on the relationship between the changing nature of state sovereignty in Egypt and the production of both tomatoes and the culinary publics in which they circulated.

The second half of the book follows the tomato into the home as the site of "kitchen sovereignty," a distinct but related form of authority that played an equally important role in shaping modern Egypt. Amy Kaplan points out that the term "*domestic* has a double meaning that not only links the familial household to the nation but also imagines both in opposition to everything outside the geographic and conceptual border of the home."[45] In the same way that the public has been conceptualized in binary opposition to the private, she writes, the notion of the "domestic" (in either sense) is defined against whatever it excludes.[46] To distinguish between these linked scales through which "the domestic" operates, this book examines what I refer to as "kitchen sovereignty": a kind of modern domestic authority delegated (in theory) to housewives and practiced by home cooks—of whom most, but not all, are women in the contexts this book explores. The genre of domestic cookbooks that flourished in Egypt in the middle decades of the twentieth century (the subject of chapter 4) lays out the idealized terms of this form of sovereignty in explicit terms. The authors of these books articulated the importance of home cooking to the nation (to which it, and the unremunerated women's labor it commanded, were subordinated and instrumental). In practice, chapters 5 and 6 demonstrate, home cooks used their authority to produce a style of food that did not always accord with the dictates of cookbooks' formally articulated principles and aesthetics.

An extensive historiography documents how gender and the domestic became spheres of contestation central to discussions of nationalism and modernity in nineteenth- and twentieth-century Egypt.[47] Much of this history focuses on the vibrant women's press that materialized in Egypt starting in the late nineteenth century and women's participation in education, politics, and the formal workforce. I contribute to this scholarship by exploring the roles Egyptian women played as authors and educators; I seek to expand it by tracing "the human subjects who performed or eluded" the terms of the gender politics formally expressed in curricula and cookbooks.[48] To do so, I draw on oral histories and ethnographic methods to trace the tomato through vernacular narratives and the embodied knowledge that is central to cooking. I aim to highlight the tension that Ray observes between national culinary traditions and "the reality of everyday practices," thereby challenging totalizing and exclusionary conceptualizations of national or ethnic cuisines.[49] By locating tomatoes in formal articulations of sovereignty as well as the realm of everyday practice and experience, we can glimpse lived forms of collective identification that were often recognized as "Egyptian" but did not necessarily reflect the logics, assumptions, or priorities of nationalism or the state.

SOURCES AND METHODS

Describing the paucity of sources for studying the history of eating in the early United States, Lauren Klein writes that the "artifacts associated with eating... remain perishable in the most literal sense."[50] And yet, as the manifesto of the Italian feminist collective Rivolta Femminile states, "any history which is based on non-perishable traces" is necessarily an incomplete one.[51] The challenges of writing about embodied experiences that are not one's own and that often resist capture in textual form require an eclectic and multidisciplinary methodology.

Texts I draw on include agricultural manuals, policy reports, popular vernacular genres like protest slogans and street cries, data about tomato production, novels and poetry, film, popular magazines, and accounts written by travelers and foreign residents of Egypt. I analyze a range of cookbooks, focusing on the first century of Egyptian cookbooks in print, published between the 1870s and the 1970s.[52] These include elite manuals written for professional male chefs as well as domestic cookbooks written for housewives. To place these texts in conversation with culinary practice and vernacular forms of expression, I draw on ethnographic data and oral histories that convey the subtleties of embodied gestures and practices that are passed from person to person and seldom written down. This includes twelve oral histories that reflect the experiences and memories of Egyptian women who were born between 1940 and 1970 and currently live in Cairo and Alexandria, whom I interviewed (often multiple times) between 2015 and 2024. Most interviews were conducted in women's homes, where conversations took place in kitchens, at dinner tables, and in dialogue with family members who were also present. I supplement these accounts with oral histories published by Egyptian researchers and institutions.

While they come from a range of backgrounds, the subjects of these oral histories have several characteristics in common. They belong to a set of generations of women who learned to cook after modern domestic science was thoroughly integrated into Egypt's state school curricula but before television and the internet became prominent sources of culinary knowledge (I typically include a subject's year of birth to situate their account historically and generationally). They are also all home cooks, and nearly all are both wives and mothers. Although these women were born in various places throughout riverine Egypt, most of them established marital homes in city apartment blocks populated by families from diverse regional origins.

Because the oral histories cited here overwhelmingly reflect perspectives from Cairo and Alexandria, Egypt's two largest cities, their accounts are skewed toward urban narratives. Although there is much to be said about the culinary cultures of smaller cities and rural contexts in Egypt, they are not the primary focus of this book, except when they traveled to Cairo and Alexandria with people who migrated. Chapters that explore agricultural production tend to cluster around the vicinities of Cairo and Alexandria too, because for much of the twentieth century that is where tomato production was concentrated.[53] Even so, many of the women I interviewed invoked rural connections, either from their own childhoods or through extended family still living in the countryside. They frequently mentioned such connections in relation to culinary practices, values, and traditions—demonstrating how perceptions and memories of rural Egypt are incorporated into urban perspectives and imaginaries of what it means for something to taste Egyptian, even in Cairo and Alexandria.

Finally, oral histories capture a range of positions within what I call Egypt's "middle strata." Lucie Ryzova distinguishes between a "local Egyptian middle-class culture" that emerged in the early to mid-twentieth century and defined itself as "modern" and members of a much broader "middle strata," not all of whom identified with that culture or participated in it.[54]

Accordingly, I use the plural "middle strata" to distinguish my interviewees' social contexts from the cultural concept of the middle class. The latter reverberates throughout this book too, largely as a set of ideals that may orient desires or frame social norms but which do not always correspond precisely with the lived experiences of the middle strata. As Ryzova and others have highlighted, middle-class culture in Egypt, as elsewhere, is often identified with or as national culture. The *efendiyya*—self-consciously modern men of Egypt's new professional classes—positioned themselves as arbiters of both correct modernity and Egyptian authenticity.[55] But it does not follow that we must take their assertions for granted.

Anthropologists have pointed to the complexity of social class in Egyptian society, arguing that "class in social practice cannot be reduced to a single criterion such as income, educational level, or occupation."[56] While my oral history subjects did not share identical relationships to these criteria, they fall into a limited, "middling" range. For example, they all had some basic level of education—but some attended only primary school, while others were university graduates. Many of them (not all) could afford to pay part-time domestic workers to help with cooking, cleaning, and childcare; but none of them employed live-in domestic staff as adults, and none of them were employed as domestic workers in other women's homes. Some are the children of urban professionals; others come from working-class backgrounds and have children or grandchildren who are urban professionals. The households represented in these oral histories also enjoy proximity to Egypt's modern "middling cuisine," including access to meat (although some had more ready or frequent access than others).

My interviewees' perspectives do not represent the whole of Egyptian society—far from it. My intent is not to present this limited number of oral histories as the basis for a definitive or comprehensive account of Egyptian cuisine. Rather, I approach them as sources that illuminate aspects of Egyptian food history that have not otherwise been captured in text, mediated through individual and collective memories. Nefissa Naguib writes that memories surrounding food are "tidy and messy" at the same time: they reflect "cultural repetitions and processes," but they are refracted through an individual's experiences and preferences too.[57] These oral narratives, which are sometimes polyphonic, including the voices of other family members, offer perspectives that cannot be or have not been captured in written recipes or texts.

As Ray points out, "cooking is mostly the body doing stuff that is unarticulated."[58] In addition to the narratives themselves, I draw on fieldnotes that reflect time spent cooking, eating, and speaking about food with Egyptians since 2013—including, but not limited to, the oral history interviews. Whenever I cooked with women or discussed culinary techniques, verbal instructions were peppered with gestures and caveats that emphasized the need to monitor and influence a dish's progress with one's judgment based on its smell, visual cues, taste, and sound. My fieldnotes record and describe these embodied forms of knowledge—like the specific motion used to shake a strainer containing puréed tomato, descriptions of the texture and color of a dish, and notes about the addition of liquid to a blender when its contents are not achieving the desired consistency.

Describing observations made or memories recounted in the present is not the same as witnessing or experiencing them as they took place in the past. But Nadia Seremetakis argues that studying constellations of meaning that connect "things, spaces, gestures, and tales" can "drag the aftereffects" of past experiences into the present, offering insights into aspects of history that may be absent from conventional or official narratives.[59] She proposes that memory offers a way to study traces of history that are otherwise perishable, describing how "the senses defer the material world by changing substance into memory."[60] I approach ethnography and oral histories as one way to access otherwise unrecorded elements of history. This approach builds on a rich scholarly literature on Egypt's public and popular cultures that incorporates not only written but visual, oral, aural, and other modes of expression and experience into understandings of identity, nationalism, and "colloquial mass culture" in modern Egypt.[61]

Scholars have extended Anderson's focus on modern print vernaculars and "print capitalism" to consider the role of how Egyptian film, television, music, poetry, and theater also played a role in the formation of a modern national consciousness.[62] An expansive approach to vernacular expression is a particularly rich mode of inquiry in the Arab world because Arabic is a diglossic language, meaning that distinct registers of the language exist simultaneously. Typically these registers are categorized as "high" and "low" varieties corresponding to a formal written variety and a spoken, everyday colloquial one. While the formal variety is generally consistent across geographical contexts in a given time period, the spoken variety differs from country to country and often by region within a given country.[63] In Egypt, scholars have noted, Cairene Arabic operates as a dominant colloquial variety, frequently represented as normal, familiar, and widely understood.[64]

Scholars have also centered the body and material culture to explore how Egyptians "understood, reacted to, and shaped" major forces such as nationalism and state power."⁶⁵ Nancy Reynolds focuses on the role of consumer cultures and objects in the formation and apprehension of modern Egyptian nationalism, grounding "imagined" communities in their material contexts.⁶⁶ Khaled Fahmy highlights ordinary spaces and bodies as crucial sites of inquiry, asking "how our understanding of Egyptian modernity would differ if we examined it not by studying schools, newspapers, and printing presses, but by taking a close look at cemeteries, slaughterhouses, and cesspools."⁶⁷ These approaches invite us to ask how Egyptian-ness—a sense of community, identity, and belonging on a national scale—was not only imagined or legislated but sensed and experienced.

Building on this work, I look beyond self-evidently "public" forms of culture to consider how cultural forms associated with the domestic sphere shaped Egyptian publics. Cookbooks that prescribed visions of modern living as well as the domestic practices of buying, cooking, and eating food shaped how Egyptians connected to one another and imagined themselves as part of a larger collectivity. Drawing on both formal and colloquial Arabic sources, I describe a series of collective forms of belonging as Egyptian culinary publics. In some cases these forms of belonging were nationally oriented; in others, they convey a more nebulous sense of "we" that, while just as attentive to questions of place and identity, were less explicitly framed as national. Through these various sources and methods, I assemble a history of tomatoes in Egypt as "kitchen history." In the most basic sense this is a history told from the vantage of the kitchen. It rejects the separation of the home and kitchen from "public" realms that have more commonly served as the setting for the writing of history. Kitchen history extends tendrils of inquiry into the farm and the market, placing cookbooks and state archives in conversation with oral histories and street cries.

KITCHEN HISTORY IN EGYPT

When the tomato was first introduced to Egypt, the home kitchen as we think of it today did not yet exist, either as a concept or a concrete space with a stove, water source, and refrigerator.⁶⁸ Nor did Egypt as a territory or polity exist in anything resembling its current form. Both of these entities—kitchen and nation-state—materialized unevenly across Egyptian territory as the tomato rose to prominence there. To provide the basic context for these developments, what follows is a timeline juxtaposing the major developments in the history of the Egyptian nation-state and of its urban home kitchens.[69]

1517: Ottoman rule begins. Headed by a Turkish-speaking dynasty based in Istanbul, the Ottoman Empire incorporated Egypt in the early sixteenth century. The Ottoman territory administered from Cairo, which came to be known in Arabic by the name of its capital city, Misr, became one of the empire's most economically significant provinces. Nelly Hanna's research shows that in the seventeenth century most residents of Ottoman Cairo had, at most, a small niche dedicated to food preparation at home.[70] This was likely used to prepare food that was then brought to communal ovens for cooking or to store and arrange food purchased from one of the city's many food stalls.[71] Home kitchens featuring a permanent, built-in heat source for cooking were generally restricted to the homes of wealthier Cairenes—where paid or enslaved workers did the cooking. As chapter 1 explains, it was during the Ottoman period that the tomato first arrived in Egypt.

1805: Mehmed ʿAli assumes power. In the wake of a short-lived French occupation (1798–1801), Mehmed ʿAli, an Ottoman military officer, consolidated power as the ruler of Egypt (1805–48). Establishing a modern Egyptian army, he temporarily invaded Syria and the Hijaz and succeeded in occupying Sudan.[72] The hereditary dynasty he established ruled Egypt until 1952.[73] During that period Ottoman suzerainty over Egypt became increasingly tenuous, and Mehmed ʿAli and his descendants reorganized Egyptian society through a series of modernizing reforms. Khedive (Viceroy) Ismaʿil (r. 1863–79) carried out a particularly extensive program of infrastructure projects, including the construction of the Suez Canal. Having financed these projects through foreign debt, the Egyptian state defaulted on loan repayments, and in 1876 a debt commission composed of French, British, and other foreign actors took control of Egypt's finances. The groundwork for much of the infrastructure that would eventually support modern home kitchens was laid during Ismaʿil's reign, when parts of Cairo were redeveloped to include streets lit by gas lamps and homes with running water.[74] It was also during this period that the domestic sphere became a central topic in debates about gender, modernity, and the nation.[75]

1882: The British occupy Egypt. Unlike the Turkish-speaking ruling elite, most nineteenth-century Egyptians spoke Arabic and benefitted unevenly from the modernizing reforms implemented by the khedival state. A nationalist movement advocating for fiscal sovereignty under the banner "Egypt for the Egyptians" gained momentum in the 1870s—only to be crushed when the British invaded in 1882 to quell a nationalist uprising and protect British interests. The British kept the khedive and the state bureaucracy in place. But British officials placed within government ministries directed state policy—backed by the British army. Starting in 1899, the British and Egyptian governments nominally shared joint control over Sudan, where Egyptian control had temporarily lapsed in the wake of a Sudanese uprising. The British orchestrated an influx of novel forms of foreign capital.[76] This capital financed, among other things, the construction of the first major Nile dam, which displaced Nubians from their homelands in the south and provided perennial irrigation to the north.

Around the turn of the century, the typical urban kitchen in Egypt consisted of a set of objects that could be moved and rearranged for the purposes of cooking and dining: braziers for cooking over coals, jugs and basins for carrying water, pots and dishes handmade from clay or copper, and trays rather than tables for eating. In a sampling of thirty-seven probate records from 1881 to 1894 in the Mediterranean cities of Alexandria and Dimyat (Damietta), only one included a spirit stove, probably for making coffee.[77] During this period the transition to cooking over gas began with the introduction of the Primus-style pressurized kerosene stove.

1919: Nationalist revolution. The growing Egyptian nationalist movement culminated in revolution in 1919 as protests, marches, and boycotts united Egyptians of all backgrounds against the British occupation. Egyptians took steps toward self-rule in 1922 with the establishment of a constitutional monarchy that divided power between the British, the monarchy, and an elected parliament. Egyptians were positioned to wield more control over agriculture, education, and many other government departments. The Nile dam that had been built at Aswan under the British was raised, and education for girls and women was expanded, including a more extensive domestic science curriculum. Anxious to preserve their access to the Suez Canal, the British continued to interfere in Egyptian affairs—particularly during both World War I and II. Partly to ensure stability in Egypt, they established a system subsidizing kerosene for household use, which helped encourage a widespread shift to cooking with pressurized kerosene stoves throughout Egyptian society by the 1930s and 1940s.[78] A 1947 article from the women's magazine

Bint al-Nil (Daughter of the Nile) presents a list of kitchen items necessary for the modern housewife, including a single-burner kerosene stove, copper pots and pans, and a copper strainer—used, among other things, to juice tomatoes by hand.[79]

1952: The Free Officers' Coup. Following an intensification of popular protests, a military coup led by junior officers overthrew the monarchy and established a republic, which was soon helmed by Gamal 'Abdel Nasser (president 1954–70). With the nationalization of the Suez Canal in 1956, all Egyptian territory was free from British control. Promoting an ideology of Arab socialism, Nasser's regime oversaw nationalizations, land reforms, and industrialization projects. The conversion of Egyptian agriculture to perennial irrigation, initiated during the British occupation, was completed with the construction of the Aswan High Dam. Built with Soviet technical and financial assistance, it generated electric power for industrial and domestic use. The High Dam prompted another major wave of Nubian displacement.

The post-1952 state was committed to providing its citizens with modern consumer goods. It actively promoted the production of kitchen appliances like propane stoves and refrigerators, which had only previously been accessible to the few who could afford imported models. In 1957, *Bint al-Nil* held a contest for a kitchen makeover.[80] The prize included a multiple-burner gas range with oven and a refrigerator—a strikingly different picture of a kitchen from the one the magazine had outlined just ten years prior. Even so, many appliances remained out of reach for many Egyptians. A 1968 survey of one hundred Cairene households indicated that while four in five owned a propane stove, only 63 percent owned a refrigerator and 16 percent owned an electric blender.[81]

1974: Economic liberalization becomes a policy priority. Nasser's successor, Anwar Sadat (president 1970–81) announced an open-door economic policy in 1974.[82] Egypt embraced the United States as a strategic ally and signed a treaty normalizing its relations with Israel. Policies encouraged Egyptian migration to Gulf states where economic opportunities abounded following the development of the petroleum industry. Imported products flowed into Egyptian kitchens. Refrigerators, deep freezers, blenders, and other appliances were more accessible to Egyptians than ever before, partly thanks to remittances that increased Egyptians' spending power.[83]

CHAPTER OUTLINES

The first half of the book relates how the tomato was introduced to Egypt and integrated into its fields, markets, and food policies. Chapter 1 considers the enigma of how and when the tomato came to Egypt. Rather than making the case for a specific moment of introduction, I explore multiple possible trajectories through the Mediterranean and Red Sea regions that tomatoes, and knowledge about them, likely traveled.

The next two chapters use histories of tomato production and consumption to explain the emergence of Egyptian culinary publics that shared, among other things, an evolving set of attachments to tomatoes. Chapter 2 tells the twinned stories of the tomato's integration into Egyptian cuisine and agriculture through an exploration of three words—*quta*, *tamatim*, and *salsa*—that illustrate how the tomato became Egyptian between the late nineteenth and mid-twentieth centuries. Chapter 3 is a history of the Egyptian state's attempts to manage and regulate its citizens' access to tomatoes between the 1940s and the 1990s. While many accounts of Egypt's food system center on wheat and bread, I focus instead on the tomato as a popular staple and the subject of collective complaint.[84]

The second half of the book traces the tomato's history in the Egyptian home kitchen. It shifts from a focus on state sovereignty to kitchen sovereignty, showing how tomatoes became a vehicle for defining Egyptian tastes and flavors from and within the domestic sphere. Chapter 4 traces tomatoes in printed recipes in domestic cookbooks written for middle-class Egyptian housewives between the 1930s and the 1970s. These books called upon their reading public, primarily educated urban women, to assert autonomy over their kitchens and nourish the nation with modern food that embodied "good taste." Recipes for sauces, stews, and stuffed vegetables reveal how these texts domesticated European culinary principles and highlighted culinary affinities between Egypt and the Mashriq, or Arab East. Chapter 5 draws primarily on oral histories to explore the rise of a tomato-based stewing technique called *tasbika* as a dominant home cooking method in the twentieth century. I discuss the practical choices and strategies home cooks used to produce Egyptian flavors—a set of sensations and attachments that embody "fulfilling and satisfying food."[85] These practices and flavors are characteristic of a culinary public defined in part by refusal, as cooks disregarded or contested the dictates of cookbooks and textbooks that called for tasbika's reform.

The book's final chapter charts the relationship between the tomato and okra. Unlike the tomato, okra has been a part of Egyptian cooking for many centuries. As tasbika-style stews became the dominant Egyptian method for cooking okra over the course of the twentieth century, residual recipes that called for preparing okra otherwise became less visible in Egypt's mainstream culinary cultures. But practices surrounding these non-tomato-based okra recipes illuminate the workings of an Egyptian culinary public that complicates and contradicts understandings of Egypt's dominant cooking styles. By detailing how Egyptian home cooks negotiated the structures and discourses that dictated the terms of their contributions to society, the latter half of the book argues that domestic labor is not merely reproductive—maintaining power structures, following the scripts of home economics lessons, providing routine nourishment—but generative. Domestic labor is crucial to the ongoing production of culinary publics in which power can be wielded, upheld, refused, or contested.

ON SPELLING AND TERMINOLOGY

Tomatoes are botanically fruits, but they have been practically understood as a vegetable in many popular and culinary contexts, including in Egypt. In agricultural texts tomatoes tend to be listed a horticultural crop, a category that tends to include both botanical fruits and vegetables. Throughout the book I refer to the tomato variously as a fruit, vegetable, crop, cultivar, plant, ingredient, and staple, depending on the situation.

The spelling of Arabic terms in English presents multiple challenges. Sometimes a given word might be accurately translated into English letters in different ways depending on whether spoken or written Arabic is being referenced. For example, the word for Egypt in formal Arabic is "Misr," but Egyptians pronounce it "Masr." I do my best to use spellings that most closely approximate the context to which I am referring. When directly quoting an Egyptian speaking about Egypt, "Masr" appears in the text; when quoting a textual source, I use "Misr." Overall, I follow a version of the transliteration system of the *International Journal for Middle East Studies*, omitting diacritical marks except for ʿayn and hamza. Arabic words appearing in the *Merriam-Webster* dictionary appear without italics and according to their common English spelling (e.g., couscous, not *kuskus*). Other Arabic terms appear in italics only the first time they are mentioned in a chapter. My aim is to signal new terms to unfamiliar readers while normalizing the use of Arabic terms in the same way that French terms have been normalized in English-language writing about food. Finally, I follow conventional spellings of Arabic names in English, including the spelling of names in romanized script that people themselves have used if they are known.

ONE

Tomato Trajectories

FROM MEXICO TO MISR

IN EGYPT TODAY IT IS not terribly difficult to find yourself eating tomatoes from morning till midnight. Breakfast might be *ful mudammas* (slow-cooked fava beans topped with chopped tomatoes and herbs) or *shakshuka* (eggs poached in tomato sauce). Home-cooked lunch is often seasonal vegetables in a meaty tomato stew. Even Egypt's most famous leafy green dish, *mulukhiyya*, is sometimes prepared with a few tomatoes grated into the broth or with a side of *dimʿa*, a rich tomato sauce. *Koshari*, a popular street food and the perfect late-night snack, is a hearty mix of rice, lentils, pasta, and tomato sauce.

The core of each these dishes, however, predates tomatoes' arrival to Egypt and was once eaten without them. Fava beans have been popular in Egypt since at least the Greco-Roman period.[1] Medieval Egyptian cookbooks include mulukhiyya and detail dozens of recipes for stews and egg dishes. And koshari's name and basic components echo the Indian dish *khichri* from which it is derived—which, by all accounts, included neither tomato sauce nor pasta when it first came to Egypt.[2] Egyptian food today is an eclectic mix of dishes with deep roots in local foodways alongside newer introductions that have become "Egyptianized." But tomatoes link an extraordinary number of Egyptian dishes from diverse origins into a common culinary repertoire. Because it was introduced relatively recently, the tomato offers a means to periodize Egypt's modern history on the basis of everyday practices and sensations, rather than European incursions or top-down political structures. But it also poses a question: Precisely how and when did tomatoes first arrive? Definitive answers are elusive, but Egypt's status as a node within several trade and travel networks means that there are multiple plausible trajectories the tomato might have followed to Egypt—each of which tells us something about how tomatoes became incorporated into Egyptian cooking.

The tomato's wild ancestors originated in the highlands of western South America; it was domesticated in what is now Mexico, where Spanish conquistadors encountered it in the early sixteenth century.[3] By the end of that century it had traveled to the western end of the Mediterranean and likely to the eastern reaches of the Indian Ocean as well. It might have then been conveyed to Egypt from either direction, or from both. As to when exactly this took place, the historical record is not forthcoming. The earliest source I have found definitively placing the tomato in Egypt is a list of flora compiled in the wake of Napoleon's 1798 invasion of Egypt.[4] Therefore the tomato's introduction to Egypt must have occurred sometime after the Spanish conquest of Mexico (1519–21) and before the Napoleonic occupation (1798–1801). This timeframe, a span of about 280 years, places the tomato's introduction within the period of Ottoman rule, which began in 1517 and lasted into the nineteenth century.[5]

Given the pace of early modern travel and how perishable their fruits are, tomatoes probably made their first intercontinental journeys as seeds.[6] Evidence also suggests that as it journeyed beyond the Americas, the tomato was accompanied by horticultural and culinary knowledge that likely facilitated its integration into new landscapes and cuisines. Therefore I approach the story of the tomato's journey to Egypt as an object embedded in context. When I refer to a possible vector for "the tomato," I mean the movement not only of the fruit or its seeds but of knowledge about how to cultivate and cook with tomatoes too. Following from this approach, and to scaffold a narrative that is at times highly speculative, this chapter interweaves the tomato's possible journeys to Egypt with the histories of shakshuka and koshari, two dishes in which tomatoes are prominent. Although both are indisputably part of Egyptian cuisine today, neither dish originated within the borders of modern Egypt—and they followed very different paths to get there, one through the Mediterranean and the other through the Red Sea. Their histories speak to the many global connections that likely brought the tomato to Egypt and the combinations of ingredients and flavors that might have accompanied it.

Shakshuka, a dish of eggs poached in tomato sauce, usually with peppers and onions, is generally accepted as originating in the Maghrib (present-day Morocco, Algeria, and Tunisia). Although today Maghribi influence on Egyptian cuisine is not always obvious, the continued presence of shakshuka and couscous in Egypt attests to historical patterns of migration and cultural diffusion across North Africa. Subsequent chapters of this book focus on the nineteenth and twentieth centuries, when the influence of Maghribi cuisine in Egypt was minimal compared to that of European, Ottoman, and

Levantine cuisines (the Levant here refers to present-day Syria, Lebanon, Palestine, and Jordan; Arabic *Bilad al-Sham*).[7] But shakshuka is a reminder of the significance of Egypt's North African ties—which, as this chapter explains, likely played a role in bringing tomatoes to Egypt.

The many layers of koshari, meanwhile, index the stages of the dish's historical development as it traveled from India to Egypt. Egyptian koshari has several key differences from its South Asian forebear, khichri, including the addition of chickpeas, dried pasta, tomato sauce spiked with hot red pepper, a tangy acidic dressing of vinegar or lime juice, and thinly sliced onions fried to a crisp. A commonly repeated origin story for koshari points to the British occupation of Egypt in 1882 as the impetus for the introduction of khichri's rice-and-lentil template to Egypt (proponents of this theory often point out that the British occupying forces included Indian troops). But there is no direct evidence supporting this narrative. Koshari's history in Egypt is both older and more complex.

Sami Zubaida has demonstrated that koshari's presence in Egypt in fact predated the British occupation.[8] In addition to identifying a description of a dish resembling koshari in the Egyptian port of Suez in the mid-nineteenth century, Zubaida charts a family of connected dishes along trade routes that connected India and Egypt for millennia. The dish's addition of pasta speaks to Egypt's legacy of Mediterranean culinary influences: durum wheat had been introduced to Egypt thanks to Greek influence during the Ptolemaic period (ca. 332–30 BCE), and dried pasta was popularized in Egypt much later, likely through the presence of a sizable Italian community in nineteenth- and twentieth-century Egypt.[9] But the history of koshari's rice-and-lentil core is oriented south and east through the Red Sea. Koshari therefore provides a corrective to histories of Egypt that are oriented singularly toward the Mediterranean, or that presume that anything modern or new must be due to European mediation. Tracing the geographies of koshari and its predecessors highlights the routes that tomatoes may also have taken through the Indian Ocean and the Red Sea, looking south and east to reveal "what is missed when our head is turned one way."[10]

WHAT WE DON'T KNOW

Details about the early centuries of the tomato's journey beyond the Americas are, in the words of one food writer, "hazy."[11] In none of the many places where it was introduced, it seems, was the tomato immediately embraced either as an agricultural commodity or an element of elite cuisine.[12] This limited its appearance in the historical record for some time.[13] Alfred Crosby, who chronicled the fifteenth- and sixteenth-century transfer of plants, animals, and pathogens between the Americas and the rest of the world, declared in 1972 that "there is no area in which the story of American foods is as obscure and yet as vital to the understanding of world history as in the Middle East."[14] Although scholarship in Middle East food studies has expanded considerably since then, the early histories of peppers, potatoes, tomatoes, maize, and other American foods in the region have not yet been the object of extensive study.[15]

Given the scarcity of sources and evidence, this chapter aims to tell the story of the tomato's introduction to Egypt as a set of possibilities rather than a single moment. After all, as Ho Ping-ti argues regarding the introduction of the chile pepper to China, "it is foolish to believe that a certain plant can be introduced into a new area only once, and then only by a certain route. A new plant may score an immediate success in one region and remain neglected in another for a considerable time."[16] Following this line of argument, this chapter presumes that the tomato most likely journeyed to Egypt along multiple routes. I explore two possible points of entry for the tomato to Egypt: Alexandria, on the Mediterranean, and Suez, on the Red Sea.[17]

In what follows, I imagine multiple paths the tomato might have taken to Egypt that often include Christian European actors but rarely center them. In doing so, I build on scholarship that has challenged framings of the global spread of American biota as a "simplified, bidirectional, Atlantic-centred, historically unprecedented transaction between the Americas and Europe."[18] Contesting narratives that center European "discovery" and neglect the agency of non-Europeans, scholars have highlighted long-distance diffusions of foods that took place beyond the early modern Atlantic sphere—for instance, throughout the histories of monsoon Asia.[19] Botanists and historians alike have pointed out that soon after Europeans first encountered them, chile peppers and other American foods traveled across the Pacific and through the Indian Ocean world as well as across the more frequently represented and discussed Atlantic routes.[20] This chapter consequently builds on work that questions the assumption "that transnational connections are modern and Western."[21]

As Alexis Wick points out, despite the long-standing significance of the Red Sea, including its status as a corridor linking Egypt and the Arabian peninsula to the Indian Ocean world, it has received a fraction of the attention that the Mediterranean Sea has enjoyed in modern historical scholarship.[22] In the Euro-American academy the Indian Ocean world has also been "less visible to nonspecialists" than the Atlantic world.[23] This chapter explores the idea that the tomato, or knowledge of it, traveled to Egypt through the Indian Ocean and the Red Sea as well as the Atlantic Ocean and the Mediterranean Sea. It therefore intends to counter the unevenness of the historiographical landscape when it comes to writing global histories of the tomato and other American foodstuffs more generally.

In examining the pathways the tomato might have taken through the Mediterranean and Red Seas during the sixteenth, seventeenth, and eighteenth centuries, my goal is not to argue for the importance of one route over another. Rather, it is to emphasize the contingency of the tomato's probable plural arrivals. I embrace the fragmentary and circumstantial nature of the evidence available as an invitation to speculate in multiples—to foreclose, rather than suggest, the possibility of certainty. The point is not to hedge but to prioritize "perplexity in the face of the real," creating an archive of possibilities that includes uncertainties and loose ends, rather than claiming to write a definitive account of what "actually" happened.[24] When it comes to food history, Krishnendu Ray points out that "most claims of origin are uncertain because the textual record is inadequate and when available provides only second order claims to novelty"; he adds, "wherever there are claims to primacy there is probably some propaganda."[25]

Moreover, even if the moment the first tomato arrived in Egypt were obvious, the circumstances of that historical event would offer scant insight into how the tomato came to embody the tastes and flavors of modern Egypt. In his study of maize in Africa, James McCann writes that "searching for the initial introduction of maize is amusing but beside the central point—namely, how to understand and gauge early African reactions to it as a food and as a crop."[26] Lines of cultural and culinary influence extended into early modern and modern Egypt from the Mediterranean, the Red Sea, the Nile Valley, North Africa, and the eastern Ottoman Empire. All of them informed Egypt's modern food culture, regardless of which delivered the tomato first. Unsatisfying as this unresolved state of affairs may be, it is a convenient reminder of the many rich critiques of the search for pristine origins.[27] Making the case for a singular, definitive origin implies a linear narrative with a tidy beginning and end. The versatile and adaptable tomato—at once sweet, sour, and umami, eaten raw, pickled, concentrated, and stewed, granted dozens of names that obscure as much as they illuminate, cultivated into a hundred varieties for a thousand purposes—could never be captured by a simple or linear history.

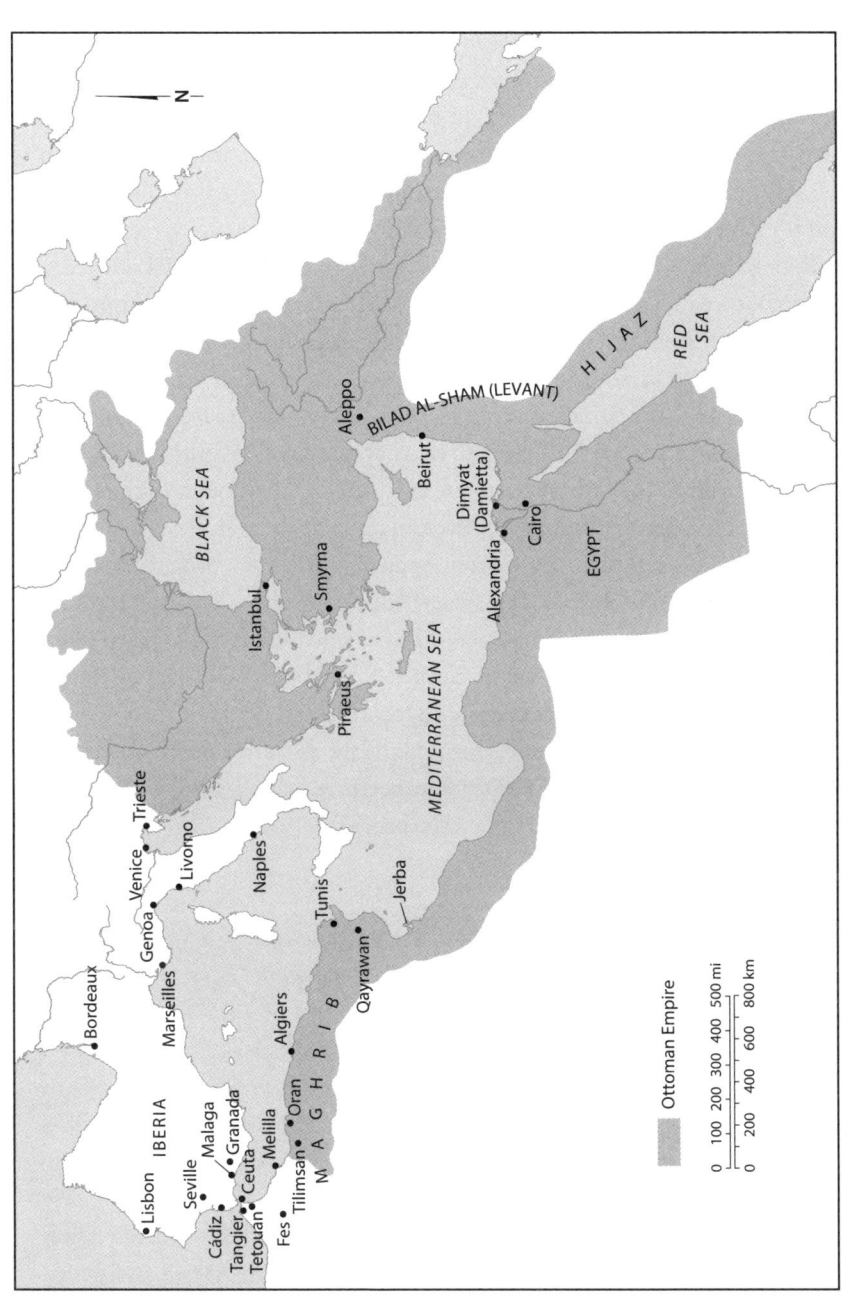

MAP 2. The Mediterranean Sea, ca. late seventeenth century. The Ottoman Empire is shown at its greatest extent. Map by Bill Nelson.

MEDITERRANEAN JOURNEYS

The Spanish were the first Europeans to encounter the tomato in its original context; therefore each of the possible routes the tomato may have taken through the Mediterranean to Egypt begins with Spain. When the tomato first arrived there, the Mediterranean was a densely interconnected space; in the words of Fernand Braudel, "the [Ottoman] Turkish Mediterranean lived and breathed with the same rhythms as the Christian."[28]

Sixteenth-century Spaniards acquired botanical and culinary knowledge about the tomato during their conquest of Mexico: texts describe the tomato's use in Aztec cooking, including as an acidic element of sauces, stews, and casseroles, and its frequent pairing with peppers.[29] Rudolf Grewe suggests that based on Spain's climate and the fact that Seville had "a virtual monopoly on New World trade" in the sixteenth century, the city was "probably the first place in Europe where the tomato was cultivated."[30] Although indirect evidence suggests a gradual embrace of the tomato in Spain over the course of the seventeenth century, the first written Spanish recipes for tomatoes do not appear until the mid-eighteenth century.[31] Spanish rule is, however, credited with introducing tomatoes to southern Italy, which led to the tomato's first appearance in European culinary literature: a cookbook published in Naples in 1692 featuring three recipes made with tomatoes, all of which are described as "in the Spanish style."[32] How, then, might the tomato have traveled eastward to the other end of the Mediterranean, where Napoleon's savants found it in Egypt at the end of the eighteenth century?

MORISCOS AND MERCHANTS: TOMATOES BEYOND IBERIA

The first set of possible routes for this trajectory was traveled by Moriscos—Iberian Muslims and their descendants who were expelled from Spain between 1609 and 1614. The last Muslim stronghold in Spain, Granada, had fallen to the Christian monarchs Ferdinand and Isabella in 1492, ending more than seven centuries of Muslim rule in Iberia. Shortly after, in the early sixteenth century, Spain's Muslims were forced to choose between conversion to Christianity and expulsion. Many resettled in North Africa and maintained connections with Moriscos in Spain, exchanging messages and information across the Mediterranean.[33] Those connections were forged during the very period that tomatoes and other American foods were introduced to Spain for the first time; it is not unthinkable that word of tomatoes or peppers might have passed through their lines of communication. It is also possible, of course, that tomato seeds or recipes traveled with Moriscos themselves when they were expelled en masse in the early seventeenth century. Most of them resettled in the Maghrib—although some also went to present-day Turkey, Libya, and Egypt.[34]

Indeed, scholars have suggested that the Moriscos played a significant role in the circulation of American cultivars, perhaps including the tomato, across the Mediterranean to North Africa.[35] Evidence to support this theory is promising, if not definitive: a travel account written by Englishman Lancelot Addison places tomatoes in Morocco by 1671, more than two decades before the publication of the first European tomato recipes in Naples. In a passage about fruits and vegetables in Moroccan towns, Addison describes tomatoes as grown "in the common fields," from which they are "pluckt and eaten with oyle." He refers to tomatoes as a kind of "Sallad" that was "rarely to be met with in Europe," and suggests that the word Moroccans used for tomato resembles the Spanish "*Tomátos*."[36] Some fifty years later Thomas Shaw, an Englishman who lived in Algeria and Tunisia in the 1720s and 1730s, reported that the "tomata" was present in "kitchen and fruit gardens" there.[37] Addison and Shaw are silent on the subject of how the tomato was first introduced. But given the timing and the fact that a Spanish term appears to have traveled with the tomato to various points in western North Africa, it seems plausible that the Moriscos brought tomatoes with them from Spain.

The history of shakshuka may mirror the movement of tomatoes from the north to the south shores of the western Mediterranean. Anthony Buccini has observed, for example, "the strong similarity between north Africa's *shakshouka* and the *pistos* of Castilian Spain," suggesting that they may both represent early iterations of a wider family of western Mediterranean vegetable stews that appeared in the early modern period and integrated newly introduced American vegetables like tomatoes, peppers, and zucchini.[38] Noam Sienna proposes that the Turkish *menemen* and shakshuka likely "share a common ancestor, along with similar dishes like the Basque *piperade*, Spanish *pisto con huevos*, and Italian *uova in purgatorio*."[39] Partly owing to the prominence of the recently introduced American ingredients in these dishes, Buccini argues that "there is a good chance that all these regional stews that feature the same exotic vegetables did not involve independently but rather are reflections of an original dish from one region which subsequently was spread from region to region."[40] Following from this premise, it is easy to imagine expelled Moriscos traveling to Istanbul, Alexandria, Tunis, or Tangier and sharing a novel technique for poaching eggs in tomato sauce with their new communities. Even if the Moriscos were not the first to introduce the tomato itself, perhaps their culinary knowledge helped to popularize it.[41]

While the case of the Moriscos offers a compelling possibility for the tomato's transmission to North Africa, it is plausible that tomatoes (or the stews and dishes that incorporated them) also traveled to Morocco, Algeria, and Tunisia with Spanish or other European Christians.[42] Between the late fifteenth and eighteenth centuries, Spain and Portugal occupied a number of port cities along the North African coast.[43] In addition, the port of Tunis, La Goulette (Wadi al-Halq), was known for being relatively open to European trade in the seventeenth and eighteenth centuries compared with other North African ports like Alexandria and Algiers; and southern Italy, where the tomato enjoyed relatively early popularity compared with the rest of Europe, had geographical proximity to and deep historical ties with Tunisia.[44] Multiple actors, in other words, might have brought the tomato, or word of it, to the Maghrib.

EAST TO EGYPT

The next piece of this possible trajectory is the question of how tomatoes traveled from the western half of North Africa, where they had been adopted by the seventeenth and early eighteenth centuries, eastward to Egypt. Numerous pathways might have served this purpose. There had been a significant Maghribi presence in Egypt since the Fatimid era (969–1171), but migration from various parts of the North African coast to Egypt increased after 1492.[45] Many of those migrants were merchants who settled permanently in Egypt, establishing commercial ties between Egypt and North African ports like Algiers, Jerba, Oran, and Tilimsan.[46] By the 1560s and 1570s, Egypt's port city of Alexandria was host to a number of "resident Maghribi merchants" who traded spices, textiles, and other goods.[47]

Multiple factors drove Maghribi migration to Egypt, including political persecution, educational opportunities, and travel to Mecca on pilgrimage, or hajj.[48] The latter was particularly influential in consolidating ties across North Africa, ensuring that Maghribi merchants in Egypt had "uninterrupted contact with the ancestral homelands."[49] Maghribi pilgrims commonly booked passage by sea to Alexandria, traveling overland from there to the shores of the Red Sea and the Hijaz beyond; they often brought goods with them to trade along the way.[50] Scholars, pilgrims, and other travelers from the Maghrib therefore had ample opportunities to pass through Egypt to visit or trade with their compatriots, establishing circuits of people and goods that moved east and west across North Africa.

Thomas Shaw's travelogue provides some insight into the transmission of culinary and agricultural knowledge through these circuits. According to a story told to Shaw in the Algerian city of Tilimsan, an Ottoman official—the Amir al-Hajj, responsible for protecting pilgrims en route to Mecca—once sent a sample of Algerian wheat to the "bashaw of Cairo" in order to settle a dispute about "the respective fruitfulness of Egypt and Barbary."[51] What other cultivars might have traveled the same path, unrecorded in the happenstance observations of foreigners? Might the tomato have been one of them? While this eighteenth-century episode may postdate the tomato's initial introduction to Egypt, it offers a concrete example of how edible plants traveled across early modern North Africa. At some point Tunisians began steaming their couscous with a broth spiced with harissa made from peppers indigenous to the Americas, and Moroccans began adding tomatoes to their couscous and *harira* (a popular soup). Innovations like these might have traveled with Maghribi traders, migrants, or pilgrims as they journeyed east to Egypt.

The tomato might also have taken any one of a number of maritime routes that connected Egyptian and European ports. Michael Reimer writes that during the Ottoman period "a dense web of Ottoman and European maritime trade connected Alexandria with ports throughout southern Europe, the Levant, and the Maghrib."[52] Even if they were not traded as commodities, tomatoes and other American foods might have traveled in a less formal capacity as provisions for ship merchants and their crews. Judith Carney and Richard Rosomoff have argued that in the context of the Atlantic world "the foodstaples that provisioned slave ships provide the bridge for understanding the means by which African dietary staples arrived in New World plantation food fields."[53] Ship provisions might similarly explain the dispersion of American foods eastward throughout the Mediterranean.[54] European Christian and Levantine merchants are both possible conduits for this kind of diffusion. European merchants maintained a presence in Alexandria through the eighteenth century.[55] And Syrians were prominent players in the commercial life of Egypt's Mediterranean ports, particularly Dimyat (Damietta).[56] Strikingly, an Egyptian horticulture manual from 1930 states that the residents of Dimyat used the Syrian Arabic word for tomatoes, *banadura*, rather than the more common Egyptian words (*tamatim, quta*).[57] If nothing else, this discrepancy in usage could be evidence of multiple routes of tomato transmission, each accompanied by its own tomato lexicon.

The Sephardic Jewish diaspora represents another potential site of maritime circulation for the tomato. This diaspora community emerged after an increase in anti-Jewish violence in Spain in the late fourteenth century and accelerated after 1492, when Spain's Jews were forced to convert to Christianity on pain of expulsion.[58] Most of those who left fled to Portugal, where they were either expelled or forcibly converted only a few years later.[59] In subsequent centuries these forcibly converted Portuguese—who came to be known as "New Christians"—settled around the Mediterranean and beyond, including in northern Europe, the Americas, and Portuguese outposts in Africa and Asia.[60] Thus, although their expulsions from Iberia predate the introduction of the tomato there, many Sephardim and their descendants established themselves in other places where American foods became increasingly common.

Various branches or groups within Sephardic Jewish and New Christian communities might have conveyed the tomato between various points—for example, from Mexico to Spanish and Italian ports where they had established communities and trading centers, or between European and North African ports.[61] In her study of the Sephardic community in seventeenth- and eighteenth-century Livorno, Francesca Trivellato explains that Livornese Sephardic Jews "thrived" on both "American goods and Asian products," redistributing them throughout the Mediterranean.[62] Their number included "a group of families based in Tunis, Cairo, and Algiers" who "became active in the region between the northern and southern coasts of the western Mediterranean" from the late seventeenth century on.[63] One can imagine tomato seeds or recipes passing through Spanish or Maghribi ports to Alexandria and Cairo on ships run by these families.

Once more, the history of shakshuka provides clues about how foods and culinary knowledge moved through the various Mediterranean networks sketched above. Sienna describes a Judeo-Arabic cookbook published in Tunisia in 1909 that includes shakshuka recipes; the book reflects the culinary culture of Tunisia's Jewish community, which had long-standing connections with Livornese Jews dating back to the seventeenth century.[64] Two notable characteristics of the cookbook include the presence of American ingredients, including tomatoes, and a number of loanwords from Italian.[65]

These factors suggest the strong possibility that American foodstuffs—or recipes that used them—circulated through Jewish trading networks in the Mediterranean. One can easily imagine a flavorful permutation of tomatoes and eggs, affixed to the Maghribi term "shakshuka", traveling from Tunisia to Egypt with Muslim pilgrims, Jewish traders, or both.[66]

The most famous Egyptian cookbook of the twentieth century offers a hint about the role of Maghribi and Mediterranean connections in the introduction and Egyptianization of shakshuka. Nazira Nicola and Bahia Osman's *Fundamentals of Cooking: Theory and Practice*, was published in 1941 and remained in print until the 1980s. It includes a recipe whose title, "Alexandrian-Style Eggs (Shakshuka)," suggests the dish's association with the food culture of the Mediterranean port city Alexandria—where Maghribis formed a distinct community in which Tunisian Arabic was still spoken even into the early twentieth century.[67] The recipe calls for roughly a half pound of tomatoes grated into pulp and then used as a cooking medium. Regardless of how tomatoes were first introduced to Egypt, shakshuka may very well have been an important vector for new knowledge about this specific culinary use of the tomato—as a medium for stewing, poaching, or braising other foods. Although conjectural, this possibility is significant because it attests to the influence of Maghribi cooking on Egyptian cuisine, which is not always easy to discern.

An Egyptian colleague of mine whose Tunisian ancestors, members of the Tuwayyar family who moved from Qayrawan to Egypt in the late eighteenth century, recounts a family story that attests to the culinary dimensions of Maghribi connections in Egypt as well as their elusiveness in the historical record. The story goes that in the late nineteenth century, his Tuwayyar ancestor found himself unable to obtain properly hand-rolled couscous in Cairo. To remedy the situation, he sent for specific Tunisian couscous artisans to be brought to Egypt (the family had maintained ties with Tunisia, which must have made the task easier). The story suggests that if at one time rolling couscous by hand and other long-established Maghribi culinary practices were once common in Egypt, at least some of those traditions were fading by the nineteenth century.[68] This inference accords with findings from a cross-section of late nineteenth-century probate records from Dimyat, Alexandria, and elsewhere in the Nile Delta that include inventories of household objects owned by Muslim men and women of varying wealth. In more than forty inventories dating from 1880 through 1901, I encountered just one single *kiskas*—the specialized utensil used to steam couscous—amid

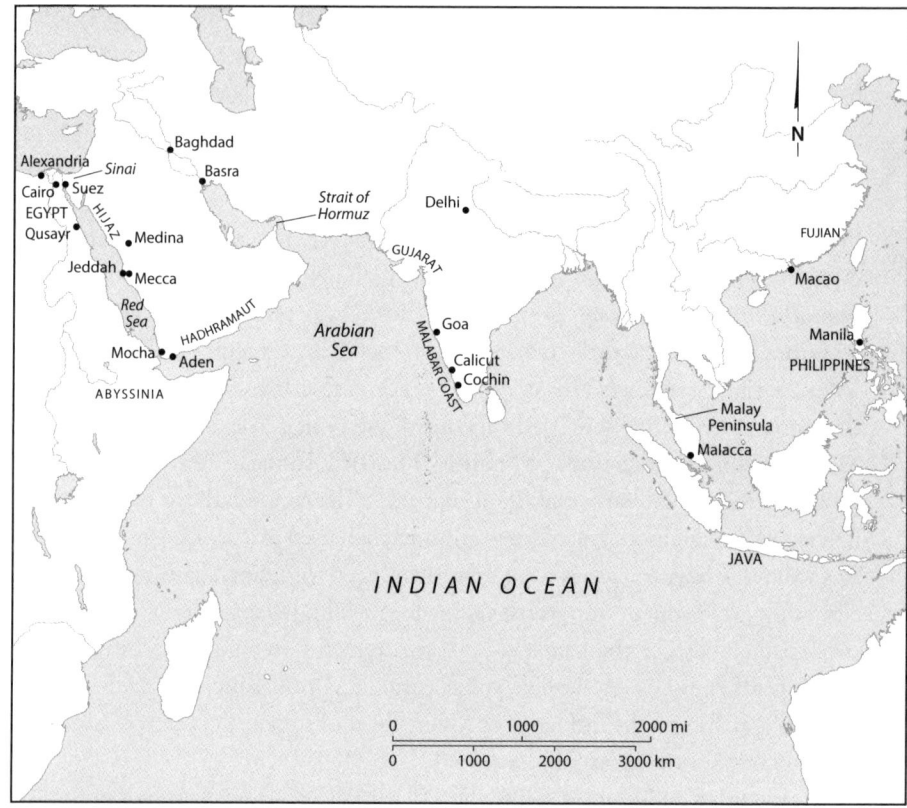

MAP 3. The Indian Ocean. Map by Bill Nelson.

hundreds of other kitchen items. It was owned by a man who died in Alexandria in 1888.[69] Couscous is still made in Egypt today, but it is often prepared as a sweet dish rather than the savory vegetable and meat dish more common in the Maghrib. Shakshuka, however, has become firmly established as one of Egypt's' *baladi* or "local" foods. In a song from the 1990 movie *Crabs*, it appears in a list of local dishes alongside *bisara* (made from fava beans), *kamuniyya*, and mulukhiyya—all of which are construed as local, authentic, and popular and directly contrasted with "expensive imported foods."[70]

The details of how, precisely, new foods filtered east across the North African shores of the Mediterranean remain with us only in fragments: an anecdote in a travelogue, family lore, a lonely kiskas in the archive, and the name of a recipe linking the port city of Alexandria to a Maghribi dish. But those fragments are clear reminders of the many vibrant connections that once animated these routes.

INDIAN OCEAN ROUTES

While Mediterranean connections might have brought the tomato to Egypt's northern ports, an equally intricate set of cultural, religious, and commercial links could have carried it to a Red Sea port like Suez, located about 80 miles east of Cairo.[71] Long before the Suez Canal was built, Egypt's Red Sea ports were thriving centers of trade. Since antiquity, spices and other Asian goods had been shipped through the Red Sea to Egyptian ports, then transferred overland to Cairo then Alexandria and the Mediterranean beyond.[72] The history of how khichiri became koshari speaks to these historical connections, which may also have brought the tomato to Egypt. Koshari is descended from an older dish that combines rice with a pulse (e.g., mung beans or lentils) and originated in South Asia, where it is still known as khichri. Usage of the word "koshari" in Arabic to describe this dish dates to at least the fourteenth century, when medieval traveler Ibn Battuta encountered khichri in the Sultanate of Delhi.[73] In Arabic koshari and khichri are both spelled using the same letters: k-sh-r-y.[74] Ibn Battuta describes it as a dish made with mung beans, a pulse similar to lentils, which the locals "cook . . . with rice and eat with clarified butter."[75]

According to David Waines, khichri was "a traditional favourite among Hindus and readily adopted by Muslims" in medieval South Asia.[76] Composed of light and shelf-stable ingredients, it would have been an ideal component of the provisions of Indian Ocean Muslims as they piloted ships along trade routes or journeyed to the Hijaz on pilgrimage. It likely also circulated among the many trading communities (including Armenians, Sephardic Jews, Syrian Christians, Hadhramis, and others) operating in the Indian Ocean world. Indeed, a thirteenth-century Arabic travelogue describes a dish of "mixed rice and mung beans" called *kijri* at the port of Aden (present-day Yemen), named in a list of goods from India "for which no customs dues are taken."[77] This suggests that khichri (here spelled in Arabic as "kijri") was consumed by seafarers along the trading routes that connected India to the Red Sea at that time—and possibly for many centuries prior. From there it is easy to imagine how the dish entered circuits that had long carried Asian spices and aromatics to Egypt's Red Sea ports.[78]

The word "koshari" remained in Arabic usage in the centuries that followed Ibn Battuta's travelogue: Nawal Nasrallah notes that in the sixteenth century, medical scholar Dawud al-Antaki, who lived most of his life in Cairo, defined "koshari" as a synonym for mung beans and specified that the best could be found in India, the next best in Yemen, and the worst in the Levant, mapping out the spread of the crop and perhaps also the word.[79] In the modern period variations of dishes made on the khichiri/koshari template appear all along the maritime trade routes that linked India with Egypt via the Strait of Hormuz, Yemen, and the Red Sea. These attest to the significance of the Red Sea as a conduit for ongoing connections between the Indian Ocean world and Egypt—connections that also perhaps conveyed tomatoes.

THE TRANSOCEANIC TOMATO BEYOND THE ATLANTIC WORLD

Although to my knowledge no scholar has made an argument for the Red Sea as a potential corridor of tomato diffusion, there are numerous reasons to take seriously the notion that tomatoes may have reached Egypt's Red Sea coast by way of the Indian Ocean as swiftly or effectively as they reached Egypt's Mediterranean ports by way of the Atlantic. As Krishnendu Ray, Kathleen Burke, and Stephanie Jolly put it: "The Indian Ocean was an ocean of comestibles for a very long time," with multiple established circuits along which foodstuffs traveled.[80] Black pepper, native to India's Malabar Coast, was found in the mummy of Ramses II around 1200 BCE, and trade routes between Egypt and India thrived during later eras, especially between the Fatimid and the late Ottoman periods.[81] Numerous scholars have argued that Spanish and Portuguese expansions were responsible for introducing various American foods to the Indian Ocean as early as the sixteenth century; some have argued that the Ottoman Empire played a significant role in their global spread.[82]

In a widely cited article, botanist Jean Andrews argues that "the Portuguese and the Turks were far more influential than the Spaniards in the diffusion of the Mesoamerican plant complex."[83] She suggests that these plants traveled with the Portuguese to the Indian Ocean and thence to the Ottoman Empire by the 1530s.[84] Andrews focuses on peppers and mentions tomatoes only in passing, but her argument nevertheless highlights the role of the Portuguese in the transoceanic transmission of American foods through their early dominance of both African coasts and the Indian Ocean. After establishing garrisons in coastal Africa in the fifteenth century, the Portuguese made inroads on the west coast of India in the early sixteenth; by 1580 they had established a settlement on India's east coast that "became a meeting place for vessels from other parts of India, China, Malacca, and the Philippines."[85]

Following the broad lines of Andrews's argument, other accounts have suggested—though with varying levels of substantiating evidence—that Portuguese trading networks conveyed multiple American foods to various locations in Africa and Asia in the first half of the sixteenth century. The peanut is believed to have been introduced by the Portuguese to China by 1539, either directly or indirectly from Southeast Asia.[86] A Portuguese account describes maize cultivation on the Cape Verde Islands and the nearby West African coast by 1540.[87] The Portuguese are credited with introducing chile peppers to Malacca, on the Malay peninsula, by 1540, and to Goa and Calicut in India the same century.[88] Scholars have speculated that the tomato was another early arrival to Goa.[89] But as James McCann points out, just because the Portuguese recorded the existence of a food in a particular place, or because their presence coincided with an American cultivar, does not mean we should necessarily credit them for bringing it there.[90]

It is very likely, however, that Portuguese traders encountered tomatoes in multiple places and only very shortly after the Spanish did. By the mid-sixteenth century Portuguese merchants operated in Seville as well as New Spain (now Mexico).[91] They leveraged their knowledge and control of the West African coast to supply enslaved Africans to the Spanish empire, securing their integration into the expanding sphere of Atlantic trade.[92] Daviken Studnicki-Gizbert writes that by the second half of the sixteenth century—a crucial period for the spread of the tomato—the various spheres of Portuguese trade were linked: "[Merchant houses] that had made their fortunes in the Asian trades allied themselves with up-and-coming houses with connections to Brazil, Africa, and the Spanish empire, to the mutual benefit of both."[93]

Andrews, whose argument centers on foods that Europeans encountered in the 1490s like peppers and maize, focuses on African routes that might have brought these foods around the Cape of Good Hope and to Asia from there. But given the slightly later timeline of the tomato, which could not have left the Americas before the 1520s, trans-Pacific routes would have been just as likely conduits for its conveyance to Asia. With the expansion of their empire in the sixteenth century, Studnicki-Gizbert writes, the Portuguese "were instrumental in creating new routes that directly linked the Americas to the Asian economy" across the Pacific.⁹⁴ In the same century the Spanish also began crossing the Pacific regularly: they had established settlements in the Philippines in the 1560s with the aid of the "Manila Galleons," which regularly traveled between Mexico and the Philippines and continued to do so until 1815.⁹⁵ Multiple sources allege that tomatoes were present in the Philippines as early as 1571.⁹⁶ Although I have found little evidence to confirm that specific claim, early modern sources indicate that "in 1658, the Portuguese of Java used the word *tomatas*" and attest to the usage of *tomatte* in Malay in 1755.⁹⁷ We might reasonably assume that word usage is a proxy for some acquaintance with the actual plant or its fruit.

Scholars have suggested that Spanish galleons, whose crews likely included sailors of Indigenous and mestizo origin, facilitated the diffusion of Mesoamerican foods across the Pacific.⁹⁸ Although peppers did not yet appear as a commodity to be traded during this period, Dott suggests that "multiple people on the galleons had reasons for bringing chiles across the Pacific for personal consumption," including crews who would likely have been "accustomed to eating chiles regularly and thus stocked the kitchens on the galleons with chiles for their food preparation."⁹⁹ The same might be true for the tomato—which was frequently paired with the chile peppers in Aztec cuisine.¹⁰⁰ It stands to reason that the tomato could have entered the trade routes of the Indian Ocean world as soon as the late sixteenth century or early seventeenth century—most likely through trans-Pacific sea routes, perhaps not as a commodity but as a component of ship provisions.

Within the Indian Ocean world, the diverse composition of ship crews may have helped convey the tomato further westward through the Indian Ocean, facilitating culinary exchange. Dott points out that "even though it is convenient to refer to Portuguese, Fujianese, or Dutch merchants or ships, most ships conducting trade in Asia during the sixteenth century had multi-ethnic crews."¹⁰¹ According to Giancarlo Casale, the pilots of both Ottoman and Portuguese ships in the Indian Ocean during the sixteenth century "were commonly Indian Ocean Muslims … because of their privileged knowledge of local conditions."¹⁰² If the tomato's nightshade cousin, the chile pepper, was indeed known on the west coast of India in the sixteenth century, perhaps the tomato accompanied it there and beyond as a silent partner—not only within the scope of European empires but within Muslim and other networks that connected the shores of the Arabian Sea.

We can also speculate about how the tomato might have moved through the Indian Ocean by considering the histories of some of the

Sephardic Jewish and New Christian families among the Portuguese merchants of the time. More than half of the mercantile communities that made up the Portuguese overseas empire during the sixteenth and seventeenth centuries were New Christians.[103] Jessica Vance Roitman argues that the disproportionate persecution that these Portuguese merchants of Sephardic Jewish heritage faced from the Inquisition and other authorities was a key factor underlying a "propensity for movement" remarkable even by the standards of the highly mobile Portuguese mercantile world.[104] According to Roitman, "it was a nearly a universal pattern for Sephardic merchants to live in four, five, or more cities throughout their lives, while also visiting numerous locales for the furtherance of their business interests, not to mention journeys made to escape direct harassment by civil or ecclesiastical authorities."[105] Strategic marriages within the Portuguese merchant community forged bonds between branches of families in different locations as well as between merchant houses.[106]

These networks connected places where the tomato had been known to Europeans since the sixteenth century, including Seville and Mexico City. One family, the Silveiras, had members in Cartagena de Indias, Lisbon, Madrid, Goa, and Malacca, among other locales.[107] Inquisition records attest to links between New Christian families in Seville and in Goa, and show that New Christians in Manila were in "direct contact" with those in Macao and India.[108] In places like Mexico City and Seville, Portuguese residents "formed closely knit neighborhoods."[109] One can easily imagine how visits, migrations, business trips, or marriages between branches of these merchant families might have brought tomato seeds or tomato recipes from Seville to Goa, or from Mexico to Malacca, and to parts of the Ottoman Empire from there.

Maya Petrovich charts a possible route for the tomato from the Americas to Portuguese Goa and then through Iraq to "central Ottoman lands."[110] "Italy might not have been the only (or even the first) location where a tomato sauce was combined with meats and vegetables," she writes, concluding: "This historian's hunch is that it might have been Goa instead."[111] Sephardic networks connecting the west coast of India to Ottoman lands are a strong candidate for the conveyance of the tomato or other American foods along such a route. Claudia Roden's landmark compilation of Jewish recipes includes three recipes from Queenie Hallegua, a member of a Portuguese Jewish community in Cochin, India, whose ancestors "arrived . . . in the sixteenth century from Portugal, Holland, and later the Middle East."[112] All three of Hallegua's recipes include ingredients indigenous to the Americas—peppers, tomatoes, and/or cashews.[113] Although these recipes, collected by letter in the late twentieth century, are not proof of sixteenth-century ingredients, they do add suggestive detail to our otherwise speculative imagining of the journeys these foods may have taken from Mexico to the Indian Ocean world.

Various accounts place American foods in various parts of the Ottoman Empire, including the Levant, as early as the sixteenth and seventeenth centuries.[114] That said, it appears that American foods like corn, tomatoes, and potatoes were only integrated into Ottoman palace cuisine in the nineteenth century.[115] In any case, scholars who have argued for Indian Ocean pathways to explain these accounts have tended to focus either on a path through the Strait of Hormuz and overland trade routes, rather than considering pathways through the Red Sea to Suez.[116] Here, I consider the possibility that tomatoes took the latter route to Egypt.

TOMATOES ON AN OTTOMAN LAKE

Passage through the Red Sea would have been the final leg of the journey that tomatoes might have taken from the Americas through the Indian Ocean to Egypt. Botanical remains at the Egyptian Red Sea port of Qusayr al-Qadim show that it was a key transshipment point during the Roman period, when Asian foodstuffs like black pepper, rice, and mung beans passed through the port. In addition to serving as a shipping lane for goods moving between the Indian Ocean and the Mediterranean, the Red Sea has been characterized since antiquity by a high volume of internal trade and exchange.[117] Although spices are perhaps the most storied and studied goods that traveled the sea, there was a considerable volume of trade in items like cloth and grain as well.[118] The Hijaz region of the Arabian peninsula (on the Red Sea's east coast) had long been sustained through regular shipments of agricultural products across the sea from the Nile Valley.[119]

Once the Hijaz became host to Islam's two holiest cities, Mecca and Medina—and therefore the destination of Muslim pilgrims performing the hajj—this internal trade took on increased religious and political significance. Starting with the Fatimids, successive Islamic dynasties sought to consolidate their control over the sea for both economic and religious reasons. It was during the Fatimid and later Islamic periods that the variety of Asian spices and other foodstuffs that passed through appears to have increased, with spices like cardamom, ginger, and turmeric appearing in archeological remains at Qusayr for the first time between the eleventh and thirteenth centuries.[120] As Islam spread through Asia, the hajj attracted pilgrims from throughout the Indian Ocean world, just as it drew pilgrims across North Africa to Egypt.

With the Portuguese incursion into the Indian Ocean in the late fifteenth century, control of the Red Sea became a matter of renewed urgency for Muslim rulers. The Ottomans secured key positions in Egypt and in Yemen in 1517, shortly after the Portuguese had made their first attempt to cut off Red Sea access to the Indian Ocean in 1507 and besieged Aden in 1513.[121] By the mid-sixteenth century they transformed the Red Sea into "an Ottoman lake closed to any Portuguese incursion."[122] Despite the Portuguese presence in the wider Indian Ocean world, their control was neither permanent nor absolute, and "the arrival of the Europeans in the Indian Ocean did not fundamentally disrupt the age-old dynamism of the Red Sea as an integrated space of exchange."[123] After the Qasimi imams of Mocha, on the Yemeni coast at the southern end of the sea, expelled the Ottomans in 1635, the Red Sea was effectively divided into an Ottoman northern half and a Yemeni-ruled southern half throughout the late seventeenth and eighteenth centuries. As a result, separate merchant networks operated in the two halves of the sea, but this division did not halt the movement of goods between them.[124]

In addition to the flow of food supplies from Suez south to Jeddah (the port of Mecca), foodstuffs and other edible commodities also moved the opposite direction, from south to north, through the early modern Red Sea. The history of coffee illustrates how new commodities, and the cultures of consumption that they engendered or accompanied, proliferated through "the thorough and longstanding internal integration of the Red Sea world."[125] From its initial sites of cultivation in Abyssinia (present-day Ethiopia and Eritrea) and Yemen at the southern end of the sea, coffee spread north, "added to the ancient dispersal routes of frankincense" during this period; the first textual record of its consumption is from 1497 in the Sinai, at the sea's northern end.[126] This is not to suggest that tomatoes necessarily followed an identical path, but to point out that once tomatoes were a known entity in the early modern Arabian Sea, conditions would have existed to convey them north to Egypt. Had the tomato indeed arrived in India by the sixteenth century and become incorporated into the provisions of seafarers and traders based there or operating in the Arabian Sea, it could have traveled with them to the Red Sea and thence to Egyptian ports. Just as pilgrims traveling from the Maghrib eastward may have carried the tomato with them to Egypt, Muslims from around the Indian Ocean world might have done the same on their pilgrimage westward, bringing the tomato to the Hijaz, a place that enjoyed frequent contact with Egypt.

The history of koshari offers some insight into how this speculative trajectory might have wound its way through the Arabian and Red Seas. Unlike shakshuka, which appears to have incorporated tomatoes from the start, tomatoes were added to koshari (and its forerunners) at an unknown date and time. Even so, the rice-and-lentil khichri template and the tomato may have traveled similar paths between the Arabian Sea region and Egypt, even if they did not travel in concert. Sami Zubaida recalls eating khichri in Baghdad in the 1930s and 1940s. His family's version of the recipe included rice, lentils, garlic and cumin fried in butter—and tomato paste. He notes that Muslim and Jewish families alike ate the dish in Baghdad as well as the port city of Basra.[127] A travel account from the late 1930s describes a similar dish among the rations of Arab sailors who moved between the east African coast and the ports of the Arabian Peninsula. Their evening meal, "often just rice and ghee," sometimes included "dhall . . . which was boiled with peppers or chilis."[128] The account notes that tins of "tomato essences" were among the dhow's provisions, although it does not mention whether they were eaten with lentils and rice.[129]

Zubaida points to another travel account placing a version of khichiri/koshari in Suez in the mid-nineteenth century: a British official stationed in Suez between the 1840s and the 1860s describes locals eating a "mixture of lentils and rice, with clarified butter poured over it," seasoned with "pickled lime or stewed onions."[130] The account was quoted in 1897 travelogue that included an explanatory note identifying this mixture as the "Kichhri" of India, popular in both the Hijaz and in Suez, and specifying "Al-Kajari" as a local Arabic name for the dish (a similar term to the one used in the thirteenth-century travelogue mentioned earlier).[131] Koshari's history confirms that the networks that connected India, Yemen, the Hijaz, and Egypt can be traced not only through the trade in luxury goods but through the shared culinary cultures of ordinary people.

The earliest printed recipe I have found for koshari from Egypt, from a 1934 cookbook written by two male chefs, includes neither pasta nor tomatoes, which suggests that the dish arrived in Egypt bearing a strong resemblance to its Indian and Arabian forerunners. The recipe is titled *aruzz koshari* (literally "koshari rice") and calls for lentils (type unspecified), rice, butter, broth, and onions.[132] Nicola and Osman's 1941 cookbook, meanwhile, includes two koshari recipes that offer a snapshot of a dish in transition. One recipe resembles the 1934 recipe and specifies the use of yellow lentils, while the other is more obviously identifiable as the Egyptian koshari of today. It is made with brown lentils and includes tomato sauce, hot pepper, vinegar, and fried onions.[133]

The Indian Ocean histories of both koshari and the tomato are fragmentary and speculative. But exploring the edges of possibility is one way to decenter the role of European influence on the formation of Egypt's modern cuisine and, by extension, in framings of history more broadly. The impulse to assume that the British were responsible for the advent of a modern Egyptian dish is the same impulse, I suggest, that animates the framing of the history of the tomato through the lens of European imperial conquest rather than Indigenous sailors, Muslim pilgrims, or Sephardic merchants. My aim has been to offer a history of the tomato that rejects Western European modernity as its "sole yardstick" and in which "local vistas can be amplified" through global perspectives, to echo Petrovich.[134]

CONCLUSION

The tomato has never been just one thing. Since its initial domestication in what is now Mexico, it has been coaxed into myriad varieties to emphasize different qualities of texture, taste, and appearance—including eventually by Egyptian farmers and horticulturalists.[135] The tomato that first arrived in Egypt is not the tomato of today; the remaining chapters of this book tell the story of how the tomato became Egyptian after its arrival. Telling that story also entails acknowledging that the "Egypt" that first tomato encountered is not the Egypt of today either. During the Ottoman period the Arabic word for Egypt, *Misr* (Turkish *Mısır*), referred most immediately to Cairo, a term that extended by implication to the wider province following "the Ottoman naming of provinces through administrative centers."[136] As the notion of Egypt as a modern state and nation concretized, so did a new spatial geography that metonymically identified the territorial entity with its capital city's name. To paraphrase Amitav Ghosh, Cairo became Egypt's metaphor for itself.[137] The shifting relationship between Misr the capital city and Misr the territory it rules will be a recurring theme throughout this book. But for the purposes of this chapter, it suffices to say that the tomato entered an Ottoman Egypt in which diets were highly differentiated by region and class. In this sense the tomato is perfectly poised to reveal how modern Egypt and the culinary publics that defined it emerged not from a vacuum or a primordial past but amid a dense and complex web of global connections.

The remainder of this book explores the tomato's role in the formation of culinary publics in Egypt the nineteenth and twentieth centuries, focusing more on Ottoman, Italian, and Levantine than Indian or Maghribi culinary influences and tracing Egypt's transformation through modern forms of state sovereignty and capital. But starting with the many unknowns within the histories of koshari, shakshuka, and the early modern tomato centers Egypt in the richness of multiplicity. Aztec knowledge about how to cook with tomatoes might have traveled with Spanish colonizers to Seville the same decade that it was carried by Indigenous sailors to Manila. Traders might have brought tomato seeds to Alexandria and Suez simultaneously. Perhaps Muslim pilgrims brought tomatoes to Egypt eastward across the Mediterranean and westward to the Red Sea the same year. This diversity of potential narratives underpins an understanding of Egypt's place in the world that cannot easily be parsed by binary categorizations: it was connected to the Maghrib to its west even as Ottoman rule bound it to the Mashriq in the east; Mediterranean routes linked it to Europe while Red Sea routes linked it to Asia. The fact that tomatoes could have come to Egypt from multiple directions highlights Egypt's potential in a field of food studies that is pushing "beyond its North Atlantic limits of conception," recentering both the temporal scales and the spatial framings we adopt to write the history of food.[138]

In exploring Egypt's place in the tomato's early history, I am struck by the resonance throughout that history of what Ella Shohat calls "the two 1492s"— the commencement of more than a century of expulsions and forced conversions of Jews, then Muslims, and concerted attempts to eliminate vestiges of their Arab culture from Iberia, at the same time that the European conquest of the Americas was launched.[139] We do not know precisely which Iberian exiles might have carried the tomato with them and when, but their role in the circulation of American species around the world haunts the historical record. So do the violent foundations of the spectacular scale of Iberian imperial expansion, whereby the "success of Portuguese networks rested on their control of the slaving stations of western Africa, an increasingly important source of coerced labor as disease decimated the indigenous populations."[140]

As Shohat points out, the stories of the "two 1492s" are more intertwined than is often acknowledged. Before it entered Egypt, the tomato made its way around the globe amid multiple layered histories of violence, expulsion, enslavement, and genocide. By connecting those histories to the food history of Egypt—a place that may on the surface appear relatively disconnected from them—this book aims to tap into the "frameworks of encounters and exchanges that allow history to work against current cultural hegemonies."[141] The chapters that follow center the tomato in order to build narratives that cut across and challenge multiple categories that profess to order our world, from nation-states to the regional boundaries of area studies to imposed divisions between "public" and "private."

TWO

How Do You Say "Tomato" in Egyptian?

WHENEVER AND HOWEVER THEY HAD been introduced, tomatoes were familiar to Egyptians by the mid-nineteenth century—cultivated seasonally and eaten in much the same way that other vegetables were. But by the middle of the twentieth century the tomato stood out among other vegetables as a mainstay of Egyptian life—ubiquitous in markets and kitchens, cultivated year-round, and commonly used as a cooking medium for other foods. The context for this transformation included multiple nationalist revolutions and uprisings fueled by popular movements as well as the British occupation and the gradual severing of Egyptian agriculture from the rhythms of the annual Nile flood. These historic events did not simply serve as the backdrop for the tomato's story; they were central to its production as Egyptian.

To trace this history across agricultural and culinary spheres, this chapter is organized around three terms that Egyptians developed to talk and write about tomatoes. The first is *quta* (OOH-ta), a distinctly Egyptian word for tomato.[1] Today it is largely used in speech and not writing—although as I will show, it was once used in written Arabic too.[2] The second term is *tamatim*, a word derived, like the contemporary English, Spanish, Portuguese, Turkish, and French words for tomato, from the Nahuatl *tomatl*. Tamatim eventually became the standard word for tomato in the register of Arabic used in written and formal contexts across the Arabic-speaking world. I also discuss a third term, *salsa*, which in modern Egyptian usage typically refers to tomato purée, often concentrated or seasoned. Salsa might be fresh, frozen, bottled, or canned. This chapter tracks the shifting meanings of these three terms in cookbooks as well as botanical and agricultural texts produced in Egypt between the mid-nineteenth and mid-twentieth centuries.

Tracing the tomato across these genres helps explain how tomatoes ensconced themselves in both food cultures and agricultural production in Egypt during this period. The cookbooks discussed in this chapter show how professional cooks integrated the tomato into the cuisine of Egypt's urban elite—a cooking style and culture that borrowed from local, Ottoman, and European influences but was increasingly labeled as Egyptian. Agricultural sources, meanwhile, document the rise of the tomato as Egypt's most lucrative and widely cultivated horticultural crop. Multiple factors made this latter development possible, including Egypt's soil and climate conditions and dramatic changes to the country's economy and infrastructure. The tomato's history illustrates that Egypt's dominant culinary styles did not simply trickle down from elite urban kitchens or appear as an accident of culinary fashion; they were produced in tandem with massive interventions carried out by successive iterations of the state across Egyptian territory. Juxtaposing culinary history with accounts of agricultural and industrial production, I use the tomato to explore the political economy underlying the culinary publics that arose in modern Egypt.

Looking at the tomato from these different perspectives also helps to disentangle and differentiate the two primary scales at which the modern Arabic term *Misr/Masr* operates—referring simultaneously to the territorial nation-state of Egypt and its capital and largest city, Cairo. Tracking the terms "quta" and "tamatim"—where they appeared, who used them, and how usage changed over time—allows us to follow tomatoes across the geographical and social divides that defined the nascent Egyptian nation. While "quta" is understood throughout Egypt, for example, it came to be associated with Cairene Arabic and working-class vegetable vendors; and the standardization of the term "tamatim" coincides with the expansion of Egyptian agricultural expertise and technocratic control projected from Cairo and Alexandria to their rural hinterlands and to Upper Egypt. The histories of these terms therefore help us to understand how tomatoes connected Egyptians across a shared culinary public; they also clarify the introduction or exacerbation of stratifications and inequalities within that public. On one hand, focusing on uniquely Egyptian usages of words like "quta" and "salsa" shows how Egyptians came to be united through common experiences, such as encountering tomatoes in fields, markets, and kitchens, as well as through the shared vernacular that they used to describe those experiences.

On the other hand, the uneven distribution of the cultural and material capital that produced Egyptian tomatoes and normalized them as a standard

Egyptian ingredient demonstrates how nationalist imaginings of Egypt reflected certain voices and perspectives while construing others as marginal. Urban actors in Cairo (and to a lesser extent, in Alexandria and other large cities) played an outsized role in producing cookbooks, shaping urban culinary tastes, setting the policies that transformed irrigation and agriculture, and establishing Egypt's food processing industry. Tomato cultivation was also uneven across time and space in the period this chapter discusses (roughly 1850 through 1950). It expanded gradually from north to south along the Nile, tracking the distribution of water resources across Egyptian territory. The introduction of perennial irrigation through the construction of Nile dams took place at the expense of Egypt's Nubian population, whose homes and lands in the south were flooded to provide reliable irrigation to the north.

Underlying most modern food cultures is a tension between production and consumption—between the regions, land, and labor that produce edible ingredients and the urban chefs and elites who decide how ingredients are combined to form dominant cuisines. Tracing tomatoes across these spheres clarifies that the stakes of food cultures, as Sucharita Kanjilal puts it, "are always about struggle, land and people."[3] Tomatoes illuminate the material factors underpinning the dynamics of inclusion and exclusion at work in the formation of Egypt as a modern nation-state.

QUTA: RED NIGHTSHADES

In Egypt today the words "quta" and "tamatim" both refer to tomatoes (*Solanum lycopersicum*). But this was not always the case. The word "quta" predates the tomato's introduction to Egypt; it is likely derived from the Coptic "outeh," meaning fruit, crop, or produce.[4] Before the tomato became popular, "quta" referred to *Solanum aethiopicum*, a plant species of African origin known in English as the African eggplant, Ethiopian eggplant, or bitter tomato, among many other names (I refer to it here as the African eggplant).

By the nineteenth century, however, texts produced in and about Egypt used "quta" to refer to both the tomato and the African eggplant—presumably because both are nightshades and although their interiors differ, their round fruits are strikingly similar in outward appearance: both sometimes feature ribbed or lobed exteriors and redden when ripe.[5] As tomatoes' popularity grew in the late nineteenth and early twentieth centuries, the

FIGURE 1. African eggplant (*Solanum aethiopicum*). *Source*: iStock.com/weisschr.

usage of "quta" shifted in two ways. First, it came to refer exclusively to the tomato.[6] Second, even though it remained common in spoken Arabic, especially in Cairo, the word was seldom used in written Arabic after the 1930s. Over the same period the African eggplant became less common, disappearing from culinary and agricultural texts alike.

Little is known about the history of the African eggplant in Egypt; it appears to be native to present-day Ethiopia and Eritrea and to have been introduced to Egypt as a cultivated plant.[7] Although the sparse documentation of nonelite foodways makes it difficult to be certain, it is likely that before the tomato was introduced, the African eggplant was known in Egypt as a component of humble and rural diets. It does not appear, for example, in Egypt's fourteenth- and fifteenth-century cookbooks, which largely reflected the cuisine of urban elites.[8] The earliest instance of the word "quta" I have encountered in an Egyptian text suggests that in Ottoman Egypt the word referred to an African eggplant and was associated primarily with the countryside.

This mention of "quta" appears in Yusuf al-Shirbini's *Brains Confounded by the Ode of Abu Shaduf Expounded*, a satirical account of rural Egypt composed in colloquial Arabic in the 1680s.[9] Shirbini was a scholar from a small town who spent much of his life in the cities of Cairo and Dimyat.[10] *Brains Confounded* ridicules Egypt's rural population, frequently through references to food.[11] Shirbini uses dozens of culinary examples to draw exaggerated comparisons between the refined eating habits of Egypt's city-dwelling elites, particularly those of Turkish descent, and the coarseness of peasants.[12] His satirical portrayals of the latter often include crude scenes that violate the boundaries of propriety by mixing sexual deviance with cooking or eating. The work's only quta appears in one such episode, in which a peasant offers a woman a bunch of onions and an quta in exchange for sex.[13] Based on the rest of the passage and its pairing with onions, which index vulgarity throughout the work, we can infer that the quta was a feature of rural Egyptian life in the seventeenth century, at least as far as Shirbini understood.[14] Although it is impossible to say for certain, I suspect that Shirbini's "quta" referred to an African eggplant rather than a tomato—although, given the word's etymology, it may have simply been selected because it was a culinary term that fit the rhyme (while many foods occur repeatedly throughout the work, "quta" appears just once).[15]

At some point Egyptians recognized the African eggplant as a nightshade cousin of the more familiar eggplant (*Solanum melongena*). Eggplants had been introduced in Egypt by the eleventh century, either through Persian intermediaries or directly from India by Arab merchants, and they became a popular component of Egyptian diets.[16] In nineteenth-century texts the word "quta" was frequently affixed to the Arabic word for eggplant, *badhinjan*, to form the compound term *badhinjan al-quta*. (The Arabic word for the nightshade family of plants is *badhinjaniyya*.) This term initially referred to the African eggplant, although by the late nineteenth century it was also used to refer to the tomato.

Egyptians' identification of tomatoes and African eggplants as nightshades is also reflected in French botanist A. R. Delile's inventory of Egyptian flora, which he produced as a member of the Napoleonic expedition that invaded Egypt in 1798.[17] It includes the earliest attestation of a tomato in Egypt that I have yet to find. Delile provides Latin classificatory and local Arabic names for both the tomato and the African eggplant. In Arabic the tomato is identified as *bydingân toumaten* and the African eggplant as *bydingân el-qoutah*.[18] To the extent that Delile's information is correct, it suggests that when the tomato was introduced, Egyptians recognized it as a nightshade—while distinguishing it from the African eggplant with a term derived from the Nahuatl *tomatl* (probably via a Spanish or other intermediary version of the word).

Evidence suggests that the Egyptian term "quta," along with the African eggplant itself, was transmitted to Turkey at some point, perhaps in the seventeenth century.[19] In Ottoman Turkish the African eggplant and tomato were referred to by separate names that paralleled the Arabic terms in Delile: *kavata* and *domates*, respectively. Although "kavata" and "quta" are transliterated differently in English, their respective spellings in Ottoman Turkish and Arabic (both of which use the Arabic alphabet) are very similar. The African eggplant first appeared in Ottoman palace records in the 1690s—over a century before tomatoes were first mentioned in Ottoman Turkish cookbooks.[20] The elite food cultures of Cairo and Istanbul were deeply connected during the Ottoman period, and influence moved in both directions. Priscilla Mary Işın notes that a 1701 document describing ingredients in the sultan's kitchens groups the African eggplant with okra and the Egyptian leafy green *mulukhiyya*, each of which is referred to by a Turkish version of its Arabic name; it seems highly likely that these African ingredients made their way to Anatolia together from Egypt, along with their Arabic names.[21] The African eggplant continued to appear in Ottoman palace records in the seventeenth and eighteenth centuries—although in Anatolia, as in Egypt, the tomato eventually eclipsed the African eggplant.[22]

Meanwhile, "quta" was used to refer to *both* red nightshade species in multiple sources published in Egypt between the mid-nineteenth century and the 1930s.[23] In each of these sources it is clear that the authors were fully aware of the distinction between the two species, despite using the same term to refer to both.[24] But it was also during this period that the African eggplant became rarer in horticultural, botanical, and culinary texts. During the same time frame, for instance, multiple sources used "quta" to refer to the tomato alone. A list of vegetables cultivated and eaten in Egypt published by Antoine Barthélemy Clot in 1840 identifies the tomato as "*Tomate* (Solanum lycopersicum, Linn.), *Bydingân el ooutah*."[25] Clot makes no mention of *Solanum aethiopicum*. The Arabic edition of a 1911 agriculture textbook compiled by two British experts occupying prominent posts in Egypt includes a section on "al-tamatim or badhinjan al-quta."[26]

A final shift in usage appears to have taken place in the 1930s, when "quta" began to disappear from written texts and "tamatim" became standard—rendering "quta" a term that was primarily spoken rather than written.[27] At some point along the way its spoken usage became differentiated by geography: "quta" became a word for tomato associated with Cairo—pronounced "oota," in keeping with the Cairene practice of dropping the "q" sound—while "tamatim" was used by Egyptian Arabic speakers elsewhere. After the 1930s "quta" ceased to be the word specifying a red nightshade in texts and became "oota," a marker of social difference.

The next section grounds this tomato lexicon in its material context. Tracing the increasingly standard "tamatim" through culinary and agricultural texts illustrates how a combination of cultural, economic, and political changes set the stage for the tomato's rise to become Egypt's most popular vegetable.

TAMATIM: TOMATOES BECOME A PERENNIAL FAVORITE

By the middle of the nineteenth century, European sources reported that the tomato was commonly cultivated in Egypt. In 1840, Clot wrote that Egyptians ate tomatoes "raw and cooked, the same as other vegetables."[28] An 1848 account described them as "abundantly cultivated," and in 1878, C.B. Klunzinger listed tomatoes among the vegetables grown in "the gardens of the country people" of Egypt alongside okra, mulukhiyya, taro, and eggplant—though he does not include tomatoes in his list of foods eaten by "ordinary inhabitants" of the towns of Upper Egypt.[29] These accounts suggest that while the tomato was a familiar vegetable in nineteenth-century Egypt, particularly in the north, it was not yet central to Egyptian cooking styles and diets. But by the start of the Second World War, tomatoes were Egypt's most significant horticultural crop and the only vegetable cultivated in all of Egypt's growing seasons. They also came to play a singular role in Egyptian cooking, particularly as carriers of flavor in stews and sauces. This change took place as "tamatim" was supplanting "quta" as the primary word used to refer to tomatoes in print. It unfolded within two distinct yet connected spheres: urban culinary cultures and the agriculture of Egypt's Delta and riverine provinces.

The foundations of the tomato's journey from novel import to popular staple were laid between Mehmed 'Ali's rise to power and the British occupation of Egypt in 1882. Although Ottoman political sovereignty diminished over this period, Ottoman cuisine remained influential. Sami Zubaida identifies "common themes" of a food culture shared between the elites of Istanbul and nineteenth- and early twentieth-century Egypt.[30] These included many dishes in which tomatoes eventually played a prominent role, such as pilafs, stews, and stuffed vegetables with rice-based fillings (Turkish *dolma*, Arabic *mahshi*). Accordingly, I use "Ottoman cuisine" as a broad umbrella term indicating a sphere of shared cultural influence, rather than a geographical designation or a strict canon of recipes. Ottoman cuisine during this period was not simply a cooking style moving unidirectionally from Istanbul; it represented the integration and circulation of dishes and ingredients throughout the empire, visible in a shared cuisine of elites across the region—including in Egypt.[31] The category of mahshi is a case in point. The technique of stuffing vegetables dates back to medieval Arab cuisine; stuffed eggplants appear in Arabic recipes at least as early as the thirteenth century.[32] The Ottomans embraced the technique with great enthusiasm, developing recipes for dozens of types of stuffed and wrapped vegetables.[33] Mahshi remains a hallmark of the cuisines of many former Ottoman provinces, including Egypt, Iraq, Jordan, Lebanon, Palestine, and Syria.[34]

In many cases Turkish words for these foods linger in the spoken Arabic of those places.[35] Over time, mahshi recipes began to incorporate tomatoes. By the turn of the twentieth century cooks in Cairo and Istanbul alike prized the tomato for its ability to produce a tart and savory sauce, and juiced or puréed tomatoes became increasingly common in both places, particularly among elites. Menus, travel accounts, and cookbooks suggest that Ottoman cuisine played an important role in the popularization of tomatoes as a sauce and stewing medium in Egypt.[36] While some elements of Egyptian court culture had shifted from Ottoman practices to embrace more French influence in the mid-nineteenth century, French cuisine by no means supplanted Ottoman cuisine in the kitchens of Egypt's elites, either in Cairo or the provinces.[37] It appears that it was not European but Ottoman influence that granted tomatoes a prominent place in elite Egyptian kitchens, particularly in stews, sauces, and stuffed vegetables, as well as in the new realm of printed recipes. Edward Lane's observations of Egyptian culture in the 1820s and 1830s, for example, mention the "red eggplant" (glossed in a footnote as "the tomata") alongside eggplants and zucchinis as vegetables commonly served with rice-based stuffing in middling and elite Cairene households—though not among poorer Cairenes.[38]

Emmeline Lott, an Englishwoman working as a governess in the khedival palace in the 1860s, was served not European foods but rather (to her dismay, and apparently despite her protests) a number of local tomato-heavy dishes, including rice with tomato sauce and "tomatoes, with the insides scooped out, and filled with boiled rice and minced mutton."[39] Klunzinger's travel account includes a detailed menu of a dinner served to him by a "well-to-do" resident of Manfalut in Upper Egypt in 1876.[40] Although the host is identified as an Egyptian and most of the names of dishes are given in Arabic, the meal also has several markers of Ottoman influence: courses are presented "alla Turka" (i.e., sequentially), two dishes, a stew and a pilaf, are annotated by Klunzinger as "Turkish," and there are many stuffed vegetables.[41] One of the courses is identified as "batingân kûta" and translated as "tomatoes boiled with flesh [meat]."[42] And an 1882 dinner given by the governor of Qena in Upper Egypt featured two dishes garnished with tomato sauce: stuffed zucchini and a chickpea dish.[43] The menu was recorded by Charles Edwin Wilbour, an American Egyptologist, who described his host as "half Turk, half Arab," with a Turkish-speaking wife.[44]

The clearest evidence of Ottoman influence on elite Egyptian cuisine during this era, however—particularly where tomatoes are concerned—is in the new genre of printed cookbooks. An early example is *The Refuge of Chefs*, translated in 1878 by Muhammad Sidqi from an 1844 Ottoman Turkish cookbook by Mehmed Kamil.[45] It includes about a dozen recipes that call for tomatoes and uses both "quta" and "tamatim," often interchangeably.[46] Tomatoes frequently appear in the form of "tomato juice" or "tomato water," used to flavor kebabs, quail, rice pilaf, and stews.[47] Even so, juiced tomatoes are not as common in this book as they would become in Egyptian cookbooks over subsequent decades: many of the stews in *The Refuge of Chefs* are made without any tomatoes at all, using meat broth or "onion water" instead. One recipe titled "red stew," *al-yakhni al-ahmar*, which one might reasonably expect to be made with tomatoes, contains none.[48] Notably the stews in this cookbook that do use tomatoes, including a Turkish stew translated into Arabic as *turli* (from the Turkish *türlü*), also feature a distinctive flavor profile: they do not include garlic and are seasoned with cinnamon—a point to which I will return.

The tomato's rise to prominence in Egypt was not merely a function of elite culinary style, however; the expansion of tomato cultivation also played an important role. This was made possible through the modernization of Egyptian agriculture starting in the nineteenth century. Repairs and expansions of irrigation works began in the 1830s under Mehmed ʿAli (r. 1805–48) and continued under his grandson Ismaʿil (r. 1863–79). A series of barrages and canals were constructed with corvée labor in the Nile Delta, and by 1873 there were a million more cultivable feddans in Egypt than there had been in 1813.[49] Such projects played a major role in the provincialization of the Saʿid (Upper Egypt), concentrating resources in the cotton-producing regions of the Delta.[50] Once connected to the economy of the Indian Ocean world and ruled by local tribal authorities, the Saʿid became peripheral in an Egyptian economy dominated by the north and a state ruled from Cairo.[51] The labor that built canals and other irrigation works was performed by peasants forced to migrate from their home villages, of whom "a disproportionate number... came from the Saʿid."[52] The chief objective was expanding cotton cultivation, which the state managed intensively. But these projects also extended the arable land and growing seasons for other crops, including vegetables. One effect was that tomato cultivation became highly concentrated in central Egypt and the Nile Delta, the first regions to benefit from improved irrigation works.

Egypt's rulers financed the outlays for these projects with foreign loans, and in 1876 a debt commission of non-Egyptians was established to manage their repayment. A nationalist movement calling for the rejection of foreign encroachment culminated in a revolutionary uprising led by Egyptian military officer Ahmed ʿUrabi. In response, the British occupied Egypt in 1882, eager to secure the repayment of their loans and maintain access to the Suez Canal. They left the ruling family in place but assumed effective control of the state.

TOMATOES UNDER OCCUPATION: BETWEEN NATIONALISM AND CAPITALISM

Between the start of the British occupation in 1882 and Egypt's provisional independence in 1922, tomatoes became newly legible as an economic commodity while gaining prominence as a foundational ingredient in an emergent Egyptian culinary style. Both trends were concentrated in the country's north.

Egypt's first comprehensive agricultural census was conducted in 1929, so conclusions about tomato production before then must be inferred from patchy or indirect evidence.[53] But several indicators suggest that in the early years of the British occupation, tomatoes were an economically significant crop in the Nile Delta—particularly near Alexandria. Between 1889 and 1909 tomato exports from the port of Alexandria remained relatively steady, averaging around 2,300 metric tons annually.[54] The transport of fresh tomatoes across long distances remains a challenge in Egypt even today, so it is likely that most of these tomatoes were grown relatively near the port. One French authority on Egyptian agriculture wrote in 1903 that of the tomato varieties grown in Egypt, only one, the "Skandarani" (Alexandrian), was of "economic importance."[55] It stands to reason that this variety was named after the location where its production was concentrated—and perhaps even developed specifically for export.

Two factors that likely contributed to these production and export trends included the demand for tomatoes across the Mediterranean and Black Sea regions as well as the continued modernization of irrigation infrastructure under the British. Egypt had been active in Mediterranean trade long before the British occupation, and, as I argued in chapter 1, those connections may have in fact facilitated the tomato's introduction to Egypt. In the 1870s the top recipients of Egyptian exports included British, French, Greek, Italian, Ottoman, and Russian ports.[56] Although one khedival source indicates that foodstuffs were the fourth-largest category of Egyptian exports by quantity in the mid-1870s, it does not contain breakdowns by specific food items, so it is difficult to tell whether Egypt was exporting tomatoes that early.[57] We do know, however, that the tomato's popularity among these trading partners significantly increased in the late nineteenth century, a time when tomatoes were becoming more integrated into cooking styles in places like Greece, Italy, and Turkey. Export manifests show that around the turn of the twentieth century, Egyptian tomatoes were being exported from Alexandria to a range of familiar destinations including Genoa, Istanbul, Liverpool, Naples, Marseilles, Odessa, Piraeus, Sebastopol, Smyrna, Trieste, and Venice.[58]

As mentioned earlier, tomatoes began to appear in Ottoman Turkish cookbooks in the mid-nineteenth century. They were also experiencing new levels of popularity in Italy, where they were eaten raw and cooked and integrated into many existing dishes, including as tomato sauce.[59] David Gentilcore notes that from the late 1870s, Italian agronomists began investing resources in refining tomato cultivation and processing methods—partly to meet local demand and partly to compete with places like Greece, Portugal, and Turkey.[60] The rise of the Mediterranean as a zone of tomato trade helps to explain Egyptian tomatoes' remarkable value as an export crop: between 1889 and 1909 tomatoes were nearly three times as lucrative as either wheat and onions by weight.[61] In the first decade of the twentieth century, tomatoes were one of the most profitable horticultural crops in Egypt, accounting for an average of 63 percent of the value of fresh vegetable exports between 1903 and 1905.[62] These dynamics of regional demand may also explain, at least in part, why the African eggplant, which was not widely consumed among Egypt's northern trading partners, did not enjoy the same investment and expansion in production that tomatoes did.[63]

Yet the regional market for tomatoes alone does not account for the expansion of tomato production in twentieth-century Egypt. Egypt's soil and climate conditions were particularly conducive to growing tomatoes, but irrigation remained a limiting factor: ripe tomatoes are at least 90 percent water, and growing them requires plentiful and precise irrigation. These requirements are explained at length in a 1922 manual published by Egypt's Royal Agricultural Society titled *The Tomato in Egypt*.[64] Convened in the 1890s by one of Khedive Isma'il's sons, the society's founding members included many Egyptian landowners as well as French and British experts.[65] Of the twenty-one publications the society produced between 1899 and 1921, seventeen were devoted to major field crops like cotton, sugar beets, and wheat.[66] The society's publication of a volume dedicated to tomatoes is indicative of their profitability in the early decades of the twentieth century. The manual offers a snapshot of the challenges of tomato cultivation in the early 1920s: it warns of the "extensive care and moderation in irrigation" that tomatoes require, "as too much or too little water can cause harm."[67] It documents irrigation experiments at the society's facility in Giza, which was becoming a major tomato-producing region.[68] And it discusses methods for fertilization and protecting seedlings from frost—a major threat to tomato crops in the Delta.[69]

By hastening the spread of perennial irrigation in Egypt, British policies created the conditions for the expansion of tomato cultivation throughout Egypt (although there is no reason to believe that this was intentional). Paying down Egypt's debt was a key priority of the British administration; to that end, the British worked to expand Egypt's taxable land and increase cotton production. This was accomplished in part by repairing and expanding irrigation works in the Delta, which in turn supported the tomato-producing regions closest to Alexandria starting in the 1890s.[70] Aaron Jakes emphasizes that although the economic history of this period is often narrated in terms of "long-term continuities of the cotton economy," the British occupation was also characterized by novel forms of economic development facilitated by massive influxes of foreign capital.[71] These included the financing and construction of the Aswan Dam (later called the Aswan Low Dam, after the construction of a new High Dam in the 1960s) in southern Egypt—the "first modern dam on the Nile River," completed in 1902.[72]

Previously, Egypt's farmers had depended on the annual Nile flood to inundate fields with water and mineral-rich silt in a system known as basin irrigation. The Aswan Dam introduced a new kind of water supply more subject to human control—and, consequently, a new dependence on imported fertilizers to compensate for the loss of the silt deposits. The dam, 37 meters high, "severed the relationship between agriculture and the flood" in the

Delta and parts of central Egypt.[73] It was shored up and heightened between 1907 and 1912, extending perennial irrigation to "all the land that lay between Cairo and Asyut."[74] By this point 3.3 million of Egypt's 5.3 million cultivable feddans (more than 60 percent) had access to perennial irrigation.[75]

The dam exemplifies the uneven distribution of resources under the British. The benefits of perennial irrigation were routed first to the Delta and then extended south from there, exacerbating inequalities between regions. Its construction created what Jennifer Derr describes as an "irrigation frontier" in Asyut, north of which "the state provided perennial irrigation" from the dam's reservoir in late spring and early summer.[76] This water flowed to fields near Alexandria where tomatoes were grown for export and to the Giza facility that hosted the Royal Agricultural Society's tomato experiments, as well as to the rest of Lower Egypt. But south of Asyut, farmers still depended on basin irrigation. The dam also displaced a first wave of Egyptian Nubians from their farmland and villages clustered around the Nile. By the end of the 1960s the dams constructed near Aswan would displace an estimated total of 135,000 Egyptian Nubians.[77] The dam's unintended effects, from Egypt's dependence on imported fertilizer to the spread of malaria and other infectious diseases due to the transformation of the Nile's riparian ecology, have been thoroughly chronicled.[78] The prominence of tomato cultivation in Egypt might be counted among them. Controlling the Nile's water through the construction of dams and canals extended the tomato's growing seasons and provided the reliable water supply that tomatoes needed. In a sense, given how much water they carry, tomatoes are a literal embodiment of the "perennial Nile."[79]

TOMATOES AS VEHICLES FOR EGYPTIAN CUISINE

As the material conditions for tomato production in Egypt transformed, so did Egyptian cultures of tomato consumption. Cookbooks and other texts written during the British occupation suggest that tomatoes were becoming more common in Egyptian kitchens and that cookbook authors recognized them as hallmarks of a distinctly Egyptian cooking style. Tomatoes feature prominently, for instance, in an 1893 cookbook titled *Advice from Mankind on the Delectability of Food*. It was written by Ahmad Ibrahim, a former chef to Khedive Isma'il and self-described "Food Philosopher."[80] After leaving the palace, Ibrahim made a career preparing feasts for Egypt's upper classes; his book was reprinted into the early twentieth century.[81] His recipes reflect the continued influence of Ottoman culture and cuisine: one calls for a fish only available in Istanbul; another offers an Istanbuli variation of the desert *mahallabiyya*.[82] Many recipes feature parenthetical notes indicating what a term is called in Turkish, or offering an Ottoman versus Arab variation of a dish; the Arabic word "mahshi" and Turkish "dolma" both appear.[83] Ibrahim also incorporates a number of European dishes and many recipes from across the Arabic-speaking world, including Morocco, Sudan, and the Levant.[84] In addition, the book features recipes or variations attributed to religious minority communities in Egypt and the Ottoman Empire, with a section with recipes suitable for Coptic, Greek Orthodox, and Armenian Christian fasts and a reference to a method for cooking eggs used among the Jewish community.[85]

One of the most striking aspects of *Advice from Mankind* is Ibrahim's articulation of an Egyptian culinary style amid this complex milieu. Sometimes this style is identified explicitly, by labeling a dish or technique as either "Misri" (Egyptian) or "Arab" (as opposed to Turkish).[86] Elsewhere it is implied by invoking specific ingredients or communities: several recipes call for fish that are specialties of Dimyat or Alexandria, and a section is devoted to Egyptian freshwater fish.[87] Multiple references are made to the eating customs of Egyptian Copts. A "fellahi" (peasant) variation is given for one recipe.[88] Tomatoes are a key conduit through which Ibrahim articulates an Egyptian mode of cooking; referred to as both "quta" and "tamatim," they are used in at least twenty-five of the book's recipes, about double the number of tomato appearances in the 1878 *Refuge of Chefs*. The majority (about 60 percent) of the recipes that call for tomatoes instruct the reader to sieve them into "tomato water."[89]

To understand how Ibrahim's recipes convey an Egyptian cooking style, it is illustrative to compare his turli recipe with the turli recipe in the earlier *Refuge of Chefs*. While the older recipe, translated directly from the Turkish, included both sieved tomatoes and cut pieces of African eggplant, the later recipe, originally written in Arabic, appears to include only tomatoes.[90] The two recipes are also seasoned differently. Whereas the earlier Turkish turli is seasoned with cinnamon and has no garlic, Ibrahim's version is seasoned with garlic and cumin. Elsewhere in *Advice from Mankind*, Ibrahim uses this flavor combination in a fish recipe prepared in an "Arab *tajin*," with onion, garlic, and cumin.[91] Tajin is an Arabic word for a clay dish widely used in Egypt and is also used to refer to the category of dishes cooked in them, similar both to the word "casserole" and to the corresponding vessel. These elements signal the emergence of an Egyptian cooking style within Ibrahim's text. Although articulated in a cookbook reflecting urban elite cuisine, this style includes a combination of dishes and ingredients particular to Egypt's diverse geography (fish from the Mediterranean coast and the Nile) and communities, including peasants as well as Copts and other religious minorities. It emphasizes Arab over Turkish flavor profiles in certain recipes. And tomatoes play a prominent role throughout, particularly when processed into juice or sauce and used as a medium for stewing or seasoning other ingredients.

There are indications that by the early twentieth century, tomatoes were consumed beyond the elite circles for whom Ibrahim cooked. A domestic manual written by Fransis Mikha'il in 1910–11 for an audience that included girls of both the middle and upper classes states that the tomato "is used in all kinds of dishes and rarely absent from our kitchens throughout the year."[92] It is difficult to gauge whether "our kitchens" extends beyond the relatively limited reading public of Egypt's reformist elites, although his invocation of an implied "we" through "our kitchens" is notable.[93] Salma Serry points out that Mikha'il's works were adopted by the Ministry of Education as textbooks in girls' schools, so they would have been guaranteed a certain level of circulation.[94] The text describes the tomato as an item to be taken for granted within the domestic kitchens supervised by a new generation of educated women—hinting at the emergence of a culinary public identified, in part, through tomato consumption.

Texts published in the wake of the 1919 revolution indicate the tomato's growing prominence and its association with Egyptian cooking even more overtly. The 1922 *Tomato in Egypt*, although chiefly an agricultural manual, describes the tomato (glossed here by a range of Arabic names: quta and tamatim as well as *banadura* and *al-badhinjan al-ahmar*, or "red eggplant") as "one of the most frequently used vegetables in Egypt" and "used in large quantities, both fresh and cooked."[95] Its authors offer some insight into the range of tomato varieties available in local markets, describing the influx of European varieties as well as the practice of mixing cultivars among Egyptian growers.[96] In addition, they write that the way tomatoes are used in Egypt differs from how they are used elsewhere, which in turn requires Egyptian tomatoes to have "specific qualities" to suit local needs.[97] In their discussion of the merits of various tomato varieties, they refer to one as *baladi*. Meaning "local" in an implied opposition to imported varieties, the identification of a "baladi" tomato (which the authors single out as in need of development and reform) is an indication of the extent to which the

ثمرة قوطة بلدى تظهر التجعدات السطحية الكثيرة الغير المرغوبة

FIGURE 2. Image of a *baladi* tomato from *The Tomato in Egypt* (1922). The caption reads: "The fruit of the baladi tomato features many undesirable wrinkles."

tomato had been Egyptianized as both a staple culinary ingredient and a modern crop.

Thora Stowell's 1923 *Anglo-Egyptian Cookery Book*, written for British women managing households in Cairo and Alexandria, offers another snapshot of the state of the tomato in Egyptian cooking toward the end of the British occupation.[98] Although it chiefly consists of British recipes, the book includes a chapter of Egyptian dishes that begins with a method for preparing vegetables in a rich tomato sauce to produce Egypt's "typical stew" (a technique discussed in detail in chapters 4, 5, and 6). Stowell notes that this category of stew is common to all Egyptian social classes, writing: "The poorer classes make the stew only two or three times a week, and re-heat for other meals."[99] The consumption of tomatoes among nonelites in Egypt is also mentioned in a series of narrative poems written by the Egyptian-Tunisian writer Bayram al-Tunisi in the early 1920s—in a passage depicting a poor Egyptian family eating a simple meal of bread and tomato sauce.[100]

Shortly after Stowell's book was published, Egypt's first elected parliamentary government took power and Egyptians gained unprecedented (though incomplete) control of their country's territory and affairs, including agriculture, under a new constitutional monarchy. Agricultural manuals published in Egypt after independence were far more likely to be written by Egyptians and published in Arabic compared with earlier periods.[101] Egypt's print culture expanded, providing new fora in which the present and future of modern Egypt were debated. The tomato played a role in both developments.

TOMATOES AND NEGOTIATIONS OF EGYPTIAN SOVEREIGNTY

Between the revolutions of 1919 and 1952 tomatoes consolidated their place as Egypt's most prominent vegetable. Data from Egypt's first national agricultural census, carried out in 1929, offers a snapshot of where tomato cultivation stood in the early years of Egypt's provisional independence. During this period the vast majority of Egypt's cultivated land was still dedicated to profitable field crops.[102] But within the acreage allocated to horticultural crops like fruits and vegetables, tomatoes enjoyed particular prominence. Only watermelons had more feddans devoted to their cultivation in either 1929 or 1939; no other horticultural crop came close.[103]

Average yields for tomatoes were up from 100 cantars of tomatoes per feddan reported in 1910 to an average of 135 cantars per feddan in 1929.[104] Tomato cultivation also expanded into all of three Egypt's growing seasons by 1929, up from the two seasons reported two decades prior—making them the only agricultural product in Egypt to be grown year-round at the time.[105] Census data also indicates that tomato yields differed by geographical region during certain times of the year: the Delta had much higher yields in summer and Upper Egypt had higher yields in winter.[106] In 1929, 72 percent of tomato-growing acreage was in the Delta, and the two governorates with the greatest number of feddans devoted to tomatoes were adjacent to Alexandria and Cairo.

Figures from the 1939 census are broadly similar, although total production had dropped slightly. The Delta's share of tomato acreage decreased from

TABLE 1. Feddans used for tomato cultivation in Egypt, 1929

Governorate	Feddans	Percentage of countrywide total (%)
Beheira	8,756	27
Qalyubiya	3,882	12
Gharbiya	3,620	11
Sharqiya	3,288	10
Daqahliya	2,699	8
Minufiya	1,150	4
Lower Egypt total	**23,395**	**72**
Giza	4,668	14
Beni Suef	1,165	4
Minya	1,143	4
Faiyum	913	3
Asyut	469	1
Girga	257	1
Qena	412	1
Aswan	113	< 1
Upper Egypt total	**9,140**	**28%**

NOTE: Names of governorates reflect spelling in the source document.
SOURCE: 1929 Agricultural Census of Egypt.

72 percent to 69 percent of the total, with small increases in the land area devoted to tomato production in Giza and Fayyum.[107] In the early 1930s another heightening of the Aswan Dam had converted four-fifths of Egypt's agricultural land in the Nile Valley to perennial irrigation.[108] In 1937 the Egyptian Ministry of Agriculture declared that the tomato was grown "almost all year round" and described it as "a vegetable commonly consumed by all classes of the population," as popular in the salads of peasants as it was upon the "tables of the rich."[109] Export figures remained relatively consistent between 1889 and 1929 at around 2,300 metric tons a year; but by the mid-1950s exports had dropped to less than half that.[110] These trends suggest that the growth in tomato production between the 1930s and the 1950s was driven by (and ultimately served) local demand, rather than exports.

Between 1919 and 1952 tomatoes appeared more prominently in cookbooks and agricultural texts alike, and they continued to be associated with an Egyptian style of cooking. The 1930 horticultural manual *Vegetables in Egypt* describes the tomato as "the most widespread and used of all vegetables ... used in the cooking of all other vegetables, cooked by itself, and used in salads."[111] It includes detailed information on the regional variations in tomato-growing patterns, including seasons, markets, and varieties—suggesting that across the country, consumers' access to tomatoes depended largely on local conditions. For example, in Dimyat tomatoes were grown almost the entire year, with harvests taking place from July through March.[112] In Fayyum, in central Egypt, the authors note four different plantings annually, and that local farms supplied the district's markets with tomatoes throughout the year (though most abundantly in April and May).[113] They mention two harvests in Saqqara, not far from Cairo, one in winter and one in the flood season, noting especially high demand for the winter crop.[114] By contrast, in the Upper Egyptian regions of Sohag, Qena, and Esna, the tomato was only planted once a year, after the Nile flood waters receded.[115]

Tomatoes also appeared more frequently in the work of the next generation of Egyptian cookbook authors. This included *Guide for the Modern Chef* (1932) and *The Arts of Modern Cooking* (1934), which, like Ibrahim's cookbook, primarily reflected elite cuisine.[116] The authors of both books had worked in palace kitchens and trained with European chefs, including those who ran the kitchens of luxury hotels in Cairo and Alexandria. They also explicitly labeled more recipes as Egyptian in style than their predecessors had. Their Egyptian recipes featured tomatoes prominently, and they never referred to them as "quta"—reflecting the growing status of "tamatim" as the standard word for tomato in Egyptian texts.

Muhammad 'Ali Abu al-Sunun, the author of *Guide for the Modern Chef*, frames his work in terms of service to the nation and addresses his "esteemed compatriots [*abna' watani*]" (literally "sons of my homeland").[117] The majority of the book's recipes are for French foods, but it also features about thirty non-European recipes, of which ten are labeled "in the Egyptian style [*'ala al-tariqa al-Misriyya*]." Many recipes labeled "Eastern" or "Turkish" include tomatoes, and six of the ten "Egyptian" recipes do as well, including recipes for rice, okra, chicken, and salad.[118] *The Arts of Modern Cooking*, published two years later, features significantly more "Eastern" (*sharqi*) recipes, which are given their own section comprising about 20 percent of the book. Its coauthors include a handful of recipes labeled "Misri" or named for Egyptian cities like Dimyat and Rashid (Rosetta). They include several more ordinary Egyptian foods like *ful mudammas*, *ta'miyya*, and *koshari* (see chapter 1 for a discussion of their koshari recipe). Tomatoes are especially prominent in the "Eastern" section of the book, where they are incorporated into recipes appearing in nearly every category of savory dish.

Comparing the tomato content in stews labeled *yakhni* in this book with those appearing in *The Refuge of Chefs* is illustrative. Yakhni, a Turkish word of Persian origin, is a rough indicator of a residual Ottoman influence. The earlier cookbook, translated from Turkish in 1878, has fifteen yakhni recipes, of which three call for tomatoes.[119] In the 1934 book, six of eight yakhni recipes in the chapter on stews call for tomatoes; the remaining two imply their use.[120] It was also in the 1930s that the African eggplant appears to have faded from urban Egyptian culinary literature. *The Arts of Modern Cooking* contains the latest Egyptian recipes calling for African eggplant or any ingredient called "quta" that I have seen in print.[121] Thus the 1930s saw both the standardization of "tamatim" as the word for tomato in formal Arabic writing and the tomato's eclipsing of the African eggplant in printed recipes.

In sum, between the late nineteenth and mid-twentieth centuries Egyptian "tamatim" had come into their own. From a vegetable used in Ottoman recipes alongside various other nightshades, the tomato evolved into a hallmark of a modern cuisine that was increasingly identified as Egyptian. This arc tracked contemporaneous expansions of Egypt's domestic tomato production as perennial irrigation made tomatoes available in more places and in more months of the year, particularly near Cairo and Alexandria. The combination of these trends in cultures of consumption and practices of agricultural production together vaulted the tomato—now consistently represented in print as "tamatim" rather than "quta"—to new levels of popularity. Production picked up significantly after World War II—between 1939 and 1949 tomato production more than doubled, from 162,245 to 379,000 metric tons—and continued to climb for the rest of the century.[122] By the time Egyptians achieved full political independence in the 1950s, the tomato was unlike any other vegetable either in the country's culinary culture or its agricultural economy. It had become a perennial ingredient and a vegetable used to cook other vegetables. In 1952, 30 percent of land used for growing vegetables was dedicated to tomatoes, producing 563,930 metric tons.[123]

Tracing "tamatim" through culinary and agricultural sources reveals how the standardization of the written term went hand in hand with the consolidation of Egyptian expertise and sovereignty as well as articulations of a national culinary style that reflected those developments. As Egyptian cooks navigated political and economic changes that impacted how kitchens were supplied, tomatoes eclipsed other ingredients and ushered in new techniques for preparing and processing food, including converting tomatoes from solid into liquid or puréed form.

SALSA: TOMATOES IMPLIED

As we have seen, the practice of sieving or juicing tomatoes was increasingly common in printed recipes starting in the nineteenth century, when the resulting product was commonly referred to as "tomato water." In the early decades of the twentieth century, however, Egyptians developed their own word to refer to this newly popular and common tomato-based substance: salsa. Over time, salsa became shorthand for tomatoes processed into liquid form and concentrated either prior to cooking or during the cooking process via reduction. *The Tomato in Egypt* (1922) described salsa as a substance well suited to local flavor profiles and culinary tastes: "[The tomato] is used in the preparation of Eastern foods [*at'ima sharqiyya*] in the form of salsa, which provides flavor [*al-ta'm*], the red color that Easterners prefer, and a unique acidic taste [*madhaq hamid*]."[124] Salsa became more accessible to Egyptians over the next several decades—not only because tomato production expanded, but through the dissemination of new preservation practices and a nascent Egyptian tomato-processing industry. Both developments owed much to Italian influence.

The word *sals* had been used in Arabic culinary literature since at least the thirteenth century, and it appears in Egyptian manuscript cookbooks produced in the fourteenth and fifteenth centuries.[125] Maxime Rodinson speculated that the term was borrowed "from the Romance *salsa*, meaning 'sauce.'"[126] Among the first tomato recipes printed in Europe, published in Naples in the 1690s, was one titled "salsa di pomodoro," or tomato sauce.[127] Ahmed Ibrahim, the author of the 1893 *Advice from Mankind*, used the word "salsa" as a translation for the modern French concept of a culinary sauce—at its simplest, "a liquid seasoning for food."[128] Other Egyptian cookbook authors often used "salsa" similarly in subsequent decades. But by the 1920s and 1930s, "salsa" began to carry a tomato-specific connotation, and some Egyptian authors began to use the word alone as a shorthand for tomato sauce.

The Arts of Modern Cooking (1934), for example, includes two recipes for *salsat tamatim* (tomato sauces) within the "Eastern Cooking" section of the book.[129] Sometimes the authors shorten the phrase to just "salsa," however. For example, one stew recipe is titled simply *Lahm bi-l-salsa* (literally, "meat with sauce"), but the instructions reveal the title's generic "salsa" to be tomato sauce.[130] The book also has a short chapter dedicated to turli, the (originally) Ottoman vegetable stew. It begins with an overview paragraph describing the general template of the dish with a list of vegetables that are typically used to cook it, including tomatoes. Some subsequent recipes within the turli chapter specify "salsat tamatim," while others shorten tomato sauces to simply "salsa."[131] In spoken Egyptian Arabic today, when you say "salsa" on its own, the tomato is typically implied.[132]

SALSA AS PRESERVATION TECHNIQUE

Salsa was not just an ingredient in elite cookbooks; it was also a technique for expanding Egyptians' access to tomatoes throughout the year. Although tomatoes were becoming more popular in the early decades of the twentieth century, numerous factors limited their accessibility to consumers. Availability and prices fluctuated considerably by season. Stowell noted that in the early 1920s tomatoes were available but expensive in Cairo markets in April and May and completely unavailable between June and September.[133] Most Egyptian tomatoes were still consumed fresh and close to where they were grown, meaning that access depended on one's proximity to tomato-growing areas and was limited by seasonal restrictions, which varied from region to region, as we have seen.[134]

In this context Egyptians began to develop methods for processing and preserving their own tomatoes. A 1910 agricultural textbook, describing the tomato's popularity, explained that "the dead-ripe fruits are often crushed, and the concentrated juice is salted and canned for use in time of scarcity."[135] Mikha'il's household management textbook, published around the same time, names several culinary uses for the tomato with salsa at the top of the list. When in season, Mikha'il writes, the tomato's price is quite low, "but when supply dwindles, its price goes up . . . for this reason, we must explain how to preserve them."[136] A detailed recipe follows. A text devoted entirely to homemade preserves (undated but perhaps printed in the 1930s) includes an even wider array of recipes for preserving tomatoes, beginning with the basic "salsat al-tamatim."[137] The practice of producing salsa at home, further explored in chapters 4 and 5, would soon revolutionize Egyptian home cooking. Meanwhile, the commercial potential of processing and preserving tomatoes did not go unnoticed. In the 1920s and 1930s culinary and agricultural experts voiced a shared concern: the tomato varieties produced in Egypt were not ideally suited to canning and preservation. The authors of *The Arts of Modern Cooking* instructed readers to use only Italian tomatoes when making tomato conserves.[138] Agricultural experts sought to import varieties developed in the United States and Italy to ensure the breeding of Egyptian tomatoes that were well-disposed to making high-quality salsa.[139]

By the end of the nineteenth century, Italy had a burgeoning tomato-processing industry.[140] One of its most popular techniques involved simmering and straining tomatoes into a concentrated sauce then bottling them and sealing them in a bain-marie. Although now the end-product of this process is called *passata* in Italian, in the early twentieth century some manufacturers called it "salsa."[141] Egyptian agricultural scientists noted the prominence of tomatoes as an industrial crop in Italy, where "factories specifically for manufacturing sauces [salsat] are everywhere, and experimental stations have been established specifically to improve existing varieties and to find new other varieties that exhibit characteristics beneficial for producing sauce."[142]

By the early decades of the twentieth century, Italian tomato products were exported to countries with large Italian immigrant populations—most prominently, the United States, Argentina, Brazil, and France—where they developed tomato-processing industries.[143] Although the Italian population in Egypt at this time did not rival the populations in those countries, Italians had formed a significant part of Egyptian society since the nineteenth century. According to the 1917 census, there were 41,198 Italians living in Egypt; many spoke Arabic and worked in skilled trades.[144] Their impact on everyday life in Egypt is reflected in the incorporation of many Italian loan words into Egyptian Arabic, included many related to food, cooking, and eating: *wabur* (a pressurized stove or an engine, from *vapore*, steam), *kustaleeta* (from *costoletta*, a meat cutlet), and *fatura* (from *fattura*, an invoice or bill).

In addition to borrowing the word, Egypt also began to import literal salsa from Italy, producing something of a tomato trade deficit: in 1929 Egypt *exported* more than 2,300 metric tons of tomatoes valued at more than 19,000 Egyptian pounds (LE). In the same year it *imported* more than 865 metric tons of salsa valued at over LE36,000—more than 99 percent of it from Italy.[145] Experts pointed out that not only were Egyptian farmers not prioritizing tomato varieties that had been optimized for salsa, but varieties within Egypt were not standardized across governorates.[146] In response, the Egyptian Ministry of Agriculture took steps to encourage and improve salsa production within Egypt. The horticulture department established a small station to pilot the domestic manufacture of tomato sauce and promote the best quality tomato varieties for producing salsa—with the aim of distributing and scaling its findings nationwide.[147] The pilot program appears to have worked: salsa import figures dropped sharply after 1930, at least for several years.[148] By 1937 the pilot salsa station had expanded and several factories for processing and canning tomato sauce had been established.[149] Between 1930 and 1940 six additional factories were built in Cairo and Alexandria to produce salsa and other canned vegetable products.[150] The 1939 Pact of Steel, which diverted 90 percent of Italian tomatoes to Germany, likely provided further incentive for expanding Egypt's salsa production capacities.[151]

Both tomato cultivation and processing advanced considerably following the Second World War. A 1949 Ministry of Agriculture pamphlet titled "Tomato Products" boasted that Egypt's expanding tomato-processing industry produced salsa that "resembles the best salsa imported from abroad."[152] The pamphlet was published under the auspices of the Egyptian Agricultural Museum, a public-facing project of the Ministry of Agriculture, and was presumably intended for public distribution and consumption: it includes instructions for making salsa and other tomato products at home. Five of the eight sources in its bibliography are Italian, indicating the sustained Italian influence on Egypt's nascent tomato-processing industry—despite tense geopolitical relations following Italy's invasion of Ethiopia in 1935 and the Second World War.[153] By the end of the 1940s tomato cultivation and processing industries in Egypt were well established and the word "salsa" had become synonymous with tomato sauce in Egyptian Arabic.

REVISITING QUTA AND TAMATIM

While working on this chapter, I had many conversations with Egyptians about the connotations of quta ("oota," when spoken) and tamatim in contemporary Egyptian Arabic. No two explanations were identical, but several recurring themes emerged. They demonstrate the role that tomatoes continue to play in connecting Egyptians across time and space while simultaneously marking forms of difference—whether of generation, regional origin, or social class. I discuss them here not to claim any definitive, generalizable explanation but to demonstrate the multiplicity of ways that the distinction between quta and tamatim can be used to explain both belonging and difference in Egypt.

Perhaps the most common explanation of the difference in meaning between quta and tamatim was geographical: namely, that "oota" means tomato in Cairene Arabic, while tamatim is used in spoken Arabic everywhere else in Egypt. The slippage between "Cairene" and "Egyptian" was evident here: some explained to me that "oota" was a word "that we say here in Masr," by which they meant, most immediately, "here in Cairo" (the site of most of these conversations), even though technically one might express the idea "here in Egypt" using the same words. This would sometimes be clarified—perhaps for my benefit, as a foreigner—with the example that "oota" would be used "here" and "tamatim" in Alexandria. Others explained the dichotomy as one between Cairo and the countryside (*al-aryaf*).

The divide between oota and tamatim was also explained to me as a matter of generational difference. In this line of interpretation "oota" was described as an old-fashioned word whose usage was slowly giving way to tamatim in spoken Arabic (which, as this chapter has shown, is a shift that took place in printed Arabic texts a hundred years ago). But where that generational shift took place seemed to vary, even among Cairenes from comparable educational and class backgrounds: a woman born in 1962 told me that "oota" was a word from a long time ago (*min zaman*), as a way to explain that she herself did not use it; but a woman from the subsequent generation reported her disappointment that her nieces insisted on using "tamatim" and declared her continued attachment to the use of "oota."

Many Egyptians also invoked social class to explain differences in usage. One working-class man living in Cairo but originally from Upper Egypt told me that "the *fellahin* [peasants] say tamatim and in Cairo they say oota," an explanation that maps onto both social and geographical difference. "Maybe they still say oota in the *sha'bi* [popular, working class] neighborhoods," an affluent Cairene speculated when I asked her who used which word and why. A friend who lives in a city in the Delta reported that people there use tamatim in everyday speech, but that street vendors use the word "oota" to announce they are selling tomatoes; she suggested that this might explain the perception of "oota" as a working-class term. All these attempts to parse the meaning of these two words should be taken with a grain of salt: I found that even though Cairenes were more likely than other Egyptians to say they used the word "oota" in everyday speech, their generation or social class was not a reliable predictor of their relationship to the word. And many insisted there was no difference between the two terms or indicated that their families used them interchangeably.

Like questions of what it means to be an Egyptian or to cook Egyptian food, understandings of these words vary based on context as well as individual inclination; meanings, even of the basic terms used to refer to tomatoes, are not stable over time. But while there was little agreement on the interpretation of these two words, every Egyptian I asked had something to say about them. Tomatoes, and the shared (if at times differentiated) vernacular lexicon used to talk about them, contribute to a "world of shared banalities," producing an Egyptian public held together by "proximities and intimacies across difference" and formed through everyday and ordinary experiences.[154]

CONCLUSION

Tracing the histories of tomatoes and tomato sauce through three key terms that Egyptians used to discuss them illustrates the roles the tomato played in constructing overlapping culinary publics. The trajectories of quta, tamatim, and salsa illustrate how the tomato was integrated into Egyptian society in the form of a new ingredient and through specific forms of vernacular expression. Tomatoes linked Egyptians who may have had very different relationships to the plants and their fruits—farmers in the Delta, chefs in elite households, women preserving tomatoes at home, and vegetable sellers who pushed carts through the streets—yet who also collectively developed a shared and uniquely Egyptian vocabulary used to talk about this newly popular red nightshade. Tomatoes thus shaped twentieth-century Egypt as a community that was not only imagined but sensed, tasted, and uttered into being.

At the same time, tracing the tomato's ascendance as a hallmark of Egyptian horticulture and cuisine underscores the fact that the category "Egyptian," while signaling or implying a unifying identification on a national scale, often masked the uneven distribution of resources. Excavating how such a label came to be asserted illuminates the dynamics of marginalization, displacement, and erasure required to produce something as avowedly coherent as a national culture or cuisine. The expansion of perennial irrigation in northern and central Egypt went hand in hand with the marginalization and displacement of Nubians and other southern Egyptians. Because of the displacements prompted by the inundation of Nubia as well as the broader peripheralization of southern Egypt in the nineteenth and twentieth centuries, thousands of Nubians and other southern Egyptians migrated to northern cities in search of work.[155] Many performed domestic labor in elite and bourgeois households, where they cooked, ironically, with tomatoes plump with the water that had flooded their homeland.

This was the context in which cookbook authors took up the tomato as a vehicle for conveying an explicitly Egyptian style of cooking. In printed cookbooks and urban kitchens, local, Italian, and Ottoman practices converged to produce a repertoire of dishes and flavors that were labeled Egyptian—and that drew upon an increasingly abundant tomato supply. Some cookbook authors highlighted the importance of modern cooking to the advancement of the nation, but their taste largely reflected (and shaped) the eating habits of a limited urban elite. Even though access to tomatoes throughout Egypt continued to expand in the second half of the twentieth century, urban consumption outpaced rural consumption well into the 1970s.[156]

Chapter 3 picks up the history of tomato production in the second half of the twentieth century and explores tomatoes' notoriously unpredictable prices. Anchoring that history is the Egyptian street cry used to advertise tomatoes, *magnuna ya oota* ("crazy tomatoes"), a phrase that continues to resonate through popular culture and everyday life.

THREE

Magnuna ya Oota

TOMATO AS COMPLAINT

"IT'S NOT JUST TOMATOES that are crazy!" proclaimed the title of an article in a popular Egyptian magazine in 1975.[1] The headline was a reference to the street cry *magnuna ya oota* ("crazy tomatoes"), which Egyptian vendors have used to advertise tomatoes since at least the 1950s.[2] The epithet "crazy" refers to the notorious volatility of tomato prices: the street cry embeds both a warning and a complaint about how much tomatoes might cost. "In our grandfathers' day," the article opens, "everything in life seemed stable. Prices rose and fell at the speed of a tortoise. But even in the old days, there was one product that rebelled ... Once, its usual price even doubled." The authors were referring, of course, to the tomato, presented in this nostalgic narrative as a sign of the hardships of modern life and a harbinger of more widespread uncertainty to come. They continue: "Our grandfathers... called [the tomato] 'crazy' and ever since, [it] has stood alone in a world of madness."[3]

The article goes on to discuss the causes of the high vegetable prices from which Egyptians suffered in 1975. It describes challenges faced by producers (such as inadequate transportation and marketing infrastructure) as well as the role of middlemen—wholesale vegetable merchants notorious for dodging regulations and profiteering. Citing government reports and the concerns of ordinary Egyptians struggling to manage household budgets, the authors attempt to explain the disconnect between the objectives of state policies designed to provide the public with affordable vegetables and the realities of the vegetable market in Egypt. This chapter explores that disconnect, examining both policy and popular culture to trace the history of vegetable production and supply, with a focus on tomatoes, between the 1940s and the 1990s. Building on scholarship that highlights the porous nature of the boundary between "state" and "society," I approach the Egyptian food system as a realm in which the relationship between the state and its public is negotiated and experienced.[4] To avoid narrating a history that renders Egyptians as passive objects of state policy, I discuss examples of vernacular culture and expression—oral narratives, protest slogans, poetry, film, and the street cry "crazy tomatoes"—that show how Egyptians understood their relationship to the state through food.

FOOD AND THE EGYPTIAN STATE: BREAD AND BEYOND

A central feature of Egypt's modern food system is the expectation that the state will ensure its citizens' access to certain foods. This is most evident in the provision of subsidized wheat bread, which has been the centerpiece of state food policy since the late 1940s "and has become an expected part of the state's social contract with its people."[5] Scholars have taken up bread as a rich frame of analysis for studying the relationship between political economy and everyday life in Egypt and elsewhere in the Arab world.[6] The history of bread in Egypt illustrates the stakes of popular protest about food. Public demonstrations in response to flour and bread shortages helped drive the establishment of the bread subsidy in the first place.[7] In 1977 thousands of Egyptians took to the streets to protest subsidy cuts in an uprising popularly known as the "bread intifada." Sherene Seikaly describes how in the wake of the uprising, state officials and elites portrayed "the people" not as actors making legitimate claims on state authority but "passive objects duped by external forces or dangerous masses capable of destroying the nation."[8] By contrast, she writes, the popular poet Ahmed Fouad Negm (among others) described the bread intifada as the people awakening from "a lengthy period of sleep and ignorance."[9] In Negm's framing, the Egyptian people (*al-sha'b*) are a public to whom the state owes basic sustenance.

The legacy of the bread intifada therefore underscores the durability of food as an arena in which state-society relations are configured and contested in Egypt. Jessica Barnes details how the myriad practices required to produce and distribute subsidized wheat bread continue to operate across scales, linking households, individuals, and a range of government authorities through a shared set of anxieties and commitments.[10] The bread subsidy was not untouched by the series of liberalizing reforms initiated in the 1980s, but it is arguably the food item that remained the most shielded from them.[11] And yet significant as it was (and is), bread was not the only food that straddled the seam of state and society in the period discussed here. Tomatoes were also impacted by state policy, albeit in less direct ways.

Unlike wheat, rice, and sugar—staples that were regulated by production quotas, subsidies, and rationing systems—horticultural products, a category that includes most fruits and vegetables, including tomatoes, largely escaped these direct forms of state regulation and intervention.[12] As discussed in chapter 2, modern Egyptian agricultural production had historically been concentrated in field crops like wheat, cotton, and rice. The post-1952 state focused the most intensive controls on those crops. Although the production of horticultural crops like tomatoes was not directly regulated, it was indirectly affected by state policies that directed resources and scrutiny elsewhere. Effectively this meant that producing fruits and vegetables required farmers to invest more of their own capital into the process—and that they stood to earn higher profits from horticulture compared with what they could make growing controlled crops. Tomatoes and other vegetables were also subject to less intensive pricing and distribution mechanisms than subsidized foods. Although the state did make some efforts to regulate and stabilize tomato prices, those attempts repeatedly failed—hence "crazy tomatoes" in the market.

From the standpoint of ordinary Egyptian consumers, however, tomatoes became a popular staple food over the course of the twentieth century—even if the state did not treat them that way. Drawing on an extensive ethnographic literature on staples, Barnes identifies three qualities that make a food a staple: it is "a food that defines a meal," serves as "a vehicle for or accompaniment to other foods," and "carries a deep symbolic resonance."[13] Other chapters in this book address how the tomato exhibits the first two qualities; here I argue that the tomato also embodies the third as an essential public good. Barnes describes the significance of bread in Egypt using the concept of "staple security," which entails practices undertaken by state actors as well as ordinary Egyptians to ensure the supply of quality wheat bread.[14] But whereas there is a shared consensus between state actors and the public about the importance of bread, the Egyptian state has not treated tomatoes in the same way. The primary metrics of state food policies during the period discussed here were calories and protein; while they did not ignore fruits and vegetables entirely, state planners and officials devoted far more of their time and energies to cereals and proteins.[15]

As Emiko Ohnuki-Tierney points out, foods tend to acquire staple status not merely because they meet a quantitative caloric baseline but because of

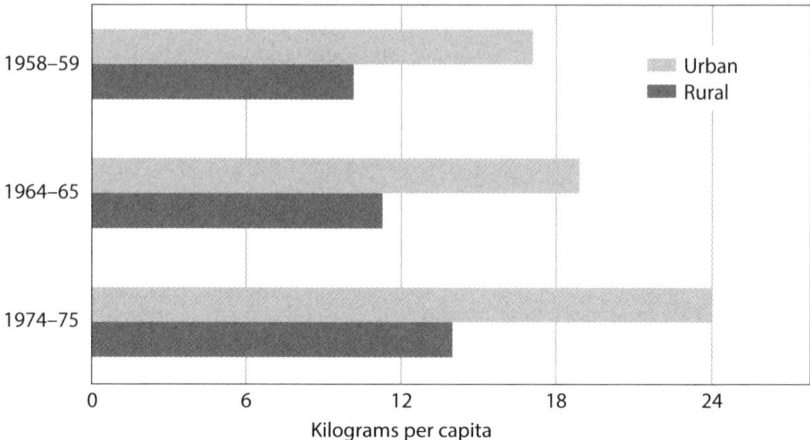

FIGURE 3. Tomato consumption in Egypt, 1958–59, 1964–65, and 1974–75. Figure by Bill Nelson. *Source*: Central Agency for Public Mobilisation and Statistics; cited in Alderman, von Braun, and Sakr, "Egypt's Food Subsidy," 50.

their role in commensality—social eating practices that define communities and connect their members to one another.[16] As the relatively new tomato became identified with Egyptian cooking and integrated into Egyptian diets, it assumed its own symbolic importance. Discontent over tomato availability and pricing did not prompt uprisings, but it did produce a specific popular mode of critique and complaint. In this sense tomatoes tell us less about the Egyptian state than they do about how its citizens came to form a public defined by a set of attachments to specific foods—including tomatoes—in the second half of the twentieth century.

For their part, Egyptian consumers prized tomatoes for their culinary utility and flavor. Per capita tomato consumption increased throughout the 1950s, 1960s, and 1970s, which helped make tomatoes a desirable crop for farmers to produce for domestic markets. Tomato production doubled between 1961 and 1975 then continued to climb before peaking in 2009.[17] Tomato exports were minimal throughout this period, and domestic tomato production (rather than imports) provided the vast majority of Egypt's tomato supply. By contrast, while Egypt had been a net exporter of wheat in the early nineteenth century, it became a net importer of wheat in the twentieth.[18] Throughout the second half of the twentieth century in particular, the state went to great lengths to procure imported wheat, manage domestic wheat production, and minimize increases in bread prices.[19] Meanwhile, consumer prices for tomatoes climbed. Because of its ambiguous position in the food system with respect to state policy and regulation, the tomato is apt for thinking beyond binaries of state and society and of domination and resistance, inviting us to examine instead "the vast political terrain that lies between quiescence and revolt."[20] Hovering at the limits of state capacity, suspended between popular demand and state priorities, the tomato and its fellow vegetables are poised as vehicles less for revolution or resistance than for popular critiques of state authority and the routine rehearsal of complaint.

This chapter presents an overview of Egypt's modern food system, situating tomatoes and other vegetables within it. I alternate between describing the details of Egypt's food policies and Egyptians' critiques of those policies' shortcomings; and I conclude with readings of a classic film and a street cry. Using popular accounts of food production and provision, I illustrate the emergence of an Egyptian culinary public that defined itself by contesting the contours and effects of state sovereignty.

EGYPT'S MODERN FOOD SYSTEM: WARTIME ROOTS

Much of Egyptian food policy in the second half of the twentieth century was shaped by the Second World War. Egypt was commandeered as a base for Allied troops (as many as two hundred thousand were stationed in Egypt and Sudan by 1942) and became a key source of food for the Allies.[21] This caused major disruptions to supply, which led to dramatic increases in the prices of basic food and household items. In Cairo between August 1939 and February 1942 the price of flour quadrupled, the price of onions doubled, and the price of tomatoes rose by 700 percent.[22] Prices in Upper Egypt rose too: between August 1939 and January 1944 the prices of flour and onions more than doubled and the price of tomatoes tripled.[23]

In response to these developments the Egyptian parliament declared a "state of siege" in 1939.[24] This empowered the state to impose new measures of control over agricultural production in order to ensure civilian food supply.[25] Elements of these policies outlasted the war, informing the state's management of agricultural production and food subsidies for decades.[26] After the war's end institutions and mechanisms designed to oversee wheat supply and bread production remained in place; wheat bread became "a cornerstone of welfare and public security."[27] Other lasting effects of the wartime food regime included rationing policies on certain consumer goods and government cooperatives that sold food at set prices.[28] These measures were critical in defining the relationship between Egyptian society and the state as it moved toward independence, shaping popular expectations of what the state should provide. They also tangibly affected what Egyptians ate. Habiba Hassan-Wassef credits the national system of cooperatives with introducing rice, historically cultivated in the Delta, to Upper Egyptians.[29] And rural Egyptians who had long subsisted largely on maize bread "began consuming far more wheat than they had in a century" after the introduction of the state-subsidized "national loaf," which came to be perceived as a "national right."[30]

In addition, wartime shortages had negative effects on public health, which prompted state interventions into citizens' diets. In a 1943 lecture 'Ali Hassan, an Egyptian expert in the relatively new field of modern nutrition, cited recent studies documenting "malnutrition and undernourishment, especially in the young."[31] He blamed this partly on the increased prices of fruits and vegetables due to the presence of troops during the war—when Egyptian factories had supplied the Allied armies with salsa and other canned vegetable products.[32] In response to these deficiencies, the Egyptian government initiated a program that provided free meals designed by "a qualified dietitian" to Egyptian students starting in the early 1940s.[33] Alongside wheat bread, tomatoes were a prominent component of these meals. Hassan-Wassef notes that at the time Egyptian nutritionists "sometimes referred to [the tomato] as the poor man's apple since it was rich in vitamin C and was available all year round."[34]

Of the school meals served in the 1947–48 schoolyear, 84 percent were simple "dry meals" consisting of some combination of bread, protein (boiled eggs, cheese, precooked beans), and fruits and vegetables.[35] Reports indicate that in the kinds of schools that the majority of Egyptian students attended, bread and tomatoes were the top two ingredients by weight in these "dry meals."[36] Insofar as the reports were accurate, the program would have provided a steady supply of free tomatoes (among other foods) to young Egyptians during and following the war. The program expanded each year, serving more than nine hundred thousand students in 1951–52.[37] Hassan mentions similar schemes in urban public kitchens and factories as well as programs that promoted vegetable production in rural areas in the early 1940s.[38]

FOOD POLICY AFTER 1952

The Free Officers' coup of 1952, which overthrew Egypt's monarchy and established a republic, ushered in a new era for Egypt's food system. By the late 1950s a military regime gave way to one in which "civilianized ex-officers administered the bureaucratic apparatus along with technocrats."[39] The state, helmed by Gamal 'Abdel Nasser from 1954 through 1970, imposed a state ideology of "Arab socialism" from the top down in a system that Zeinab Abul-Magd describes as "socialism without socialists."[40] By the mid-1960s the regime began to embrace free-market policies and to rely increasingly on foreign aid—a shift that accelerated after Egypt's disastrous 1967 military defeat.[41] Throughout this period certain aspects of the food system that had been established in the 1940s were maintained and expanded, like food subsidies and cooperatives, and new elements were introduced. All these measures consolidated popular expectations of the state's role in food provision.

Land reform was one of the regime's first major undertakings. In addition to setting limits on land ownership, reforms established agricultural cooperatives controlled by the Ministry of Agriculture through which "the state gradually became the dominant supplier of seed, fertilizers, pesticides, and rural credit."[42] Reforms did not radically reorganize agricultural production or rural social structures, but they did position state-controlled cooperatives as conduits for "the extension of new production techniques" within the agricultural sector.[43] As a condition of receiving redistributed land and access to inputs like seeds, fertilizers, and pesticides, farmers were required to join state cooperatives and deliver specified crops such as cereals, onions, and potatoes to the government at fixed prices.[44] Most fruits and vegetables, however, including tomatoes, were excluded from this scheme, making them more expensive to produce but also more profitable to sell.

As a result, state interventions did affect tomato production beginning in the Nasser period, but indirectly. Only farmers with enough capital to purchase fertilizers and other inputs outside the state cooperative system could invest in horticultural production.[45] Because most horticultural crops fell outside state regulation, they were "lightly taxed and highly profitable."[46] Accordingly, intensive controls on major crops "indirectly distorted the allocation of resources to horticultural crops."[47] Because the prices that the government paid for controlled crops were low, many farmers "diverted [state-provided] fertilizers and pesticides for use on alternative, higher-profit crops or sold them on the black market."⁴⁸ Per one 1968 study, 10 to 20 percent of the value of fertilizer provided through government cooperatives was resold at a profit.⁴⁹ Yahya Sadowski notes that many farmers "worked outside cooperatives, and those who worked within them often evaded government exactions."⁵⁰ Therefore, "the effects of state policy were thus often quite different from their intended objectives."⁵¹

Some Egyptian experts argued that it was important to expand fruit and vegetable production in order to improve the nutrition of Egypt's growing population and thereby support the country's capacities for "agricultural and industrial progress," as one professor of agriculture wrote in 1970.⁵² The state did implement measures intended to support tomato production in the 1950s and 1960s, investing resources in technocratic solutions aimed at supporting horticultural production—not only to meet domestic demand but to make more fruits and vegetables available for export and processing.⁵³ Ministry of Agriculture agronomists imported, tested, and distributed new varieties of fruits and vegetables, supporting producers through "research, extension, and services."⁵⁴ Experiments were developed to optimize fertilization and irrigation methods in order to increase horticultural yields and combat diseases and blights.⁵⁵ In 1964 the ministry established a five-year research program focusing on improving vegetable production with a "special emphasis" on tomatoes.⁵⁶

Vegetable cultivation area, production, and value increased significantly between 1950 and 1972, and tomatoes remained Egypt's top vegetable crop in terms of land allocation and annual production.⁵⁷ Tomato production nearly tripled between 1952 and 1970, from 563,930 to 1,553,000 metric tons.⁵⁸ But tomato yield rates remained fairly stable through the 1960s, indicating that these increases in tomato production reflected an increase in the amount of land dedicated to growing tomatoes, rather than advances in the amount of tomatoes produced per feddan.⁵⁹ It therefore appears that the primary drivers of expanded tomato production during this period were the indirect incentives created by production controls and the market demand driven by the tomato's popularity, rather than technocratic interventions. Horticulturalist Saʿid Hamdi, professor of agriculture and a technical advisor to the government in the 1950s, argued that the tomato's dominance in Egyptian horticulture was "fundamentally attributable to the fact that the people [al-shaʿb] have embraced it to such a great extent, using it to cook most other vegetables and in some meat dishes as well."⁶⁰ According to figures from Egypt's Central Agency for Public Mobilisation and Statistics, per capita tomato consumption in both urban and rural Egypt increased between 1958 and 1965—and continued to rise into the 1970s.

Beyond the realm of agriculture, policies aimed at regulating supply also shaped how Egyptians purchased and prepared food. The new regime continued the rationing and subsidy policies begun during the war, although economic pressures led to a restructuring of the subsidy system in 1965. Ration cards were issued for kerosene, cooking oil, sugar, and tea, with additional items added in 1967.[61] Another cornerstone of the regime's social justice agenda was education. As enrollments expanded, so did the universal school meal program, which served more than one million students in the 1953–54 school year and 1.6 million at its peak in 1954–55 (although it was interrupted in 1956 and scaled back at some point thereafter).[62]

Under Nasser the state also invested heavily in industrialization through centralized planning and spectacular infrastructure projects. The most famous was the Aswan High Dam, constructed in the 1960s with Soviet financial and technical assistance. The High Dam had significant implications for agriculture and industry alike. Its construction completed Egypt's conversion to perennial irrigation, flooding what remained of historical Nubia and forcibly displacing an estimated one hundred thousand Nubians who still lived there.[63] Unlike previous Nile dams, it also generated electricity for industrial and consumer use. By the mid-1970s the electricity the dam generated "was equivalent to the electricity produced from all sources in the mid-1960s."[64] The project formed part of a broader economic policy of self-reliance through industrialization and import substitution. A major focus of that policy was the production of modern consumer goods, including refrigerators, gas stoves, and water heaters.[65] In the early 1960s the state nationalized multiple industries, including fertilizer and pesticide manufacturers, home appliance manufacturers, and food-processing companies. The latter included Edfina and Kaha, the companies that dominated the production of Egyptian salsa into the 1990s. Salsa production nearly quadrupled between 1952 and 1970, from 314 to 1,235 metric tons annually—although most tomatoes produced in Egypt continued to be consumed fresh domestically.[66]

COMPETING NARRATIVES OF PROGRESS AND DECLINE

When it came to horticultural production, state planners and technocrats measured progress in terms of expanded production and increased yields. But in oral history interviews urban Egyptians from a range of backgrounds narrated changes in food supply during their lifetime by invoking narratives not of progress but of decline—of the flavor, safety, and nutritional value of food, especially fruits, vegetables, and animal products. The most vivid descriptions of this sense of decline often came from mothers and fathers of my primary oral history subjects, who frequently participated in interviews, meals, and conversations about food memories. The discussion that follows therefore primarily reflects the narratives of urban Egyptians born before 1952 who remember life before the construction of the High Dam and other transformations of the Nasser era.

Assertions that "nothing tastes as good as the past" are so universal they have become cliché.[67] But my concern is not so much why or whether the flavor and quality of fruits and vegetables empirically changed in twentieth-century Egypt as the specific themes that arose as Egyptians of a specific generation explained their perceptions of change. Their critiques sometimes cited direct acts of corruption, but they also frequently identified a misalignment of priorities between popular opinion and state policy when it came to the production of food. Two common points of discussion were perceived changes in irrigation systems and the widespread use of "chemicals" (*kimawiyyat*), a generic category that included pesticides, fertilizers, and hormones, in agricultural production.[68] Rather than describing these factors as enhancers of productivity, Egyptian consumers and home cooks tended to explain them as corrupting and spoiling the quality of Egypt's water, farmlands, and produce. One woman, a housewife born in 1939, told me that "the taste of food from the past is not the same as the food now, even the vegetables—because of the soils. Cucumbers have no taste anymore."[69]

Another Cairene born in 1951 spoke about the vegetables of his childhood in more detail: "The food, tomatoes and cucumbers and legumes were all, oh my God, beyond delicious. The land, the soil was so clean, it was untouched . . . you would eat the tomatoes, you wouldn't even—of course it's nice to put olive oil and salt or lemon, but you could eat [them] as such, the irrigation water was so clean."[70] A kebab-maker born in 1938, meanwhile, told me that life was good "back then," explaining that "food was fresh and clean and the land was naturally fertile."[71] He attributed the changes in produce to changes in the way the land was used. When I asked about when things changed from how they were "back then" to the current state of things, he dated the change to his late twenties—incidentally, the period when the High Dam was being constructed. As though responding to the rhetoric of state agronomists, he acknowledged the need to transform land use to feed a growing population and meet society's needs. But in his view the intended effects had not been achieved. Decrying the sacrifice of quality for quantity in food production, he said, "Back then, you would eat food and sleep an hour and wake up, and feel like you'd slept six hours." The food of today, he said, produced no such effect. "Now, you can sleep twelve hours and still feel tired."

Others cited the connection between pesticides and cancer as a major factor distinguishing the foods of the past from those of the present. Referring to her childhood in rural Upper Egypt in the 1940s, Hanan explained, "There was ... nothing that would cause cancer or things like that, everything was natural. There was no pollution. You could go to a farm and eat food straight away, without washing it!"[72] What is striking across these narratives is the way that urban Egyptians, themselves largely alienated from agricultural production, voiced their critiques of the quality of their food by commenting on specific aspects of domestic agricultural production—and framing their commentary in terms of decline.

FOOD SYSTEMS AND LIBERALIZATION

Nasser's successor Anwar Sadat (president 1970–81) initiated an "open-door" economic policy known as *infitah*. Starting in 1974, the state relaxed regulations and encouraged privatization and investment. The Sadat era also saw a rise in Egyptian labor migration, much of it to Gulf countries, as well as a shift in Egypt's foreign policy away from the Soviet Union and toward the United States, which became a major source of food aid. Notwithstanding the significance of these changes, many scholars have pointed out that infitah policies simply expanded and accelerated a number of changes that had already begun under Nasser.[73] Highlighting certain continuities between the Nasser and Sadat era, Sadowski notes that "Nasser was never a rigid, doctrinaire socialist, and Sadat's support of the private sector was always tempered by his ongoing enthusiasm for state intervention in the economy."[74] Another point of continuity was the steady increase of domestic tomato production, even as food imports rose overall.

The expectation that the state should subsidize access to key foods was another major continuity between the Nasser and Sadat eras. The cropping and price controls instituted by Nasser's government remained in place under Sadat, as did the subsidy system, which expanded to include eighteen different food items, including "beans, lentils, rice, frozen fish, meat and chicken."[75]

Embodying these contradictory continuities was the influential official Sayed Marei, who served in the administrations of both presidents. Marei was the minister of agriculture twice under Nasser and a key figure in the implementation of infitah.[76] Robert Springborg describes Marei as "the undisputed overlord of the agricultural sector," under Nasser "the Arab World's most prominent agronomist," and "probably Sadat's closest confidant."[77]

There were also significant changes under Sadat, however. The early 1970s witnessed a global food crisis; Egypt's food system became more dependent on food imports and foreign aid and consumers were plagued by inflation, as the article discussed at the start of this chapter attests.[78] Egypt "became a net importer of agricultural commodities for the first time in its history" in 1974.[79] Egypt's debt soared. Pressure from the IMF led Sadat's government to announce cuts to several subsidized commodities in 1977, sparking the bread intifada. For two days Egyptians protested throughout the country. The uprising ended after a violent crackdown, and the government agreed to reinstate subsidies—for the time being.[80] Subsequent reforms and subsidy cuts were rolled out more gradually and quietly by Sadat and his successor Hosni Mubarak (president 1981–2011).[81] Throughout the 1970s and 1980s government interventions in agricultural production continued to focus on major crops like cotton, rice, wheat, maize, and sugarcane—leaving the production of fruits and vegetables largely unregulated.

OPEN-DOOR TOMATOES

According to government survey data, per capita tomato consumption continued to increase between 1964 and 1974. In 1974, Egyptian farmers produced over 1.7 million metric tons of tomatoes; when Mubarak came to power in 1981, that figure had risen to more than 2.4 million metric tons, and ten years later, to nearly 4.7 million metric tons.[82] Tomato production also increased per capita over this period.[83] Exports of tomatoes and tomato products remained insignificant.[84] In other words, Egyptians both produced and consumed increasing amounts of tomatoes through the second half of the twentieth century.

Although locating detailed agricultural statistics from the 1960s and 1970s proved challenging, I assembled partial agricultural census data from 1961 and 1981 to formulate some tentative observations about where tomatoes were produced. Comparing figures from three significant tomato-producing

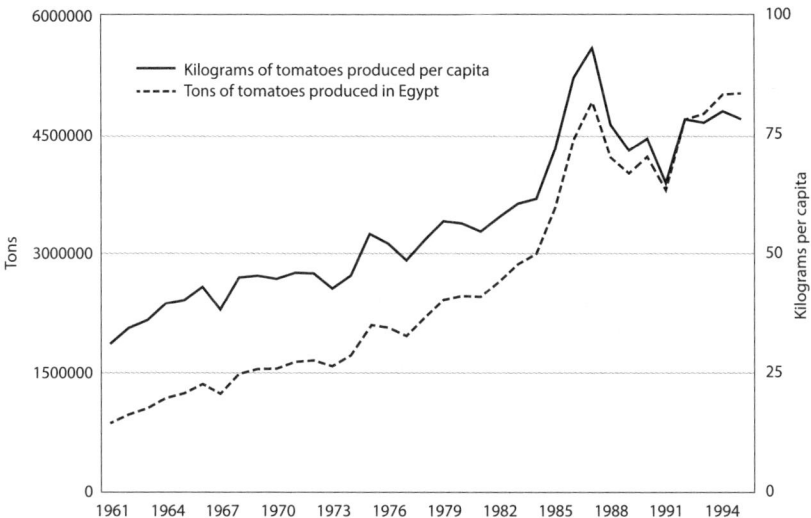

FIGURE 4. Total and per capita tomato production in Egypt, 1961–94. Figure by Bill Nelson. *Source*: FAOSTAT; World Bank Open Data.

regions (Sharqiyya in the Delta, Giza in central Egypt, and Qena in Upper Egypt) offers some insight into overall trends.[85] First, tomato production became more evenly distributed across Egypt's riverine governorates during these two decades. Census data shows that in 1961, about 20 percent of the total land used to grow tomatoes was in Giza (up from 14 percent in 1929).[86] According to one study, "nearly two-thirds of the total tonnage" of tomato production still took place in the Delta and areas surrounding Cairo, like Giza, in the early 1970s.[87] But thereafter the distribution of tomato production became more diffuse: between 1961 and 1981 the land area devoted to tomatoes more than doubled in both Sharqiyya in the Delta and Qena in the south; and proportionally Giza's share of Egypt's total tomato-growing area fell to 8.8 percent of the countrywide total, less than half of its share two decades prior. In the 1980s and early 1990s, Upper Egyptian governorates expanded their winter production, and Qena became a key source of winter tomatoes.[88]

Census data also points to increased tomato production on small farms (defined as fewer than 5 feddans) over this period.[89] In Giza half of the area used to grow tomatoes was on small farms in 1961; by 1981 it was 71 percent.[90] The share of land devoted to tomato production on small farms also increased between those years in Sharqiyya and Qena, rising to 46 percent and 59 percent

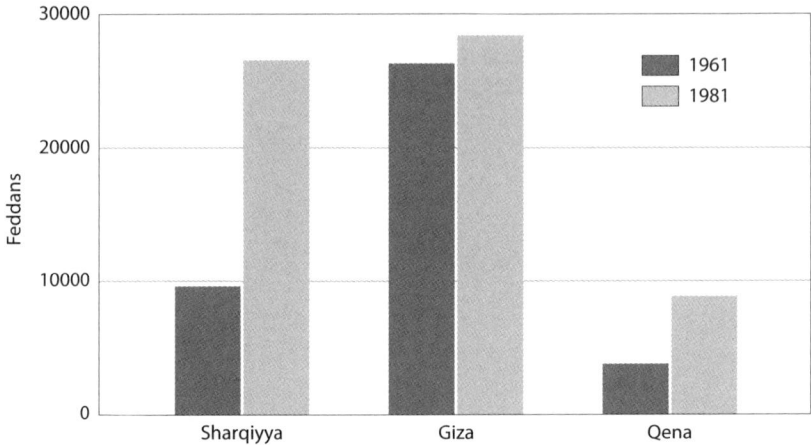

FIGURE 5. Feddans used for tomato cultivation by region in three major tomato-producing governorates, 1961 and 1981. Figure by Bill Nelson. *Source*: 1961 and 1981 Agricultural Census of Egypt.

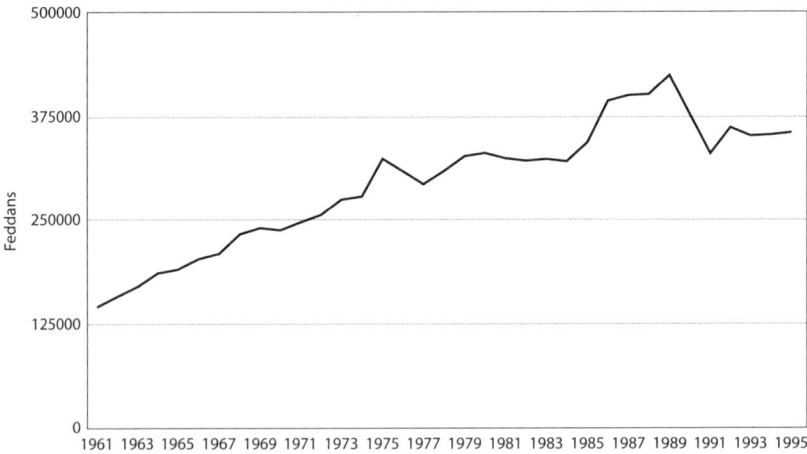

FIGURE 6. Total feddans used for tomato cultivation in Egypt, 1961–94. Figure by Bill Nelson. *Source*: FAOSTAT.

of all tomato-producing land, respectively. These shifts were likely due to several factors. To begin with, land reforms meant there were simply more small farms in 1981 than there had been in 1961.[91] That said, one of the defining characteristics of farms consisting of fewer than 5 feddans, according to Mahmoud Abdel-Fadil, is that they do not produce enough to generate capital

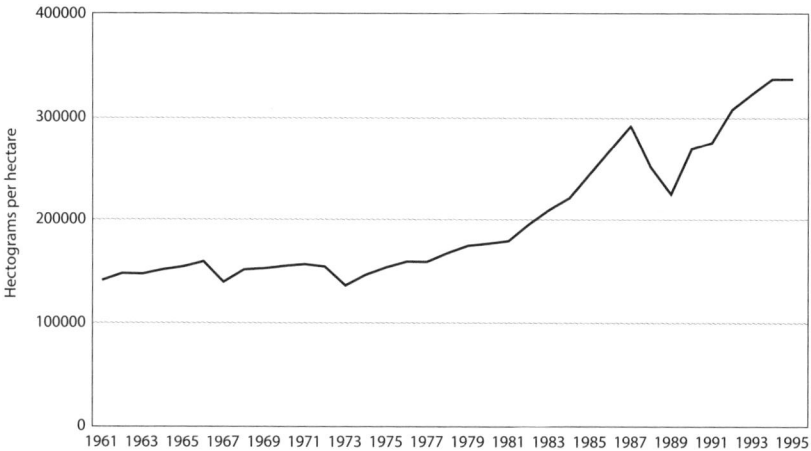

FIGURE 7. Tomato yields in Egypt (hectograms per hectare), 1961–94. Figure by Bill Nelson. *Source*: FAOSTAT.

for investment, meaning that small farmers would have had difficulty accessing the fertilizers, pesticides, and seed necessary to invest in tomato cultivation.[92] Thus there must have been additional factors enabling smaller farms to increase tomato production by 1981. These likely included a combination of cheaper inputs and the introduction of higher-yield varieties, both of which would have incentivized expanding tomato production.

In the 1970s increased governmental subsidies made inputs like fertilizer and pesticides more accessible to farmers.[93] And after remaining stable at around 15 metric tons per hectare throughout the 1960s and early 1970s, tomato yields increased steadily between 1974 and 1981, from 14.8 metric tons to 18 metric tons per hectare.[94] Thereafter they rose more dramatically, reaching 30.9 metric tons per hectare by 1992.[95] From 1980 through 1986 tomato production was the largest driver of growth in the agricultural sector, which some analysts attributed to the availability of new varieties that responded well to fertilizers, thereby producing higher yields.[96] One study described the most significant changes in Egypt's agricultural production in the 1980s as "a major shift upward of tomato production and a decline in cotton production."[97] The practice of diverting limited fertilizer resources toward lucrative crops like tomatoes was nothing new, but the changes described here made it easier and more lucrative to do so in the 1980s.[98] Ministry of Agriculture agronomists continued to develop methods to combat diseases and blights that threatened tomatoes, which also benefitted farmers.[99]

Meanwhile public sector companies continued to dominate the tomato-processing industry. Salsa production peaked in 1982–83 at over 9,000 metric tons but maintained significant levels thereafter, exceeding 6,000 metric tons in 1984–85 and 5,100 metric tons in 1991–92.[100] Around the time that Heinz established its first tomato-processing facilities in Egypt in 1992, salsa accounted for a sixth of the total production of all public food-processing companies in Egypt.[101] With structural adjustment programs implemented under Mubarak, the state's hand in the provision and distribution of food—including tomatoes—became less visible.

FOOD AND DISSENT

The threatened dismantling of subsidies under Sadat prompted overt forms of collective dissent. Egyptians across the country protested the state's handling of the food system, affirming the public's expectation that the state would provide fair and equal access to basic foods. One protest slogan from the 1977 bread intifada accused the powerful of robbing the people of bread: "First we're wearing burlap clothes, now they're coming for our loaves."[102] Another blamed hunger and poverty specifically on infitah: "O thieves of the open door, the people are hungry and poor."[103] And at least one slogan chanted during the protests directly addressed a state official, Sayed Marei: "Sayed Marei, Sayed Bey, a kilo of meat now costs a geneih!"[104]

Elliott Colla argues that we should read slogans not as "literary texts whose meanings can be reduced to a purely semantic level," but as "part of a performance—embodied actions taking place in particular situations."[105] In the context of social movements, slogans like the ones just described embody a set of demands developed and articulated collectively against the state. While so-called "food riots" have sometimes been interpreted as the "spasmodic" actions of mobs, E. P. Thompson's study of eighteenth-century protests in England argues that they should be understood instead as "a highly-complex form of direct popular action, disciplined and with clear objectives."[106] Food riots are not simply reflexive responses to hunger, corruption, or high prices, Thompson writes; they express outrage about violations of "social norms and obligations" perceived to be a matter of "popular consensus."[107] Chanted and performed publicly in the wake of the announced subsidy cuts, Egyptian protest slogans voiced collective claims on the state made in the name of the people.[108]

Ahmed Fouad Negm, whose verses celebrated the political agency of the people during the 1977 uprising, also composed satirical verse criticizing Marei in the form of a *fazzura* (pl. *fawazir*), a kind of riddle that describes an unknown person. Unlike the traditional form of the riddle, Kamal Abdel-Malek writes, the fawazir that Negm wrote did not aim to obscure their subject; rather, they were designed to be obvious to Egyptians who heard them.[109] Negm's riddle about Marei presents the subject as a man of irreconcilable contradictions: both "rooted in wealth" and yet taking it upon himself to implement purportedly socialist policies.[110] Amir al-'Amri explains that during the Sadat era, when the fazzura was written, Marei was well-known in Egypt as a landowner and capitalist who reared foxes for fur at the same time he was, ironically, the head of the Arab Socialist Union.[111]

Negm then deploys food metaphors to critique his subject with even more specificity, invoking zucchini, okra, and squash—three vegetables used as metaphors for corruption in Egyptian Arabic.[112] Decrying the corruption that has sprung up across "our country [*baladna*]," the final lines of the poem describe the vegetables scattered "across the face of the *tasqiyya*," invoking a word referring to a dish made with hot broth that also connotes the irrigation of crops.[113] The riddle thus invokes a collective "we" to criticize a figure responsible for food and agriculture policy as hypocritical and corrupt. The fact that this critique was designed to be easily recognizable to Egyptians suggests that Negm's riddle, like protest slogans and collective action, expressed a popular consensus about the moral obligations of the state and its officials. And while tomatoes did not become metaphors for corruption the way other vegetables did, the invocation of zucchini, squash, and okra hint at the way that popular demands upon the state did not stop at caloric staples like bread. The public's vision of the good life—and popular critiques of the state's failure to provide it—extended to vegetables too.

PRICING TOMATOES

As the magazine article at the start of this chapter indicates, tomatoes' propensity to double in price without warning was a problem in Egypt long before 1952. A consistent factor has always been tomatoes' notoriously high spoilage rate—stemming from the fruits' fragility and exacerbated by Egypt's hot summers and lack of transportation and storage infrastructure. Some estimates suggest that as much as 50 percent of the Egyptian tomato crop is lost between the farm and the consumer.[114] Seasonal fluctuations in production have historically also contributed to price volatility: tomatoes were the first vegetable to be grown year-round in Egypt, but that did not mean that supply was steady throughout the year.

Discussions of the challenges of tomato supply appear as early as the 1910s, when, as discussed in chapter 2, one textbook advised readers to preserve tomatoes to safeguard against high prices in times of scarcity.[115] A 1930 agricultural manual observed that in some cases, the cost of transporting tomatoes to the market alone could exceed the proceeds from their sale.[116] Perhaps the most notorious problem facing tomato producers and consumers alike, however, was the concentration of the vegetable trade in wholesale markets in Cairo and Alexandria. The Rawd al-Farag market in Cairo had a reputation for profiteering wholesalers dating as far back as the 1920s.[117] The market was monopolized by a small group of powerful merchant families who controlled vegetable wholesaling for decades, defying attempts at regulation. Sadowski notes that although hundreds of wholesalers worked at the market, "all but ten percent of them came originally from the same three villages in Suhag" in Upper Egypt.[118]

Having inherited this state of affairs, the military officers in charge of the post-1952 government were anxious to get tomato prices under control. In his memoir Muhammad Naguib (president 1953–54) wrote that one of his fellow Free Officers was so zealous in his insistence that the Ministry of Supply protect the public from unscrupulous merchants that the minister resigned in frustration.[119] Another (perhaps apocryphal) story relates that one of the Free Officers declared that getting tomato prices under control was "more important than the departure of the English."[120] The officers did appoint market inspectors, but the phenomenon of volatile and sometimes prohibitive vegetable prices persisted, especially when it came to tomatoes.

Although horticultural crops were largely exempt from production controls, the state did attempt to influence the supply and pricing of vegetables starting in the 1950s.[121] This proved challenging, however. In 1958 Sa'id Hamdi explained that even though tomatoes could be grown year-round, seasonal variations in production levels meant that their price fluctuated throughout the year "more than any other vegetable."[122] Although some changes in tomato prices could be attributed to the laws of supply and demand, Hamdi wrote, "sometimes they fluctuate unexpectedly [*fuja'iyyan*]."[123] He included a chart depicting the supply quantities and prices of tomatoes at Alexandria's wholesale market in 1955–56 and 1956–57.

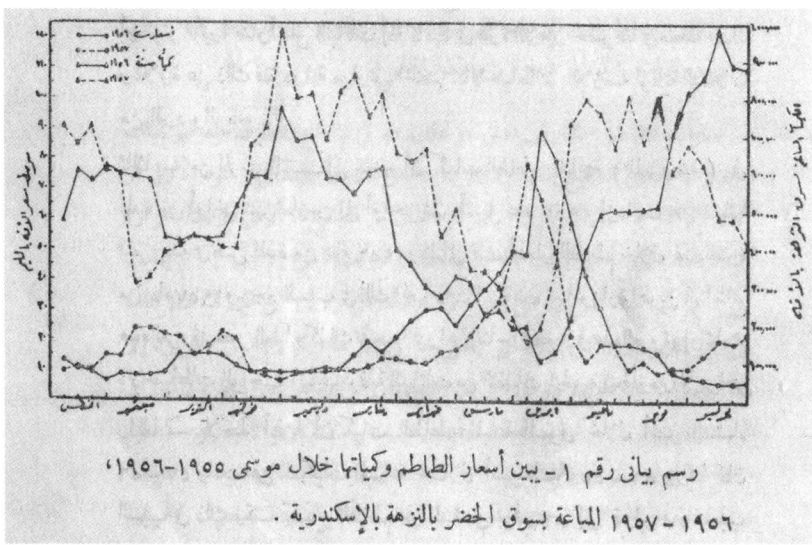

FIGURE 8. Tomato supply and prices at Alexandria's Nuzha vegetable market, 1955–56 (solid lines) and 1956–57 (dotted lines). The horizontal axis runs chronologically from left to right (August–July). The pair of contrasting lines that starts on top represents tomato supply; the other represents prices. *Source*: Hamdi, *Intaj al-tamatim*.

Although the chart perhaps obscures more than it clarifies, Hamdi explained some of its data points, offering a sense of the state interventions in the mid-1950s that sought to stabilize tomato supply throughout the year. He wrote that higher quantities of late winter and spring tomatoes had been brought to the market in 1957 compared with the previous year, resulting in lower prices. Hamdi attributed the increased supply (and indirectly, the lower prices) to measures undertaken by the Ministry of Supply that included encouraging farmers in Upper Egypt to plant tomatoes in winter in order to counter the typical seasonal drop in supply in spring, and offering guidance on protecting plants from weather fluctuations and disease—although he also mentioned the Tripartite Aggression of late 1956, which temporarily halted tomato exports, as another possible factor.[124] In any case, the seasonal variation of supply (and therefore prices) appears to have been a perennial issue; farmgate prices for tomatoes were consistently higher in winter than summer between 1964 and 1983, with the difference between summer and winter prices growing greater over time.[125]

In the 1960s, as the state turned to more concerted planning mechanisms, it consolidated additional controls over food supply—establishing "public companies for importing, exporting, and retailing agricultural products," for example, and mandating price ceilings on fruits and vegetables, including tomatoes, setting "different price levels for producers, wholesalers, and retailers."[126] Although the Ministry of Supply "was never able to completely suppress black market trade in agricultural goods," Sadowski suggests that the price ceilings did reign in price fluctuations to some degree.[127]

But price controls appear to have done little to curb the power of the merchants, who retained control over pricing, with the result that costs were passed on to the agricultural sector.[128] This is clear from a 1966 memo prepared by the National Planning Institute that describes the inner workings of Cairo's Rawd al-Farag market.[129] "The prices announced at the market do not reflect the prices at which goods are actually sold most of the time," the author notes, adding that most vendors did not maintain any official records that would document those discrepancies.[130] The memo details how merchants wielded power over farmers: while producers with smaller farms near Cairo could sell their vegetables themselves as ambulant vendors, those who lived farther away or produced larger quantities were forced to deal with the wholesale market system, paying a commission to the merchants who sold their produce.[131] Merchants were also frequently involved in financing production, particularly among smaller farmers, and therefore profited not only from their commissions but from interest on the money they loaned to farmers.[132] "The way the market currently operates does not protect [vegetable] suppliers from the dishonest dealings of some merchants," the memo concludes.[133]

Sadowski notes that the Ministry of Supply helped facilitate the merchants' oligopoly in the 1960s, having "encouraged the concentration of fruit and vegetable wholesaling" in major Cairo and Alexandria markets because "it lacked the manpower to police hundreds of scattered markets."[134] Yet this did not translate into effective control of prices at those markets. Officials from the Ministry of Supply knew which families controlled the wholesale market and coordinated with them in their efforts to control prices.[135] For decades merchants operated in secret, making deals that undercut official prices. A scene from the 1957 film (discussed further in the next section) depicts one of these deals, portraying how wholesale merchants colluded to restrict the tomato supply and thereby drive prices up.

An inspector from the Ministry of Supply quoted in the 1975 magazine article explains that merchants did not cooperate with government inspectors, and that "many illegal deals are struck at dawn, far from the market."[136] Moreover, he said, the fine for those caught violating price controls was too low to disincentivize illegal activity. In 1983 the chief of the Supply Police stated that "because the wholesale merchants deal only with a limited number of people known to them personally and in advance . . . it is hard to uncover their transgressions, particularly since those who deal with them fear to inform on them or be witnesses against them."[137] Effective regulation was also thwarted by technocrats who consulted "foreign development experts," and not the inspectors tasked with implementing regulations, when setting policy.[138] Despite the expansion of tomato production and increased yields in the 1970s and 1980s, therefore, tomato prices remained a thorny issue. An American agricultural economist working in Egypt in the 1980s observed that the system of official fixed prices for fruits and vegetables remained "generally ineffective" and that "in practice, prices for these perishable commodities are determined by competitive auction at levels that clear the markets daily."[139]

Youssef Wali, the minister of agriculture who oversaw the liberalizing reforms of the 1980s and 1990s, was a staunch advocate of removing controls on crop production and pricing, and in May 1985 the Ministry of Supply lifted all price controls on fruits and vegetables.[140] A crisis ensued: the price of tomatoes more than tripled, and many Cairenes could not afford vegetables. Months later "the government invoked its emergency powers to reduce the price of tomatoes, squash, and potatoes."[141] Eventually the controls were lifted for good, but the wholesale merchants retained their influence.[142]

TOMATOES AT THE MOVIES

The tomato crisis at Rawd al-Farag was dramatized in Salah Abu Seif's 1957 film *The Thug* (*al-Futuwwa*), which highlights the oppressive effects of the wholesale merchants—and the corrupt government officials who enabled them—on producers and consumers alike. Revisiting this classic film highlights the tomato's role as an element of Egyptian life that united farmers and workers, Cairenes and southerners, in a shared set of collective demands upon the state. In the film's opening scenes, the hero, Haridi, journeys to Cairo from the countryside for the first time.[143] His city-dwelling cousin 'Abdallah asks his wife to purchase food and prepare a meal to welcome the newcomer. Soon after, Haridi overhears her negotiating prices with a nearby vegetable seller. "That's crazy!" he exclaims when he hears the price of tomatoes in Cairo. Haridi makes his way to Cairo's wholesale vegetable market in search of work. Before long, the secrets of the tomatoes' high prices reveal themselves.

When Abu Zayd, one of the market's most powerful merchants, arrives at the market, he is met by a lackey who reports that the price of tomatoes is falling. Abu Zayd orders him to restrict the supply of tomatoes to drive up the price—and to send word to two other merchants to do the same. In time, Haridi learns the inner workings of the vegetable trade, including the merchants' alliances with powerful government officials who provide the necessary cover for their collusion. Shocked and angry, Haridi devises a plan to pool resources, source tomatoes directly from the countryside, and sell them at reasonable prices. But he is thwarted by Abu Zayd's thugs, who sabotage the trucks carrying his tomatoes. Eventually Haridi's increasingly elaborate ruses to overcome the oligopoly corrupt him, and he becomes the very kind of predatory merchant he once rallied the neighborhood against.

Although at first glance the film's central focus is the corruption of the merchants, a closer reading suggests a broader critique of the state structures that keep the merchants' corrupt system in place. The film's opening credits include an epigraph: "The events of this film took place at a time when the few controlled the livelihood and sustenance of the many." Various visual elements of the film's set and costumes place its story in the pre-1952 era. It could plausibly be understood by its initial audiences as depicting the corruption of the recently overthrown monarchy—a common trope in national narratives of the 1950s, and one that served the political interests of the Free Officers who now controlled the government.[144]

Yet the film's history suggests that this was not the only way it was received by the public. As discussed earlier, the change of regime had little impact on the wholesale market or the unpredictable and sometimes exorbitant price of tomatoes. In other words, the merchants depicted in the film were not figures from the past but characters with real-life analogues in Cairo in 1957. Just before the film was released, the merchant upon whom Abu Zayd's character was based brought a defamation lawsuit against the film's writer and its star, Farid Shawqi.[145] The case was defeated and the release went ahead, but the incident demonstrates how relevant its story and characters remained in post-1952 Cairo. The neorealist style of filmmaker Abu Seif underscored the connections between the story's fictional past and the tomato prices that its audiences experienced. His films frequently featured stories in recognizable Cairene settings; the market set in *The Thug*, for instance, was a replica built for the film and modeled after the actual Rawd al-Farag market.[146]

Given the persistence of high and unpredictable tomato prices before and after 1952, *The Thug* might also be read as a commentary on the continuities between Egypt's past and present governments. In this reading, the film's fundamental critique is leveled not at the corrupt merchants but at the political system that enables them. This reading draws on and resonates with a broader history of a statist politics of complaint in twentieth-century Egypt, whereby citizens across the ideological spectrum have looked to the state to address the problems of society.[147] Like food subsidies and tomato racketeering, this popular orientation toward the state existed before 1952 and survived long after it. This interpretation is affirmed by the film's closing scene. Haridi and Abu Zayd have by this point developed a rivalry that eventually escalates into violence between the two merchants' factions. Chaos descends on the market as tomatoes fly across the screen. Haridi and Abu Zayd, locked in hand-to-hand combat, become trapped in a walk-in refrigerator. Abu Zayd dies; Haridi barely escapes with his life. A policeman arrives to restore order (too little too late, one might add) and pronounces that the problems of the market are not caused by this or that individual; they are systemic and inevitable. "Abu Zayd and Haridi may go," he intones, "but a thousand more like them will come." A newcomer promptly arrives on the scene, presumably to take up the mantle of the corrupt wholesale merchant.

The film's ending renders its epigraph about a time gone by ironic in retrospect: although it implies that the concentration of power in the hands of the elite is a thing of the past, Egyptian audiences would have recognized the statement as a reflection of the present as well—at least when it came to tomato supply. The policeman's monologue confirms this, suggesting that the fundamental inequalities structuring society have not budged. As Samih Fatih puts it, the message of the film's final scene is that "the faces may change but the story remains the same."[148] In this sense the film prefigures the persistence of the tomato pricing problem despite the changes in regimes and their prevailing ideologies over the course of the twentieth century. Its conclusion implies that so long as the agents of the state are resigned to the status quo, corruption will persist and the people will continue to suffer from unjust tomato prices.

Ouissal Mejri describes *The Thug*, along with the earlier film *The Black Market* (*al-Suq al-sawda'*) as Egypt's first political films, and as foundational to the establishment of a genre of Egyptian films focused on *futuwwa*—literally, "youthful masculinity," or the figure who embodies it—an Egyptian cultural type that lends the film its name.[149] The content of *The Thug* underscores how these two observations are connected: "futuwwa" is not only a reference to the behavior of certain characters in the film; it also resonates through understandings of power and authority in modern Egypt. The term "al-futuwwa" has a complex genealogy; it originally implied a man's "honor, generosity, courage, and solidarity with his confreres."[150] Over time, however, it acquired negative overtones connoting the qualities of a bully, thug, or gangster—like the racketeering tomato merchants.[151]

Wilson Chacko Jacob describes futuwwa in the modern period as an ambivalent model of masculinity vying with a new kind of national subject, the self-consciously modern *efendi*—who is in turn the principal agent of bourgeois national sovereignty in Egypt.[152] Jacob highlights the figure of the futuwwa in modern Egypt not as a remnant of the past but as a present and ongoing manifestation of an "internal Other" who provided a foil to the efendi within "competing repertoires of authority."[153] Given this context, and the reading of the film proposed here, we might interpret the "thug" of the film's title as referring not only to the various characters that embody this type but also as a comment on a kind of authority that rules by force and fails to enact justice in the context of the modern market.

COUNTRY TOMATOES, CITY TOMATOES

The film *The Thug* also portrays this authority, and the figures who wield it, as attached to a particular place. Underpinning the film is a system of oppression in which control over the supply of a perishable commodity (tomatoes) is concentrated in the Cairo wholesale market. The film reveals how urban-rural divides fragmented Egyptian society during an era of rapid urbanization and the processes by which a wider Egyptian public—often overly identified with Cairo in dominant forms of popular culture—was brought into being through contestations over food supply in general and tomato prices in particular.

Haridi's journey as a naïve villager who is corrupted by life in Cairo is a familiar one in Egyptian cinema of the period. The plot of *The Thug* both critiques the relationship between the countryside and the city and continually attempts to remake and repair that relationship. The countryside does not appear as a static repository of Egyptian authenticity contrasted with the cosmopolitan modernity of the city, nor as a site of reform, but rather a site of production crucial to the fate of society. Samah Selim explains that beginning in the nineteenth century, the Egyptian peasant "came to represent Egypt itself."[154] With the rise of the modern state, increased rural-to-urban migration, and the consequent transformation of urban-rural relations, however, the figure of the peasant became a "potential (if problematic) national subject" in need of reform by elites.[155] By the second half of the twentieth century, "fiction, poetry, film and television soap operas depicted the village and the peasant in graphic detail in an attempt to describe the ills of Egyptian society and to point to a better future."[156] Selim observes that "even properly urban [Egyptian] fiction is almost always haunted by the presence of the village."[157]

In the world of *The Thug* it is not the countryside, but the urban vegetable market that requires reform. About halfway through the film the action breaks and cuts to a musical interlude. A chorus sings a song composed by Mahmud al-Sharif with lyrics by ʿAbd al-Fattah Mustafa, as scenes play of farmers laboring in the fields.[158] The interlude appears as Haridi is developing his first plan to undercut the wholesale merchants' oligopoly by sourcing tomatoes directly from the countryside. Both Haridi's scheme and the song lyrics highlight the way that injustice and corruption extend beyond Cairo, pervading Egyptian society as a whole.

A phrase from the song's refrain—"like us, our lands are dear and generous"—asserts farmers' claims as the rightful owners of the land, particularly agricultural land. This reflects "the idea of *al-ard wal-fallah* (Land and Peasant)," which Selim identifies as a motif running throughout twentieth-century Egyptian fiction.[159] By identifying farmers *with* the land, the song transcends the very framework of land ownership, modifying the land and the farmers with the same pair of adjectives. Those adjectives, *hinayyin* and *karim*, embed a range of meanings. "Hinayyin" signifies a person who is kind or tender as well as the physical quality of something soft or yielding.[160] "Karim" can refer to nobility or honor—a clear counterpoint to the "futuwwa" at work in the urban market—but it also refers to the linked value of generosity. The land is easy and pleasant to work and gives abundantly, in other words, and the farmers are honorable and generous.

The series of couplets that alternate with the song's chorus provide a clear indictment of those who have abused the land and its rightful custodians. Bewailing the loss of the land's bounty, the singing peasants blame the corrupt land ownership regime that controls it: "The Nile always rises, but the crops are not ours." As Ayman Khalil writes, "the song emphatically conveys the injustice, despotism, and corruption that citizens suffer from at the hands of those who have monopolized the markets, the land, and the farmers."[161] In the context of the film, the song invites us to consider the moral economy of the Egyptian food system beyond Cairo, looking to the rural spaces where tomatoes and other foods are produced. Finally, the song reflects the film's representation of the country and the city as sites of contestation over the heart of Egypt itself. This is clearest in the way that both country and city are personified in the character of Haridi, the rural outsider in the city. Embodying the struggle of the everyman against authority and the corrupting power of authority, inhabiting elements of both urban and rural types, and subject to the vicissitudes of the market, the character represents the emergence of a modern Egyptian public and the contradictions and elisions it entails.

One consistent marker of Haridi's rural origin is his speech: certain features mark his Arabic as rural rather than Cairene. He refers to tomatoes as "tamatim," whereas the Cairene vegetable seller he encounters in the first scene—as well as his local customers—refer to tomatoes as "oota."[162] As explained in chapter 2, the distinction between these two words for tomatoes is seldom straightforward; but in this case "tamatim" clearly identifies Haridi as an outsider in Cairo. The film's opening scene includes a clear reference to the street cry "magnuna ya oota," when Haridi calls the price of tomatoes "crazy," although he pronounces the word "majnun," with the soft "jeem" of the countryside rather than the hard "geem" of Cairene Arabic—another linguistic marker of his outsider status. Even so, for the film's audience a reference to tomato prices as "crazy," regardless of its pronunciation, would have been recognizable as a reference to the refrain proclaiming the ongoing problems of tomato prices.

CRAZY TOMATOES: ANATOMY OF A STREET CRY

Both *The Thug*'s emphasis on continuity and its statist critique were prescient. Although Cairo's wholesale vegetable trade was redistributed to three new sites in the 1990s, the volatility of tomato prices has persisted.[163] Ongoing complaints about tomato prices remain an aspect of Egyptian life, and they have a refrain: magnuna ya oota. Jayeeta Sharma describes how food vendors' street cries are historical sources that can illuminate food cultures' role in constructing the social fabric of urban environments, in part through the way that they contribute to "overlapping acoustic communities."[164] Like other forms of vernacular forms of expression, street cries help stitch together a collective sense of identity—less through protest and chanting than through a shared set of interactions that includes sellers, customers, and anyone else in earshot. The street cry is an urban working-class genre that was often performed, Sharma notes, by newcomers to cities, many of whom worked as street vendors upon their arrival (a phenomenon illustrated in *The Thug* through the trajectory of Haridi, whose first job upon arriving in Cairo is pulling a vegetable cart around the city).[165]

With this in mind we can understand how street cry "maguna ya oota," reverberating through urban Egypt in Cairene Arabic, has helped shape the Egyptian public in the era of the tomato.[166] Bruce Smith notes that in early modern England the street cries of different vendors "were distinctive not just in content but in rhythm, rhyme and sometimes cadence."[167] "Magnuna ya oota" is no different: the phrase is in two three-syllable halves whose cadence repeats (mag-NU-na ya OO-ta) and features internal rhyme ("nu" and "oo"). As rural migrants began selling tomatoes, their use of the cry would have signaled a linguistic shift by which they performed Cairene Arabic, at least in their roles as vendors, and contributed to the making of a Cairene public defined in part by the sound of their refrain.

I suggest that the meaning of the street cry "magnuna ya oota" embodies a specific form of critique best understood not as resistance or even refusal but complaint and disavowal. With it, the seller announces he is selling tomatoes while affirming he can make no promises about their price, which might be unexpectedly high compared to yesterday's. Through "ya," a vocative particle of address, the crier is technically addressing the tomato itself; "ya" effectively imposes a distance between the seller and the tomato, insisting, perhaps, that he is not responsible for their price. And while "craziness" signals a complaint that protests the price and proclaims its irrationality, its embodiment in a street cry also affirms that the seller and the customer are participating in the tomato market anyway—largely because they have little choice. For the most part Egyptians in the second half of the twentieth century could depend on the government to ensure an accessible bread supply; but the failure of the state to control the price of tomatoes was an open secret. Tomatoes were not deemed important enough to merit the kinds of state interventions reserved for bread. Yet as a popular staple that Egyptians relied on to convey flavor and cook other vegetables and meat, they were important enough that the most common public reference to them was a refrain of collective, if resigned, complaint.

José Ciro Martínez describes citizens' engagement with the state-run system that produces subsidized bread in Jordan. He observes that outright resistance or rejection of the system is generally impossible because of peoples' dependence on the state for basic sustenance and survival. But where rejection and resistance are not possible, he notes, people engage with the system through a range of tactics in order to actively participate in a state process and "to prevent the disappearance of bread as a public thing."[168] The complaint of crazy tomatoes in Egypt is also a claim on the state, although it operates somewhat differently. As a refrain, it names the state's failures and limitations while affirming, implicitly, a moral economy of welfare that the state has failed to uphold. As it circulates through Egyptian society, it forges a sense of shared experience across differences of social class, livelihood, and geography.

CONCLUSION: TOMATOES AND THE PUBLIC

Between the Second World War and the reforms of the early 1990s, the Egyptian state assumed a visible role in ensuring its citizens' food supply. As a result, food played a major role in constructing a statist culinary public in Egypt defined by a collective understanding of the relationship between the people and the state. This public took shape not only through material arrangements that shaped Egyptians' diets, but within the range of forms of popular expression by which Egyptians voiced disagreement, complaint, and sometimes dissent about the state's role in the food system.

As a popular staple and a beloved food that nevertheless fell outside of the state's most concerted efforts to regulate its food system, tomatoes offer insight into the ways that the relationship between state and society has been understood and experienced in Egypt. Street cries might not occasion policy changes, but they illuminate collective everyday experiences and sentiments—and how these cohere a kind of public defined against the state. In between moments of widespread protest and overt revolt, from demonstrations in the early 1940s to the bread intifada of 1977 to the revolution of 2011, lie mundane rehearsals of complaints about the prices of tomatoes. In Egypt in the second half of the twentieth century the tomato was part of the interface between Egyptians and various aspects of the state, uniting them collectively through shared experiences: complaining about tomato prices, haggling over their purchase, buying salsa produced by public sector companies.

But what happened when tomatoes were brought home from the market or released from a can plucked from the store shelf? How were they transformed into homecooked meals that furthered a sense of Egyptian-ness as something tasted and felt? The second half of the book traces what happened to tomatoes once they were in the hands of Egyptian cookbook authors and home cooks. From prescriptive recipes that instructed women how to use tomatoes to exhibit refinement to the everyday know-how that processed tomatoes into satisfying meals that tasted Egyptian, the chapters that follow explore tomatoes as ingredients in forms of belonging that were forged in Egyptian kitchens.

FOUR

Defining Egyptian Taste

TOMATOES IN DOMESTIC COOKBOOKS

IN 1937, HUDA SHAʿRAWI (1879–1947) received a letter containing two recipes.[1] One was for *sharkasiyya*, a walnut-based chicken dish. The other was a dolma recipe that called for stuffing vegetables with a mixture that included a generous quantity of tomatoes. Shaʿrawi was a prominent anticolonial activist who campaigned against the British occupation and advocated for women's rights; contributions to the field of cookery do not typically rank in lists of her accomplishments. And yet her interest in cooking was not confined to her personal correspondence; it was intimately connected to her nationalist and feminist politics. Her influence helped shape a genre of women-authored cookbooks that flourished in Egypt in the middle decades of the twentieth century. This chapter discusses these cookbooks as an entry point for the second half of this book, which traces how tomatoes entered Egypt's home kitchens.

Shaʿrawi herself was born into an elite family and only learned to cook as an adult. Her memoir recounts an epiphany she had in 1914, when she happened to be traveling in Italy during the outbreak of World War I. Temporarily stranded, she realized that she had no practical skills she could rely on to support herself. "I realized that I was neither a proficient cook nor a skilled seamstress . . .," Shaʿrawi recalled. "[A]nd I recognized that this was a lesson I should learn from. So after that I worked hard to learn how to cook and to improve my sewing skills."[2] In the large household in which she was raised, cooking was performed by a vast staff, some of them enslaved.[3] Shaʿrawi's education, typical for a woman of her generation and class, focused on Arabic, Turkish, French, and music.[4] But over the course of her lifetime, norms around domestic labor and the nature of girls' education in Egypt were changing. Advice urging elite and middle-class women "to reclaim domestic tasks," rather than delegate them to servants, was a fixture of the Egyptian press starting in the late nineteenth century.[5] This approach was increasingly institutionalized over the first half of the twentieth century. Domestic education, introduced to girls' school curricula in the nineteenth century, was expanded; textbooks incorporated increasingly detailed and extensive culinary content; new institutes were established dedicated to training teachers of domestic science (later home economics).[6] Practical domestic education was presented in public debates as an important aspect of (and justification for) girls' education, which expanded significantly between the late nineteenth and mid-twentieth centuries.

Shaʿrawi played a role in many of these developments. With a group of other nationalists she cofounded the Egyptian Feminist Union in 1923, the same year Egypt's first post-independence parliamentary elections took place. One of the organization's priorities was lobbying the government to expand women's access to secondary and higher education.[7] A major barrier was the lack of qualified female teachers, so Shaʿrawi helped assemble a delegation of Egyptian women to study at teaching colleges abroad.[8] In the 1920s Egyptian women studied a range of subjects in British institutions, including nursing, physical education, English literature, childhood development, and domestic science and cookery.[9]

The inclusion of the latter subjects reflected growing anxieties about the effect of women's education on Egyptian domestic life, which was widely debated in the press. In 1927 an article attributed to a woman named "Layla" claimed that the more highly educated Egyptian women were, the less likely they were to know even the most basic cooking skills, like frying an egg.[10] A 1934 cookbook review in a prominent newspaper emphasized the importance of domestic cookbooks at a time "when Egyptian girls are placing less and less value on working in the kitchen," insisting that even educated girls should know how to cook.[11] Shaʿrawi herself wrote an open letter endorsing the reviewed book and praising its author, Basima Zaki Ibrahim, for her "public service."[12] Teaching women how to properly manage the domestic sphere was commonly described as central to the fate of the nascent Egyptian nation.

In the 1930s and 1940s Egypt's Ministry of Education expanded and revitalized its approach to domestic subjects. The Higher Institute of Domestic Science, a teacher training college, was established in Cairo in 1937. The building included four large teaching kitchens and aimed to support the integration of domestic science into Egypt's secondary school curriculum (it was already being taught at the primary level).[13] Its faculty included many of the women who had studied in England, including Nazira Nicola and Bahia Osman, who were teaching there when they wrote their 1941 *Fundamentals of Cooking*—which was destined to become an Egyptian classic. Nicola, Osman, and Ibrahim were part of a cohort of Egyptian culinary professionals active between the 1930s and 1970s. Many had graduated from British domestic science colleges or from Egypt's own High Institute and worked as educators.[14] Several of them also produced content for magazines and radio in addition to writing cookbooks and textbooks. Their work merged the domestic science principles espoused in their British colleges with Egyptian and other "Eastern" recipes. And most of their books were written for an educated, middle-class housewife who cooked for her nuclear family within her own home kitchen, neither supervising a paid cook nor working as one—despite the fact that for most Egyptians, this framing reflected ideology more than reality.

Sha'rawi's trajectory offers a scaffold for charting the rise of home cooking as a specialized field at the intersection of specific norms of "gender, class, and collectivity."[15] When she was born in the late nineteenth century, the importance of domestic subjects to girls' education was a central point in debates about gender reform in Egypt.[16] School curricula and the periodical press emphasized that elite and middle-class women needed to acquire the proper kinds of knowledge to take an active role in managing their household, including their servants. As Sha'rawi rose to prominence in public life, domestic education was becoming institutionalized in Egypt's school system, and cookery emerged as a modern field of learning with its own texts, curricula, and specialist educators.

With domestic science and women's education in general expanding under the aegis of state institutions after Egypt gained political independence, cookbooks began to dictate new configurations of space, labor and knowledge in the home. The ideal housewife they envisioned nourished the nation single-handedly, aided only by the advantages conferred by a modern kitchen and a modern education. Cookbooks emphasized hands-on knowledge over managerial acumen, eliding the labor and culinary expertise of paid domestic workers and implying that even women who could afford to hire a maid or a cook needed to acquire modern, practical culinary knowledge.

Although Sha'rawi and her correspondents (like most middle- and upper-class women in Egypt) almost certainly employed domestic workers in their homes, the letter she received models the display and circulation of precisely this kind of knowledge. The letter makes no mention of servants; the culinary knowledge it contains appears to circulate only between elite women. Although written by hand, the recipes are formatted in the same style as recipes in contemporaneous printed cookbooks, listing precisely quantified ingredients followed by detailed instructions in formal Arabic. The recipes in the letter also mirror contemporaneous Egyptian cookbooks' repurposing of recipes from a range of sources, including Ottoman, Levantine, and European cuisines as well as local culinary traditions, into a modern *Mashriqi* (eastern Arab) sphere. The name of the dish "sharkasiyya" literally means "Circassian," suggesting its origins in the Caucasus; more locally, it would have signaled associations with the Turko-Circassian elites dominant in nineteenth-century Egypt (Sha'rawi's mother, for example, was a Circassian refugee who married a wealthy Egyptian landowner). Dolma, meanwhile, is a Turkish word for a category of foods with Arab roots and a rich Ottoman history (discussed in chapter 2). This chapter explores how women authors and educators framed Egyptian and other "Eastern" foods in much the same way that Sha'rawi's correspondents did: women's knowledge to be mastered and practiced within the home and expressed in formal Arabic.

Tomatoes, of course, featured prominently in this process. The books discussed here were published at a time when Egyptian tomato production was plentiful and rising steadily. According to one horticulturalist, Egypt produced enough tomatoes in 1956 for each family to have 125 kilograms for the year, a rate comparable to that in the United States—"the largest tomato producer in the world" at the time (for reference, this equates to about 2.4 kilograms, or a little more than a pound, per family per week).[17] Tomatoes offer an interpretive throughline connecting domestic practices with formal politics in midcentury Egypt.

MIDCENTURY DOMESTIC COOKBOOKS: A NEW GENRE

I focus here on the generation of cookbook authors active between the 1930s and the 1970s, although they were preceded by an earlier genre of domestic manuals that sometimes included recipes.[18] Of the eleven titles cited directly in this chapter, eight were written or coauthored by two of the genre's most prolific and prominent authors, Nazira Nicola and Basima Zaki Ibrahim. I purchased all of these cookbooks in the used book markets of Cairo and

Alexandria.[19] Many bear signs of use: notes and annotations, clipped and handwritten recipes tucked between their pages, and stains from the kitchen. Their presence in the book market and these markings offer some sense of the genre's circulation among a reading (and cooking) public.

These domestic cookbooks were different from previous Egyptian culinary texts in several ways: first of all, they were all written by women and intended for use by women home cooks.[20] And while most earlier domestic manuals were written for the benefit of elite or middle-class women presumed to be managing at least one servant, nearly all of the midcentury domestic cookbooks discussed in this chapter were written for a housewife working alone in her kitchen.[21] Midcentury cookbook authors also formatted their recipes into divided lists of ingredients and instructions. By contrast, none of the four cookbooks written by professional chefs discussed in chapter 2 organized recipes this way. Designed for the housewife, the divided recipe was pioneered by British cookbook authors to maximize efficiency and economy, encourage planning, and provide detailed instruction.[22]

The genre spans a major rupture in Egyptian history: the transition from a constitutional monarchy to a republic following the 1952 Free Officers' coup. Although certain aspects of these books' focus and emphasis shifted—for example, kitchen appliances were updated, and women's participation in the formal labor force was eventually acknowledged—the continuities across the decades are striking.[23] Many authors of the 1930s and 1940s continued to publish cookbooks and contribute recipes to women's magazines into the 1970s. And some cookbooks, particularly those authored by Nicola and Osman, were reprinted for multiple decades after their initial publication (the latest edition I have seen of their 1941 cookbook dates to 1981). New generations of cookbook authors followed, and eventually television and the internet became influential spheres of food media.[24]

SOVEREIGNTY IN THE KITCHEN

The Arabic term *tadbir al-manzil*, literally "household management," had been in use for centuries, originally borrowed from Greek sources.[25] In its original formulation "tadbir al-manzil" referred to a male property owner's material management of his estate—including his wife, children, and slaves; but in the modern period the phrase came to refer to a set of knowledge and skills that all women should cultivate to act as a manager of the home in her own right, rather than as the object of, or a proxy of, her husband's management.[26] Scholars have shown that in nineteenth-century Egypt the domestic sphere emerged "as a space that claimed attention" in a new way.[27] Eventually Egyptian educators used the phrase "tadbir al-manzil" to translate the English term "domestic science" into Arabic.[28] Thanks in part to this shift, by the mid-twentieth century the domestic kitchen had become a space saturated with new norms connected to modernity, gender, class, and the nation. It was not only important *that* women performed culinary labor; *how* and *what* they cooked mattered. This chapter explains how cookbooks contributed to the discursive construction of the kitchen as a private space of public concern.

I take up the concept of "kitchen sovereignty" to describe the power delegated to women working in home kitchens in the twentieth century. Just as conventional understandings of modern sovereignty confer authority on a particular entity (the state) within a defined space (a territory with borders), kitchen sovereignty also applies to a specific kind of actor and space. It is a modern form of authority granted to housewives—meaning, in the idealized terms of Egypt's midcentury cookbooks, married, middle-class women raising children in heteronormative nuclear family homes. The home kitchen was central to prescriptions of the importance of this authority and how it should be wielded. The idea of a permanent, dedicated space for cooking within the home was novel in Cairo, where only the homes of the wealthy reliably featured a dedicated kitchen with ventilation and a built-in heat source before the modern period.[29] Ambulant vendors and stalls selling prepared food were vital in a city where home kitchens were historically not the norm. The appearance of modern kitchens in urban middle-class homes across Egypt took place unevenly and gradually over the middle decades of the twentieth century—the same span during which the cookbooks discussed in this chapter were published.[30] Cookbooks specified how kitchens should be constructed and which appliances and fixtures they should feature—most importantly, a refrigerator, gas stove, and a sink with running water.

Unsurprisingly, the kitchens described in these cookbooks share many features with British kitchens that had appeared in the curricula many Egyptian cookbook authors had studied in England. But they included some uniquely Egyptian elements too: *Fundamentals of Cooking* includes a list of necessary equipment for a kitchen in a "middling" or "middle-class" home (*matbakh bi-manzil mutawassit*).[31] It includes a Primus stove, which was common in urban Egypt by the Second World War, as well as a *makhrata*, the mezzaluna-type blade Egyptians use to mince the leafy green *mulukhiyya*, and items made from copper—a historically common material for Egyptian cookware, prized for its cultural and practical value. The copper items include "a copper sieve for tomatoes," which was used to juice and grate tomatoes before the advent of the electric blender.[32]

These texts highlight the importance of home cooking performed by a specific kind of woman: the middle-class housewife. This ideal figure has been educated in the principles of modern scientific household management and nutrition (or is at least educated enough to access these texts' explanations of them) and cooks within her own home as an unremunerated form of domestic and affective labor—she is neither cooking for wages nor managing someone who is. These qualities are often highlighted in cookbook titles and front matter: one 1953 cookbook is titled *Fundamentals of the Art of Cooking: The Most Modern Methods*, with a title page promising that its recipes are written using "a scientific method." It is dedicated to "the virtuous wife who seeks to make her husband happy."[33]

Authors referred to the "housewife" as *rabbat al-bayt* or *sayyidat al-bayt*.[34] These Arabic terms encode social class more explicitly than their English equivalent: "rabba" and "sayyida" translate to "lady" or "mistress." "Sayyida" is from the same root as the Arabic word for "sovereignty," *al-siyada*. The terms underscore that within the idealized kitchens of these texts, a particular kind of woman was construed as sovereign, and culinary authority (i.e., kitchen sovereignty) accrued implicitly to a woman of the educated classes. In this sense domestic cookbooks formed part of a global trend whereby "the home became a site for the fortification of social hierarchies."[35] Sherene Seikaly notes that in mandate Palestine the construction of an idealized "model middle class" was defined against its "others"—Bedouins, peasants, maids, and workers—rendering them either invisible or "as stock figures that threatened the social order."[36] By the 1950s Egyptian cookbook authors had adopted the former approach, omitting all references to maids and domestic workers.[37]

Equipped with the right appliances and the correct modern knowledge, the subject of the midcentury domestic cookbook was empowered to maintain distinctions of culture and class. Cookbooks purported to set up their readers as arbiters of good taste, positioning middle-class housewives as producers of a national culinary culture that was modern, refined, and authentically Egyptian.[38] In her endorsement of Ibrahim's first book, Sha'rawi praises Ibrahim's "good taste [*husn dhawqiha*]."[39] Nicola and Osman frame *Fundamentals of Cooking* as a response to a consensus in "public opinion" that young women should be equipped with an understanding of "refined domestic life [al-hayat al-manziliyya al-raqiyya]."[40] These cookbooks therefore embody what Amy Kaplan describes as "part of the cultural work of domesticity"—namely, charging women with "defining the contours of the nation and its shifting borders with the foreign," regulating distinction on the national level (defining which are "our" foods versus foreign foods, for instance) as well as within a society.[41] Egypt's domestic cookbook authors dictated the contours of a prescriptive cultural and class identity, identifying which elements of European, Eastern, and Egyptian cuisines were suitable and on what terms.

The idealized vision of domesticity outlined in prescriptive texts cannot be read as a straightforward representation of actual kitchens or configurations of domestic labor. Even among their educated readership, Egyptian discourses of modern domesticity were often at odds with reality.[42] Laura Bier observes the largely aspirational nature of images of kitchens in Nasser-era periodicals, noting that access to the kinds of spaces and technology they depicted "was necessarily uneven, differing not only by economic class but also by location."[43] Following the 1952 revolution, the Egyptian state prioritized making items like refrigerators and propane stoves more accessible through domestic production and financing schemes.[44] Yet access to these appliances remained relatively limited: a 1968 survey of one hundred Cairene households representing a cross-section of socioeconomic levels indicated that while four in five households owned a propane stove, only 63 percent owned a refrigerator and 16 percent owned an electric blender.[45] It was not until the 1970s that appliances such as refrigerators, deep freezers, water heaters, and blenders became more widely accessible—largely thanks to the rise of labor migration, which increased many families' purchasing power significantly.[46]

Despite the many cookbooks written for households in which only housewives carried out the cooking and other housework, paid domestic labor was common in the homes of Egypt's urban professional classes, where the books' readers were most likely to reside.[47] Beth Baron notes that "more Egyptian women were employed as domestic servants than in any other capacity in the late nineteenth and early twentieth century."[48] In 1960 more than one-fifth of urban workers in Egypt were categorized as "household servants."[49] That year one million Egyptian girls attended primary school, but fewer than twenty-nine thousand were enrolled in secondary school; even in 1976, 71 percent of Egyptian girls and women were illiterate.[50] It is true that the structures of domestic labor in Egypt were changing during the period these cookbooks were written, shifting away from a model of live-in servants toward part-time waged labor.⁵¹ But in a context in which most middle-class households continued to employ some form of domestic labor, these cookbooks—intentionally or not—effectively elided both the labor and culinary knowledge of the domestic workers responsible for cooking in Egypt's elite and middle-class homes. Although their authors often addressed themselves to all Egyptian women and couched their contributions in national terms, in practice these books were written for a comparatively narrow reading public of educated women.

Kitchen sovereignty therefore shares some features with modern state sovereignty. Both are tied to new ways of conceptualizing space (the territory contained within the borders of a modern map; the newly permanent space of the home kitchen).⁵² Both concepts encompass a set of ideals that tend to contrast with the messier reality of how they are put into practice: as Lauren Benton puts it, "sovereignty is often more myth than reality," at times functioning "more as a story that polities tell about their own power than a definite quality they possess."⁵³ Egyptian cookbooks similarly tell a "story" about a gendered form of authority within the domestic sphere. Even when they were "more myth than reality," however, these cookbooks played an important role in shaping Egyptians' aspirations and desires. I therefore approach them as mediators between reality and experience.

EXTRACTING WESTERN KNOWLEDGE, PRESCRIBING EASTERN TASTE

While cookbook authors used introductions and other paratextual material to dictate the proper management of domestic space and labor, most of their books were of course devoted to recipes. The specific foods that authors chose for their readers speak to how they envisioned Egyptian good taste in culinary terms. Authors across the genre positioned Egyptian cooking within a broader "Eastern" sphere that frequently emphasized Arab elements.⁵⁴ They also integrated "Western" culinary knowledge and recipes in specific ways.⁵⁵ Accordingly, the most basic culinary categorization running throughout these cookbooks is a dichotomy between Eastern (*sharqi*) and Western (*gharbi, afranji*) foods.

Following Japan's defeat of Russia in 1905, intellectuals across Asia and the Islamic world took up a new paradigm of East and West, citing the

Japanese victory as a refutation of Orientalist assertions of Western superiority.⁵⁶ Marilyn Booth notes that abstracted notions of East and West were frequently invoked in Egyptian debates about nationalism and modernity after 1905, adding that "as Egyptian nationalisms became more sharply defined, the layers of meaning these terms contained multiplied."⁵⁷ The cookbooks discussed here were published during a specific period in the history of these debates: the 1930s saw the rise of a new generation of *efendiyya* (male members of Egypt's urban professional classes) whose discussions of the nature of Egyptian nationalism incorporated a range of broader "Eastern" formations.⁵⁸ Participants in these debates often produced overlapping, rather than mutually exclusive, visions of Arab, Eastern, Egyptian territorial, and Islamic identities and affinities, although "Egyptian Arab nationalism" was a consistent theme.⁵⁹

The content of Egypt's midcentury domestic cookbooks illustrates that educated women also engaged in these discussions.⁶⁰ Incorporating multiple influences, including those from beyond Egypt's borders, the genre functioned not to canonize a narrow vision of "national cuisine" but instead operated within a broader framework of "culinary nationalism." Michelle King describes this framework as "a dynamic process of creation and contestation" that entails both signifying boundaries between nations and marking internal distinctions within them.⁶¹ In Egypt's midcentury domestic cookbooks, certain foods are identified as "Western" not to exclude them from their readers' repertoires but to present them as one tool among many for enacting modernity and refinement through cooking.

Of the authors discussed here, Ibrahim articulated the relationship between Egyptian and other Eastern identities, as well as her opinion of Western cuisines, most explicitly. In *Eastern Cuisine* (ca. 1940?) she describes the Japanese as a people who have "made great strides in civilization, progress, and culture, but without shunning their past or their customary ways of cooking and serving food." Exhorting her fellow Egyptians to follow the Japanese example, Ibrahim calls for systematizing and refining aspects of their food culture while "protecting its national character . . . preserving its Egyptian-ness first, followed by its Eastern-ness."⁶² This nesting of Egyptian identity within a broader Eastern identity is echoed in one of her later works, from 1958, which addresses "Egyptian women in particular, and Eastern women in general," as well as "the daughters of the Arab nation."⁶³

When it came to Western cuisine, Ibrahim insisted: "Truly, there is nothing remarkable about the cooking of the West [literally, cooking among

Westerners, *al-tabkh ʿind al-gharbiyyin*] apart from the way it is organized in accordance with the principles of health."[64] Her books present both concepts and recipes from "Western" cuisines as resources for reforming and refining "Eastern" cooking practices, encouraging readers to exercise careful judgment so they may dispense with the "inferior elements of the heritage of the past" but without allowing their tables to become "purely Western."[65] Her 1958 cookbook instructs "Egyptian ladies [*sayyidat*]" to cook foreign dishes in order to diversify their culinary repertoires; the book includes, alongside many Egyptian and other Eastern dishes, recipes for French sauces and American-style fish.[66] Like other Egyptian midcentury cookbook authors, Ibrahim presents Western dishes as simply one part of a diverse and refined menu.[67] Not all authors described cultural categories so directly, but all of them adopted an instrumental approach to "Western" knowledge, selectively incorporating frameworks from European and North American domestic science. Many open their books with introductory material that references concepts from modern nutritional science (like the categories of fat, protein, and carbohydrates), and most adopt a sequence of chapters based on categories that mirror those of British domestic science texts. And of course, all of them divide their recipes into ingredients (*al-maqadir; al-mawadd*) and instructions (*al-tariqa*).

Cookbook authors also integrated a wide range of foods, both Eastern and Western, into their recipe collections. *Fundamentals of Cooking*, for example, includes Egyptian regional specialties (*kishk Saʿidi* from the south, Dimyati cheese from the Mediterranean coast), street foods like *ful mudammas* and *koshari*, and foods associated with regional and global elites (from French sauces to dishes connoting Ottoman Turkish influence). According to Omar Taher, upon her return from England, Nicola "went into the field in order to master Eastern cooking," gathering culinary knowledge from sweet shops, restaurant kitchens, and Ministry of Agriculture labs (where she studied preserves and dairy products).[68] British domestic science provided a framework for consolidating and organizing this vast local knowledge—elevating local practices and domesticating elite dishes into a modern culinary repertoire to be wielded by middle-class housewives.

Authors also positioned themselves as authorities who adjudicated the terms of good "Eastern" taste. The category of "Eastern" foods was relatively consistent in domestic cookbooks between the 1930s and 1970s, comprising a wide range of dishes but with an emphasis on the Arab East. Ibrahim's

Eastern Cuisine is illustrative: about 80 percent of the book's recipes are in a section titled "Egyptian Dishes [*al-alwan al-Misriyya*]." This is followed by a shorter section, "National Dishes in Different Eastern Countries." Nearly half of this shorter section comprises recipes from former Ottoman territories in the Eastern Mediterranean, among which Syrian cooking is singled out for particular praise. The remaining pages include foods from other countries in Africa and Asia.[69] This balance reflects the definition of "Eastern" cuisine in other midcentury domestic cookbooks—which is to say, notwithstanding the occasional couscous or curry, there is a strong emphasis on foods of the Eastern Mediterranean. While earlier cookbooks often framed such dishes as Turkish, midcentury cookbooks favored labels that highlighted Arab affinities instead. In addition to the general label "sharqi" (Eastern), authors often used "Shami," referring to the Levant (Syria, Lebanon, Palestine, and Jordan).[70] Comparatively very few Maghribi dishes are included, and besides the Ibrahim chapter mentioned here, none of the other books I discuss name Sudanese recipes or invoke the label "African."[71]

This pattern illustrates how these authors situated Egyptian cooking within a Mashriqi culinary sphere, highlighting Egypt's affinity with certain parts of the Arabic-speaking world over others. Although this tendency has an obvious resonance with the pan-Arab politics of the late 1950s and 1960s, it is also rooted in older political, cultural, and culinary histories. These include the influence of Ottoman Turkish cuisine discussed in chapter 2 and debates over Egyptian nationalism mentioned in this chapter. In addition, following the opening of the Suez Canal in 1869, many merchant families relocated from Syria to Egypt as trade was routed to Cairo rather than Aleppo. They brought their recipes with them, which entered the repertoires of the Egyptian cooks who staffed their kitchens as well as the restaurants of Cairo and Alexandria.[72] Parallel to these culinary infusions was a set of intellectual and cultural connections between Egypt and the Levant, including in education and publishing.

In summary, midcentury cookbooks centered a middle-class subject conversant in a cosmopolitan repertoire of modern cooking that included both Eastern and Western foods. They yoked recipes from the Levant and Egypt into a Mashriqi culinary category, which was positioned as a means for creating and maintaining social and cultural distinctions within and beyond Egypt. In doing so, authors outlined a vision of modern Egypt defined not only in territorial terms, but within a transnational Mashriqi sphere. Tomatoes were central to the construction of this layered vision.

TOMATOES AS VEHICLES FOR EASTERN-EGYPTIAN TASTE

By the time this genre of domestic cookbooks was being written and published, tomatoes had consolidated their status as a key component of Egyptian diets—particularly in the urban areas where many of the cookbooks' readers lived. Twentieth-century agricultural manuals identified the tomato as a central ingredient in "Eastern" cooking, which paralleled the way that cookbooks incorporated Egyptian cooking within a wider Eastern context. As discussed in chapter 2, the authors of *The Tomato in Egypt* (1922) highlighted the tomato's use in "Eastern foods [*at'ima sharqiyya*]," particularly as *salsa*, or tomato sauce. Another manual from 1972 states that the tomato is "among the most consumed vegetables in our Arab countries [*fi baladna al-'Arabiyya*]."[73] Its title, *al-Tamatim: al-Banadura*, also bridges regional varieties of Arabic, invoking both the Egyptian and Levantine Arabic words for tomato.

Similar claims about the tomato appear in domestic manuals published in the early twentieth century, when tomatoes were already playing key roles in the repurposing and reframing of Ottoman dishes as Egyptian and Arab. Fransis Mikha'il's household management textbook (1910–11) lists common uses of the tomato as "*salsa*, *mahshi*, cooked with rice, or in salads" (using the Arabic term "mahshi" rather than the Turkish "dolma").[74] A contemporaneous manual by Ibrahim 'Abd al-Ra'uf adapts two Ottoman dishes and presents Egyptian versions of them. Whereas "red stew" (*al-yakhni al-ahmar*) had appeared in nineteenth-century Ottoman cookbooks *without* tomatoes, 'Abd al-Ra'uf's recipe by the same name calls for tomato sauce as the cooking medium.[75] His *turli* recipe is subsumed under a broader, Egyptian-coded category, *tawajin* (casseroles; singular *tajin*), and includes diced tomatoes and cumin (recall Ahmed Ibrahim's substitution of cumin for cinnamon in a turli recipe some years earlier).[76] In other words, even before Nicola, Osman, and their colleagues were sent to England, authors writing recipes for home cooking were using tomatoes to establish Arab Egyptian versions of a range of Eastern dishes in a trend that was continued and expanded by the next generation of cookbook authors.

TOMATO SAUCES AND STEWS

Tomatoes appear most prominently in midcentury domestic cookbooks within sauces and stews, which were central to the way that authors modeled a vision of Egyptian taste that was refined, modern, and Mashriqi. To understand what this looked like in practical terms, I discuss examples from Nicola and Osman's *Fundamentals of Cooking*. At over nine hundred pages, their book is by far the longest and most comprehensive cookbook of its kind. It is also the best-known cookbook within Egypt; most Egyptians I know are familiar with it—or at least with Nazira Nicola, the more famous of its two authors, who is popularly known as Abla ("Auntie") Nazira.

Known colloquially as "Abla Nazira's book," *Fundamentals of Cooking* played a dual role as both a textbook for the institute that trained Egypt's domestic science teachers and a popular household object. It appears to have circulated more than other books of its genre; I was often told that it was commonly given to brides in middle-class circles in the 1950s and 1960s. One copy I found in a used book market was inscribed with a dedication from a husband to his wife; another was embossed with its owner's name. It remained in print until at least the 1980s. Its authors cowrote several other books together and had their own careers as educators and public figures: Osman contributed recipes to the women's magazine *Hawwa'* and Nicola hosted a radio show. It is not just a cookbook but a cultural touchstone.[77] For all these reasons *Fundamentals of Cooking* is an ideal case study for understanding how tomatoes operated within the broader genre.

Tomato sauces and stews appear in numerous guises throughout the book; but in each case a systematic framework organizes some combination of Egyptian, Mashriqi, and European recipes. The way they are structured mirrors aspects of British domestic science texts and curricula, but they also introduce culinary aesthetics specific to the Arab world, particularly when it comes to vegetable stews. The authors repurpose older Arabic culinary terms and introduce them into a framework of explicitly "modern" cooking. Tomato sauces first appear in a chapter devoted to sauces ("salsa," here used in the broad sense rather than referring narrowly to tomato sauce). Nicola and Osman's chapter on sauces hews closely to the models provided by British domestic science curricula. Its structure resembles the sauce chapter in one of the textbooks used at Berridge House, the college where Osman studied.[78] Both chapters follow a similar sequence and center roux-based and emulsified French sauces like béchamel, hollandaise, and mayonnaise (though often renamed, in the original English and in Arabic translation, with British labels like "white sauces" and "brown sauces").[79]

The only "Eastern" sauces included in the chapter appear toward the end. One is a vinegar and garlic sauce described as a garnish for *fatta*, a dish prepared throughout the Arab world. Many variations exist, but it generally features a carbohydrate base, protein, and sauce. Egyptian versions typically feature a vinegar-based sauce, meaning that the recipe would likely have been familiar to the book's readers.[80] The chapter includes two sauces that can be classified as "Eastern": *tarator*, a tahini-based sauce popular throughout the Levant, and a sauce to dress sharkasiyya, the Turko-Circassian dish included in Sha'rawi's recipe letter.

Finally, the chapter presents two very different tomato sauce recipes, one British and the other Egyptian. The former, called simply "tomato sauce [*salsat al-tamatim*]," appears to be adapted from the British textbook, with minor adaptations to suit an Egyptian readership (e.g., the substitution of *samna*, or clarified butter, for bacon fat).[81] The second is titled "tomato sauce, known as *dim'a*."[82] "Dim'a" is a common Egyptian colloquial term for a kind of tomato sauce.[83] The recipe in the cookbook is made with garlic and samna. It concludes with a note in parentheses: "it is used to cook many types of foods."[84] Such remarks are rare in the book; this one suggests that the authors assumed that it was known to their readers. We might read Nicola and Osman's inclusion of Egyptian and Mashriqi sauces within a British-style framework emphasizing French-style sauces as an assertion that they are just as sophisticated, refined, and modern as any European sauce.

STEWS FOR STOVETOP AND OVEN

While tomatoes play a minor role in the cookbook's sauce chapter, they are the star of sections containing recipes for stews, braises, and casseroles. These are grouped under the umbrella category of *tasbik*, which includes all three types of dish. Throughout the book "tasbik" is integrated into a sequence of cooking techniques (boiling, stewing/braising, frying, grilling, roasting, steaming) that corresponds to the sequence taught at the British domestic science college that Nicola attended, albeit in a slightly different order.[85] After its appearance in a preliminary chapter that presents an overview of each technique, the sequence recurs in a pattern throughout the book.[86] In any given chapter, recipes involving boiling precede those for stewing, which are followed by frying and so forth.

In their preliminary overview of tasbik as a cooking technique, Nicola and Osman present it in a favorable light, particularly compared to boiling. They define "tasbik" principally as a method that entails a long cooking time over low heat.[87] They point out several additional comparative advantages: the technique preserves both the nutritional value and the flavors of the ingredients while maximizing efficiency through the use of a single cooking vessel.[88] They explain that tasbik is adaptable to various kitchen configurations: it can be achieved either using a stove with a very low flame or in the oven in a clay tajin. The vegetables chapter of the book opens with a brief section about boiling vegetables that is primarily focused on how to do so without sacrificing their texture and color, before moving onto a much more elaborate explanation of the range of braises, stews, and casseroles that can be used to prepare vegetables.

An account by Esmat Rushdi, an Egyptian educator living in England in the late 1940s, offers some context for these pointed comparisons with boiling. In a 1948 article written for a British audience about Egyptian domestic science education, Rushdi includes a tomato stew recipe. Describing the technique as "the basic method of cooking Egyptian vegetables," she emphasizes its superiority to the British preference for boiling ("Your basic method of cooking vegetables is boiling, as I who have suffered for the first time from the boiling of potatoes and cabbage know").[89] Reading between the lines of Nicola and Osman's cookbook and Rushdi's account, one can imagine a generation of Egyptians arriving in England to study cooking only to be horrified by the boiled vegetables that appear at lunch. Nicola and Osman's defense of their favored cooking techniques on the basis of nutrition, superior flavor, and efficiency might be read as a vindication of their native cuisine using the principles of their British training.

In the introduction to their chapter on vegetables (which includes many recipes featuring meat), Nicola and Osman detail three foundational techniques under the heading "tasbik."[90] All of them involve tomatoes. The techniques are organized into two primary categories: *matmur* (for which an alternate spelling is given, *makmur*) and *musaqqaʿa* (often spelled "moussaka"). Matmur/makmur is further subdivided into two categories: with and without a technique called *basliyya*.[91] This basic outline is followed by numerous notes and variations, including a list specifying which vegetables should be cooked with the addition of garlic and cumin. While all three techniques have layered histories (and nomenclatures) in Ottoman, Egyptian, and Arab cuisines, Nicola and Osman generally prioritize Arabic terminology. Where Turkish terms do appear, they are subsumed within Arabic categories. *Yakhni*, a Turkish word of Persian origin, is listed as a type of makmur; turli appears as a subcategory of musaqqaʿa; dolma is positioned as a type of mahshi. Recipes applying each of these techniques share a common set of ingredients (meat, tomatoes, samna, onion, and various vegetables) but in different configurations.

Two of the three basic techniques—musaqqaʿa and the first type of matmur/makmur—are essentially layered casseroles and have clear links to older, pretomato dishes. The Hinds-Badawi dictionary of Egyptian Arabic defines makmur as "a kind of stew prepared in an earthenware pot buried in hot ashes."[92] This technique is common to many Arab cuisines; in Egypt it was historically used to slow-cook fava beans in the ashes of communal ovens and bathhouses. Nawal Nasrallah traces the origin of musaqqaʿa in precursors that date back to tenth-century Baghdad, and notes that the other words used to refer to the dish and its forerunners include *medfune*, a word that connotes burying or covering a dish during the cooking process.[93] These cooking methods existed long before tomatoes arrived to the region, but when Nicola and Osman present their versions of them, tomatoes are a prominent—even a dominant—feature.[94] The middle technique, "matmur/makmur," made with a step the authors term "basliyya," is described as suited only for stovetop cooking. It is most clearly identifiable with the stewing technique that Egyptian cooks refer to in spoken Arabic as *tasbika* (the subject of chapter 5). It includes similar ingredients to the other techniques but adds a number of steps that will be familiar to any Egyptian cook today: begin with a base of minced onions browned in samna, add cubed meat, cover with tomatoes sieved into a liquid form, add vegetables and seasonings, then place over heat "until the tomatoes are finished cooking, which you will know by the separation of the samna [from the surface of the stew]."[95]

This theoretical introduction to the three tasbik methods is followed by seventy-three pages of recipes for cooking vegetables. Multiple recipes are offered for each vegetable, typically beginning with a cursory recipe for boiling and sometimes including a European recipe or two (e.g., garnishing with a white sauce) as well as Egyptian and other Eastern cooking techniques, including recipes with and without tomatoes. In addition to the various tasbik techniques, all of which involve tomatoes, some recipes pair vegetables with dimʿa, the garlic-based tomato sauce described above. Of twenty-two vegetables, fifteen are presented with one or more tomato-based options.

The inclusion of so many tomato-forward recipes points to the popularity of these techniques in the early 1940s; their variety suggests that tomatoes were being integrated into a cuisine in transition, as dishes that had been historically prepared in casseroles in ovens or buried in ashes were being adapted to kerosene and other types of gas stoves. But it is also striking that Nicola and Osman did not include these recipes within a theoretical framework and structure based in European cooking principles, as they had done in the sauce chapter. Instead, they present them within their own theoretical framework and structure based in Eastern cooking. I read this approach as their assertion of Egyptian cuisine as a sophisticated culinary culture equal to European cuisine in its variety and technicality—a site of modern, nutritional, economical, efficient cooking and a means for purveying good taste with tomatoes as a major throughline.

Naguib Mahfouz's Cairo Trilogy offers context for the cultural resonance of "tasbik" as an Egyptian and implicitly Arab category. Part national epic and part family saga, the three novels of the trilogy begin in the lead-up to the 1919 revolution and were published in the 1950s. They revolve around the ʿAbd al-Jawad family, helmed by an upwardly mobile Egyptian merchant and thought to be based on Mahfouz's own childhood home.[96] One of the signs of the family's upward mobility is its children's intermarriage with elite families of Turkish origin. Cultural differences between the Arab Egyptian ʿAbd al-Jawad family and the Turkish-descended elites with whom they intermarry are occasionally represented through food. A scene in the second installment of the trilogy suggests the association of "tasbik" with a local, Egyptian mode of cooking. Khadija, one of the daughters of the ʿAbd al-Jawad family, has married the Turkish-descended Ibrahim Shawkat. At a meal hosted by Khadija's mother Amina, Ibrahim offers enthusiastic praise for his mother-in-law's cooking, calling it the "most appetizing and delicious food" and singling out her tawajin in particular. It's not only the ingredients that Amina uses that make her cooking so delicious, he explains to the family members gathered around the table, but her mastery of tasbik—the technique with which they are prepared. "The tasbik is everything," he cries, describing it as the product of superb work(wo)manship and "a miracle."[97]

It is significant that an elite, Turkish-descended character swoons so dramatically over a mode of cooking clearly associated with the traditional, local Egyptian culture that Amina embodies throughout the trilogy—as opposed to more prestigious dishes like sharkasiyya that would have been associated with households like the one he grew up in (indeed, in the first novel in the trilogy, sharkasiyya is a point of difference between Amina's cooking and the elite cuisine of her Turkish daughter-in-law).[98] Did Amina's tasbik involve tomatoes? It is impossible to know for certain. But Nicola and Osman's invocation of the term to refer to a category of dishes that featured tomatoes so prominently highlights tomatoes' status as a marker of authentic, delicious, home-cooked Egyptian food by the middle of the century.

STUFFED VEGETABLES AND LEAVES

Finally I turn to the category of *mahshuwwat*, popularly known as mahshi. This set of foods demonstrates how midcentury cookbook authors used tomatoes, Arabic terminology, and the organizational frameworks of modern domesticity to repurpose Ottoman and other regional foods into a Mashriqi repertoire with Egyptian variations. Nicola and Osman devote a nineteen-page section to "mahshuwwat" toward the end of a chapter on grains and legumes.[99] Unlike the vegetable and sauce sections discussed above, the mahshi section includes no European elements whatsoever. It opens with a rare descriptive headnote: "Stuffed foods are an important category of dish, particularly in Eastern countries [al-bilad al-sharqiyya]. They vary based on the type of vegetable used and may be served individually or on a platter featuring several different varieties."[100] The chapter outlines four categories of filling. The first two are made with ground meat, samna, and rice, and seasoned with parsley, mint, and tomatoes; the only difference between them is whether one cooks the filling before stuffing and cooking the vegetables with it. The fourth is labeled with the Turkish term "dolma" and is a vegan version of the first two fillings (no meat; oil rather than samna).[101]

The final stuffing is labeled ʿassaj. As far as I am aware, this is a word unique to Egyptian usage; the Hinds-Badawi dictionary lists it as "cooked with onion (and sometimes tomato sauce, parsley, etc.) until the juices are absorbed (of minced meat to be used as a component in stuffed vegetables etc.)."[102] This definition closely resembles the recipe that Nicola and Osman provide for ʿassaj, which appears earlier in the cookbook.[103] The stuffing incorporates this basic ʿassaj recipe as well as tomatoes but does not include rice. While tomatoes are included as a possible ingredient for all four types of stuffing, the ʿassaj stuffing—arguably the most obviously Egyptian variation, at least linguistically speaking—is the only one for which the use of tomatoes is not listed as optional.

Following this overview of stuffing styles are twenty-eight recipes for a variety of types of leafy and other vegetables. Seventeen of those, a little more than half, call for tomatoes to be used as a cooking medium for the vegetables once they have been stuffed. Usually this takes the form of "sieved tomato," but in a handful of instances recipes call specifically for the use of dimʿa.[104] One of the recipes for stuffed grape leaves is identified as "Levantine-style [ʿala al-tariqa al-Shamiyya]"; it does not call for tomatoes.[105] Compared to the rest of the cookbook, the most unusual feature of this section is the authors' deference to their readers' preferences and tastes. For instance, one of the four types of stuffing is described as "a mixture of desired ingredients, according to taste [al-dhawq] and the type of vegetable."[106] Similarly, the recipe for ʿassaj filling includes a note next to the parsley and pinenuts in the ingredient list: "these may be omitted."[107] The invocation of the cook-reader's taste suggests faith in both the reader's culinary acumen and taste level. Only rarely in the cookbook are readers granted so much discretion. Incidentally, the dolma recipe sent to Huda Shaʿrawi embeds a similar flexibility: its otherwise exact ingredient list includes the option of stuffing pepper or eggplant, as the cook prefers.[108]

It is perhaps unsurprising that as a category Nicola and Osman could expect their readers to be familiar with, this section includes more flexibility than anywhere else in the cookbook. Embracing variations of a favorite category of dishes shared across the Levant and Egypt, the mahshi section exemplifies the authors' idealized model of Egyptian taste envisioned as part of a Mashriqi culinary sphere—while revealing the importance of tomatoes, particularly in anchoring its Egyptian elements.

RECIPES FOR A NATION

Throughout the genre of midcentury domestic cookbooks, tomato-forward dishes were a central arena in which authors highlighted local techniques as important markers of Egyptian and Eastern cultural identity while simultaneously singling them out for improvement and refinement. Across the decades discussed in this chapter, cookbook authors exhibited a remarkably consistent critical stance toward tomato-based stews in particular, singling them out for modernization and reform—perhaps because they were by this point so strongly identified with local culinary practices and traditions. One of the most common critiques was that these dishes included too much samna and that their fat content should be reduced. Ibrahim (ca. 1940) calls on her readers to refine their Eastern dishes, specifying that "care should be given to reduce the amount of fats mixed into them."[109] In a later cookbook (1958) she laments that "nearly all food in Egypt is the same" in what is likely a reference to the practice of cooking so many foods in tomato sauce.[110]

These critiques reverberate in later decades too: in 1970, Samiha ʿAbd al-Latif wrote in the introduction to her cookbook: "I have intentionally refrained from combining Eastern dishes (such as makmur, musaqqaʿa, and mahshuwwat) into a single section to avoid calling attention to them and to encourage the housewife to free herself from them. In truth they are not well-suited to our hot climate, and their inclusion of so many spices, samna, and tomatoes can impact a person's overall health over time."[111] She cites several afflictions that can, allegedly, result from eating too many tomato stews. In a 1977 cookbook Nicola instructs that diabetics may consume "vegetables cooked in the traditional way [*ʿala al-tariqa al-taqlidiyya*]" so long as they are not made with the excessive amount of fats typical of food that has been prepared tasbika-style (which she describes using the passive participle: "what we call *al-akl al-musabbak*").[112] None of these authors is seeking to replace tomato stews—merely to reform them or incorporate them into a more varied repertoire. Tomato stews and related dishes thus recur throughout the genre as a site where authors actively sought not merely to reflect Egyptian taste, but to shape it.

Besides the role played by Eastern tomato dishes, another striking continuity across the four decades of these domestic cookbooks is the authors' consistent articulation of the knowledge they present, and the practices that this knowledge will theoretically enable, as a matter of public concern. Authors framed the home as a place where the national community was shaped. Even Nicola's later cookbooks, which fully embrace the Nasser-era figure of the "working woman" who contributes to national development through workforce participation, never questioned the assumption that women bore sole responsibility for "cooking and serving nutritional meals" to their families.[113]

Historians have noted how shifts in the configurations of the domestic effectively interwove the public and private sphere together, even as discourses of domesticity sought to affirm the gendered separation of "domestic" and "public" spheres.[114] Sherene Seikaly describes how Palestinian elites in the interwar period used the concept of the "new Arab home" to frame "new norms of class, gender, and collectivity," promoted in radio and print, that construed managing the home with efficiency and economy as "a national obligation."[115]

Mona Russell argues that in early twentieth-century Egypt, even as textbooks and other prescriptive literature dictated boundaries between the supposedly separate masculine sphere of productive labor and feminine sphere of reproductive labor, those boundaries "were actually in the process of erosion." She points out that "the rationalization and modernization of housewifery necessitated greater contact with the world outside the home," with women and girls called to be both students and consumers.[116]

By the time Ibrahim, Nicola, Osman, and others began to write their cookbooks in the 1930s and 1940s, the home kitchens of Egypt's urban elites concretized and sharpened these contradictions. In practical terms, kitchens were increasingly networked into expanding urban and national infrastructures that supplied them with electricity and running water and furnished them with a growing range of consumer products. State interventions played an important role in structuring the "private" sphere. Domestic science education inserted state-sanctioned instruction into the transmission of culinary knowledge; and after 1952 the state became more involved in supplying kitchens with food staples and modern appliances. Meanwhile prescriptive texts like cookbooks and textbooks described kitchens as the heart of a domestic sphere where women were sovereign *and* as spaces crucial to the development, productivity, and cultural identity of the Egyptian public. The sovereignty of the kitchen, and the labor women performed there, was ultimately construed as instrumental to that of the state.

Domestic cookbooks and their proponents described the public import of domestic culinary labor in various ways that frequently tracked the dominant political rhetoric of the time they were written. Shaʿrawi's endorsement of Ibrahim's first cookbook described it as an example of "public service to the nation [*al-umma*] and homeland [*al-watan*]."[117] Nicola and Osman describe writing *Fundamentals of Cooking* as a duty to their homeland (*al-watan*) and present it to both Egyptian society (*al-mujtamaʿ*) and their reading audience or public (*al-jumhur*).[118] Although Ibrahim's later works recycled recipes and cooking advice from her earlier books, the framing shifted to reflect the populist rhetoric and pan-Arabism of the late 1950s; the title of her 1958 cookbook is *The People's Table*, and it addresses both "the people" (*al-shaʿb*) and "the Arab nation" (*al-umma al-ʿArabiyya*).[119]

In 1959, Egypt's Higher Institute for Domestic Science hosted a series of events during the Afro-Asian Youth Conference. A pamphlet that the Institute produced afterward underscores the significance of cooking to a political sphere that did not necessarily stop at Egypt's national borders:

below a photograph of two young women cooking, a caption identifies one as Egyptian and the other as Palestinian, asserting that the institute's mission includes strengthening the ties of pan-Arab solidarity and sisterhood.[120] Reflecting another political shift, Nicola's cookbooks in the 1970s invoke developmentalist rhetoric, describing the importance of happy, well-nourished families to the health of society and the nation writ large. One of these texts describes the role of modern household management in "uplifting the country [*al-balad*] by uplifting the family."[121] Another describes the importance of nourishing food to both the well-being of the nation (*al-umma*) and its cultural, agricultural, and industrial progress.[122]

In summary, midcentury domestic cookbooks invoked a range of terms and concepts to articulate the wider stakes of their vision of modern Egyptian taste, framing culinary labor as a matter of broad political importance. They called upon their readers to shape the Egyptian public from within a supposedly "private" space. Like the physical territory of the nation, the kitchen—according to these texts—was a site where the substance of modern Egypt itself was produced and defined. At the same time, their largely implicit class politics positioned a specific kind of educated middle-class subject as the crucial repository of knowledge needed to nourish the nation with the right sorts of foods.

CONCLUSION

Food historians have long cautioned that we cannot read domestic cookbooks as windows into how people actually cooked or what they ate.[123] Despite their limitations, Egypt's midcentury domestic cookbooks are nonetheless significant historical and cultural texts as evidence of how an influential cohort of authors sought to define the culinary contours of an emergent Egyptian public, and of whose agency they centered in its construction. They outlined an idealized paradigm of culinary knowledge and labor addressed to a relatively limited reading public—middle-class housewives deputized to produce modern cooking and exercise good taste on behalf of the nation. In doing so, they repackaged knowledge that had once been the provenance, at least in part, of a subaltern category of domestic workers as the domain of a mythical middle-class housewife, as other cookbook authors had done elsewhere.[124] Ironically, employing at least part-time domestic labor during the period these cookbooks were published would have been seen as a marker of middle-class status; and yet the cookbooks designated for middle-class women conspicuously omit any reference to it. Tomatoes appear throughout these cookbooks as a prominent ingredient that grounds Egyptian food in a Mashriqi culinary sphere construed as both modern and authentically Arab.

It is now common sense to associate Egypt with the "Middle East" rather than "North Africa," and with the "Mashriq" rather than the "Maghrib." We might attribute this tendency to a range of factors, from histories of migration and conquest to Egypt's role in pan-Arab politics to patterns of European imperialism in the region. But these cookbooks offer insight into another dimension of that "common sense," portraying Egypt as affiliated with the Mashriq through everyday foods cooked in Egyptian homes, from mulukhiyya to mahshi to tomato stews. It is in these cookbooks that we can glimpse an implicit positioning of Egypt as Arab and Eastern rather than African or North African. Tracing patterns in everyday foods makes sense of an Egypt imagined and experienced not in connection with the Maghrib or the greater Nile Valley but with the Mashriq. These texts remind us that the domestic is not only a sphere in which hierarchies within a society are fortified, but one in which boundaries of public identities are negotiated—and what constitutes "our food" is distinguished from the foods of the other.

It is also in these cookbooks' tomato-forward recipes that the limitations of their paradigms of modern knowledge and middle-class taste begin to show. The fact that authors decried the amount of samna used in Egyptian tomato stews decade after decade suggests that cooks persisted in using large amounts of it. Why? The flexibility that Nicola and Osman built into their mahshi recipes hints that at some point a cook must rely on practical experience and judgment. Can these really be captured in a cookbook and distilled in a written recipe in formal language? What can we learn from the culinary knowledge and practice that resides beyond that realm? Chapter 5 takes up these questions, exploring how Egyptian home cooks born in the decades in which these cookbooks were published used tomatoes to make foods that their families would perceive as "fulfilling and satisfying."[125] To understand that process, we must examine how kitchen sovereignty worked through tomatoes in the realm of practical consciousness—not in cookbooks, but in kitchens, in practice.

FIVE

Creating Egyptian Flavor

TOMATOES IN HOME KITCHENS

ANNY: Did you study domestic science in school?

ZAYNAB: Yes, there was a big kitchen at the school ... but those lessons were very simplistic and theoretical. It was all empty talk. Home was where you learned things in a practical way.

ANNY: Did your grandmother know tasbika?

RANIA: Of course! Where do you think my mother learned it?

Despite the proliferation of cookbooks and domestic science education, formal educational texts and spaces did not supplant the home as the most important site of culinary learning for Egyptian women in the twentieth century. Although women's education in Egypt expanded significantly through the mid-twentieth century, the number of formally educated women remained limited—meaning that most women's culinary education continued to take place entirely within the home.[1] Furthermore, oral histories with women who did study domestic science in Egyptian state schools—like the two women quoted above—emphasize the importance of maternal culinary authority over formal domestic education. This was particularly true of dishes and techniques that home cooks considered part of a traditional Egyptian culinary repertoire passed down over generations like the leafy green *mulukhiyya* and the tomato-based stewing technique known as *tasbika*.

This chapter turns from the formal realm of written recipes to the knowledge and practices of Egyptian home cooking during the mid-twentieth century. I argue that these practices were foundational to the formation of a culinary public in Egypt that was distinguished not by discourses of distinction but the production of a constellation of specific flavors. Drawing on oral histories that I conducted with women born between 1940 and 1970 from a range of backgrounds within Egypt's middle strata, I trace the emergence of this culinary public through a history of tasbika, a cooking technique that became the default method for preparing vegetables in twentieth-century Egypt. "Tasbika" is derived from the same root as *tasbik*, the word invoked to describe Amina's excellent cooking in Naguib Mahfouz's Cairo Trilogy and used by Nicola and Osman as a category comprising stews, braises, and casseroles.² Although it appears in the titles of thousands of YouTube videos and blog posts today, before the internet most written accounts of the technique did not use the word at all.³

This chapter contends that tasbika is not just a vernacular word but a vernacular technique—that is to say, although formalized, written instructions for tasbika exist, in practical terms it inhabits the realms of embodied knowledge and oral tradition. As such, it offers a different perspective from the cookbooks explored in chapter 4. My aim is not to impose a binary or hierarchy between these two types of culinary knowledge, but to highlight the practical realm of everyday cooking as its own site of meaning-making. To study the details of how something like tasbika is learned, reproduced, and adjusted over time is to refuse to take women's culinary know-how for granted. Taking up the home kitchen as an important site of social and cultural production opens up a new way of understanding modern Egypt beyond the "formal consciousness" of nationalism. Everyday foods like tasbika speak to an understanding of Egyptian-ness as it is "actively lived and felt," as a structure of feeling rather than a formal ideology or concept.⁴

My conviction that tasbika is an apt culinary example for exploring this line of thinking stems from what I have learned about it from speaking to Egyptians about their own cuisine. In 2016 an employee of Egypt's national archives told me candidly that if I really wanted to understand the Egyptian kitchen, I should devote my energies to studying tasbika. During my fieldwork one person told me tasbika was "the mother of all dishes"; another called it "the most basic Egyptian food."⁵ In her ethnography of food and masculinity in Egypt, Nefissa Naguib identifies a desire for "fulfilling and satisfying food" as a unifying theme in the many conversations she had with Egyptians about food.⁶ Again and again, I heard Egyptians describe tasbika this way: as a quintessentially Egyptian way of cooking that connected them with their family's culinary roots amid the changes of the twentieth century and transformed raw ingredients into "good food": satisfying, nourishing, flavorful meals. This chapter details how tasbika achieved its status as a central technique for the production of "fulfilling and satisfying food" in Egypt's home kitchens over the course of the twentieth century.

INGREDIENTS AND INSTRUCTIONS

Before proceeding further, it is worth pausing to explain what precisely tasbika entails and how I define it. I approach tasbika as a flexible method for cooking vegetables rather than a single dish or a fixed, stable recipe. That said, there is a general structure with features that are common to most accounts of it. The first step is to chop an onion finely and brown it in *samna*, or clarified butter. "Pay attention; this meal takes a lot of samna," begins an ethnographic account of a tasbika-style recipe for okra relayed to Naguib.[7] Next come additions of cubed red meat (usually lamb or mutton), an in-season vegetable, seasonings, and *salsa* (depending on the cook, this might be concentrated store-bought salsa, freshly prepared tomato purée, or a combination). The timing and order of these additions as well as the specific seasonings—for example, combinations of salt, pepper, coriander, and garlic—vary depending on who is cooking and which vegetable is featured. The presence of meat is also not an absolute requirement. "Tasbika" sometimes simply refers to a thickened, seasoned tomato sauce that can be used for various purposes, like cooking *mahshi*.[8] Coptic Egyptians who are fasting might prepare a version without meat, using oil instead of samna. But for many, tasbika implies meat unless specified otherwise. Rania, who was born in 1952 and grew up in Alexandria, explained this to me matter-of-factly: "You can't make vegetables without meat."[9]

Tasbika has an intriguing relationship to seasonality: while the central vegetable cooked in it (okra, peas, green beans, etc.) tends to be whatever is in season, tomatoes are used year-round.[10] Most cooks agree that the most important "ingredient" in a good tasbika is time, often multiple hours of stewing. Once the tomato has been added, the mixture should be left over a low flame until the liquid is significantly reduced. One interviewee told me that "the most important thing is the heat: [make it] as low as you can!"[11] An acquaintance explained that the tomato medium should be almost sticky in texture, like jam, when finished. This process requires not only time and patience but attention: various cooks warned me that the pot must be closely monitored to prevent its contents from burning. This means that the cook must judge whether to stir or add water, as needed, until the dish is finished.

Several factors may indicate that sufficient time has passed: Naguib's interlocutor explained that at the end of the cooking process "the meat must be very tender, falling apart."[12] And almost without fail, cooks explained to me that the final proof that a tasbika is finished is that the liquid fat separates from the tomato mixture, rising to its surface. At that point the onions, samna, meat, vegetables, seasonings, and tomato form a newly cohesive dish that is flavored with a rich red sauce and served with bread or rice.

The noun "tasbika" and its related passive participle, *musabbak*, which is used to refer to a dish prepared "à la tasbika," are by no means the only way of referring to tomato-based saucing and stewing techniques. As discussed in previous chapters, *dimʿa* and salsa also refer to kinds of tomato sauce (and are more common in printed sources). In everyday parlance it is common for a dish that is "musabbak" to be referred to simply by its primary vegetable ingredient—in Naguib's account, for example, the resulting dish is described as "meat with okra"—that tomatoes are used as the stewing medium is implied.[13] By its very nature tasbika is always being remade, tweaked, and reinvented, and each cook approaches it slightly differently. My focus on "tasbika" as the word I use to define this cooking method and its culinary philosophy also reflects, in large part, the term's scarcity in written texts (even those that describe the technique) and, conversely, its resonance in spoken Egyptian Arabic. Centering the term reflects my deliberate privileging of the vernacular sources at the core of my understanding of it.

TASBIKA, WRITTEN AND REMEMBERED

Although written recipes tell us little about the affective qualities of tasbika and of Egyptians' attachments to it, they do help to approximate the history of its ascendance within Egyptian home cooking. The first recognizable detailed description I have found of tasbika that contextualizes it this way is in Thora Stowell's 1923 cookbook, first discussed in chapter 2.[14] Although written for British housewives in Egypt, the book includes a chapter of "some of the commoner dishes to be found on Egyptian tables." It emphasizes a technique recognizable as tasbika, a stew she describes as "highly seasoned with garlic and spice, and richly dosed with tomato, and with plenty of 'semn' [samna] floating on its surface." Stowell also indicates that tomatoes are not reliably available year-round. She emphasizes the importance of samna to producing the distinctive flavors of Egyptian cooking—which continues to be the case today, with samna a key factor differentiating Egyptian stews from tomato-based stews made elsewhere in the Mashriq.[15]

Nicola and Osman's 1941 cookbook includes a comment that tomato sauce "is used to cook many types of foods," indicating that cooking foods in tomato sauce was widespread by the early 1940s—at least among their reading audience.[16] This is confirmed by the suggested weekly menus published in the women's magazine *Bint al-Nil* (Daughter of the Nile) between 1946 and 1955, which frequently feature seasonal vegetables prepared in tomato sauce—reflecting the tomato's shift from seasonal ingredient to perennial cooking medium.[17] The rise of the tomato as a focus of popular complaint in the 1950s and 1960s, discussed at length in chapter 3, suggests that by midcentury they had become a popular culinary staple upon which Egyptians from a range of social classes relied. When Nicola criticized the overuse of samna in the 1970s, she referred to vegetables prepared tasbika-style as "cooked in the traditional way."[18] None of the texts mentioned here use the exact term "tasbika."[19] But they offer a clear description of the technique that came to be associated with that word and place it on a timeline: common in some urban households for part of the year by the 1920s, more widespread as a year-round recipe by midcentury; glossed as traditional by the 1970s.

Oral histories conducted with Egyptian women who grew up during tasbika's rise to prominence suggest a somewhat different historical narrative, however. Born between 1940 and 1970, the women whose voices are represented here come from a range of class and geographical backgrounds; but all of them ran households in Cairo or Alexandria, nearly all of them had some exposure to formal domestic science or home economics education, and all of them had strong childhood memories of tasbika. They all described a close association between tasbika and their grandmothers' cooking. These memories informed a widespread assumption that tasbika was a technique whose history stretched back countless generations. And yet based on what we know of the tomato's history in Egypt, tasbika—in its current, tomato-centric form—can only have taken its place in the Egyptian home kitchen relatively recently. The tradition of making it can only stretch so far into the past: at some point, probably in the late nineteenth or early twentieth century, it was introduced into home-cooking repertoires and thereafter became increasingly widespread.[20] Since then, it has been passed down intergenerationally.

In other words, women who came of age in the 1950s and 1960s were likely among the first to experience tasbika as a key point of continuity between their grandmothers' cooking and their own. It is unlikely that their grandmothers' grandmothers had access to enough tomatoes to prepare tasbika regularly, if at all. Drawing on these women's narrations of their food memories and ethnographic observations of their current culinary practices, this chapter explains how tomatoes, expressed through tasbika, came to embody a set of flavors popularly understood as a long-standing tradition shared across multiple segments of Egyptian society. It describes how that process unfolded not in modern classrooms or cookbooks but within the home kitchen.

I analyze tomatoes and tasbika as key elements of a "culinary vernacular": cooking and eating practices shared by members of a wider community linked by shared attachments to specific culinary flavors and textures.[21] They offer insight into the construction of an Egyptian public not merely through language, laws, or public institutions but everyday experiences of feeling and tasting. As a popular and vernacular cooking technique that has thrived outside of the formalized realm of texts, tasbika is best studied through oral history and ethnography, which reflect observable practices and narrated memories of sensory experience that convey Egyptians' own understandings of how to make a proper tasbika and why it matters.

My intent is not to present these oral history narratives as the basis for a definitive account of tasbika—indeed, I would argue that no such thing exists.[22] Tasbika's contradictions and flexible nature are central to its significance and analytic richness. Each oral history is a unique narrative that helps us understand the complexity, adaptability, and significance of Egypt's tomato-based cooking techniques, capturing what written recipes cannot. Tasbika's history must be sought in narrated memories and observed gestures because it is the sort of cultural material typically omitted from "public culture, official memory and formal economies," to quote Nadia Seremetakis.[23] Tasbika exemplifies the kind of cultural history that is typically disregarded or ignored, in large part because it cannot be written based solely on "nonperishable traces."[24] And yet histories of practices and narratives like those that surround tasbika are essential to understanding how culinary publics are formed and sustained.

KITCHEN SOVEREIGNTY IN PRACTICE: PRODUCING FLAVOR

Because tasbika resides in a different culinary realm from the cookbooks of the previous chapter, it reflects a different understanding of the gendered labor that makes food both Egyptian food and "good food." In contrast to cookbooks' focus on refinement, modernity, and variety—and their consistent, pointed dismissal of samna-heavy, tasbika-style cooking—home cooks' narratives around tasbika focus on continuity and tradition as well as specific material qualities of the richness that makes food satisfying.

In studying tasbika, we also see home cooks wielding a kind of prowess that I describe as kitchen sovereignty in practice. It appears in narratives as an everyday form of authority exercised by home cooks making decisions about how to manage (often scarce) resources and feed their households. This practical and practiced dimension of kitchen sovereignty is akin to what Lauren Berlant describes as "lateral agency," typical of reproductive labor like providing and consuming food: it consists of practices that are not necessarily explicitly counterhegemonic but still conscious and meaningful.[25] Tasbika is therefore not only the realm of the vernacular—of shared unofficial, quotidian, and oral forms of culture—but the affective: it embodies the kinds of cultural knowledge and inclinations that reside in the body, inhere in particular techniques and ingredients, manifest in emotional attachments, and become naturalized as instinctive.

This practical culinary form of agency often expresses itself through selective instances of refusal.[26] Unlike resistance, typically theorized as "the act of standing against" state and other hegemonic forms of power, refusal accommodates acts of avoidance as well as practices that are generative and social. It offers a framework for describing the actions of those not necessarily construed as outsiders or consciously acting subversively.[27] In making tasbika, I argue, home cooks practiced culinary techniques and perpetuated aesthetics that often refused formally articulated understandings of what it meant to create "good food."

I explain this difference by drawing a distinction between articulations of Egyptian *taste* and the production of Egyptian *flavor*. While the former can be traced in domestic cookbooks, the latter, I suggest, unfolds through culinary practices like making tasbika. The distinction mirrors one in Egyptian Arabic between the word *zooq*—"taste" in the sense of abstracted aesthetic value judgments and distinctions; *al-dhawq* in written Arabic—and *al-taʿm*, which corresponds more closely to the English word "flavor" and often refers to the sensory perception or gustatory qualities of an ingredient or dish.[28] This was the term invoked by one acquaintance who explained to me, describing the significance of tasbika, "we believe tasbika gives a better flavor to food." Flavor also has the advantage, in English, of being an action verb performed by cooks rather than eaters. In contrast with this sense of flavor, cookbook authors and their proponents were concerned with modeling what Egyptian housewives ought to cook to meet standards of "good taste" (*al-dhawq al-salim*), as detailed in chapter 4.

Admittedly the English word "taste" presents something of a conundrum in writing about this distinction: it slips too easily between its various meanings, from an act of gustatory perception to personal preference to a mode of judgment (e.g., deeming something to be "in good taste" or "in poor taste"). In differentiating between "taste," which I locate within discourses of distinction, and "flavor," which I locate in the affective realm of experience and attachments, I am drawing what is perhaps an overly deliberate contrast. In doing so, however, I am building on the work of food scholars who have critiqued the separation of "literal/palatal taste"—that is, the sensory experience of physically tasting something and perceiving it with one's body—from discussions of taste as a construct for aesthetic judgments that are abstracted from sensory experience.[29]

By taking up tasbika as a site of the production of Egyptian *flavor*, I aim to bring questions of sensory experience and internalized practical know-how to bear on the role of tomatoes (and food in general) in the construction of a culinary public. The narratives and observations about tasbika that I describe here explain how specific flavors came to signify an expression of Egyptian-ness that was not merely represented or written but also "actively lived and felt."[30] The rapid rise of tomatoes and tasbika as vehicles of Egyptian flavor shows us that understandings of what it means to be Egyptian, and the practices through which Egyptians construct and understand themselves as members of a shared culinary public, are always in flux. In what follows, I show how home cooks actively engaged with elements of Egyptian social experience, from the modernization of the food system to the imperatives of cookbook authors and curricula. Wherever possible, I endeavor to relate how Egyptian home cooks described and understood tasbika in their own words.

SOURCING AND PROCESSING INGREDIENTS FOR FLAVOR

Looking at the individual components of a tasbika-style stew, it is easy to identify them as the natural result of relatively recent transformations in Egypt's agriculture, economy, and food system. Perennial irrigation provided year-round access to tomatoes, while the Egyptian food industry provided canned salsa to cooks pressed for time. Other ingredients associated with the technique and the meals it produces (like meat, oil, rice, and flour) are inputs whose production was regulated by the state and whose purchase was facilitated by a food subsidy system that expanded between the 1940s and the 1970s.

But the state's modernization and industrialization projects merely made these ingredients accessible to home cooks; it was their practical know-how that transformed them into tasbika. As they selected and processed ingredients for their tomato-based stews, Egypt's home cooks, most of them women, made countless decisions about how to source ingredients, adapt to new technologies, and provide their families with good food through a gendered practice that Noha Fikry calls "bread-nurturing": the labor entailed in "securing ... food of trusted quality and taste for their households."[31] As bread-nurturers, Egyptian home cooks developed strategies for cooking seasonally, for maintaining the home as a key site of food production, and for sourcing trusted *baladi* (local) ingredients in the face of industrialized inputs.

Tasbika is one of a small number of dishes that women frequently told me they prepared exactly as their grandmothers had. While I did not take this claim at face value per se, I did not dismiss it either: with follow-up questions I sought to clarify what specifically home cooks saw themselves as replicating from their grandmothers' recipes.[32] If the kitchen technology differed, for example, what other aspects of their cooking process rendered it equivalent to the tasbika of their childhood? What gestures or strategies did they learn from mothers and grandmothers (and aunts and sisters) and continue to practice today? What specific sensory qualities marked continuities between the food of the past and the present? The responses to these questions help explain how tasbika came to be understood and experienced as traditional Egyptian cooking, despite its relatively recent emergence.

Tasbika became more popular as the kitchen appliances available to women in Egypt's urban middle strata were changing. Gas stoves, refrigerators with freezers, and electric blenders all promised to liberate women by saving them time and reducing the burden of domestic drudgery. Yet feminist scholars have long argued that labor-saving domestic appliances seldom fulfill their liberatory promises.[33] Studying how these appliances played a role in producing tasbika reveals a different dimension of their function: facilitating the reproduction of tradition in the face of change. In particular, the question of how women approached processing whole tomatoes into salsa—the most labor-intensive step of tasbika's preparation—offers insight into

FIGURE 9. Advertisement for Kaha tomato sauce, *al-Musawwar*, February 24, 1956.

women's responses to these modernizing and allegedly time-saving technologies. Among those I interviewed, women held various attitudes toward salsa. These all, however, involved some selective negotiation of the use of state-produced or subsidized inputs and products, starting with the matter of whether to use canned salsa.

As chapters 2 and 3 document, Egyptian companies produced and marketed canned vegetable products, including salsa, with significant state support starting in the 1930s. A 1956 magazine advertisement picturing a cascade of scarlet sauce falling abundantly into a bowl boasted that it was made from the "choicest varieties of fresh tomatoes."[34] Advertisements like these—run by companies that were eventually incorporated into the public food sector—promised women the best of both modern convenience and the luxurious flavors of a seasonal diet: unencumbered by the time and labor required to pickle, ferment, or preserve and free from the threat of seasonal scarcities.

Skipping the process of grating or blending the enormous quantity of tomatoes tasbika requires by purchasing canned salsa is an enormous time-saver. In the face of new constraints on their time (as more women entered the formal workforce) and newly available consumer goods, it is no surprise that many women embraced canned salsa.[35] Its widespread availability was doubtless a key factor in making tasbika a cornerstone of daily cooking—and a perennial rather than a seasonal technique. Salsa has been described as such a staple that today "no truly Egyptian fridge or pantry" lacks it.[36] And yet women's discussions of how and when they incorporated items like ready-made salsa reflect an ambivalence toward the state's production and promotion of canned and processed food products. Even those who did use canned salsa year-round employed it as a medium for stewing other ingredients that they ate only seasonally, like green beans, okra, taro, and spinach, even though many of these other vegetables were also available in cans that promised to deliver farm freshness. Many cooks also used a combination of fresh and canned tomatoes in their tasbika. We might read this balancing of fresh produce with the perennially available salsa less as a wholesale adoption of the state's promotion of canned foods than a strategic negotiation—a compromise position that depends upon a canned version of one ingredient in order to present a rotation of flavorful and varied seasonal dishes throughout the year. In other words, using industrially processed tomatoes as the base for tasbika made it possible to cook dishes that otherwise embodied freshness, seasonality, and variation: okra in summer, spinach in winter.

That said, many women still opted to make their own salsa. This was explained to me not as a blanket rejection of modern food-processing technologies so much as a prioritization of the home kitchen as the best site for their application. Nobody boasted to me that they puréed tomatoes by hand, like their grandmother had, rather than using a blender. In making their own salsa, women did not reject the use of new appliances to process tomatoes. Rather, it was through the practice of making salsa at home that women said they replicated the flavors of their mothers' and grandmothers' cooking.[37] Women who produced their own salsa highlighted a range of reasons for doing so that speak to how flavor embodies specific ideas about good food through sensory and affective qualities. Reem, born in 1967, explained the excellence of her grandmother's cooking by stating that she never used canned tomatoes and obtained her samna from a local, reliable source. "[My grandmother] used real tomato. Of course the smell was completely different," she told me.[38] For Reem, producing a good tomato stew that reflected her family's culinary heritage required "real" ingredients, meaning that they were sourced and processed in trustworthy ways. Hanan, a woman of the same generation as Reem's mother, explained to me in detail how she makes her own salsa to this day, describing how changes in technology have affected the way tasbika has been cooked over time.

While invoking the ethos she associated with the cooking of her childhood, Hanan explained that she had learned her method for making and preserving salsa from scratch not from her mother but from her sister, whose kitchen setup had more closely resembled her own: "I take off the skin and boil [the tomatoes] with only water. I put them on the Butagaz [propane stove], add some salt, and then I put them in the blender. Then I put it in the freezer: that's salsa. You can get it at the supermarket. But I make it at home." Excitedly leading me to her kitchen, Hanan opened her freezer, which was full of frozen bags of salsa. This practice has the advantage of protecting against fluctuating prices—tomatoes can be purchased and processed when prices are low. It also saves time by having salsa ready to go when it is time to cook, but without sacrificing the quality associated with home cooking. And although tomatoes are available all year-round, their quality varies; so making and freezing salsa at home offers a way to optimize the use of tomatoes when they are best.

When she first married, Hanan had grated her tomatoes by hand with a sieve (*masfa*, in Egyptian Arabic). It was only later in life, when she prepared it for children and grandchildren in large batches, that she used an electric blender to make salsa and store it in her freezer. Despite the shift in technologies used, for Hanan this is a story not of change but of continuity: the fundamental aspects of her preparation rendered her tasbika consistent over time, because regardless of the technology involved, the salsa was being produced by her and within the home.[39] Hanan's refusal of canned salsa was not a matter of nostalgic intent to re-create the cooking of her childhood step-by-step, or to do things by hand for the sake of it; it was an active adaptation of an inherited rural practice of sourcing one's own food that took advantage of the modernization of kitchen technology to ensure a steady supply of salsa. For both Reem and Hanan, the practice of producing salsa at home connected previous generations' rural tasbika in Upper Egypt to their own urban tasbika in Cairo and Alexandria through the production of what they perceived as a similar kind of flavor, even though it was produced in a very different kind of kitchen.

Meanwhile Maryam, a Coptic woman originally from a village in Giza who now lives in a so-called informal settlement in southern Cairo, integrated several Coptic elements into her preparation of fresh salsa for tasbika. She emphasized to me that the practices that I witnessed were symbolic (*ramzi*) rather than strictly religious (*dini*) practices.[40] These illustrate how the cultural concepts that tasbika signifies are not uniform across contexts, even if they are expressed through the same basic ingredients. Like many others, Maryam blended the tomatoes for her salsa in an electric blender. But the electrical grid on her block was unreliable and could at times be pushed to its limits by the voltage demands of the blender. After tossing a finely chopped onion into a pot sizzling with samna on the nearby gas stove, she placed the tomatoes into her unplugged blender, grabbed the pronged end of its cord, and touched it briefly to a religious icon on the wall of the kitchen before plugging it in and switching it on.

I must have looked puzzled; the family swiftly explained that this action was meant to guard against the faulty electrical grid. When the tomatoes refused to blend into a liquid right away, Maryam added a splash of water from an unmarked bottle. She explained that it was holy water, blessed by a priest; it allowed the blender's blades to swiftly pulverize the tomatoes into a liquid that would soon be added to the stew pot and cooked down into tasbika. The emergence of tasbika in its modern form depended not only on certain appliances but also the integration of Egypt's urban home kitchens into infrastructure that furnished them with gas, running water, and electricity. Maryam's appeal to an icon and integration of holy water are implicit testaments to the insufficiency of state infrastructure development alone to produce homemade salsa and quality tasbika today—and the existence of additional factors that contributed to the making of good food in Maryam's kitchen.

In addition to salsa, the animal-based ingredients of tasbika are a subject of much debate. While some home cooks critiqued tasbika as overly heavy because of its rich ingredients like red meat and samna, others insisted that good food was not a matter of whether or how much meat and samna were included, but of sourcing the correct *kinds* of meat and samna. It was in discussions of these ingredients that cooks and their families most frequently drew links between producing quality flavor and concepts related to health. These discussions embodied home cooks' desire to practice what Emily Yates-Doerr and Megan Carney call "culinary care," the practice of mediating various understandings of health into care practices surrounding meal preparation.[41] For many women a key element of this form of care entailed sourcing milk, butter, or meat from other individuals or families who could be trusted to produce quality products. Many families avoid state-subsidized or industrially produced food products whenever possible—for example, seeking out butchers that sell quality "baladi" (local) meat for their stews rather than industrially farmed meats or procuring the right inputs for producing "baladi" clarified butter, or "samna baladi."

"Baladi," meaning local or literally "of the country," is a term that signals a range of meanings associated with high-quality and locally authentic food. In discussions around tasbika, samna, and animal fats in general, Egyptians frequently invoked the word as a contrast to anything imported as well as anything produced industrially or on a mass scale: baladi butter was contrasted with imported butter; factory-farmed meat was compared unfavorably with heritage breeds and home-raised baladi meats.[42] The use of the term "baladi" connoted not only superior flavor and nutritional content; it also implied a connection to a known source within Egyptian territory.[43]

For many urban women, the samna baladi they use might be the only element of a tasbika-style meal whose origin they can definitively trace. Producing samna baladi often entails clarifying butter from a known source, ideally from the milk of a water buffalo rather than a cow and from a village to which one has family connections. In oral history narratives samna was often foundational to establishing a link between a woman's own tasbika and her mother's or grandmother's cooking. Maryam's mother died young, so she learned to cook from her grandmother. While her cooking practices reproduce what she learned from her grandmother's outdoor village kitchen in Maryam's own urban kitchen, it is through samna that she maintains a material link to her village. She acquires water buffalo butter either from her own home village or from "another person she knows"—a trusted source—then prepares large batches of samna at a time, as her grandmother did. Another woman, Magda, who lives in central Cairo, still receives samna regularly from her mother in Giza, who purchases large quantities of butter from the countryside and clarifies it herself before distributing to family members.

Underscoring the significance of quality butter was the belief, expressed to me by multiple people, that health concerns applied to some samna but not to high-quality samna baladi. Magda dismissed concerns over the cholesterol content of samna, insisting: "My mother has lived her whole life on samna. She has never had diabetes or high blood pressure . . . samna is not the problem."[44] Hanan highlighted the difficulty of attaining good samna today: "Now there are so many kinds of samna," she said, but added that even the best kinds are not as good as the samna of the past. She explained that the true "samna baladi baladi [twice for emphasis]" of her childhood memories was "yellow, and tasty, with a pleasant aroma." These are among the qualities that make samna central to memories of an idealized midcentury tasbika and to attempts to re-create it today. In the face of warnings about cholesterol and processed foods, many Egyptians seek to reproduce the tasbika of their grandmothers by sourcing quality samna and meat. It is with these ingredients that they produce good flavors and satisfying food through bread-nurturing practices that produce flavors recognizable as traditional, nourishing, and unmistakably Egyptian.

TASBIKA AS TECHNIQUE: COOKING FOR FLAVOR

Tasbika's production of Egyptian flavors did not only involve sourcing the right ingredients. Specific cooking practices were also essential to the transformation of those ingredients into flavors that embodied nourishing, traditional Egyptian food. Just as home cooks selectively engaged with industrial and processed ingredients, the material and technical dimensions of cooking tasbika frequently entailed the (typically tacit) refusal of various principles enshrined in cookbooks and domestic science textbooks. In making and remaking tasbika, home cooks favored and perpetuated culinary techniques and aesthetics inherited through maternal lines of transmission, even when they contradicted those most prized by cookbook and textbook authors. As a result, the tomato became a primary ingredient that Egyptian cooks used to re-create certain kinds of flavors and textures that predated the tomato's introduction to Egypt. I contend that this continuity of flavor and texture (in the face of changes in ingredients and kitchen technologies) was one factor in the swift construction of tasbika as a remnant of the Egyptian past and an expression of what was perceived as traditional flavor—despite its reliance on the relatively new tomato. The unique material qualities of tomatoes and tasbika, including the relationship between texture and fat content and the tomato's chemical makeup, help explain this phenomenon.

FAT: TO SEPARATE OR TO INTEGRATE?

A consistent refrain of the tasbika recipes that were narrated to me out loud was the final step that signals that the dish is finished: the samna or fat "rises above" or separates from the rest of the stew. In other words, the liquid fat content of the stew is suspended, floating on the stew's surface. Although the melted fat remains liquid, by this point the tomato sauce itself has transitioned to a much thicker medium—not exactly solid, but close. This sign that the stew is done speaks to the high samna content that tasbika conventionally includes—as well as the importance of embodied knowledge to making tasbika: the dish is not finished based on a particular time or temperature; it takes as long as it takes (and the longer the better), but "you know the tasbika is finished when the oil rises to the top of the tomatoes."[45] The liquid content of the sauce must be carefully monitored so that the tomatoes are the correct consistency by the time this occurs. The separation of liquid fat as a marker of a successful tasbika is also significant because it is strikingly different from the culinary aesthetics detailed and promoted in prescriptive culinary texts, including cookbooks and domestic science textbooks. As chapter 4 explained, cookbook authors consistently criticized the high fat content of Egyptian dishes between the 1930s and the 1970. The material qualities of tasbika, particularly the separation of the fat just described, also contrasted directly with other culinary aesthetics that these cookbooks explicitly promoted.

Midcentury culinary texts drew recipes from a wide range of sources, but one common feature was the inclusion of French culinary techniques. French sauces were especially prominent in cookbooks and textbooks destined for Egyptian homes and schools from the 1930s on. In these texts the word "salsa" corresponded not to the Egyptian term for puréed tomato but to a broader category of sauces that blended French culinary aesthetics with the ideals of modern domesticity. A cooking textbook written by Fatima Fahmy, a domestic science educator who trained other teachers, explains that "sauces render the foods they are served with more versatile, increase their nutritional value, shape their appearance, and make them more appetizing."[46] Nicola and Osman's *Fundamentals of Cooking* outlines the optimal characteristics of a sauce as follows: it should "be free of solids or suspended fats," and "all of its ingredients must be combined equally and not separate out."[47] Sauces may be thickened "with the addition of a small amount of cornflour, flour, clarified butter, eggs, butter, cream, etc."[48]

These instructions reflect the aesthetics of modern French sauce-making, intended to enhance foods with smooth, blended sauces prepared separately from a dish's main ingredient.[49] Many of the French "mother sauces," codified by Auguste Escoffier by the early twentieth century, appeared frequently in Egypt's midcentury cookbooks. They were in the curricula that Egyptian authors had studied in England and part of an aesthetic that circulated globally in domestic science circles.[50] Fahmy and Osman attended the same British college, and Fahmy wrote her cookbook upon her return from an international domestic science conference in Rome in 1927 (an invitation had initially been extended to Huda Sha'rawi but because of a scheduling conflict, Fahmy attended instead).⁵¹

The white sauce béchamel became thoroughly Egyptianized and remains a beloved component of Egyptian cuisine. A 1964 Egyptian school textbook translated from English into Arabic includes a recipe headnote emphasizing the simplicity and versatility of white sauces, noting that correct technique is essential to produce a sauce in which "all of the components have been blended to produce a homogenous consistency."⁵² Nicola included béchamel in her cookbooks through the 1970s. And yet its aesthetic directly contradicts many fundamental aspects of tasbika, which is defined by the suspension and separation of the liquid fat from the thick tomato sauce, rather than its incorporation or emulsification, and which is thickened not with the addition of a particular ingredient but through the process of reducing tomatoes over a long period of time. Of course, these books and their French-derived sauce aesthetics neither dictated nor necessarily reflected what home cooks chose to do in their kitchens, or the reasons they made the choices they did. And of course, as chapter 4 detailed, these texts also included non-European recipes that did not necessarily conform to French culinary aesthetics. But the genre's overall theorization of sauces helps clarify the meaning of the choices that home cooks made. Domestic cookbook authors, many of whom also worked as educators, highlighted specific kinds of sauces as paradigmatic. They emphasized uniformity of texture and the full incorporation of fat into a sauce as hallmarks of modern, desirable, and aspirational cooking.⁵³

In doing so, these texts helped to construct smooth sauces like béchamel as "modern" while implying that differently textured sauces like those produced by tasbika were their "traditional" foil. Both approaches to saucing are popular across Egypt today, and both were introduced relatively recently. But tasbika is the one that has come to signify traditional Egyptian home cooking, in cookbooks as well as in oral history narratives. Even if a home cook rejected the notion that béchamel was preferable to tasbika, the opposition between tasbika and a "modern" béchamel helped to produce an understanding of tasbika as traditional. This process reflects what Raymond Williams calls "selective tradition," by which cultural phenomena like tasbika construct "a version of the past which is intended to connect with and ratify the present," offering in practice "a sense of predisposed continuity."⁵⁴ By electing to prepare it again and again, Egypt's home cooks forged an understanding of tasbika as a traditional contrast to the culinary interventions introduced from European cuisines. Facilitating this perception were material dimensions of the tomato that resonated with Egyptian culinary techniques that long predated its introduction.

WHAT TASBIKA REPLACED

Tasbika did not emerge from a vacuum. Setting aside the tomato, tasbika continues a long tradition of one-pot stews and casseroles that historian David Waines describes as "the most characteristic method for creating substantial dishes" in medieval Arabic cookbooks, "where the ingredients (e.g. meat, vegetables, seasonings) were cooked in a liquid in a pot over the heat of a fire."[55] Paulina Lewicka notes multiple reasons this kind of dish was prevalent in medieval Cairo: stewing offered a way to tenderize meat in a hot climate, and it made efficient use of fuel and water because only one pot was required.[56] Medieval cookbooks include many stew recipes that include acidic notes from the addition of vinegar or the juices of citrus, pomegranate, and other fruits. A term was even coined specifically for the category of sour meat stews, *hawamid*.[57] Edward Lane describes a similar approach to stewing among Cairenes of the middle and upper classes in the early nineteenth century; among that milieu he describes a typical meal as "stewed meat, with chopped onions or with a quantity of 'bamiyehs' [okra] or other vegetables."[58] He notes that fruits are frequently added to meat stews and that "most of the meats are cooked with clarified butter."[59]

Although these earlier stews differ from tasbika in many respects, there are also points of commonality—particularly the use of acidic notes and the transformation of various components, including meat, vegetables, liquid, and seasonings, into a single flavor profile in a stewing medium that blends and intensifies elements of each of its ingredients.[60] This general aesthetic was shared across medieval European and North African cuisines through which "sauces fused with principal ingredients," reflecting an "understanding of cooking as the art of transforming raw material into wholesome, digestible, invigorating food."[61] It was this aesthetic, food historians have noted, from which modern French cuisine's smooth, separately prepared sauces, were a deliberate departure.[62] It offers a template adaptable to regional and seasonal variations. And it is a technique that distributes even minimal amounts of meat into flavor for an entire meal, making it appealing to those for whom meat was both desirable and expensive. Harold McGee explains that cooking meat slowly at a simmer "allows the meat enzymes to tenderize and flavor the meat," meaning that this technique transforms even a tough cut into an edible portion, distributing its flavors to the sauce that seasons the dish.[63]

TOMATO CHEMISTRY: SWEET, SOUR, UMAMI

What was it about the tomato that led to its collective embrace as the base for the twentieth-century version of this kind of stew? Previous chapters have suggested that the tomato's status as a familiar nightshade likely paved the way for its adoption and outlined how Egypt's climate and soils are optimal for tomato production, particularly after the conversion to perennial irrigation. We have seen that Egyptian nutrition experts prized tomatoes for their nutritional content, and horticulturalists identified tomatoes as uniquely well suited to carry Eastern, Arab, and Egyptian flavors.[64] To expand upon this latter point, I consider the distinctive material qualities of tomatoes—what anthropologists call its "embodied qualia"—that help explain why that is the case.[65]

To understand how the context of Egyptian food history and the embodied qualia of tomatoes were such a powerful combination, I take up Ian Hodder's idea of "affordances." These are specific properties of objects related to the kinds of relationships that those objects invite, "entangling" humans and objects in various configurations with one another.[66] Hodder points out that these entanglements are not merely brought about by the affordances inherent in objects but are "also the product of concepts and ideas."[67] In this case tomatoes have specific affordances that predisposed them to produce or enhance certain effects already prized within Egyptian cuisine: an acidic and umami flavor profile and high water content. These helped tomatoes find their place in a culinary culture that prized meat and rich animal fats and had a long history of slow-cooking them with acidic notes. In other words tomatoes' affordances meant they had unique value to Egyptian cooks and eaters, which incentivized their integration within Egyptian cooking practices.

A focus on these affordances in context can help us to explain culinary change over time as the interaction of material and social factors. Tomatoes are not inherently predisposed to the production of flavors that came to be perceived as traditional; rather, tasbika became a vehicle of traditional flavor because of the relationship between existing Egyptian culinary principles and preferences and the tomato's affordances. Conceptualizing tasbika in this way helps us imagine how cooks fluent in an existing Egyptian culinary vernacular may have adapted tomatoes to their use through the exercise of their practical know-how, applying their culinary inclinations to whatever ingredients happened to be available.

The first set of these affordances lies in the tomato's distinctive flavor profile, which food science writer Harold McGee describes as a "balanced sweetness and acidity."[68] Lilia Zaouali has argued that the presence of tomato juice in a range of modern Arab dishes is "a survival of the medieval practice of adding a sour fruit juice to stews."[69] Tomatoes' enzymes contribute to the texture as well as the flavor of stews and are effective thickening agents. Sucharita Kanjilal writes that tomatoes' acidity and their ability to thicken and emulsify other ingredients when heated facilitated their adoption in India as an ingredient "amenable to local culinary traditions that favored cooked curries, stews, and dals" as well as various dishes flavored with souring agents.[70] A similar process was at work in Egyptian cuisine, in which stews had featured sour notes for centuries, as discussed earlier. Professional chefs working in Egypt in the nineteenth century clearly recognized this; two of the cookbooks discussed in chapter 2 call for a combination of "tomato water" and other souring agents like lemon juice and sour grape juice in preparing stews.[71] One of them also suggests that "onion water" (puréed onions) and "tomato water" are interchangeable in a kebab recipe, indicating tomatoes' introduction as a sometime substitute for existing ingredients rather than as an entirely novel element of cuisine.[72]

The molecular structure of tomatoes also reflects higher amounts of both glutamic acid and sulfur compounds more commonly associated with meats than with fruits and vegetables. These in turn "predispose them to complement the flavor of meats, even to replace that flavor, and certainly to add depth and complexity to sauces and other mixed preparations."[73] In other words tomatoes bring a rich umami flavor to a dish that few ingredients other than meat can convey, and can amplify a stew's capacity to infuse its ingredients with a meaty richness. They therefore provide a cost-effective way to produce and extend the umami flavors of expensive red meats—an advantageous quality in Egypt, where meat is generally desirable and prestigious. David Gentilcore relates an Italian example that illustrates how one early nineteenth-century innkeeper used this feature of the tomato to his advantage in a "poor-man's meat sauce" that included "leftover meat, along with potatoes, onions, herbs, and tomatoes." The innkeeper claimed that the sauce was indistinguishable from "an authentic meat ragout."[74] Similarly, another nineteenth-century recipe printed in Egypt suggests that either meat broth or salsa could be used in a vegetable stew.[75]

FROM LIQUID TO SOLID: A RECIPE FOR CULINARY EXCELLENCE

Tomatoes' high water content and its use in tasbika also make them an apt base for a specific a kind of stew that, like tasbika, depends upon changing a liquid concoction into a solid (or nearly-solid) one. The etymology of the word "tasbika," like the older related category "tasbik," can be traced to an Arabic lexical root (*s-b-k*) whose association with this kind of material transformation—from solid to liquid—predates the arrival of the tomato to Egypt. Classical Arabic lexicons indicate that this root and its derivations connote smelting, purifying, and casting molten metal into solid shapes.[76] Connotations in contemporary Egyptian usage include the metallurgic meaning but extend to more abstract definitions, including to do something well or to express an idea with eloquence and economy of language, as well as those related to cooking something in concentrated stock or juice.[77] Together these material dimensions of tasbika, embedded in the word's root, coalesce (literally) in the conceptualization of a good tasbika as *jamid* ("gamid," in spoken Egyptian). This term has a range of meanings in Egyptian Arabic: it can simply mean solid or congealed, like the texture of tasbika when it is finished cooking. More abstractly, it can mean strong, robust, or intense, reflecting the intensity of the flavors concentrated through reduction, the richness conveyed in tomatoes' glutamic acid, and the infusion of meat juices throughout the tomato sauce and other vegetables.

Many women highlighted the importance of samna as well as the significance of extended cooking time to lending the dish its robustness (indeed, these two points are linked, as the proper level of solidity is achieved when the samna, itself a source of gustatory solidity, separates from the condensed tomato content of the dish). The material robustness of the dish in turn embodies its conceptual meanings as a filling, satiating, and nourishing food. Through the texture of suspended fats, the acidic and umami notes lent by heated tomatoes, and the intense solidity of a slowly stewed reduction, tasbika came to embody traditional Egyptian flavors—in ways that were often at odds with formal, elite, and state-sanctioned culinary discourses.

NARRATING EGYPTIAN FLAVOR

Tasbika's coherence as both a recognizable technique and a cultural concept is notable given the range of backgrounds of women who learned it as young girls and still regularly prepare it today. While no two women's experiences are identical, tasbika was a striking throughline in the oral histories I conducted. Take two different stories from women whose perspectives we have already heard from, Hanan and Maryam. Hanan was born in 1940 in a village outside of Minya in Upper Egypt. Her family employed a full-time domestic staff that did the food shopping and most of the culinary labor. She moved to Alexandria when she married a judge originally from the Delta city of Mansura, setting up a nuclear family home in a multistory apartment building far from the natal homes of either side of the family. There she employed a part-time maid and took on significantly more of the cooking and shopping duties than her mother had. Hanan acquired most (though not all, in her recollection) of her culinary knowledge after marriage, learning many foods, like the new and modern béchamel, from friends and neighbors.

Maryam, by contrast, was born around 1970 in a village in Giza, just outside of Cairo. Her mother died young, and as a result Maryam learned to cook mostly from her grandmother and stepmother. When she married into a working-class family living in Cairo, she learned new dishes from her mother-in-law, who lived nearby but had Saʿidi (Upper Egyptian) roots. Maryam and her family members have always done all of the cooking labor in their home kitchens. Despite being from different generations, religions, social classes, regions, and educational backgrounds, these two women had a strikingly similar relationship to tasbika. Each of them cited it as a technique central to their own culinary repertoires, prepared it almost identically, and remembered learning to make it in their childhood homes via maternal lines of culinary transmission. Their narratives illustrate how tasbika came to embody a form of flavor that resonated on the scale of the anonymous and expansive social imaginary of a modern public, shared among people whose paths would likely never cross but recognizable as elements of a common, and in this case, nationally oriented identity.

Like many other women I interviewed, as they narrated their memories of tasbika to me, Hanan and Maryam described lines of culinary knowledge transmission that connected their urban households to their homes and families of origin—even as they cooked far from home and in drastically different kitchens from those of their mothers and grandmothers. These narrative themes, I suggest, were another major factor contributing to the construction of tasbika as an embodiment of traditional Egyptian cooking. Equally Saʿidi and Alexandrian, rural and urban, tasbika appears in a range of oral histories as a common strategy for producing Egyptian flavor. Women emphasized tasbika's consistency over generational, spatial, and social divides, implying a much older, continuous history than the political economy of tomatoes could have supported.

"FROM THE HOUR I WAS BORN": MATERNAL LINES OF CULINARY TRANSMISSION

Nobody I spoke with attributed her knowledge of tasbika to a peer; all of them credited the maternal authority of their mothers or grandmothers. When I asked Rania, born in Alexandra in 1952, whether her grandmother had been familiar with tasbika, she laughed. "Of course! Where do you think my mother learned it?" she asked. For Rania the fact that the dish was something passed down directly from grandmother to mother to daughter was self-evident.[78] Hanan described tasbika as something learned so early in childhood as to be nearly innate. "I knew tasbika my whole life, from the hour I was born," she told me.[79] Hanan also contrasted this with more recent introductions to the Egyptian kitchen, like béchamel sauce, which she had learned as an adult from a neighbor—a distinction that other oral history subjects described as well.

This privileging of maternal knowledge is particularly striking given the many obstacles to this kind of intergenerational knowledge transmission facing Egyptian women who came of age after the Second World War. More Egyptian women had access to education than ever before, not just at primary but at secondary and postgraduate levels; in many cases mothers who had not had access to education encouraged their daughters to focus on their studies rather than on perfecting the art of cooking. Many women from these generations, regardless of their educational level, also migrated away from their natal homes in their teenage years, often moving to a city where a husband or brother had found work or seeking work themselves.

Because most of them had attained at least some level of secondary education before they were married, most of the women I interviewed only knew a handful of basic dishes—including tasbika—when they left their natal home for their husband's. But this did not stop them from continuing to learn from their mothers and grandmothers. "Before I married I didn't do anything in the kitchen," Rania told me. But as a married woman, she said, "I would pick up the phone and say [to my mother], what do I do? And I worked like this... until I became like a professor [*ustaza*] of cooking." The phenomenon of Egyptian brides learning to cook only at the point of marriage was common enough to be the subject of a cartoon in the magazine *al-Musawwar* in 1959, which pictures a woman in a wedding gown gesturing at a pot on a stove and proclaiming to her new husband: "Of course I know how to cook! Mama taught me this just yesterday."[80]

For many (though not all) women within the middle strata of Egyptian society, culinary knowledge transmission was also complicated by the fact that domestic workers, rather than their mothers, had borne the primary cooking responsibilities in their childhood homes. Nadia, who had lived in her grandfather's palatial villa in the 1960s, moved with her mother to a nuclear family–sized apartment when she was a teenager in the mid-1970s. In the villa none of her family members had participated in the day-to-day cooking, which had taken place in the basement kitchen. When Nadia and her mother moved out following her parents' divorce, they hired a cook to come on Fridays to prepare the more elaborate, time-consuming meals that her mother, who now worked outside the home, did not have time to prepare during the week. In the apartment the cook they hired shared the same kitchen space as the family. Fridays "became a ritual" that offered a space for Nadia to learn how to make more time-consuming traditional dishes.[81] Her narrative points to the significant role played by domestic workers in preserving culinary knowledge throughout Egypt's modern history.[82] This was sometimes mentioned by interviewees from more elite backgrounds but seldom emphasized to the same degree as the culinary knowledge and preferences of their mothers and grandmothers, even (and sometimes especially) when I asked about the role played by paid domestic staff. Tasbika was consistently narrated and claimed as something passed directly down from mother to daughter.

Although nearly all the women I interviewed had received some form of instruction in domestic science (or home economics, as it was called later) as a part of their formal schooling, none of them credited it with their knowledge of tasbika. None of them, in fact, thought very much of formal domestic education at all. Zaynab, born in 1943 in Alexandria, waved her hand dismissively when I brought up the subject. "Those lessons were very simplistic and theoretical," she said. "It was all empty talk."[83] The public school she had attended did have a teaching kitchen, but lessons were largely limited to lectures from the teacher: "We would listen to what the teacher said but that would be it," Zaynab told me. "Home was where you learned things in a *practical* way." She emphasized that the home was a more significant site of culinary transmission. "The things you learn from your mother are more important. They're inherited, passed down from one mother to the next," she explained. Right on cue, our interview was interrupted by a phone call from a relative seeking her advice on a family recipe.

Women who had owned *Fundamentals of Cooking* and other cookbooks also directly contrasted the rationalized and precise approach of written recipes with the sensory forms of embodied knowledge used within home kitchens. "It was too complex," Reem told me when I asked if her mother had actually cooked from the copy of *Fundamentals of Cooking* she had owned. "Everything was measured in grams. Nobody cooked like that."[84] Women emphasized how, when learning from their mothers, sensory cues, not predictable or precise instructions, were essential: Is the liquid reducing too quickly? Do the tomatoes feel ripe to the touch? Has the fat separated yet from the stew? What are the sounds and smells telling us?

As this chapter has explained, tasbika did not traverse time or space unchanged. Home cooks like Hanan and Maryam and countless others were forced to re-create familiar dishes with new ingredients and technology. Some women learned to cook tasbika over a new kind of stove, while others found themselves in strange cities that posed challenges to sourcing quality ingredients. But these changes are precisely what makes narratives about the continuity of tasbika from grandmother to granddaughter so compelling: they harness the narrative power of invoking maternal knowledge and early childhood experience to construct an alternative to the dominant narratives of progress and modernization that marked the mid-twentieth century, looking instead to conceptualizations of tradition and in many cases a rural past.

Their narratives feature several common themes. Many women described tasbika as a way for cooks in the present to access an older and superior way of cooking. "Long ago all the food *had* to be made that way," said Rania, crediting the constraints of past technology for producing superior food rather than describing them an obstacle for technological progress to overcome. She added, though, that preferences and culinary fashion played a role as well; in the past, she said, "all Egyptians cooked with samna baladi; there wasn't a house without it."[85] Ghayda, born in a similar generation as Rania but to a less wealthy family, expressed a similar sentiment. "Now we [cook] so quickly, but things tasted better back then," she told me.[86] Her husband concurred. "Before, the food was rich in fat, even though money was scarce," he said. "Now there's money [referring to a higher standard of living]. But there's no fat!"[87] "The food of the past was all cooked in the tasbika style," sighed Hanan. "And that is what gave it a better aroma and flavor [ta'm]." For all these home cooks tasbika represented a bulwark against the negative changes they perceived in the modern food system (described in chapter 3); it was a way to drag the best of Egypt's culinary past into the present.

In this sense these narratives situate tasbika as traversing what Michelle King refers to as "one of the most powerful of internal boundaries" entailed in the construction of culinary nationalisms: the temporal boundary between past and present, which separates "imagined, often nostalgic, 'traditional' culinary pasts from contemporary, 'modern' foodstuffs and eating practices."[88] Yet doing so required imposing a novel genealogy on a relatively new ingredient and technique, modeling how communal visions of food cultures are often "riddled with forgetfulness."[89] Women, accordingly, emphasized tasbika's consistency across time, space, and social class. Hanan went so far as to insist that "the peasants of Minya and people in Alexandria make it exactly the same."[90] Nour, who was born in the mid-1960s, described her grandmother's and mother's versions of tasbika as identical, although the former was born in a southern governorate and the latter in Cairo.[91] Although it would of course be empirically impossible for all of these iterations of tasbika to be *exactly* the same, claims that they are underscore tasbika's significance as a marker of a distinctly Egyptian culinary public—an umbrella of identification shared across time, space, and social difference.

Tasbika thus emerges in narrated memories to index a kind of flavor described as uniting Egyptians across difference through a homogenizing stew, rather than a means for constructing or upholding social distinctions between Egyptians. Much like its culinary structure, tasbika's narratives absorb a diversity of elements and present them as a unified whole. In describing tasbika's origins, women emphasized maternal lines of knowledge over the innovations and ruptures of modernization and across spatial and generational divides. Their stories actively reframed tasbika as a quintessential example of domestic Egyptian cooking: a practice that takes place within the home, uses ingredients and practices sourced throughout the territory of the nation, and which is a defining element of that nation's culture.

TASBIKA RECONSIDERED: RAW AND THE COOKED

None of this should be taken to imply that tasbika was universally embraced or beloved. Sofia, who was born in the mid-1950s, recalled it with disgust and told me that as children she and her siblings sometimes threw their tomato-stewed vegetables out the window in desperation. Many criticized tasbika by citing health concerns over cholesterol or diabetes and other diet-linked conditions.[92] These concerns led to a meatless version of the technique referred to as *nayy f-nayy* (literally "raw in raw") in which vegetables are prepared in a tomato purée or with chopped tomatoes but with less cooking time and little or no fat. As a child, Sofia recalled, although her grandmother and mother prepared everything in tomato sauce, they both opted for a much lighter version than a typical tasbika approach, skipping the initial step of frying the onion in fat. "It was always much lighter, with very little fat. Ultimately she eliminated [the fat] and used just a droplet of vegetable oil. Not even butter," she told me.[93] Sofia attributed this to her grandmother's health problems, which led the entire family to shift to lower-fat cooking. Other interviewees connected the rise of this "raw" approach to tasbika both to awareness about cholesterol and a rise in cultural preferences for lighter food.

Egyptian cookbook authors had been calling for these changes since the 1940s, but it appears that they were not widely embraced until some decades later. Malak Rouchdy describes this "reformist and modernizing" approach to Egyptian cooking as rising to prominence from the late 1980s on.[94] She describes a twenty-first century cookbook author who typifies this approach as an example of someone who values older, traditional cooking but calls for its modernization through "decreasing the amount of fat, simplifying certain preparation and cooking steps, and adjusting the aesthetic of the dish."[95] Rouchdy describes this trend as a new means to enact social distinction, offering a way for the upper-middle class in the late twentieth century to maintain a connection to "traditional" food while distinguishing themselves from the "popular" taste with which tasbika had come to be associated. Her analysis centers on the role of tasbika in discourses of taste in Egyptian society, in which it appears as a means to name and uphold class distinctions. But the "nayy f-nayy" trend can equally be read as a testament demonstrating tasbika's staying power—its persistence as a mode of cooking to be reformed, rather than replaced, and its establishment as a "traditional" mode of cooking in the space of a century. Above all, tasbika has retained its cachet not as a Cairene or Saʿidi technique but an Egyptian one. Its staying power is

FIGURE 10. Tomato products, Cairo supermarket, 2024. Photograph by author.

evident on the shelves of high-end supermarkets in affluent areas of Cairo, which feature a range of tomato products—from Heinz tomato paste to local brands that boast "tasbika" in a jar.

CONCLUSION

Tasbika—a rich, tomato-based stew technique used to cook meat and seasonal vegetables—became a dominant mode of Egyptian cooking amid the social and political transformations of the twentieth century. Charged by the state to act as sovereigns within their kitchens, women took up a plentiful tomato supply and used it to create the template of a recipe that would soon be considered a key embodiment of traditional Egyptian flavor—even as home cooks adapted inherited knowledge to a changing array of domestic technologies.

Anne Meneley explains how the specific qualities associated with ingredients can become associated with the properties of associated places and narratives, forging connections between their individual consumers and those wider frames of meaning.[96] In the case of tomatoes a number of specific material properties, magnified through tasbika, served to connect Egyptians to Egyptian landscapes outside of Cairo and Alexandria and to narratives of family heritage preserved and passed on through culinary practice.

The culinary labor of home cooks making tasbika was not merely reproductive but generative. Exercising "kitchen sovereignty" in the face of social and economic change, they contributed to a shared culinary repertoire that resonated across social, geographical, religious, and generational differences. Selectively incorporating new ingredients and technologies into a living, evolving culinary tradition, home cooks forged a culinary public through Egyptian flavors that existed beyond the representational modes of cookbooks and written recipes. The women who created and popularized it drew on vernacular, embodied and inherited knowledge to produce a dish that was adaptable to changes in season, culinary technology, and market scarcity. As they cooked meat and vegetables in a rich tomato base, they determined what it meant for something to "taste Egyptian," defining dominant flavors within the bounds of the domestic authority that had been delegated to them.

Even so, assertions of coherence across time, space, and social difference do not necessarily reflect historical reality. Understandings of "Egyptian" flavors that circulate in Cairo and Alexandria do not reflect the full diversity of cooking within the borders of the state. Like the emergence of any dominant cultural form, tasbika's rise entailed the marginalization of certain practices and perspectives and the privileging of others. That is not to say that the intention of home cooks was to perpetuate that marginalization—but tasbika illustrates how the effects of structural inequalities became naturalized and normalized in the everyday spaces and practices of the home kitchen.

As cooks shifted toward cooking more dishes with tomatoes, they necessarily cooked other foods less often. The prizing of hearty meat stews within a dominant urban culinary style helped sideline regional and rural culinary cultures that featured more pulses and less animal protein and older approaches to cooking vegetables, for example. Chapter 6 considers how the dominance of tomatoes, produced in part through the uneven development and distribution of national resources, also enacted forms of culinary and cultural displacement that at times relegated elements of Egypt's richly diverse cooking heritage to the margins.

SIX

Red Stew, Green Stew

COOKING OKRA IN THE NILE VALLEY

BEFORE THERE WERE TOMATOES in Egypt, there was okra (*bamiya*). Today it is commonly prepared in a tomato stew; but Egyptians were eating okra long before the tomato arrived, and okra recipes without tomatoes have remained part of Egyptian home cooking. Okra is therefore—somewhat paradoxically—a testament both to the tomato's transformation of Egyptian cuisine and to the limits of that transformation. Okra's historical associations with African cuisines also ground Egypt's food history in its African context—which has not featured prominently in most of the material examined in the preceding five chapters.[1] This chapter considers Egyptian okra over the longue durée to write the end of this book's tomato-centric story into a wider temporal and geographical framework. Along the way I explore how okra embodies and engenders experiences of social and cultural difference.

By the twelfth century, Arabic sources described okra as thoroughly integrated into Egyptian agriculture and cuisine.[2] In the historical record of the medieval and early modern periods, okra featured in the high cuisine of Egypt's successive ruling elites as well as in the "humble fare of the common people."[3] Nawal Nasrallah includes okra in a short list of foods characteristic of medieval Egyptian diets, noting that social distinctions in medieval Egyptian cuisine were often expressed not through different dishes and ingredients but through the quality and mode of their preparation.[4] Premodern sources highlight two aspects of okra's reputation in Egypt that persist to this day: its viscous, slippery texture and its frequent association with the Saʿid, or Upper Egypt.[5] Nasrallah notes that from the corpus of medieval Arabic cookbooks only one okra recipe survives; it first appears, so far as we know, in an anonymous fourteenth-century Cairene cookbook. The recipe calls for okra to be cut into pieces, cooked with red meat or pigeon, and seasoned with onion, black pepper, fresh cilantro, and garlic. It specifies that once cooked, the okra should be flavored with "the juice of one lime ... so that the broth does not become viscous."[6] The addition of acidic ingredients (like citrus and tomato) to okra for the purposes of minimizing its mucilaginous texture is a recurring piece of advice in instructions for cooking okra to this day, in Egypt and elsewhere.[7]

Yusuf al-Shirbini's seventeenth-century satire (discussed in chapter 2 because it mentions the "quta") includes a passage that links bamiya with *mulukhiyya* and associates both with the cuisine of Upper Egypt. Mulukhiyya is a leafy green and, like bamiya, it is part of the mallow family (Malvaceae) and known for its slippery texture. Shirbini relates a story about an Upper Egyptian man who journeyed to Cairo to purchase an enslaved cook.[8] He met a woman who "was for sale at an extremely high price because of her knowledge of different dishes." But upon learning that he was from the Saʿid, she told him: "You have no need of fine food, for the diet of the people of Upper Egypt is six months a year okra and six months a year [mulukhiyya]."[9] The juxtapositions of geography and social standing are striking here; the presumably Cairene urban cuisine that the enslaved cook has mastered becomes a point of superiority so pointed that it is wielded by a female slave over a free man of means. Her disdain satirizes the culture of the Egyptian south for an audience of elite readers in northern Egyptian cities. Shirbini's anecdote and the medieval recipe underscore that although okra was evidently integrated into a range of medieval and early modern Egyptian cuisines, it could at times index a sense of otherness—whether through a particular texture that required culinary management or geographical associations that imposed a hierarchy between Egypt's northern cities and its southern periphery.

Even so, okra remained widely popular in Ottoman and khedival Egypt. A seventeenth-century travelogue attested that okra was "ordinary and popular" among Egypt's nonelites.[10] In the early nineteenth century Edward Lane described okra as a common dish in the meat stews of Cairo's "higher and middle orders," who served it with citrus juice like their fourteenth-century predecessors.[11] An 1876 account of Upper Egypt places okra at the top of a list of the "most common" vegetables grown in "the gardens of the country people" as well as in descriptions of elite and humble cuisines.[12] A 1910 agricultural manual describes okra as "one of the most popular and most esteemed native pot-herbs" of the country.[13] In other words, as the tomato was making its way into Egyptian fields and kitchens in the nineteenth and early twentieth centuries, okra continued to be eaten throughout Egypt and across social classes—as it had been for centuries. Discussions of okra's texture, the use of acidic flavors and meat stews to cook it, and its associations with both mulukhiyya and Upper Egypt continued into the modern period.

Against the backdrop of these continuities, however, the tomato revolutionized dominant approaches to cooking okra in Egyptian kitchens. Indeed, okra has appeared frequently in this book's accounting of the tomato's rise to prominence: it appeared, for example, in early print recipes for Egyptian-style dishes (chapter 2) and as a tomato-based comfort food in an ethnographic account (chapter 5). In this chapter, I use cookbooks, oral histories, and ethnography to explore how tomatoes transformed the way Egyptians cook okra—and how Egyptians have continued to cook okra otherwise.

RED OKRA: CULTURE AS (SELECTIVE) TRADITION

"In my house, I only make [okra] with [tomato] *salsa* and lamb; it has to be filling, slow-cooked, and rich [*ti'ila wa misabbika wa dasima*]," Reem told me when I asked her how she prepares okra.[14] This tomato-centric approach to cooking okra is relatively new, but it swiftly became prevalent: although absent from nineteenth-century cookbooks, it is ubiquitous in twentieth-century sources. Cookbooks and oral histories help explain how this approach became construed as a traditional means of okra preparation in Egypt's dominant culinary cultures. Throughout this chapter I refer to the range of tomato-based okra recipes as "red okra," a direct translation of the Arabic phrase *bamiya hamra*, which my interlocutors often invoked to describe it.

Red okra, like many other tomato-based Egyptian dishes, emerged in the twentieth century as a "selective tradition": an "intentionally selective" version of the past that is "powerfully operative in the process of social and cultural definition and identification."[15] Over the course of a few generations, cooking okra with tomato became identified as the "normal" or default way of preparing okra in Egypt. I trace where and how this transition took place first through a survey of cookbooks that framed red okra as Egyptian okra, then by exploring the construction of red okra as traditional through oral histories that detail its transmission and significance within the home.

We do not know who first cooked Egyptian okra in a tomato stew. But Thora Stowell's 1923 cookbook (discussed in chapters 2 and 5) offers an account suggestive of the circumstances under which red okra was integrated into the kitchens of Egypt's elites. Like other foreigners before her, Stowell identifies okra as a "specimen dish" of Egyptian cooking (alongside mulukhiyya, which she describes as "perhaps the greatest favourite with Egyptians").[16] In a departure from earlier accounts of okra in Egypt, however, the okra dish Stowell presents as an exemplar of Egypt's "typical stew" is tomato-based, including equal parts tomatoes and meat by weight, and described as a template for other vegetable and meat stews.[17]

Presumably Stowell's knowledge of Egyptian dishes came from her Nubian cook. Although she never names or credits him, Stowell indicates that all the book's recipes "have been made either by a [Nubian] cook alone or with my aid."[18] Stowell's text includes extensive advice for managing local servants and a chapter of Egyptian recipes that, we can infer, reflects those domestic workers' knowledge of Egyptian cuisine. Her book is a reminder of the significance of domestic workers and enslaved cooks, particularly those from Nubian and other Upper Egyptian backgrounds, within the elite food cultures of Cairo and Alexandria.[19] Stowell's chapter on managing servants advises speaking to Nubian servants only in Arabic, which Stowell claims helps to preserve the distinctions of rank within the household.[20] To that end, the book includes a glossary of "Kitchen Arabic" to be used with Egyptian servants, which includes a list of "the imperative mood of some useful verbs."[21] It is worth noting that Nubian languages are distinct from Arabic; Nubians working either in an Anglo-Egyptian home like Stowell's or an Arab Egyptian home would likely not have spoken with their employers in their mother tongue.

Stowell's advice aligns her work with the wider genre of nineteenth- and twentieth-century advice manuals for British colonial wives in India, Malaysia, Singapore, and elsewhere in the British empire.[22] Maintaining and policing boundaries between colonizers and their local servants was central to the ideology of domesticity these books promoted. Stowell's book includes the hackneyed colonial stereotypes about local domestic servants that British colonizers had repeated elsewhere for decades (even as, Cecilia Leong-Salobir points out, they entrusted those servants with the critical labor of food preparation).[23] But it also provides a glimpse of the particulars of domestic labor in Cairo and Alexandria in the early twentieth century. Stowell assumes that suitable domestic servants are of Nubian origin and notes, for example, that it is easier to find servants in Cairo than Alexandria because Cairo is comparatively closer to their homeland in the south.[24] Her cookbook thus helps to contextualize the nature of culinary knowledge in elite urban domestic contexts in this period in Egypt and highlights (however indirectly or inadvertently) the role played by southern Egyptians in developing and transmitting that knowledge.

Nubians, displaced from their home villages due to the construction of a series of twentieth-century dams, are an ethnolinguistic group whose homeland is in southern Egypt and northern Sudan. The exchange of culinary traditions between Egypt and Nubia has taken place since antiquity; cookware and traces of food residue at one Egyptian fortress near the Nubian frontier indicate historical shifts "towards Nubian foodways... and mirroring the adoption of Nubian cookpots" that often tracked political alliances—such as during the Second Intermediate Period (1650–1550 BCE) when the area came under Nubian rule.[25] (Perhaps this is how okra was first introduced to Egypt, though no documentation has yet proven it.) By the time the tomato arrived to Ottoman Egypt, an active slave trade traversed historical Nubia, linking Egypt and Sudan and enslaving populations in and beyond Egypt's southern periphery.[26] Under Mehmed ʿAli the Egyptian state centralized its control over Upper Egypt and colonized Sudan.

Eve Troutt Powell notes that "by the 1870s, more and more Sudanese and Nubian people had moved into the cities of Lower Egypt, sometimes as slaves but increasingly as merchants and traders or doormen and gatekeepers."[27] Powell describes how the modern relationship between Egypt and Sudan emerged from this legacy of political domination as well as economies of racialized domestic labor rooted in what was by then a centuries-old slave trade; she documents how these dynamics gave rise to, and found expression in, Egyptian stereotypes about Sudanese inferiority.[28] Although the slave trade was abolished in Egypt in 1877, slavery as an institution was not, and "African slaves continued to make up significant parts of the domestic labor force" in the late nineteenth century, particularly in elite households (including Huda Shaʿrawi's childhood home).[29] Emancipated slaves and their descendants often continued to work in domestic service.

After 1902 the construction of dams at Aswan drove even more Nubians north in search of work as irrigation projects submerged their agricultural lands. One outsider's account from 1911 notes that "most of the men, some time or other, visit Egypt and enter domestic service there or go even further afield.... A large amount of money is sent back to Nubia as the result of the money-earning abilities of the men who go to Egypt for work."[30] Elite northern Egyptian households employed Nubians and other southerners as cooks and servants well into the twentieth century, as Idris ʿAli's autobiographical novel *Under the Poverty Line* attests. ʿAli recounts his own exploitation in the labor market as a Nubian newly arrived in Cairo around 1950, where he was employed by "a humble middle-class Coptic family."[31] His account speaks to the racialization of various southern populations (Sudanese, Ethiopians, Nubians, Upper Egyptians) who found that in Cairo their identities were treated as interchangeable. The book's narrator protests the dehumanizing treatment that he faces in the capital, addressing the Egyptians and demanding: "Why have you taken a farming people and made them into servants and doormen for your palatial villas and homes?"[32]

One consequence of these historical hierarchies and entanglements is that at the time the tomato was being integrated into Egyptian cooking—transforming the way okra was cooked in the process—much of the culinary labor in the households of northern urban elites would have been performed by men from the south. Although their culinary contributions have yet to be studied in detail, Taylor Moore's work shows that in the late nineteenth and early twentieth centuries, Upper Egyptian and Black African women from similar backgrounds were deeply influential in other aspects of Egyptian domestic culture as "occult healers and spiritual guides."[33] It is clear that not just the culinary labor but the culinary knowledge of southern cooks was central to the production of red okra as an Egyptian dish, at least within certain households.

There are striking parallels here with the history of the southern United States. As Jessica B. Harris, Michael Twitty, and others have documented, the cuisine of the American South depended upon the knowledge and labor of enslaved Africans.[34] They brought their knowledge of (among many other things) cultivating rice and cooking with okra, enriching southern agriculture and producing a complex cuisine "under situations that ranged from the unpleasant to the unspeakable."[35] The significance of the labor of the enslaved was twinned with the denial of their cultural and intellectual importance. Harris writes that although "for centuries, black hands have tended pots, fed babies, and worked in the kitchens of [the United States'] wealthiest and healthiest," their contributions have been historically underdocumented in cookbooks and other sources.[36] For example, Mary Randolph's 1824 cookbook *The Virginia House-wife* is often credited as a key early source for published recipes for tomatoes and okra in the United States.[37] Yet Randolph's kitchen was run by enslaved cooks whose presence her text obscured. Marie Pellissier writes that Randolph referred euphemistically instead "to the 'household' as the dominion over which the Virginia housewife had control—over labour, over knowledge production and over household management."[38]

Stowell's knowledge about okra stew, mediated through her Nubian cook, is just one sliver of the history of the relationship between tomatoes and okra in Egypt. Her perspective is limited and her prejudices are plain. But her cookbook offers some clues about the relationship between the marginalization of Egypt's southern regions and the rise of a tomato-based stew as the dominant approach to cooking Egyptian okra. While chapter 2 documented how an unequal material relationship between Upper Egypt and Cairo created a steady tomato supply through perennial irrigation, here we see how economies of migration and domestic labor also produced red okra as a culinary tradition.

RED OKRA AS EGYPTIAN OKRA: A SURVEY OF SELECTED COOKBOOKS

The next red okra recipe under discussion appears in a very different context: *Guide for the Modern Chef*, the 1932 cookbook published by chef Muhammad 'Ali Abu al-Sunun. This recipe comes not from a foreigner and her subaltern cook, but from one of the *efendiyya*—the "self-consciously modern" male subjects who positioned themselves as arbiters of Egyptian authenticity and correct modernity in late nineteenth- and early twentieth-century Egypt.[39] In his introduction Abu al-Sunun deplores the lack of adequate cookbooks in Arabic and presents his volume as an act of service to the nation within the field of modern cooking—charting a path "that all those fervently devoted to our homeland and its national character might follow."[40] Abu al-Sunun's cultural authority is expressed through his formal Arabic. His culinary authority, meanwhile, derives from his training, described in his introduction in detail, under a series of prominent European chefs in luxury hotels in Cairo and Alexandria.

Abu al-Sunun's red okra dish is one of about ten recipes that he explicitly labels "Egyptian." It appears in a chapter of vegetable dishes that includes both European and "Eastern" recipes. Recipes labeled Turkish, Eastern (*sharqi*), and Egyptian feature tomatoes prominently.[41] "Turkish-style stuffed zucchini," for example, involves a small amount of tomato sauce mixed into the stuffing.[42] A recipe for "Eastern-style green beans" calls for garlic, onion, lamb, and a quarter of a liter of tomato sauce.[43] Immediately following this recipe is "Egyptian-style okra," in which fresh peeled okra pods are cooked "according to the same method as the Eastern-style green beans"—that is, in a meat-and-tomato stew.[44] Abu al-Sunun's recipe positions okra within a wider Eastern category while differentiating it as Egyptian. He presents the dish not just as a typical "specimen" of Egyptian cooking, like Stowell does, but as properly *modern* Egyptian and Eastern cooking.

Recipes from women-authored domestic cookbooks reinscribe red okra as Egyptian in yet another context: the middle-class home kitchen. Samia 'Abd al-Hamid's 1953 *Fundamentals of the Art of Cooking: The Most Modern Methods* includes two okra recipes; both feature tomatoes and include vocabulary that identifies them as Mashriqi (eastern Arab) and Egyptian. The first is titled *al-bamiya al-matmura*, invoking the terms *matmur/makmur* used by midcentury cookbook authors in reference to tomato-based stews and casseroles. It follows the same general contours as the red okra stews discussed earlier in the chapter. Like Stowell, 'Abd al-Hamid presents okra as the paradigmatic example of this style of cooking: the recipe ends on a note to "follow this method for making matmur-style squash, green beans, and potatoes."[45]

As discussed in chapter 4, midcentury cookbook authors often used "matmur" and "makmur" to index an older cooking style that they presented in a modernized form. 'Abd al-Hamid's recipe has another notable element: the instruction to prepare the okra for cooking by a process called *taqmiʻ*, an Egyptian Arabic word used to refer to trimming okra pods in a particular way (I return to this term shortly). The name of 'Abd al-Hamid's second okra recipe, *al-bamiya al-burani*, also evokes an older category of Arab dishes that dates back to the medieval period.[46] It does not feature tomatoes as prominently as the first recipe but includes them in a dish that layers okra, meat, and tomatoes in a *diqqiyya*—an Egyptian term for a small pot historically made from copper.[47] Thus, although 'Abd al-Hamid does not confer a national label on her okra recipes, the lexicon she uses frames them as both Egyptian and Mashriqi.

Recipes for red okra cooked and served in a diqqiyya also appear in the series of cookbooks Nazira Nicola wrote for the "working woman" in the 1970s.[48] Two books in the series feature slightly different versions of a recipe titled "Diqqiyyat al-Bamiya al-Marsusa" ("Layered okra in a small pot").[49] It is similar to the recipes just mentioned, with the addition of lemon juice for serving. One of them calls specifically for *bamiya rumi*, referring to the smaller, more delicate pods preferred by cooks preparing red okra.[50] A 1903 source describes "baladi" and "rumi" (meaning, approximately, "local" and "foreign") varieties of okra in Egypt, specifying that the rumi variety is "comparatively more delicate" than the baladi.[51] Like 'Abd al-Hamid, Nicola presents tomato-based okra recipes with titles that suggest older culinary traditions—for instance, the invocation of the diqqiyya in a decade when few urban Egyptians continued to cook in copper pots—while placing the recipe in the hands of the "working woman" who is also the cook for her family. Read across the decades, these three authors' recipes define "red okra" dishes as an exemplary part of a dominant cooking style that is at once modern and authentically Egyptian.

NORMALIZING RED OKRA

While cookbooks show how tomato-based okra dishes were represented as "Egyptian okra" in texts, oral histories and ethnography detail how "red okra" became the ordinary, default approach to cooking okra in Egypt through the repetition of everyday practices. The most obvious theme that emerged in conversations I had on this subject was a near-tautological identification of the Arabic word "bamiya" not merely with "okra" but with "okra cooked in tomato sauce." This first became evident to me during a conversation with a doorman from Aswan working in central Cairo. As I asked about the various kinds of okra his family made in the Saʿid, he repeatedly and patiently clarified that "bamiya," for him, simply meant okra cooked with meat and tomato sauce; other types of okra dishes were marked by specific names. More than one Egyptian acquaintance referred to bamiya prepared in a tomato stew as *bamiya ʿadiyya* (normal, typical, ordinary, or regular okra). Even Egyptians familiar with non-tomato-based okra dishes often spoke in these terms, describing tomatoes as the default medium for cooking okra.

Memories of intergenerational culinary knowledge transfer—the passing of red okra recipes from mother to daughter—cemented this understanding of red okra in many (though by no means all) families. Hanan, who was raised in Minya in the 1940s, explained the basic dishes that she had learned to cook from her mother as "very ordinary things like okra, mulukhiyya, potatoes."[52] When I asked for more detail, she clarified that by "okra" she meant okra made tasbika-style, with lots of *samna baladi* (traditionally prepared clarified butter; see chapter 5). Notably, okra was the first food she named—a striking echo of the primacy accorded to okra in Stowell's and ʿAbd al-Hamid's explanations of tasbika-style stews, and even of Shirbini's characterization of Saʿidi cooking as dominated by okra and mulukhiyya. Regardless of whether okra was in fact the first thing Hanan learned from her mother is immaterial to the fact that in an oral narrative in 2016, sixty years later, okra in a tomato stew was first in the list of "ordinary" foods she recalled learning in her natal home. A 2018 memoir-style cookbook by Nawla Darwiche similarly associates red okra closely with her mother's cooking: her tomato-based okra recipe is titled "My Mother's Bamiya" (*al-bamiya 'ala tariqat mama*); none of the book's other recipes are labeled this way.[53] Women frequently paired okra and mulukhiyya together as they described memories of their mother's cooking to me. Rania, who was born in 1952 in Alexandria, told me that although she didn't know how to cook when she married, as a young wife she constantly called her mother on the telephone to ensure that she was preparing everything correctly. As a result, Rania said, "I make mulukhiyya and okra the way my mother did," adding, "and they're delicious."[54]

I also observed maternal affinities with red okra preserved and performed through gestures and material culture. When I asked one acquaintance about how her mother had prepared okra, she began moving her hands in a circular gesture as she spoke—mimicking the motions her mother had made when grating tomatoes over the kind of sieve that Egyptians used to produce salsa before they had electric blenders. During an oral history interview Reem, the Cairene mother and office worker who described her tomato-based okra as "filling, slow-cooked, and rich," rummaged around in a closet and produced her mother-in-law's heavy copper sieve for me to see.[55] Reem later told me that she only makes red okra because her children prefer it that way—pointing to another dimension of the intergenerational dynamics that have shaped Egyptian attachments to red okra.[56] These narratives, gestures, and objects all help explain how red okra came to be understood as a traditional dish passed down intergenerationally through matrilinear transfer, thereby becoming an obvious, ordinary, and instinctive Egyptian culinary practice.

Conversations about red okra typically also prompted discussions about how to minimize okra's slippery, mucilaginous texture. As discussed earlier, this appears to have been a preoccupation of Egyptian cooks since the medieval period. While many culinary texts (Egyptian and otherwise) mention the use of acidity to minimize this texture, Egyptian home cooks emphasized a different set of strategies, starting with the importance of cooking okra pods whole to avoid releasing the slippery texture of their interior. Today many Egyptians refer to that slippery texture using the word *zaflata* (noun; adjective *mizaflat*). Another modern technique for minimizing zaflata is the technique for trimming okra pods called "taqmi'" ("ta'mi'", in spoken Egyptian Arabic). This technique entails trimming the okra pod carefully to remove the outer layer of hard skin and produce a pointed tip, almost as if sharpening a pencil (the word literally means "to make something into the shape of a funnel"). The idea is to render the okra pleasant to chew when cooked whole but without cutting through the wall of the pod to the interior where the mucilage lies.

An important element of this approach to preparing zaflata-free okra is selecting small pods with tender outer skins so that they attain the desired tenderness even when they are cooked whole. Attentiveness to the tenderness of okra has a long history in Egypt: in the thirteenth century the botanist Ibn al-Baytar observed that the people of Egypt ate okra "with its outer skin if it is still smooth."[57] For much of the twentieth century home cooks achieved this by purchasing and eating okra in its peak season, when it is at its most tender. "Of course we had mulukhiyya in season, and the same for okra," said Nadia, describing memories of family meals in the 1960s and 1970s.[58] With the arrival of reliable and spacious freezers, home cooks also had the option of purchasing okra in season, then cleaning, parboiling, and freezing it for use throughout the year.[59] Eventually supermarkets with freezer sections began to carry what is now called "bamiya zero"—the smallest, tenderest whole okra pods, available year-round for those who can afford it. In this sense okra and tomatoes have parallel histories in the Egyptian home kitchen: some cooks buy okra and salsa ready-to-use from the store, while others prepare and freeze them at home or cook from scratch. Like tomatoes, okra has navigated the arrival of new appliances and technologies while consolidating its status as a hallmark of Egypt's traditional home cooking.

RED OKRA AND BEYOND

The history of red okra relayed thus far is in a sense the culmination of this book's argument up to this point. The material factors that rendered tomatoes into a year-round crop and a quotidian cooking medium underpinned a hegemonic understanding of modern Egypt defined primarily by and through northern elites. An Egyptian culinary style presented by cookbook authors masked multiple social structures that upheld social differences: a racialized (and in some cases displaced) labor force from a peripheralized region, a gendered approach to domestic labor that demanded women shoulder the burdens of cooking for others, and a class politics that elided the contributions of subaltern domestic workers. As it became integrated into everyday practices, red okra was recast as a tradition that rendered the novel traditional and produced a sense of continuity rather than rupture. It fit squarely within a Mashriqi-inflected understanding of Egyptian cuisine that looked east and north to the Levant rather than south and west to the rest of Africa. Red okra came to embody a sense of Egyptian identity oriented toward the Eastern Arab world that became naturalized as dominant, common-sense, and ordinary.

We could end the story here. Some accounts of Egyptian food history have effectively done so by implying that tomato-based okra replaced other okra preparation techniques entirely. One description of medieval Cairene okra written in 2011 notes: "Nowadays, it is prepared more or less the same way, with the addition of the New World tomato."[60] Another includes a footnote directing the reader to cookbook author Claudia Roden's work "for the contemporary version of [okra], in which tomatoes and tomato paste constitute important ingredients" (note the specification of red okra as *the* contemporary version, not *a* contemporary version).[61] My goal is not to suggest that these scholars, or any of my interlocutors, are deliberately imposing a teleological narrative on the rise of red okra. Rather my aim is to illustrate how easily a dominant cultural form can establish itself as normal and natural and singular in a way that confirms common-sense understandings—in this case, of Egyptian culture as defined by Cairo and Egypt as a part of the Mashriq— of the Arab East. Again, we could end the story here.

Okra, however, begs to differ. A quick glance at Roden's work—a body of recipes that reconstructs the world her Sephardic Jewish family left behind when they left Egypt in 1956—reveals a more complex landscape of okra preparation in Egypt.[62] Her okra recipes include two variations that she identifies as Upper Egyptian. Both involve mashing the okra pods rather than cooking them whole; one involves no tomatoes whatsoever.[63] The more I spoke to friends and colleagues about okra, and as I conducted follow-up interviews with many of my original oral history subjects, the more I learned about the universe of tomato-free approaches to okra—not just in the Saʿid but in the middle strata of Cairo: the very context where I had sought to understand the production of Egypt's dominant culinary cultures.

Raymond Williams writes that cultural activity can be studied "both as tradition and as practice."[64] In the same way that okra offers a means to understand the construction of a tomato-based culinary tradition in Egypt, it also opens up other ways of narrating the culinary and cultural history of modern Egypt—one that considers the persistence and significance of everyday practice. In doing so, okra helps to situate Egypt's culinary cultures within an African context.

WHITE OKRA: CULTURE AS PRACTICE

In a 2014 short story by Omnia Talaat a lonely nine-year-old girl narrates an episode from a day in her life.[65] Abandoned by her mother, she lives with her austere and unforgiving grandmother. Roused by her grandmother's demands to help her with the shopping (and with no time for breakfast), she struggles behind her through the market, weighed down with baskets holding fruits and vegetables. Teetering on the verge of exhaustion, the narrator relates: "The aroma of a meat broth infiltrated my nose, and I felt as though my sweat was mingling with the fat of the meat as it melted in the broth." Her body trembles. She passes into a state of intoxication as the smell leads her down a side street: "Powerless, I followed the desires of my nose and stomach, whose cries drowned out all other sounds." She leaves her tomatoes and cucumbers piled by the greengrocer where her grandmother is shopping.[66] Soon she arrives at the source of the smell. Looking through a window from the alley, she spies the local plumber preparing an okra dish laden with garlic over his kerosene stove. Closely following each step of its preparation with her eyes and ears, she falls into a reverie, simultaneously desiring the dish and identifying with it as her mouth waters and her cravings grow—until her grandmother yanks her back to reality once more with a shout.

The alluring dish in the story is *weeka*, a completely different kind of okra dish from the category of red okra discussed earlier in this chapter. The story attests to the ongoing presence of Egyptian okra preparation methods, including weeka, that feature no tomatoes—sometimes referred to in general as *bamiya khadra* or *bamiya bayda*—"green" or "white" okra. In what follows, to refer to the various okra dishes that are not made tasbika-style, I often use the phrase "white okra," following popular usage—an indicator less of the literal color of this category of dishes (which ranges from green to brown) than the notion that they are distinct from red okra.[67] (When quoting sources or people directly, however, I use the terminology that they used.)

Talaat's short story draws on the varied cultural resonances of weeka and other white okra dishes, illuminating multiple dimensions of okra's significance in Egypt beyond tomatoes. White okra dishes make visible the culinary connections shared across Egyptian, Nubian, and Sudanese cultures in the Nile

Valley. They also involve a set of culinary practices and aesthetics that depart from and qualify our understanding of the tomato's dominance in Egyptian cooking. These include cooking with dried okra as well as techniques that turn okra into a viscous stew, rather than minimizing its slippery texture.

GREEN DISHES IN A RED CULINARY SEA

White okra dishes are not the only green holdouts against the crimson tide of tomato dominance in the Egyptian kitchen. Summarizing the results of a longitudinal study of Egyptian eating habits over the second half of the twentieth century, Habiba Hassan-Wassef notes that "dark leafy vegetables" are, along with *ful mudammas* (stewed fava beans), "traditional food items" that "appear daily on nearly every table in rich and poor homes alike."[68] Undoubtedly the most famous of these is mulukhiyya. Although mulukhiyya is consumed across the Arabic-speaking world, different regions and countries have distinct tendencies when it comes to its preparation: whereas in the Levant the leaves are often left whole, in Egypt they are typically finally minced with a special tool, the *makhrata*, and cooked in a poultry, rabbit, or meat broth. This preparation method, like many white okra recipes, optimizes mulukhiyya's mucilaginous texture. Mulukhiyya remains one of Egypt's most beloved home-cooked foods.

Another "green" dish that has resisted incorporation into the pantheon of red stews and casseroles is the root vegetable *qulqas*, known in English as *colcasia* or taro. Although there are preparations for qulqas that involve tomato, the classic and perhaps more popular version is a greens-based recipe that entails cooking the vegetable in *khudra* (literally, "greens"), a paste made of fresh cilantro, chard, and garlic. Amira Howeidy describes qulqas as a dish that "has preserved its ancient DNA as a green minority in a red culinary constituency," drawing a parallel between it and Egypt's Coptic Christian minority.[69] The comparison is not incidental: qulqas is traditionally eaten by Copts to mark the Feast of the Epiphany, which occurs in January, when qulqas is in season. The stages of growing and preparing qulqas for consumption, Howeidy explains, are often likened to baptism (Copts celebrate the baptism of Jesus on Epiphany). Similar recipes to the contemporary version can be found in a fourteenth-century Cairene cookbook. Qulqas remains a divisive dish in Egypt today, in part because of its slippery texture, but few would deny its significance to Egyptian food heritage.

This brings us to the "green" (which is to say, nonred or "white") versions of okra. On one hand, it is not difficult to find twentieth-century Egyptian cookbooks that only provide okra recipes involving tomatoes—this was the case with all the cookbooks quoted in the previous section. Yet on the other, there are plenty of Egyptian print cookbooks that also include white okra recipes. Ahmad Ibrahim's 1893 cookbook includes okra recipes with and without tomatoes, including one for Sudanese weeka, as do Fatima Fahmy's 1931 culinary textbook and Basima Zaki Ibrahim's 1958 *The People's Table*. In the latter two books, the recipes without tomatoes resemble the qulqas recipe just described, prepared with green chard and herb paste.

The most comprehensive cataloguing of okra recipes I have encountered in twentieth-century cookbooks, however, is in Nicola and Osman's *Fundamentals of Cooking*, which includes twelve recipes for okra.[70] Half of these fall into the category of "red okra," the kind of dishes discussed previously in this chapter that involve cooking okra pods whole with tomato sauce. The remaining recipes offer a full accounting of the diversity of Egyptian "white okra" recipes. One is a chard-based preparation (*bamiya bi-l-khudra*, or okra with greens) that follows a similar mode of preparation as the book's qulqas recipe.[71] There are three recipes for weeka, the okra dish that beckons the narrator of Talaat's story. One calls for dried okra and the others for fresh; one is made with cut pieces of meat and the other two with ground meat. But all three call for *shatta* (hot pepper) and the addition of a *taqliyya* at the end—a characteristically Egyptian mixture of garlic and coriander fried in samna and drizzled over the finished dish.[72] Finally, all three recipes deploy okra in a way that releases rather than limits its slipperiness—either through the use of dried okra that is pounded into a powder or by stirring whole pods in a way that breaks them down. The addition of taqliyya and the production of a slippery texture align these recipes with dominant Egyptian approaches to making mulukhiyya.

Nicola and Osman's documentation of this wide variation of okra preparations makes it impossible to sort Egyptian okra recipes into mutually exclusive binaries—like recipes with tomato versus without tomato, or those that use dried versus fresh okra. Representations of and conversations about okra often use these binary terms as a proxy for naming difference: we make red okra and others make weeka; we use fresh okra and dried okra is a thing of the past, or something that is only done in the Saʿid. But Nicola and Osman's okra recipes do not neatly map onto these either/or categorizations. They include recipes for okra in tomato sauce that call for both dry and fresh okra, and a weeka recipe that is made with tomatoes. Their collection of okra recipes comprises complexities and forms of difference within Egypt's culinary cultures that cannot easily be reduced to binary terms.

A CULINARY AESTHETIC OF DIFFERENCE: INTERPRETING OKRA

It is by now clear that despite its dominance, red okra—tender whole pods stewed in tomato sauce—is far from the only way that Egyptian okra is prepared. How, then, should we conceptualize the relationship between red okra and white okra—or, put differently, between red okra and its others? It is tempting to read the resilience of weeka and other non-tomato-based okra preparations as a counterhegemonic narrative—a minority or minoritized practice holding out against incorporation by a dominant mode. Yet this framing fails to capture the past and present nuances of okra preparation in Egypt and risks reinscribing the dominance of red okra—casting it as inevitable rather than revealing how it is made, remade, and contested.

It is true that some narratives and texts affirm the dominance of tasbika-style red okra, describing the world in terms of those who eat okra with salsa and those who eat it without, or simply omitting alternatives to red okra altogether. But plenty of Egyptians even in my own limited circles (including within the urban "middle strata" of my interview subjects) rejected this oversimplified stance. One Uber driver shrugged when I asked him what kind of okra he preferred. "I like bamiya hamra and bamiya bayda, they're both good," he told me, gently refusing my invitation to take a stance in support of one or the other. While many of my Egyptian friends, acquaintances, and oral history subjects had little to no knowledge of Egyptian okra recipes without tomatoes, a roughly equal amount had much to share about non-tomato okra—a level of parity that is anecdotal but striking.

Drawing on observations of discursive and embodied practices, I propose that okra allows us to explore a *culinary aesthetics of difference* that operates within an Egyptian frame but also extends beyond it—offering a way to conceptualize the complexities of Egyptian okra without reinscribing the logic of the nation-state and the hierarchies of gender, race, ethnicity, and class that uphold it. In doing so, I borrow from Mary Youssef's identification of an "aesthetics of difference" in the work of several contemporary Egyptian novelists. Youssef identifies an emergent critical sensibility "towards difference and the complexity of the Egyptian population" through which novelists explore "the cultural experiences of individuals from the ethnically and religiously marginal communities whose histories and languages are often overlooked due to dominant cultural discourses and reductive historical narratives."[73] This includes the work of Idris ʿAli, the Nubian Egyptian writer whose novel *Under the Poverty Line* was quoted earlier in the chapter.

Youssef observes that ʿAli's writing, as well as the way the author has situated himself in the Egyptian literary sphere, challenges singular and monolithic conceptions of the Egyptian nation-state while also rejecting categorization under the banner of "Nubian literature." She notes that ʿAli describes himself not as a Nubian or an Egyptian writer but "as a '*katib shaʿbi*' (public/popular writer)."[74] Elliott Colla observes that as much as ʿAli's work is in conversation with the conventions of mainstream Egyptian literature, including the national romance, it also departs from those conventions in significant ways.[75] He describes *Under the Poverty Line* not as "a coherent platform of resistance or escape" but as a text that "succeeds in renaming—and reframing—geography and history in an intensely local, idiosyncratic way."[76] Menna Agha identifies a range of ways that displaced Egyptian Nubians have worked to create community beyond the limits and failures of the nation-state. After more than a century of displacement, she writes, "Nubia still exists" within a "virtual territory" created and reproduced through oral and literary traditions as well as in associations and clubs in Cairo and Alexandria where displaced Nubians gather.[77]

Building on these observations, I propose an analogous framework to interpret a set of culinary practices related to okra in order to "rename and reframe" understandings of modern Egypt—thinking of it not as a nation-state but a public informed by and experienced through a culinary aesthetics of difference. Like ʿAli's refusal to concede to the terms either of a dominant nationalism or a bounded minority, conceptualizing a culinary public through okra's complexities allows for an understanding of modern Egypt that is both "intensely local" and unencumbered by the conceptual and physical boundaries of the nation-state. I trace the way cooking okra contributes to an Egyptian culinary aesthetics through practice. Monique Scheer argues that practices, as "observable behavior," offer a way to historicize and study the affective dimensions of social worlds (like unconscious gestures accompanying sensory memories) as well as more easily traceable elements (like printed recipes). She notes that practices can occur "along a continuum from wholly conscious and deliberate to completely inadvertent," from intentional cultural practices to processes through which the body teaches and organizes feelings.[78] Building on this approach, I explore a wide range of practices to describe multiple dimensions of social and cultural difference as they are expressed and understood through okra. These include practices of narrating, transmitting, and making okra recipes.

NARRATING DIFFERENCE: HERE AND THERE

"White okra" recipes, especially weeka, sometimes signal difference when they are narrated as belonging "elsewhere." We can see how this occurs on a hyperlocal scale in Talaat's story, in which the narrator leaves the familiar culinary and cultural terrain of her grandmother's orbit (including a pile of tomatoes) and is led down an alley to the plumber's house. Her gaze and her longing transgress a boundary between the narrator and her neighbor, who is engaged in the intimate act of cooking alone in his home. She peers into a private space from the public street—although of course it was the aroma of the weeka that crossed the boundary first. Her grandmother's admonishment confirms the transgression and restores the narrator back into the more familiar space of matrilineal authority. This scene is echoed in sociologist and food scholar Krishnendu Ray's account of his own transgressive consumption of kebabs for the first time as a Hindu boy in Delhi, which happened, he recounts, when "an aroma lured me into the Muslim quarter."[79] These scenes illustrate the ways that food, in its sensory exuberance, can sometimes invite transgressions of the boundaries that humans impose.

As a foreigner trying to understand the place of weeka in Egypt, I often heard explanations of weeka as something that happened elsewhere. When I asked an Uber driver in Cairo about weeka he replied, "Oh, that's Sudanese. We don't have that here. They make it with dried okra. Here we make okra with salsa." Instantly an okra-based distinction was mapped onto an "other" that was located according to national borders: "they" meant Sudanese; "we" implied Egyptians or Cairenes. A contact in the food and hospitality industry in Cairo suggested I check out Sudanese restaurants if I wanted to learn about weeka. While acknowledging the presence of Sudanese people and food in Cairo, this remark similarly placed weeka on the other side of a boundary that was nationally, if not spatially, inscribed. The association of weeka with Sudan is not new in Egypt: a nineteenth-century travelogue written by Muhammad al-Tunisi, a member of a Tunisian merchant family living in Egypt, describes weeka disparagingly as a typical food of Darfur, with variations made from dried ingredients (although he describes the different kinds of weeka he encountered, al-Tunisi refused to try any of them).[80]

Yet other narratives—particularly those I heard from the many Egyptians whose own culinary repertoires included weeka or other white okra dishes—just as easily explained weeka as part of a culinary culture shared between Egypt and Sudan, rather than characteristic of one or the other. Febe Armanios, a scholar of Coptic history who grew up in Cairo in a family with roots in Asyut and Esna in Upper Egypt, recalls her grandmother's weeka.[81] "My Esnawiyya Teta came from a Coptic-Sudanese background, with her family roots in Sudan dating back to the early nineteenth century," Armanios writes. She describes weeka as "a garlicky pulverized okra stew-soup, eaten with loads of baladi bread. The stew is known in Upper Egypt but is also considered a national dish in Sudan."[82] Her narrative acknowledges the different place of weeka in Upper Egypt versus Sudan, while underscoring that the distinction is not a mutually exclusive one.

Armanios's narrative leads to another key point: Sudanese restaurants are far from the only place in Egypt where weeka (or other types of "white okra") can be found. Many Egyptians I spoke with or interviewed immediately associated weeka with the Saʿid. This too is a long-standing association in the context of Egypt's northern cities: in Shirbini's Ottoman-era satire, referenced earlier, which casts okra and mulukhiyya as typical foods of the Saʿid, the word used to refer to okra is actually "weeka."[83] The work frames weeka negatively through the perspective of the enslaved cook in Cairo, perhaps reflecting the opinion of Shirbini himself as a member of the educated northern elite.

In the very different context of Nicola and Osman's twentieth-century cookbook, however, white okra recipes appear as vehicles for conveying and producing a sense of culinary difference—but not in a way that excludes them from the category of "Egyptian" or the refined repertoire of foods they prescribe for their readers. Their weeka recipes are all finished with a taqliyya, the fried garlic and coriander mixture that "gives a distinctive Egyptian flavor to a number of dishes," as Claudia Roden puts it.[84] At the same time, the weeka recipes' inclusion of hot pepper distinguishes them from most other recipes in the cookbook; and the book's list of necessary kitchen items does not include the specialized tool used to break up okra for mucilage-forward okra dishes—even though it does include a sieve specifically for tomatoes and a makhrata for mulukhiyya. We might read the inclusion of these "white okra" recipes, then, as expanding the range of culinary aesthetics that Nicola and Osman are prescribing for the nourishing of Egyptian society: notably, they do not qualify weeka with any regional or national geographic designations as they do for other recipes throughout the book.

Moreover, in contemporary Egypt, associations between non-tomato versions of okra dishes and "elsewhere" are not always about Upper Egypt or Sudan. Reem, quoted earlier as making only red okra in her own home, associated a different style of okra with her father's side of the family. "Because he was from Fayyum, he would make a kind of green okra," she explained to me, which involved cooking okra in a meat broth and finishing it with a taqliyya.[85] Born and raised in Fayyum, he had settled in Cairo when he married Reem's mother, where he continued to prepare Fayyumi-style dishes, including the green okra dish, ducks, and pigeons.[86] White okra dishes thus appear in cookbooks and oral narratives as a marker of difference, but not always according to the binary logics of here versus there, us versus them, Egyptian versus non-Egyptian.

EXCHANGING DIFFERENCE

In Talaat's short story the source of the alluring weeka is not the proverbial grandmother but a working-class man. In fact, the weeka-cooking plumber forms a foil to the grandmother, who has deprived the narrator of her breakfast. Although none of my oral history subjects recounted any okra stories quite like Talaat's fictional one, weeka did appear as a counterpoint to common narratives about recipes and cooking knowledge being passed down from grandmother to mother to daughter—a key mechanism, I have argued, by which certain foods (including red okra) have been produced as traditional in modern Egypt.

Because weeka and other "white okra" dishes were so strongly associated with culinary traditions from places south of Cairo, the way they circulated in northern cities in the mid-twentieth century—a formative time and place for many of my oral history subjects—was completely different from the way that red okra recipes had been passed down. For one thing, just because a person's Saʿidi grandmother made weeka doesn't mean that she herself did the same. Nour, for example, associated weeka with the kitchen and cooking of her grandmother, who had grown up in Sohag and moved to Cairo in the early 1940s. The dish made the journey from the provinces to her grandmother's kitchen in the capital, but had not made the jump between the kitchens of subsequent generations within Cairo. Nour only made okra with red sauce.[87]

As important as intergenerational transmission of certain key dishes was for most of the women I interviewed, I found that interpersonal transmission between neighbors and friends was also a significant form of culinary learning—particularly for those who had moved away from their natal homes and extended families. Hanan, for example, learned many dishes from an older neighbor in her Alexandria apartment building who was "like a mother" to her, showing her complex culinary techniques like stuffing vegetables for mahshi and making béchamel sauce.[88] Magda's mother, born in 1941, moved from a village in the Delta to Cairo to live with her brother and attend school; she learned some recipes from her mother over the phone and picked up others—including weeka—from friends and neighbors.[89] This process echoes a dynamic Arjun Appadurai describes in India in the 1960s and 1970s by which women in the urban middle classes would "verbally exchange recipes with one another across regional boundaries."[90]

What this means for weeka is that it exists in the living memories of many urban Egyptian women born between the 1940s and the 1970s not as a static traditional dish made elsewhere or reproduced faithfully from a grandmother's recipe but as a dish passed along, shared, and remade as Egyptian in a completely new way. Some home cooks with Saʿidi roots learned to make weeka from their aunts and mothers and grandmothers. But other Cairenes learned how to make it in an intragenerational process of learning—from friends and neighbors. Magda's relationship to weeka embodied both kinds of transmission. When I asked her how she learned to make weeka, she explained:

> From my mom. She used to make it. But the origin, the real origin of the people who made it, it was people from the Saʿid in Upper Egypt. They don't eat okra like we do, red okra; they eat weeka . . . [My mom] had a neighbor from the Saʿid and she would make it for her. . . . For example, during Ramadan she would make weeka, and we'd say how do you make it, and they would tell you . . . people would exchange recipes that way.[91]

For Magda, a Cairene whose roots are in Tanta in the Delta, weeka is now a family recipe. A colleague told me a similar story about an aunt who recounted that in the 1960s she gave their family weeka recipe to at least twenty-five of her work colleagues upon their request. As they traveled into new kitchens and homes, or were passed down through generations of families that relocated to new places, weeka and other white okra recipes conveyed practices that continued to produce a sense of culinary difference in everyday Cairene cooking. This sense of culinary difference sometimes marks departures from the flavors, foods, or places of childhood. It reflects how contrasts jostle together in a city populated, in large part, by people originally from elsewhere.

This history reflects how, as Akhil Gupta and James Ferguson argue, in the wake of displacement and migration "the cultural certainties and fixities of the metropole are upset as surely, if not in the same way, as those of the colonized periphery."[92] The transmission of foods outside of biological family ties also stands against narratives that divide Saʿidi foods from Cairene ones. In doing so, they defy long-standing dictates of certain Cairene tastes that have sought to minimize okra's slippery and luscious texture—demonstrating how everyday practices preserve and reproduce certain forms of visceral difference.

EMBODIED PRACTICES OF MAKING: COOKING DIFFERENCE

In addition to narrating geographical difference through white okra dishes, home cooks described (and in some cases demonstrated) a wide range of culinary practices that produce tangible experiences of culinary difference. The practice of drying okra pods was one. For many Cairenes dried okra had been captured in their minds as an expression of generational difference—a remnant of the culinary past. Multiple women described a specific visual memory: a garland of dried okra pods strung onto a thread, hanging like a necklace in a mother's or grandmother's kitchen. One mentioned the strand tied to the knobs of the kitchen windows, and another recalled the okra hanging alongside strands of garlic. But the same basic image recurred. (Once, after explaining this in a conference presentation, an Egyptian woman in the audience told me that she had texted her mother in the middle of the panel and confirmed that her mother had the same memory.) Nor was this a vision of the past necessarily linked to Upper Egypt: one acquaintance remembered a grandmother bringing dried okra from the Delta. Another, born and raised in Cairo, reached behind her as we sat chatting in her living room and showed me a tin of okra pods she had recently dried herself. While I met few people who continue to dry okra themselves, and others who had never even seen dried okra, many named or recalled it as a fixture of kitchens "before the fridge."[93] Many also associated dried okra with the distinct brown color that it lends a dish when cooked.

When fresh okra is used to make "white" as opposed to "red" okra, a different set of practices is used to select and prepare the appropriate pods. "Weeka is just okra, you know, but [the pods] have to be really big—they should be long," Magda explained to me.[94] Often the appropriate type of okra pod was conveyed in gestures: multiple men held out their hands to indicate that an okra pod for weeka should or could be as long as a finger, compared to the much smaller pods appropriate for red okra (I could imagine their mothers, sisters, or wives teaching them the gesture with their hands before sending them to the market). Because the textural aim of preparing weeka and other kinds of green or white okra is to maximize mucilage, small, delicate pods are not necessary and the longer pods are more efficient. Typically white okra recipes call for fresh pods to be sliced through the middle and for the top to be cut clean off (not daintily shaped into a funnel), exposing the mucilage and seeds inside, and for dried okra to be crushed into a powder, which acts as a thickening agent.

Not everyone is a fan of the resulting textures. But many who said they loved it associated it with their favorite childhood memories. Khaled, who grew up in Cairo in the 1970s and 1980s, told me that in Abu Tig in Asyut, where his mother's family is from, "they love weeka a lot." Even though his mother cooked both types of okra, he said, "I loved the weeka more ... I would drink the weeka like a drink." As a child, his objection to red okra was precisely *because* the pods were left whole: "I would say [to my mom,] No! I don't want it! There are spiky bits [*shuk*]." It was only when he was older that he acclimated to eating whole okra pods in tomato sauce.[95] Similarly, a Cairo bookseller with family roots in Sohag told me that although his mother cooked both weeka and red okra, he vastly prefers the texture of the former to the rich tomato flavor of the latter.

These differences of opinion about okra mirror debates about okra elsewhere in the world. Siddhartha Mitter, who fell in love with okra as a child in Calcutta, was surprised to find that okra was a divisive food in mainstream food culture in the United States. "Its proponents seem to divide into nostalgics and militants," he writes. "Everyone else is an okra hater." The objections to okra he encountered focused on its texture, Mitter continues: "That lush, fertile consistency I loved as a child is known in the American parlance as slime."[96] Mitter observes how cookbook authors frequently emphasize the need to handle okra in a way that minimizes its slippery texture and "make certain to offer okra selection and preparation tips to help defeat the ooze."[97] By contrast, Jessica B. Harris highlights okra's texture as central to its high standing in African and African diaspora cuisines: "Prized on the African continent as a thickener, it is the basis for many a soupy stew and is served up in sheets of the slippery mucilage that it exudes," she explains.[98] Given these narratives, it is striking that in Egypt—and even more specifically, in Cairo—it is possible to find culinary and gustatory approaches that prize both approaches to okra, often in the same family or kitchen. The practices that produce the slippery texture of weeka in Cairene kitchens lend a new dimension to our understanding of the pod's sometimes divisive texture. They show that the divide between slime-minimal and slime-maximal okra does not always map neatly onto social class, generation, urban-rural divides, or even geographic origin.

Historically a key practice used to maximize okra's mucilaginous qualities was the use of the *mifrak*, a wooden tool with spokes at one end that has been used in Egypt since at least the Greco-Roman period (also called a *yay*).[99] Slicing the okra pods open helps release their texture, but mixing them in broth with a mifrak helps break up the solid pieces and maximize their viscous potential.[100] Some families still use the mifrak: Khaled told me that he had one in his house "because my mom is from the Sa'id," adding that his mother-in-law also uses one. The tool also plays a central role in Talaat's short story. It is thematized as an active component of the aspects of the dish that draw the narrator in (the "voice of the yay" confounds her) and works her into a frenzy as if she herself were the okra ("the yay crushes me"). The tool is as active an agent as the cook himself in the story, putting a point on the textural difference that the weeka offers the narrator.

For many, however, the mifrak exists only in memories of a past time or generation and a different place—a natal village or a grandmother's kitchen. When white okra recipes moved without a mifrak in tow, people developed new practices to generate the same form of textural difference. Working without a mifrak, one acquaintance told me, her mother would slice the okra especially thin, to accelerate the release of its texture. It would then need to be cooked longer in its broth than it would if using a mifrak to reach the desired consistency—which, an aunt had told her, you could tell had been achieved when the okra seeds turned pink. Others told me that they used a blender, although with the caveat that one must take care not to overblend

FIGURE 11. Wooden mifrak (hand blender), Fayyum, Egypt, Greco-Roman Period (332 BCE–395 CE). Bibliotheca Alexandrina Antiquities Museum. Photograph by Christoph Gerigk.

and produce a texture that is *too* gooey and slippery. Okra prepared in this fashion is sometimes called *bamiya mafruka*, or "beaten" okra, with the passive participle derived from the same root as "mifrak." While sometimes bamiya mafruka is used as a synonym for weeka, in other cases I found that they were used to refer to distinct dishes.[101]

I find the smooth and gentle texture of weeka and bamiya mafruka to be the most prominent aspect of the experience of eating these dishes. Egyptians use a range of seasonings to add flavor notes to what is a smoother, softer canvas than that of their vivid and rich tomato-based stews. Lemon juice is one of the most common—added in this case to brighten the flavor rather than to affect the texture. Another frequent addition is hot spice, often in the form of a small chile pepper sliced and added to the stew. As Magda told me, "You have to add hot pepper [to weeka] or there's no flavor [*taʿm*]."[102] Ironically, because peppers are also an American cultivar, this must also be a somewhat recent addition to practices of weeka preparation. This flavoring practice reminds us that the weeka of Shirbini's seventeenth-century satire is not the same as the weeka of today.

To come full circle, there are also dishes made with dried okra and tomato, undermining the notion that okra dishes in Egypt can be mapped neatly onto non-tomato/tomato or pre-tomato/post-tomato binaries.[103] In a Sudanese restaurant in central Cairo, for instance, I was served both weeka (made with dried okra, ground meat, and tomatoes) and bamiya mafruka (made with fresh okra and dill). On the side came pillowy fresh bread, lemons, fresh tomatoes and cucumbers, and a small dish of deep red chile pepper paste. And according to Nubian chef Mohamed Kamal, one Nubian preparation of okra entails cooking dried and crushed okra with onion, tomato, garlic, salt, pepper, and cumin in a stew.[104] The practices associated with producing the textures and flavors of Egypt's "white okra" dishes illustrate that they are neither frozen in the past nor confined to southern Egypt. They produce a sense of difference in Egyptian kitchens and eating practices. Sometimes these are deliberate expressions, like the act of cooking a particular recipe to pay tribute to one's Saʿidi or Sudanese grandmother. Sometimes they are a practical matter—a new cooking technique acquired from a neighbor by a young mother learning to run her own kitchen and faced with okra pods too long or tough to toss into her tasbika. And sometimes they are the kinds of intuited inclinations acquired as a child—a deep attachment to a type of culinary texture that stands against dominant global tastes about what constitutes refined food. These all inform a sense of what makes okra Egyptian. Sometimes that sense is bound up in tomatoes; sometimes it is anything but.

A CULINARY PUBLIC OF OKRA

The diverse world of Egyptian okra dishes, from red okra to weeka to bamiya mafruka, conveys the contours of Egypt as a culinary public that includes multiple layers and forms of difference rather than binary logics. In kitchens, food memories, and cookbooks okra is not a matter of either/or: tasbika-style stews sit comfortably alongside dishes that purposely break into large okra pods filled with seeds and slipperiness. Weeka is best understood not as Egyptian or Sudanese but a practice shared by both countries. Okra connects Egypt to the Mashriq but also to Africa. White okra dishes are not pre- or post-tomato but both. Okra illustrates the production of a modern sense of Egyptian-ness that is not just articulated but lived, sensed, cooked, and tasted.

However, as Anita Mannur reminds us, "a public in and of itself is not radical."[105] Just because a public facilitates or includes expressions of difference does not make it democratic. The framing that okra inspires here is one of possibilities not inevitabilities. It is possible, as the narratives discussed in this chapter show, to tell a selective history of Egyptian okra that is teleological (the modern tomato replaces what came before it) and homogenizing (preparing okra in red sauce embodies the truest or the most "normal" expression of Egyptian culinary tradition). Food, like any facet of culture, can normalize the nation not just as territorial entity but as a logic of relation to other territorial entities and wider forms of identification—naturalizing Egypt as Arab in ways that marginalize Nubian cultures or situating it in a Mediterranean or Levantine sphere rather than an African or Indian Ocean one.

But food's history and its status as a dynamic part of cultures in formation can also provide a means to understand community and belonging along different lines. Mannur writes that food offers a mode of critique with the potential to change the configuration of our world, insisting that "how one eats, consumes, and distributes food must reconfigure how we think about networks of intimacy beyond the familial, the heteronormative, the couple, and the nation."[106] The history of Egyptian okra sustains within it much of what has been erased through constructions of Egyptian nationhood as homogenous—whether the rhetorical conflation of Cairene culture as the culture of all of Egypt or the destruction of historical Nubia and the displacement of its people into resettlement sites and northern cities. When viewed through the complexities and variations of everyday practices, okra paints a picture not of a canonized national cuisine but a more capacious culinary public. Encompassing a varied set of influences and modes of culinary expression, this culinary envisioning of an Egyptian public embraces forms of belonging and identification beyond narrow understandings of nation and biological kinship. Although rooted in the particularities of the local, it also embodies food's refusal to respect borders—from the aroma of weeka wafting into an alley to centuries of stuffed eggplants circulating across languages, empires, and eras, and millennia of nightshades crossing oceans.

Conclusion

HOW TOMATOES BECAME EGYPTIAN

IN A CHAPTER ON VEGETABLES the midcentury cookbook author Basima Zaki Ibrahim described tomatoes in their dazzling range of varieties. "Some are long, or spherical, or oblong, or ribbed," she wrote. "They come in red, scarlet, and yellow. But the most common variety cultivated in Egypt is the *baladi* tomato."[1] The term "baladi," meaning at its most basic "local" or "of the country," has peppered the chapters of this book. That the Tunisian tomato-and-egg dish *shakshuka* could be described as baladi in Egypt marked its transformation from a Maghribi dish to a local one. Cooks referred to *samna* (clarified butter) as baladi to indicate that it had been made at home using butter from a trusted source. "Baladi" appears in agricultural manuals that describe Egyptian varieties of vegetables like okra and of course tomatoes. I conclude by exploring the layered meanings of the term "baladi" to ask: What did it mean for the once novel tomato to become baladi in Egypt?

I have used the tomato's history to describe a series of culinary publics in Egypt—social worlds defined by a sense of belonging experienced or articulated through food. The concept of "baladi" runs through each of these publics: it embodies a vivid and locally specific sense of connection and expresses "culinary care."[2] As relevant to fields and markets as it is to the home kitchen and the dinner table, the notion of what counts as baladi is central to the many ways that food constructs forms of collectivity. I approach the baladi as an idea that is "in a constant process of becoming."[3] By tracing how different iterations of this concept have shaped Egyptian culinary publics, I conclude this book with a focus on "processes rather than essences."[4] Much like the role of the tomato in Egypt, the "baladi" has been defined as much by the movement of people, foods, and ideas as it is by the relationship between those things and a fixed place.

The adjective "baladi" is derived from the noun *balad*, which loosely means "community"; at its most basic "baladi" means "local." But local is a relative term. It can refer to a community defined by political borders (e.g., baladi produce as opposed to imported produce) or to other spaces that define peoples' sense of belonging. In Egypt it can be applied to specific "popular" (*sha'bi*) neighborhoods in Cairo or other cities, a rural hometown or village, or to the entire country. "Baladi" is often opposed to *afranji*, which connotes a Western or European kind of foreignness in dress, values, or behavior. The adjective "baladi" is often embodied in the figure of the *ibn al-balad* or *bint al-balad* (son or daughter of the country). Like any concept, the terms "baladi" and "ibn al-balad" have histories. Sawsan El-Messiri dates the first appearance of the "ibn al-balad" to the work of al-Jabarti (1753–1825), an Egyptian scholar who chronicled Napoleon's invasion of Egypt.[5] In other words its appearance in the historical record is roughly contemporaneous with that of the tomato. In this sense the baladi and the tomato are both thoroughly modern phenomena in Egypt.

BALADI AS HEIRLOOM

One usage of "baladi" is approximately equivalent to the term "heirloom" in English—used to refer to heritage varieties of plants or animal breeds that have been bred for flavor rather than other factors like size or yield.[6] Egyptian agricultural manuals invoke baladi this way to describe locally developed varieties of vegetables, often in contrast to foreign or introduced varieties labeled *rumi*.[7] The Egyptian Agricultural Museum in Cairo features dioramas with specimens of baladi and rumi breeds of ducks and geese. The histories of "baladi" varieties of plants or animals, however, clarify that defining something as baladi does not mean it was not introduced from elsewhere. The variety of sugarcane called "baladi" in twentieth-century Egypt was imported from Jamaica in the mid-nineteenth century.[8] "Baladi" is therefore more than just the assertion of something as local to a place: it can also camouflage an underlying history of connections that link that place to elsewhere. Many of the baladi vegetable varieties in Egypt today were developed from introduced plants—including okra, eggplant, and of course the tomato. Although the first locally named tomato variety in Egypt appears to have been the Skandarani (Alexandrian), by the 1920s Egyptians described their most prominent local tomato variety as baladi.

What was (and is) the Egyptian baladi tomato? Sources in the 1920s and 1930s describe it as "ribbed, thick-skinned, and juicy."[9] Writing in the late

1930s or 1940s, Ibrahim identified it as the most common variety of tomato cultivated in Egypt.[10] Despite the baladi tomato's apparent popularity, agricultural experts have focused mostly on its shortcomings: *The Tomato in Egypt* (1922) captioned an image of the baladi tomato with a description of its "many undesirable wrinkles," followed by images of smoother, more "desirable" varieties.[11] The book details the results of an experiment comparing five different tomato varieties, of which the baladi had the lowest percentage of flowers yielding fruit.[12] A 1937 source dismisses the baladi tomato as unsuitable for export.[13] And yet the baladi tomato persisted. An Egyptian botanical work from 1960 states: "In this country, the 'beledi' which is irregular, elongated and ridged, is the most common strain."[14] An agronomist writing in 1970 dismissed the baladi, as his predecessors had: "It has little flesh and a large amount of juice and seeds; it is not suitable for preserving or for export."[15] But ordinary Egyptians seemed to disagree, and the baladi tomato was produced and reproduced for decades on Egyptian farms—eluding the requirements of agronomists and would-be exporters.

During my fieldwork many friends and interviewees gushed about the baladi tomato as a tomato of superior taste and flavor that had all but vanished. "All our tomatoes used to be baladi," said Magda, "but now they're all grown in a greenhouse."[16] People described baladi tomatoes as smaller, softer, less regularly shaped—tomatoes that still had dirt on them, that filled the kitchen with fragrance, and were red in color inside and out. They also often mentioned the short shelf life of a baladi tomato. This was confirmed by a farmer I met in 2024, when I was invited to visit a peri-urban farm in the greater Cairo area where baladi tomatoes were being grown.[17] Nestled alongside other tomato varieties in a small rented plot were the tomatoes that the farmers called "baladi." Although still ripening, their distinctive shape resembled the image printed in an agricultural manual a hundred years before, although their exact provenance was unclear. When I asked the farmer if there was high demand for them, he shrugged. "They spoil so quickly that it's difficult to get them to market in time." Even today the baladi tomato is not just one thing.

BALADI AS BULWARK AGAINST ALIENATION

This book has explained how certain practices associated with a specific place, like the home or the countryside, can localize ingredients and dishes and sustain a sense of belonging or attachment to that place. Learning a recipe from one's grandmother, for example, helps establish it as Egyptian; sourcing meat or butter from one's natal village nurtures a sense of connection to a place otherwise left behind. Often "baladi" is used to describe the products of practices like these, indicating that something is traditional, handcrafted, or authentic and defining it against what is modern, industrial, and superficial. Thus "baladi" can be interpreted as a counterpoint to alienation. This meaning of baladi appeared often in oral histories quoted throughout the book. Egyptians use it to emphasize not just the origin of a cultivar or breed but a set of practices entailed in cultivating a crop, sourcing and processing an ingredient, or raising an animal for slaughter.[18] "Baladi" often implies the valorization of an agroecological system free of industrial inputs or factory farmed animals. To call food "baladi" is to make a claim about quality, flavor, and social responsibility over quantity, standardization, and profit.

This understanding of baladi also operates at the various scales that the English term "domestic" does—defining a sense of home that emanates from the intimacy of the domestic sphere while differentiating the local from the foreign. For samna to qualify as "samna baladi," I was told, it should be clarified at home (not in a factory) from butter sourced from the milk of an Egyptian water buffalo, not imported cow butter. Samna produced this way is embodied by a specific color and smell that prefigure its flavor and contribute to its baladi sensibility. It also underscores that what counts as Egyptian is defined just as much by national borders as by what happens within the home.

The label "baladi" can also designate an object or ingredient as something that links the present with a locally specific version of the past. Walter Armbrust points out that this sense of "baladi" can be used in a derogatory manner, to indicate something is "not just 'local,' but 'unsophisticated,' 'crude,' and invariably 'pre-modern.'"[19] But, he adds, it can just as easily be invoked to describe "a much-loved food such as *mahshi* [stuffed vegetables]" or otherwise "invoke tradition in a positive sense."[20] This meaning appears occasionally in Egypt's midcentury cookbooks. *Fundamentals of Cooking* includes three lentil soup recipes: two baladi and one afranji.[21] Of course, given the context of the cookbook, both types of soup recipe are intended to be made in a home kitchen. But the baladi recipe is anchored in a local and Egyptian sense of home, expressed in the kind of soup that one learns from one's mother. For the reader the juxtaposition implies: learn a European soup recipe, but don't forget where you came from. Incidentally lentils are another Egyptian food dating back to ancient times; but the lentil soup recipe I learned from Hanan, whose life story is related in chapter 5, includes a tomato for a punch of flavor. New ingredients, technologies, and cooking techniques may cross Egypt's borders; but it is in the home that they are incorporated into the realm of the baladi.

BALADI AS (NATIONAL) CHARACTER

As explained previously, "ibn al-balad" and "bint al-balad" are cultural types that embody what it means to be baladi. Frequently represented in film and fiction, the ibn al-balad "is sometimes described as a sociological type," living in certain neighborhoods, working a trade, wearing a *gallabiyya*, speaking Egyptian Arabic (rather than a foreign language)—think of Haridi, the hero of *The Thug* (discussed in chapter 3).[22] Sometimes the figure indexes the working classes of Cairo; sometimes he is more national in scope. Marilyn Booth observes that while baladi is a label often applied "by those who consider themselves not '*baladi*,' the noun [ibn al-balad] incorporates a strong sense of self-identity."[23] The concept does not map evenly onto national identity; as El-Messiri puts it, "Egyptian nationality is necessary but not sufficient to identify one as an *ibn al-balad*."[24]

Nefissa Naguib describes the role that the self-identified ibn al-balad plays in contemporary Egypt in procuring ingredients for family meals. She relates the story of a man about to move his family from their home in Bulaq, a sha'bi neighborhood in central Cairo, to a larger apartment in a new suburb. Although the move a sign of upward social mobility, the man expresses his worries about the move, describing his perceptions of the differences between his old and new neighborhoods.[25] "[In the suburb] they spend money on showy stuff; we don't do that here," he says. "I spend on food for my family." Whereas his new neighbors buy "one tomato" at a time, "chicken full of hormones," and bread packaged in plastic from the supermarket, the man says, "I come home with two baladi [free-range] chickens, two kilos of tomatoes, twenty breads from the oven. And I will insist that my wife use all the food for one meal."[26] He refers to Bulaq as "the real and traditional Cairo," saying, "Here life is tough, but it has a taste."[27] In his story the baladi and the ibn al-balad converge in an expression of authenticity, nourishment, and abundance.

BALADI AND THE INDUSTRIAL

Histories of bread in Egypt show how understandings of the baladi can also attach themselves to culinary objects of a very different kind. Baladi bread (*'aysh baladi*) is a standardized, government-subsidized flatbread loaf produced from 82 percent extraction flour.[28] It is made primarily in commercial bakeries, where it is baked to a standard size and weight that the state determines.[29] Jessica Barnes finds that Egyptians today identify bread as baladi "primarily from the degree of refinement from the wheat flour and from whether any other grains are added," not by the source of its wheat.[30] In other words today's baladi bread might be made from Ukrainian wheat, or Egyptian wheat bred from imported strains, and still be understood and perceived—tasted—as baladi. Baladi bread illustrates that a food item can be experienced as local and authentic even if it is produced through the confluence of bureaucratic regulations, international flour markets, and industrial processing. The making of baladi bread calls to mind the way that the rise of the baladi tomato was due in part to the construction of massive modern dams that altered Egypt's human and physical geography and warranted the influx of unprecedented levels of fertilizers.

Contemporary Egyptian artist Yasmine El Meleegy's installation *Future Farms (Organic)* incorporates these contradictions into a set of giant fiberglass tomato sculptures, which she describes as a challenge to "the entrenched paradigm of contemporary agricultural progress."[31] Different tomato shapes represent "the manipulation of tomatoes' natural form over the years," from the baladi tomato to genetically modified varieties whose seeds are sold to farmers for one-time use.[32] Although every tomato is an organic-looking form in a slightly different shape, each is placed on neat stack of wooden pallets arranged in precisely ordered rows, hinting at the systematizing logic underlying their production. The installation speaks to the hidden links between the market and the home and between cultures of mass consumption, industrial systems of production, and foods' organic matter.[33] El Meleegy's work is a testament to the way the baladi tomato continues to sit at the heart of the contradictory meanings and processes that define not only what counts as baladi, but what counts as Egyptian.

FIGURE 12. AND 13. Tomato sculptures by Yasmine El Meleegy, *Future Farms (Organic)*, 2023, polyester, fiberglass, 2k-paint, acrylic, corn husks, EPAL-pallets, installation dimensions variable. Courtesy of the artist, For and Gypsum Gallery. Photograph by Gina Folly.

BALADI AND CRITIQUE

What did it mean for tomatoes to become baladi in Egypt? As we have seen, the term "baladi" stakes a claim opposing the local to the foreign; yet it is also the semantic mechanism by which the foreign is localized. In the 1920s, when agronomists were actively importing new tomato varieties from Europe and North America, the act of labeling a tomato "baladi" heralded the arrival of an emergent ingredient on its way to dominance. Through subsequent decades the term helped bind together and smooth over the asymmetries of a dominant culinary culture that materialized (in part) through tomatoes, "simultaneously recognizing and suppressing the contradictions" it contained, to borrow a phrase from Lisa Lowe.[34] Asserting tomatoes as baladi, in implicit contrast with the categories of rumi or afranji, both "admits and obscures" the uneven dynamics of their production and assimilation as Egyptian.[35] This paralleled a process by which British, French, Indian, Italian, Levantine, Maghribi, and Turkish elements were mediated through modern cooking styles, often within the home, into a cuisine recognizable as both local and Egyptian.

Examining the production of the tomato as baladi underscores the way that nation-building rests upon a set of interlocking hierarchies that render certain people and places subordinate to national progress. Egyptian tomatoes grew out of the uneven development of a territory in which Saʿidi livelihoods and the Nubian homeland were deemed expendable. Although the state supported the production and provision of staples that ensured the population's minimum caloric intake, the tomato—an essential vehicle for local flavors—was left in a political gray area, easier for more affluent farmers to produce and profit from and easier for affluent consumers to buy. The tomato was central to recipes framed as a modern form of knowledge in cookbooks that downplayed the role of subaltern domestic workers and centered a mythical middle-class housewife as the means for "uplifting the country [al-balad] by uplifting the family."[36] The effects of these material and discursive dynamics resonate powerfully, and often unconsciously, in the ordinary spaces and practices of the home. It is in everyday contexts like these that difference becomes normalized and naturalized.

The slipperiness of the "baladi" cloaks these historical changes in a deceptively self-evident coherence—not unlike the logic of the nation itself. But as this book has argued, critical histories and interpretations of culinary practices can also support critiques of those claims to coherence. The complex web of influences that made the tomato baladi reveals what nationalist logic endeavors to conceal and what the humble tomato renders obvious: that an understanding of the nation as an "undivided, homogenous, and, above all, ethnically pure entity" is a fiction.[37] Beyond critique, the tomato also provides ample material with which we might envision, describe, and inhabit different configurations of nourishing and belonging. It can, in the words of Adrienne Rich, "connect what has been dangerously disconnected" through a reassessment of how a sense of "we" and its relationship to place is constructed through food.[38] As an introduced foreign fruit, a perennial industrial product, and a beloved baladi vegetable, the tomato places Egypt in Africa and in the Mashriq alike. In the hands of cookbook authors and home cooks it can embody an incisive rejection of colonial hierarchies. It can perhaps point us to a different way of narrating and navigating difference.

NOTES

INTRODUCTION

1. Farmer, "The Humble Tomato"; "Suwwar karikatir dahika ʿan irtifaʿ asʿar al-tamatim (al-banadura)," *Farfesh Plus Online*, December 11, 2015, www.farfeshplus .online/Display2.asp?catID = 142&mainCatID = 139&sID = 177803.
2. Soghayar, "Hamra Ya Qouta."
3. For a discussion of the hyperbole common in book titles from this genre, see Robbins, "Commodity Histories."
4. According to the UN Food and Agriculture Organization, Egypt produced 6.8 million metric tons of tomatoes in 2019. The same year, its exports of all tomato products combined (fresh, peeled, juice, paste) only totaled 119,931 metric tons. FAOSTAT, "Crops and Livestock Products."
5. Williams, *Marxism and Literature*, 132.
6. Tompkins, *Racial Indigestion*, 190n5.
7. Robbins, "Commodity Histories," 456.
8. An ancestor of the tomato was carried from South America to Mesoamerica by 5000 BCE, where it was fully domesticated. Bhagat et al., "(Re)Mapping the Columbian Exchange," 77.
9. Gentilcore, *Pomodoro!*
10. King, introduction, 7.
11. François-Xavier Branthôme, "Worldwide (Total Fresh) Tomato Production in 2021," *Tomato News*, February 23, 2023, www.tomatonews.com/en/worldwide -total-fresh-tomato-production-in-2021_2_1911.html. According to FAO statistics, Egypt was ranked sixth among tomato producers in 2021.
12. The conditions of agricultural labor entailed in producing Egyptian tomatoes are regrettably beyond the scope of this book.
13. Ichijo, Johannes, and Ranta, introduction, 2.
14. Ray, "Heritage-Making," 254.
15. King, introduction, 2.
16. King, introduction, 3.

17. Laudan, "Slow Food"; Ray, "Heritage-Making."
18. Laudan, "Slow Food," 138.
19. Laudan, "Slow Food," 138.
20. Ray, "Heritage-Making," 259.
21. Tompkins, *Racial Indigestion*, 2.
22. Kashdan, "Anglophone Cookbooks," 5.
23. Kashdan, "Anglophone Cookbooks," 5.
24. For a critical discussion of the construction of imagined "Middle Eastern" and Mediterranean spaces through cookbooks, including Roden's work, see Kashdan, "Anglophone Cookbooks."
25. Roden, *Book of Jewish Food*, 11.
26. Gupta and Ferguson, "Beyond 'Culture,'" 8.
27. For a recent example of this approach see Martínez, *States of Subsistence*.
28. Mannur, *Intimate Eating*, 8.
29. Warner, "Publics and Counterpublics," 55–56.
30. Warner, "Publics and Counterpublics," 49.
31. Warner, "Publics and Counterpublics," 82.
32. Berlant, *Female Complaint*, xi.
33. Stewart, *Ordinary Affects*, 27.
34. Davidson and Hatcher, introduction, 7.
35. Davidson and Hatcher, introduction, 21.
36. Davidson and Hatcher, introduction, 19.
37. Counihan and Højlund, introduction, 1; Gertel and Samir, "Search for Security," 90.
38. Mannur, *Intimate Eating*, 5.
39. Ohnuki-Tierney, *Rice as Self*, 98.
40. Laudan, *Cuisine and Empire*, 248.
41. Laudan, *Cuisine and Empire*, 248; see chapters 7 and 8 on the rise and globalization of "middling cuisines" in world history.
42. Laudan, *Cuisine and Empire*, 248.
43. Alicia Kennedy, "On Politics and a Liberal Platitude," *From the Desk of Alicia Kennedy* (Substack), February 9, 2024, www.aliciakennedy.news/p/on-politics.
44. Anderson, *Imagined Communities*, 19.
45. Kaplan, "Manifest Domesticity," 183.
46. Kaplan, "Manifest Domesticity," 183–84.
47. Scholarship on gender in modern Egypt is exceptionally rich and includes the work of, among others, Lila Abu-Lughod, Leila Ahmed, Margot Badran, Beth Baron, Laura Bier, Marilyn Booth, Hanan Hammad, Mervat Hatem, Hanan Kholoussy, Lisa Pollard, Nancy Reynolds, Mona Russell, Judith Tucker, and Hoda Yousef.
48. Booth, "Wayward Subjects," 355.
49. Ray, "Heritage-Making," 257.
50. Klein, *Archive of Taste*, 1.
51. Rivolta Femminile, "Manifesto," 229.

52. This includes an extensive collection of out-of-print cookbooks that I assembled over years from the used book markets of Cairo and Alexandria, including titles typically not held by libraries. That collection is now housed in Cairo at the library of the Women and Memory Forum.

53. Even when it addresses aspects of Egypt beyond Cairo and Alexandria, this book focuses more on riverine Egypt—the cities and settlements along the banks of the Nile—at the expense of other parts of territorial Egypt like the Suez Canal Zone, the Sinai Peninsula, and the western oases.

54. Ryzova, *Age of the Efendiyya*, 4–5, 10–12.

55. Sofia Fenner (*Shouting in a Cage*, 20) usefully and succinctly glosses *efendiyya* as "city-dwelling professionals." Sherene Seikaly (*Men of Capital*, 12; 57) calls us to consider with caution the "global conviction that the middle class has the potential to eradicate inequality and political instability," describing the "middle-class project" as both "shifting and exclusionary."

56. Fikry, "Today's Children," 90n1; Fikry draws on Schielke, "Living in the Future Tense."

57. Naguib, *Nurturing Masculinities*, 6; 115–16.

58. Ray, "Domesticating Cuisine," 59.

59. Seremetakis, *Senses Still*, 12.

60. Seremetakis, *Senses Still*, 29.

61. Fahmy, *Ordinary Egyptians*.

62. Anderson, *Imagined Communities*, 44. Fahmy, *Ordinary Egyptians*, 3; 15. See also Armbrust, *Mass Culture and Modernism*; Abu-Lughod, *Dramas of Nationhood*; Booth, *Bayram al-Tunisi's Egypt*; Powell, *Different Shade of Colonialism*; Simon, *Media of the Masses*.

63. In practice, the linguistic situation in Arabic is more complex than the model of diglossia suggests: a widely cited paradigm for Egyptian Arabic describes it as a system of five levels arranged along a spectrum from most to least formal, rather than a clear-cut binary of low and high. Badawi, *Mustawayat al-ʿArabiyya al-muʿasira fi Misr*.

64. Fahmy, *Ordinary Egyptians*, 8–11; Haeri, *Sacred Language, Ordinary People*, 3.

65. Fahmy, *In Quest of Justice*, 25.

66. Reynolds, *City Consumed*, 8.

67. Fahmy, *In Quest of Justice*, 15.

68. For the emergence of the "modern" Egyptian home kitchen, see Gaul, "Food, Happiness," and Bier, "Pleasures of Domesticity." For a parallel account of the modern kitchen in Central Europe, see Kreklau, "Neither Gendered nor a Room."

69. The examples described here largely reflect the *urban* home kitchen, partly because it has been more thoroughly documented and partly because it was in cities that the modern home kitchen first materialized.

70. Hanna, *Habiter au Caire*.

71. Lewicka, *Food and Foodways*, 92–94; for an overview of scholarly debates about what constituted a kitchen in medieval Cairo, see pp. 88–100.

72. Khaled Fahmy (*All the Pasha's Men*, 11) describes the establishment of Egypt's modern army and the reorientation of Egyptian agriculture toward producing lucrative long-staple cotton as "the twin pillars" of Mehmed ʿAli's rule.

73. Mehmed ʿAli's successors gained the title of *khedive* (viceroy) and, after the dissolution of the Ottoman Empire, *malik* (king).

74. Russell, *Creating the New Egyptian Woman*, 22.

75. Accounts of gender reform in Egypt often highlight the significance of Qasim Amin's 1899 book *Tahrir al-marʾa* in these debates. But as many scholars have demonstrated, authors from a range of backgrounds, including men and women, had debated women's education and their role in society in the Arabic press for decades, and "questions of gender *saturated* the Arabic publishing scene of the decade before Amin's book appeared." Booth, "Before Qasim Amin," 365. See also Badran, *Feminists, Islam, Nation*, 14–17.

76. Jakes, *Egypt's Occupation*, 7.

77. These observations are based on a sampling of thirty-seven probate records from 1881 to 1894 from the *shariʿa* courts of Alexandria and Dimyat as well as a handful of probates held in the British National Archives from the 1910s and 1920s. The estate featuring the spirit stove was that of a wealthy individual whose possessions also included a Persian rug and suits made from expensive fabric, underscoring how rare stoves were when first introduced. Tarakat Mustafa Afandi Qabrawan al-Murshidi, Mahkamat Dimyat al-Shaʿriyya, 1881, DWQ, 1032–0030602.

78. This took the form of a stabilization fund to ensure prices stayed consistently low. For British archival documents concerning the stabilization funds, see Treasury (T) 236/6794, 1952, BNA. The indispensability of kerosene to poorer Egyptians was emphasized in colonial correspondence, for example, "Memorandum: Effect of Recent Increase in Prices of Petrol and Kerosene," October 11, 1952, Foreign Office (FO) 141/768, BNA; and "Memorandum: Oil Situation in Egypt," 1933, FO 141/721, BNA. A British government report on Egypt's cost of living in 1942 listed Primus stoves as a key commodity. "Report on cost of living in Egypt," April 29, 1942, FO 371/31572, BNA.

79. "Athath al-matbakh," *Bint al-Nil*, January 10, 1947, 44.

80. "Al-Faʾiza bi-hadiyyat Bint al-Nil 'matbakh Ideal' tatasallam hadiyyataha," *Bint al-Nil*, February 1957, 17.

81. Barakat, "ʿAlaqat al-taghayyur al-tiknulujiyya," 111–12.

82. Salem, *Anticolonial Afterlives in Egypt*, 164–66.

83. Amin, *Madha hadatha li-l-Misriyyin?* 107–108.

84. Schewe, "Egypt's National Bread Loaf"; Goldberg, "Killing Them Softly"; Barnes, *Staple Security*.

85. Naguib, *Nurturing Masculinities*, 1.

CHAPTER 1

1. Dorry, "Forbidden, Sprouted, Stewed," 88. She notes that "fava beans only make the occasional appearance in archaeological contexts dating to Pharaonic

times... but become a much more common component of archaeobotanical assemblages starting in Graeco-Roman times."

2. Zubaida, "Idea of 'Indian Food,'" 208.
3. Grewe, "Arrival of the Tomato," 70.
4. Delile, "Florae Aegyptiacae illustratio," 56.
5. I suspect that additional and perhaps earlier evidence of the tomato in Egypt does exist, potentially in Egyptian manuscript repositories or the Ottoman archives. While the search for that evidence is beyond the scope of my own scholarly specialization, let alone this book, I hope this chapter might lay groundwork for future explorations of the histories of American cultivars in the Maghrib and Mashriq.
6. It is also possible that they were transported, at least for part of the journey, as plants, or in dried or pickled form.
7. For a discussion of the category of "Levantine/Shami" cuisine, see Gaul and Pitts, "Introduction: Making Levantine Cuisine."
8. Zubaida, "Culinary History of 'National' Cuisine" and "Idea of 'Indian Food.'" His argument and supporting evidence are gradually gaining traction in Arabic and English media, where the theory of the British introduction of koshari is common. For an example of Egyptian media coverage that draws on Zubaida's findings, see *al-Koshari*, CBC Sofra, 2022, www.facebook.com/cbcsofra/videos/632435861575779/.
9. Dorry, "Food History in Egypt," 23.
10. Ray, Burke, and Jolly, "Food in the Indian Ocean World," 3.
11. Hyman, *Tomato*, 24.
12. Despite (or arguably, because of) the lack of direct evidence, many scholars have suggested that the tomato was largely consumed by nonelites in the Mediterranean, South Asia, and Middle East in the first centuries after its introduction. Allard, "El Tomate"; Hyman, *Tomato*, 26; Buccini, "Western Mediterranean Vegetable Stews," 136; Petrovich, "How to Navigate the Oceans," 252; Anderson, "Foreword: The History of the Use of the Tomato," 290.
13. In this sense the tomato's introduction to Egypt likely shares some broad similarities with the chile pepper's introduction to China—which, Brian Dott (*Chile Pepper in China*, 7) writes, was "more indirect and involved less fanfare than that of other American crops," despite its eventual impact on Chinese cuisine.
14. Crosby, *Columbian Exchange*, 188–90.
15. One exception is Bilgin, "From Artichoke to Corn." See also Nabhan, *Cumin, Camels, and Caravans*; and Artan, "Ottoman Elite's Food Consumption."
16. Ho, "Introduction of American Food Plants into China," 195. Building on Ho's work, Brian Dott (*Chile Pepper in China*, 20) presents evidence for no fewer than three entry points for chile peppers into China.
17. These two suggestions are not exhaustive; overland travel or Egypt's other ports may also have played a part.
18. Bhagat et al., "(Re)Mapping the Columbian Exchange," 59.

19. Ray, Burke, and Jolly, "Food in the Indian Ocean World," 3, 18; Bhagat et al., "(Re)Mapping the Columbian Exchange, 65–67. See also Carney and Rosomoff, *In the Shadow of Slavery*.

20. Anderson, "Anatolian Mystery"; Andrews, "Diffusion of Mesoamerican Food Complex"; Petrovich, "How to Navigate the Oceans"; Dott, *Chile Pepper in China*.

21. Ray, Burke, and Jolly, "Food in the Indian Ocean World," 3, 18; Bhagat et al., "(Re)Mapping the Columbian Exchange, 65–67.

22. Wick, *Red Sea*, 1–5. Among the reasons Wick cites for this historiographical imbalance are a tendency to identify the Ottoman Empire, and Islamic societies more broadly, as land-based and disconnected from all things maritime as well as the inverse: an association of the Mediterranean, and seafaring in general, with the identity of modern imperial Europe.

23. Ray, Burke, and Jolly, "Food in the Indian Ocean World," 2.

24. Hayden White quoted in Rogne, "Aim of Interpretation," 74.

25. Ray, "Foreword: Food in the Making and Unmaking of Asian Nationalisms," xiv.

26. McCann, *Maize and Grace*, 26.

27. Foucault, "Nietzsche, Genealogy, History"; Rich, "Notes toward a Politics of Location"; Enloe, *Does Khaki Become You?*

28. Braudel, "Preface to the English Edition," 1:14.

29. Grewe, "Arrival of the Tomato," 70–73.

30. Grewe, "Arrival of the Tomato," 68.

31. Whereas other American foodstuffs, like turkey and chocolate, appeared in sixteenth- and seventeenth-century European cookbooks, tomatoes were comparatively scarce. Even as the tomato appeared in more botanical texts toward the end of the sixteenth century, the three Spanish cookbooks known to have been published in the late sixteenth and early seventeenth centuries do not include it. Grewe, "Arrival of the Tomato," 67–72. The potato appears to have been adopted more quickly by comparison. Hamilton, "What the New World Economy Gave the Old," 859; Hawkes and Francisco-Ortega, "Potato in Spain during the Late 16th Century."

32. Gentilcore, *Pomodoro!*, 48–52.

33. Ingram, introduction, 13; Herrera and Pons, "Moriscos Outside Spain," 219–20.

34. Morisco destinations beyond the Maghrib have been less thoroughly documented. Herrera and Pons, "Moriscos Outside Spain," 219. For an exception, see Abd al-Rahman, "Morisco Settlement in Egypt," 158–63.

35. The Moriscos' introduction of American foods to Tunisia is a common theory, but it can be difficult to pinpoint the precise circumstances surrounding the introduction of specific crops. One exception is the chile pepper, which Mohamed Frini traces in early modern Tunisian records ("Épices, assaisonnement et changement"). John Derek Latham ("Towards a Study of Andalusian Immigration," 241–42), emphasizes that despite "a good deal of evidence to the effect that Tunisia

profited from the introduction of new cultures or new varieties of cultures already known ... the contribution of Moriscos to the transmission of new cultures introduced from the New World to 16th century Spain and cultivated in Barbary in the 17th and 18th centuries, e.g. maize, tomatoes, varieties of haricot beans, pimento, etc. is not the least point on which enlightenment would be welcome."

To his point, the reference that Latham himself cites regarding the Moriscos' role in conveying the tomato specifically to Tunisia is not a primary source but a 1939 book by a Tunisian scholar that describes a series of historically significant Tunisian mosques. A chapter about a mosque established by refugees from Spain includes a footnote describing the community that founded it, which states that "the tomato was unknown in Tunisia before their arrival," referring specifically to the final expulsions of the early seventeenth century—but without offering substantiating evidence. Ibn al-Khuja, *Tarikh ma'alim al-tawhid*, 82–83.

36. Addison, *West Barbary*, 80–81. Emphasis in original.

37. Shaw, *Travels*, iii–iv; 258. The first edition of this work was published in 1738, and Shaw died in 1751. One drawback of this source is Shaw's frequent reference to "Tunisia and Algeria" or "Barbary" rather than specific cities or regions.

38. Buccini, "Western Mediterranean Vegetable Stews," 137. It is possible, of course, that the similarities between the dishes can be explained by convergent evolution instead.

39. Sienna, "Shakshuka for All Seasons," 175.

40. Buccini, "Western Mediterranean Vegetable Stews," 132.

41. Sienna ("Shakshuka for All Seasons," 175) notes that seasonal variations of shakshuka appear in an early twentieth-century Judeo-Arabic Tunisian cookbook; the "winter" version features no tomatoes or peppers, but it does include potatoes, lending further weight to the possibility that this dish was a vector for the introduction of American foods into new contexts.

42. Highlighting both the likelihood of Morisco transmission of American cultivars and the need for additional evidence to substantiate it, Latham ("Towards a Study of Andalusian Immigration," 242–43) cautions that "the influence of European elements in Barbary ports should not be ignored" in the matter.

43. These included, among others, two port cities on the Mediterranean coast of present-day Morocco: Ceuta (occupied by Portugal in 1415) and Melilla (occupied by Spain in 1497). Spain also occupied the city of Oran and nearby port Mers El Kebir, in present-day Algeria, for various periods between the sixteenth and eighteenth centuries.

44. Clancy-Smith, *Mediterraneans*, 23–24.

45. This was partly because Spain's Catholic monarchs launched a series of attacks on Maghribi cities in this period, emboldened by their conquest of Granada. 'Abd al-Mu'ti, *al-Maghariba fi Misr*, 18–19.

46. 'Abd al-Mu'ti, *al-Maghariba fi Misr*, 19.

47. Reimer, "Ottoman Alexandria," 111.

48. 'Abd al-Mu'ti, *al-Maghariba fi Misr*, 19–24.

49. Reimer, "Ottoman Alexandria," 129.

50. Tagliacozzo, "Hajj by Sea," 114–15; Ben Ismail, "History of the Ottoman Fez," 163; Raymond, "Tunisiens et Maghrébins," 345–50.
51. Shaw, *Travels*, 252.
52. Reimer, "Ottoman Alexandria," 114.
53. Carney and Rosomoff, *In the Shadow of Slavery*, 65.
54. For a similar argument about the introduction of the chile pepper to China, see Dott, *Chile Pepper in China*, 21.
55. Clancy-Smith, *Mediterraneans*, 23–24. For more about European merchants in Alexandria, see Reimer, "Ottoman Alexandria," 119–25, 127–28, 130–31.
56. Hill, "First Arabic Translations of Enlightenment Literature," 210.
57. ʿAli, ʿAbd al-Badiʿ, and Surur, *al-Khudrawat fi Misr*, 295.
58. Ray, *After Expulsion*, 2–3; 10. Ray writes that medieval networks that had once linked Jews across the Mediterranean had begun to fade and fragment starting in the thirteenth century but reemerged "over several generations" as Jews were increasingly excluded from parts of the "Latin West."
59. Ingram, introduction, 8.
60. Although technically banned from Portuguese territories like Goa, in practice "Sephardic Jews and New Christians were active in this domain." New Christian families did not all have the same relationship to Judaism; some continued practicing or returned to it over time. To confuse matters, by the late sixteenth century, the term "the Portuguese nation" had become "the official designation of newly formed Sephardic communities in Venice, Livorno, and Amsterdam." Nonetheless, different Sephardic families had distinct networks, with some focused more on Atlantic trade and others on various parts of the Mediterranean. Trivellato, *Familiarity of Strangers*, 234; 43. For more on New Christian merchants' participation in the Portuguese empire, see Boyajian, *Portuguese Trade in Asia*, 30–33; 70–82; 142–43.
61. Studnicki-Gizbert, *Nation upon the Ocean Sea*, 27–28; 50–55; a mapping of Portuguese merchant networks on p. 103 includes nodes in Seville, Malaga, Venice, and Livorno.
62. Trivellato, *Familiarity of Strangers*, 6.
63. Trivellato, *Familiarity of Strangers*, 67.
64. Sienna, "Shakshuka for All Seasons," 174.
65. Sienna, "Shakshuka for All Seasons," 174.
66. Sienna identifies several pieces of linguistic evidence supporting the association of the word "shakshuka" with Maghribi dialects in general and Tunisian Arabic in particular. In addition to discussing its appearance in two Jewish Tunisian cookbooks, he cites an 1871 French-Arabic dictionary and an 1894 German travelogue that identify "shakshuka" as a Tunisian word for a dish featuring tomatoes, peppers, onions, and eggs. He notes that the term appeared in the French press glossed as "Oeufs à la tunisienne" in 1894. Sienna, "Shakshuka for All Seasons," 176–77. The question of shakshuka's origin would of course benefit from further research drawing on additional North African sources; it is notable, for instance, that shakshuka rhymes with *taktuka*, a Moroccan dish featuring peppers and tomatoes. Curiously,

another culinary term derived from the same Arabic root, "sh-k-sh-k," meaning to pierce or prick, appears in at least one Ottoman Egyptian source. But it is derived differently (*mushakshik*) and refers to a dish made with salted fish, onions, and oil—perhaps underscoring that the derivation "shakshuka" was introduced to Egypt via Maghribi Arabic. Shirbini, *Hazz al-quhuf*, 2:248–49.

67. Nicola and Osman, *Usul al-tahi*, 444–45. Throughout this book citations of this cookbook reference a 1953 edition. I have compared quoted material to a 1942 second edition held by Dar al-Kutub in Cairo (the earliest edition I have been able to access) and besides the pagination, the content is virtually identical. Booth, *Bayram al-Tunisi's Egypt*, 19, 33.

68. Personal correspondence, April 9, 2021, and November 30, 2024. Nawal Nasrallah suggests that couscous "was likely incorporated into the mainstream Egyptian repertoire" during the Fatimid era. A recipe for couscous appears in a fourteenth-century Egyptian cookbook. Nasrallah, trans., *Treasure Trove*, 49; 146–47. See also Lewicka, *Food and Foodways*, 169–72.

69. Tarakat Shaykh Shihab Futuh, Sijil Aylulat bi-Mahkamat al-Iskandariyya al-Shaʿriyya, 1888, DWQ 1029–002676. The 10 household inventories I accessed from Alexandria included more than 450 items for cooking and eating. For a contrasting account of the kiskas in Algeria—namely, its transformation from an indigenous Maghribi tool to a manufactured commodity in the context of French colonialism—see Durmelat, "Can the Couscous Pot Speak?"

70. Armbrust, *Mass Culture and Modernism*, 142–43.

71. The port of Qusayr is another plausible Red Sea conduit for the introduction of American foods.

72. Shipping through the Persian Gulf then overland to Syria was another route for Asian drugs and spices; but historian André Raymond ("Le commerce des épices," 115) writes that "other routes were used for circulation of these luxury goods, but the one that passed through Suez, Cairo, and Alexandria was one of the most important, and one whose activity had rarely been interrupted since antiquity."

73. Ibn Battuta, *Tuhfat al-anzar fi gharaʾib al-amsar wa-ʿajaʾib al-asfar*, 2:14. David Waines ("Ibn Battuta") notes that Ibn Battuta's stay in the sultanate of Delhi, from 1333 to 1342, was longer than his stay anywhere else.

74. Because written Arabic is not typically vowelled, only the consonants appear in most texts. In other words, the way that Ibn Battuta spelled "khichri" is identical to modern spellings of the Arabic word "koshari." Waines transliterates it as *kishri* and Nasrallah transliterates it as *kushari*. Waines, *Odyssey of Ibn Battuta*, 102; Nasrallah, trans., *Treasure Trove*, 638.

75. Ibn Battuta, *Tuhfat al-anzar fi gharaʾib al-amsar wa-ʿajaʾib al-asfar*, 2:14. Following this description, Ibn Battua writes, "they call it koshari," then spells it out using the names of the Arabic letters.

76. Waines, *Odyssey of Ibn Battuta*, 102.

77. Ibn al-Mujawir, *Traveller*, 159.

78. Sami Zubaida ("Idea of 'Indian Food,'" 208) mentions pilgrims and seafarers as possibilities for groups who brought koshari to the Hijaz and to the port of Suez.

79. Nasrallah, glossary, 638. Antaki compares them with lentils, perhaps for the benefit of readers in Egypt where lentils had been grown since antiquity. It is possible that over time the word "koshari" was used both to refer to a lentil-like pulse and metonymically to refer to a dish made with a pulse and rice—not unlike the naming of hummus after its main ingredient, the chickpea, a convention that dates to at least the thirteenth century in Arabic cookbooks. Antaki, *Tadkhirat*, 353; Nasrallah, introduction, 21.

80. Ray, Burke, and Jolly, "Food in the Indian Ocean World," 4–6.

81. van der Veen, *Consumption, Trade and Innovation*.

82. Edgar Anderson ("Anatolian Mystery," 14) asserts that Anatolia was "the chief center of diversity for one of the species [of cucurbits] along with various crop plants of the Old World." Crosby (*Columbian Exchange*, 188–89) argues that "a claim that American food plants did not find their way to the Middle East before 1600 would deserve little support," though he devotes only a few pages to the subject. See also Andrews, "Diffusion of Mesoamerican Food Complex," 194–204; Petrovich, "How to Navigate the Oceans."

83. Andrews, "Diffusion of Mesoamerican Food Complex," 194. According to Google Scholar, this article has been cited more than eighty times.

84. Andrews, "Diffusion of Mesoamerican Food Complex," 194, 203. See also Anderson, "Anatolian Mystery." Arguments along these lines are often muddled by the imprecise use of categories like Ottoman, Turk, and Arab (to begin with, not all Ottomans were ethnically Turkish, and not all Arabs were Ottoman) and overly broad references to "Turkey" or "the Ottoman Empire." At its peak in the seventeenth century the Ottoman Empire extended into much of southeastern Europe, North Africa, and of course encompassed Egypt as well. Giancarlo Casale ("Ethnic Composition of Ottoman Ship Crews," 124) points out that "European authors of the sixteenth century, in common with most historians today, habitually referred to the Ottomans as 'Turks' . . . in practice, 'Turk' was employed by Europeans . . . as an indiscriminate blanket term for a Muslim of any ethnic origin."

85. Sen, *Feasts and Fasts*, 210.

86. Dott, *Chile Pepper in China*, 17.

87. McCann, *Maize and Grace*, 23.

88. Dott, *Chile Pepper in China*, 12; Andrews, "Diffusion of Mesoamerican Food Complex," 19; Burton, *Raj at Table*, 6.

89. Burton asserts, for example, that "sixteenth-century Portuguese introductions [to India] included pineapple, papaya, cashew nut, and tomato," although without citing specific sources or evidence (*Raj at Table*, 6). Sucharita Kanjilal ("Beyond Bourdieu," 5) clarifies that "while Portuguese traders might have brought it to the subcontinent in the 1600s, the tomato's widespread adoption [in India] coincides with the consolidation of the British Empire in India."

90. McCann, *Maize and Grace*, 23.

91. Studnicki-Gizbert, *Nation upon the Ocean Sea*, 25–26. This was despite the division of the Americas into separate spheres designated for Spanish and Portuguese colonization per the 1492 Treaty de Tordesillas. For a discussion of the Span-

ish crown's attempts to assert control over Atlantic trade amid the expansion of a multinational set of actors in that sphere, see Studnicki-Gizbert, *Nation upon the Ocean Sea*, 28–30.

92. Studnicki-Gizbert, *Nation upon the Ocean Sea*, 27.

93. Studnicki-Gizbert, *Nation upon the Ocean Sea*, 34–35. From 1580 to 1640 the Portuguese and Spanish crowns were united following a disastrous Portuguese military defeat in Morocco—although Portugal retained control over its trading posts in Africa, India, and northern Europe (see Studnicki-Gizbert, *Nation upon the Ocean Sea*, 35–36).

94. Studnicki-Gizbert, *Nation upon the Ocean Sea*, 37.

95. Dott, *Chile Pepper in China*, 12–13.

96. For this claim Sen and Petrovich both cite Villareal, *Tomatoes in the Tropics*, 56. But Villareal himself does not directly place tomatoes in the Philippines in 1571. He states that "the Spanish began introducing several agricultural commodities into the Philippines from Mexico in 1571, but it is possible that tomatoes had been taken from Spain to Asia much earlier, perhaps just a few years after the discovery [*sic*] of the Philippines by Ferdinand Magellan in 1521." Villareal's book is a technical work about the horticultural conditions and techniques necessary to cultivate tomatoes in tropical places, not a work of history, and he provides no citations for what are clearly intended as speculations about the tomato's arrival to the Philippines.

97. Sturtevant and Hedrick, *Sturtevant's Notes on Edible Plants*, 343–44. Sturtevant and Hedrick, whose work was published in 1919, attribute the claim about the Portuguese in Java to the Dutch naturalist Bontius (1658) and the Malay use of *tomatte* to the German botanist Rumphius (d. 1702), as cited in an 1855 work by the French-Swiss botanist De Candolle.

98. Dott, *Chile Pepper in China*, 12–13.

99. Dott, *Chile Pepper in China*, 13.

100. Grewe, "Arrival of the Tomato," 71–72.

101. Dott, *Chile Pepper in China*, 13; see also Casale, "Ethnic Composition of Ottoman Ship Crews."

102. Casale, "Ethnic Composition of Ottoman Ship Crews," 131.

103. Studnicki-Gizbert, *Nation upon the Ocean Sea*, 10–11; 24–25. Studnicki-Gizbert writes that of the Portuguese mercantile communities spread across the globe by the sixteenth century, more than half were "New Christians." He points out the importance of attending to patterns of exogamous marriage, which affected the numbers of Portuguese merchants with Sephardic Jewish heritage over generations.

104. Roitman, "Sephardic Journeys," 209.

105. Roitman, "Sephardic Journeys," 209. Roitman's study focuses on two Sephardic families, one wealthy and the other less prominent, both with comparable global scope.

106. Studnicki-Gizbert, *Nation upon the Ocean Sea*, 74.

107. Studnicki-Gizbert, *Nation upon the Ocean Sea*, 74. Even though technically Jews were banned from overseas Portuguese colonies, they often functioned there in practice. Boyajian, *Portuguese Trade in Asia*.

108. Boyajian, *Portuguese Trade in Asia*, 142, 240.

109. Studnicki-Gizbert, *Nation upon the Ocean Sea*, 51–53.

110. Petrovich, "How to Navigate the Oceans," 253. Several scholars have published on the history of the tomato in the Ottoman context, but they tend to focus on its initial uses rather than the question of how it made its way to Ottoman lands. Artan, "Ottoman Elite's Food Consumption"; Bilgin, "From Artichoke to Corn"; Samancı, "Cuisine of Istanbul."

111. Petrovich, "How to Navigate the Oceans," 253.

112. Roden, *Book of Jewish Food*, 365.

113. Roden, *Book of Jewish Food*, 364; 371; 601.

114. Crosby (*Columbian Exchange*) mentions one European traveler who placed several American foods, including kidney beans, French beans, and maize, on the banks of the Euphrates and near Aleppo and Jerusalem in the 1570s. Andrews ("Diffusion of Mesoamerican Food Complex," 200–201) mentions accounts of beans, maize, and squash, though in some cases without full citations and in vague references to "Turkey" or the "Turkish empire." Artan ("Ottoman Elite's Food Consumption," 183n29) mentions a French traveler, Joseph Pitton de Tournefort (1656–1708), who wrote that he saw "Lycopersicon" or "love apples" in "Ottoman lands," although as chapter 2 explains, it is possible he saw a different nightshade and mistook it for a tomato.

115. Samancı, "Cuisine of Istanbul," 87–88.

116. Andrews, "Diffusion of Mesoamerican Food Complex"; Petrovich, "How to Navigate the Oceans."

117. Wick, *Red Sea*, 30. This was in part due to inhospitable terrain that required trade to support settlements, coupled with the need for settlements to sustain the transregional trade passing through this geographically strategic region. Wick describes this as part of the "paradox" of the Red Sea, which has had lasting geographic and religious and cultural significance yet whose shores are almost uniformly inhospitable and whose waters are especially dangerous to navigate because of reefs, currents, and winds: "It absolutely had to be navigated, if only to sustain the population and foster commercial exchange."

118. Wick, *Red Sea*, 33; for a discussion of the "spice trade" narrative, see pp. 33–34.

119. Wick, *Red Sea*, 28.

120. van der Veen, *Consumption, Trade and Innovation*, 41.

121. Wick, *Red Sea*, 41–42.

122. Tuchscherer, "Trade and Port Cities," 34.

123. Wick, *Red Sea*, 43–44. See also Subrahmanyam, *Green Sea*, chapter 2; and Tuchscherer, "Trade and Port Cities," 35–36.

124. Raymond, "Divided Sea"; Um, *Merchant Houses of Mocha*, 20–23.

125. Wick, *Red Sea*, 49.

126. Wick, *Red Sea*, 48; Ray, Burke, and Jolly, "Food in the Indian Ocean World," 14.

127. Zubaida, "Idea of 'Indian Food,'" 206–207.

128. Villiers, *Sons of Sindbad*, 42. Konganda T. Achaya (*Historical Dictionary of Indian Food*, 60) defines dhal as a category of pulses that includes many varieties, of which mung dhal "is recommended for everyday consumption."

129. Villiers, *Sons of Sindbad*, 404. He describes them as "used sparingly."

130. Zubaida, "Idea of 'Indian Food,'" 208.

131. Zubaida, "Idea of 'Indian Food,'" 208. The travelogue in question is Richard Burton's account of his trip to Mecca and Medina, first published in 1855. Earlier editions appear not to include this footnote, however, and include only Levick's original account. Zubaida cites an 1897 edition.

132. Amin and Saʿid, *Kitab Funun al-tahi al-hadith*, 72.

133. Nicola and Osman, *Usul al-tahi*, 351–52. Many Egyptians today refer to koshari made with yellow lentils as "Alexandrian" koshari, though neither Nicola and Osman nor Amin and Saʿid labeled it that way, despite all assigning various other recipes labels with Egyptian cities.

134. Petrovich, "How to Navigate the Oceans," 253.

135. For discussions of early practices of tomato breeding in the Americas, see Long, "Tomatoes," and Estabrook, *Tomatoland*, 10–12.

136. As Alexis Wick puts it (*Red Sea*, 85), in the Ottoman context "Mısır is the province ruled from Cairo, not some proto-national Egypt." See also Mitchell, *Rule of Experts*, 180–81.

137. Ghosh, *In an Antique Land*, 32.

138. Ray, Burke, and Jolly, "Food in the Indian Ocean World," 27.

139. Shohat, "Sephardi-Moorish Atlantic," 51.

140. Studnicki-Gizbert, *Nation upon the Ocean Sea*, 27.

141. Ray, Burke, and Jolly, "Food in the Indian Ocean World," 28.

CHAPTER 2

1. In spoken Egyptian Arabic the initial "q" of quta is pronounced as a glottal stop. Therefore I treat quta as a word starting with a vowel; hence "an quta" rather than "a quta." When referencing written texts, I transcribe the word as "quta," corresponding to the way it is written in Arabic, with the *qaf*; when referencing spoken Arabic, I refer to it as "oota."

2. There are exceptions: sometimes the word "quta" appears in written texts that represent colloquial speech—e.g., political cartoons.

3. Twitter/X post by Sucharita Kanjilal, October 30, 2023, https://x.com/KanjiSuch/status/1719005878982963300.

4. Another possible etymology stems from the word "qawta," a word for a fruit basket, derived from an older Greek or Semitic root for a cup or goblet. I thank Febe Armanios, Hany Takla, and Nawal Nasrallah for their input on this question.

5. Priscilla Mary Işın ("Kavatanın Peşinde," 204–206) went to extraordinary lengths to confirm that historical accounts of "quta" ("kavata," in Turkish) referred to *Solanum aethiopicum*, visiting a part of Turkey where it is still cultivated and

confirming samples with a botanist. She notes that African eggplants resemble tomatoes on the outside but not the inside, which tends to resemble either bell peppers or eggplants.

6. The earliest and latest botanical works where I have seen *Solanum aethiopicum* identified as "quta" are Delile's 1813 "Florae Aegyptiacae illustratio" and Bedevian's 1935 *Illustrated Polyglottic Dictionary of Plant Names*. It is possible that there are parts of Egypt where the African eggplant is still cultivated or still referred to as "quta." My fieldwork was limited to Cairo and Alexandria, and my knowledge of those places of course has its limits.

7. Royal Botanic Gardens, Kew, "Solanum aethiopicum"; Boulos, *Flora of Egypt*, 3:34–54. Boulos, whose flora covers native and naturalized but not cultivated plants in Egypt, does not include the species in his chapter on the Solanum family. I thank Hala Barakat for her advice regarding the species' botanical origin.

8. I thank Nawal Nasrallah for her advice on this subject.

9. Shirbini, *Hazz al-quhuf*.

10. Davies, introduction, xi. Davies describes Dimyat as the "second city" of Ottoman Egypt.

11. Davies, introduction, xix–xx.

12. Zubaida, "Hazz al-Quhuf"; Davies, introduction, xx, xxxii–vii.

13. The peasant addresses a woman who has had sex with multiple partners in her cooking pit, saying, "I'll give you two bunches of onions and quta/And on the Great Feast I'll bring you a futa [towel]." Shirbini, *Hazz al-quhuf* 1:366–67. Translation by the author to preserve the rhyme.

14. Other instances where Shirbini uses onions to convey a sense of disgust at rural life can be found in *Hazz al-Quhuf* 1:32–33; 2:188–89; 208–11; 266–69. Shirbini (*Hazz al-quhuf*, 2:266–67) writes elsewhere that the word used in the "quta" passage for a "bunch" of onions, *shirsh*, "is also applied to the beginning of the emergence of a silent fart."

15. I have yet to encounter a text that definitively uses "quta" to refer to tomatoes prior to the nineteenth century and suspect that "quta" would not have referred to tomatoes in a text this early.

16. Lewicka, *Food and Foodways*, 246; Nasrallah, introduction, 24–26; van der Veen *Consumption, Trade and Innovation*, 93; Watson, *Agricultural Innovation*, 70–71.

17. Napoleon invaded Egypt with forty thousand soldiers and five hundred civilians, including naturalists and other scholars. Hampikian, "Cairo," 63; 75n3.

18. These spellings reflect the pronunciation of "badhinjan" in Cairene Arabic. Delile, "Florae Aegyptiacae illustratio," 56. Also listed as names of the African eggplant are *tufah dahabi* and *tufah al-hubb*. These are literal Arabic translations of common European terms for the tomato from this period ("golden apple" and "love apple," respectively), suggesting that there was some confusion about the two species among European scientists.

19. Işın ("Kavatanın Peşinde," 199–200) demonstrates that Ottoman agricultural and culinary sources discussed kavata and domates as separate vegetables.

20. Tomatoes first appeared in Turkish recipes in the mid-nineteenth century. Işın, "Kavatanın Peşinde," 197; Artan, "Ottoman Elite's Food Consumption," 112–14; Samancı, "Cuisine of Istanbul," 87.

21. Işın, "Kavatanın Peşinde," 197; 206–207.

22. Işın, "Kavatanın Peşinde," 197; Artan, "Ottoman Elite's Food Consumption," 112–14. According to Işın (p. 204), the African eggplant is still cultivated in parts of Bursa, but it is not widely known in Turkey.

23. These include two cookbooks, a horticultural manual, and two glossaries of plant names. Kamil, *Malja' al-tabbakhin*; Ibrahim, *Nasihat al-anam*; ʿAli, ʿAbd al-Badiʿ, and Surur, *al-Khudrawat fi Misr*, Bedevian, *Illustrated Polyglottic Dictionary*; ʿIssa, *Dictionnaire*. See also Edward Lane and Stanley Lane-Poole's *Arabic-English Lexicon*, under "badhinjan."

24. In the lexical, horticultural, and botanical sources, this is evident from the use of Latin classificatory names.

25. Clot, *Aperçu général sur l'Égypte*, 185.

26. Foaden and Fletcher, *al-Ziraʿa al-Misriyya*, 252. This textbook was edited by G. P. Foaden, the secretary general of the Khedival Agricultural Society, and F. Fletcher, the head of the School of Agriculture in Giza. Originally published in English, it was translated into Arabic in 1911.

27. As a very approximate indicator, searches of the catalog of Dar al-Kutub, Egypt's national library, yielded more than a dozen works with "tamatim" in the title; I found only one publication in the catalog with "quta" in the title: the 1922 text *al-Quta fi Misr* (The tomato in Egypt), discussed below.

28. Clot, *Aperçu général sur l'Égypte*, 185.

29. Pickering, *Races of Man*, 408; Klunzinger, *Upper Egypt*, 140, 142; 158–60. He clarifies that he is not discussing "the fine gardens of many pashas and Europeans in the capital."

30. Zubaida, "Culinary History," 153.

31. Işın, *Bountiful Empire*.

32. Nasrallah, "In the Beginning," 601–602.

33. Işın, *Bountiful Empire*, 30.

34. For an account of stuffed grape leaves as emblematic of Levantine cuisine today, see MacDougall, "Embodying Levantine Cooking."

35. Examples are "dolma" (meaning "stuffed") and "yalanji" (is from the Turkish word for "liar" and refers to vegetarian versions of stuffed and wrapped foods).

36. My interpretation of these sources builds on the work of historians who have asserted that even amid growing European influence within nineteenth-century Egyptian society, the three-hundred-year relationship between Cairo and Istanbul is essential context for understanding this period of Egyptian history. Fahmy, *In Quest of Justice*, 15. Fahmy highlights other scholars who adopt a similar approach to Egyptian history, including Jane Hathaway, Ehud Toledano, Alan Mikhail, Adam Mestyan, and James Baldwin.

37. Konrad, "Global and Local Patterns." Under Saʿid (r. 1854–63) the palace kitchen staff included a French chef, and palace banquets began to feature French dishes. Russell, *Creating the New Egyptian Woman*, 13–15.

38. Lane, *Manners and Customs*, 194; 251. Notably, Lane mentions neither tomatoes as ingredients of stews or sauces nor their appearance on the tables of the poorer classes. It is also unclear whether he or the other European observers of Egypt referenced here grasped the difference between the tomato and the African eggplant; both vegetables were stuffed in this manner in Ottoman cooking.

39. Lott, *English Governess in Egypt*, 22.

40. Klunzinger, *Upper Egypt*, 54–61.

41. Klunzinger, *Upper Egypt*, 56.

42. Klunzinger, *Upper Egypt*, 59–60. This may have been an African eggplant.

43. Wilbour, *Travels in Egypt*, 153.

44. Wilbour, *Travels in Egypt*, 151.

45. Kamil, *Maljaʾ al-tabbakhin*, 69. Although the first edition of Sidqi's translation of *Maljaʾ* was published in 1878, here I reference a 1915 edition.

46. For instance, a recipe titled "quta salad" begins: "the way to make this dish is to cut a tomato into thin round slices." Kamil, *Maljaʾ al-tabbakhin*, 69. According to Özge Samancı ("Cuisine of Istanbul," 87), the original Turkish cookbook only included "seven or eight recipes that include tomatoes." Additional tomato recipes may have therefore been added to the Arabic translation, a further indication of the tomato's rising popularity in Egypt.

47. The term used for "juice" in this context in the cookbook is ʿusara, probably as a direct translation from the Turkish word *suyu*, "juice."

48. Kamil, *Maljaʾ al-tabbakhin*, 11–12.

49. Derr, *Lived Nile*, 17, 22.

50. Zeinab Abul-Magd (*Imagined Empires*, 81) refers to Upper Egypt as the "first colony" of Mehmed ʿAli's administration.

51. Abul-Magd, *Imagined Empires*; Powell, *Different Shade of Colonialism*, 69.

52. Beinin and Lockman, *Workers on the Nile*, 26.

53. I draw on records of tomato production and exports held by the Library of Congress in Washington, DC; the National Agricultural Library in Beltsville, Maryland; the Arab World Documentation Unit in Exeter, England; and Dar al-Kutub in Cairo. Foaden and Fletcher's textbook *Egyptian Agriculture* also includes some relevant data. Categories and units of measurement vary across sources, so comparisons are sometimes difficult. For example, many records that mention foodstuffs or the even more specific category of "vegetables" do not break down data into more specific categories.

54. Foaden and Fletcher, *Egyptian Agriculture*, 2:844–47. Exports ranged from a low of 1,885 metric tons (1906) to a high of 2,966 metric tons (1904). For comparison, onions averaged 81,110 metric tons and wheat 10,456 metric tons annually from 1904 to 1909, though exports of both varied more widely from year to year. Cotton, unsurprisingly, dominated the export market; in 1907 the value of exported cotton was literally a thousand times that of tomatoes.

55. Bonaparte, *Egyptian Farm Crops*, 49. He repeats this in a 1910 publication: Bonaparte, "Vegetables," 582.

56. Ministry of Interior, "Mabadi'," 50.

57. Ministry of Interior, "Mabadi'," 52. The category of foodstuffs is labeled *ma'kulat*. Aaron Jakes (*Egypt's Occupation*, 45) writes that "though Isma'il's government had created a Statistical Department in 1873, the British had cut its funding, and the government would not generate comprehensive statistics again until the mid-1890s." Thus the lack of specific data about tomato exports may reflect a lack of data, a lack of tomato exports, or both.

58. Export manifest data from *The Egyptian Gazette*, sampled from 1900 and 1905.

59. Gentilcore, *Pomodoro!*, 66–8; 95–97.

60. Gentilcore, *Pomodoro!*, 83–89.

61. Tomatoes averaged 9.06 Egyptian pounds (LE) per metric ton to onions' LE3.03 and wheat's LE3.75. The value of wheat and tomatoes (though not onions) per metric ton dropped dramatically after the financial crisis of 1907. Foaden and Fletcher, *Egyptian Agriculture*, 2:845; 847.

62. Bonaparte, *Egyptian Farm Crops*, 50; Bonaparte, "Vegetables," 533–34. Onions are not included in the category of fruits and vegetables in Egyptian statistics at the time, as they were (and are) considered "field crops" rather than "vegetables" in Egypt.

63. Bonaparte's works, for example, do not mention the African eggplant. Today the African eggplant is eaten largely in sub-Saharan African and Asian cuisines. There are also varieties grown in Brazil and the Basilicata region of Italy.

64. Royal Agricultural Society, *al-Quta fi Misr*.

65. Royal Agricultural Society, *al-Jama'iyya al-zira'iyya al-malakiyya*, 14–15; 20.

66. Royal Agricultural Society, *al-Jama'iyya al-zira'iyya al-malakiyya*, 44.

67. Royal Agricultural Society, *al-Quta fi Misr*, 14.

68. Royal Agricultural Society, *al-Quta fi Misr*, 21

69. Royal Agricultural Society, *al-Quta fi Misr*, 25, 26. Earlier agricultural texts had similarly warned about the susceptibility of Egyptian tomatoes to freezing in winter, further corroborating the conclusion that tomato cultivation in the first decade of the twentieth century was concentrated in the Delta, where winters are cooler (winter would not have posed the same problems in Egypt's southern regions). See, for example, Bonaparte, *Egyptian Farm Crops*, 49–50.

70. Derr, *Lived Nile*, 26, 40; Jakes, *Egypt's Occupation*, 44.

71. Jakes, *Egypt's Occupation*, 7–8.

72. Derr, *Lived Nile*, 15.

73. Derr, *Lived Nile*, 3, 46, 58. For an account of colonial infrastructure transformations in Nigeria under British rule during a similar period, see Larkin, *Signal and Noise*, 35–40.

74. Derr, *Lived Nile*, 61.

75. Derr, *Lived Nile*, 61; 178n105.

76. Derr, *Lived Nile*, 57. Derr notes that this was also facilitated by smaller-scale barrages built elsewhere in Egypt as well as the digging of additional irrigation canals.

77. Mahmoud, "Dashing Nubians' Hopes."

78. Derr, *Lived Nile*; Gallagher, *Egypt's Other Wars*; Mitchell, *Rule of Experts*; Schewe, "Egypt's National Bread Loaf."

79. Derr, *Lived Nile*, 3.

80. Ibrahim, *Nasihat al-anam*. I cite the 1893 first edition.

81. Kamal Inas, "Man huwa 'Faylasuf al-ta'am'? A'rif qissatahu 'huwa illi 'ashsha al-Khidiwi Isma'il,'" *Food Today*, August 23, 2022, http://bit.ly/4ipG3Oj.

82. Ibrahim, *Nasihat al-anam*, 31, 122.

83. Ibrahim, *Nasihat al-anam*, 7, 55–57, 60–61.

84. It appears that an Egyptian cookbook dedicated to European cooking, titled *al-Usul al-fanniyya fi al-makil al-afranjiyya*, was published around the same time, but I have been unable to locate a copy or obtain additional information, except that the author's son, Muhammad 'Ali Abu al-Sunun, also wrote a cookbook, discussed below in this chapter. That said, in Ibrahim's text European recipes are in the minority, scattered throughout the book's various sections.

85. Ibrahim, *Nasihat al-anam*, 19, 24.

86. Examples include an Egyptian fish recipe made with coriander, and an Arab style dish with garlic and cumin; Ibrahim, *Nasihat al-anam*, 32, 42.

87. Ibrahim, *Nasihat al-anam*, 6, 8, 32.

88. Ibrahim, *Nasihat al-anam*, 24.

89. Written as *ma' al-quta* and *ma' al-tamatim*, occasionally without the definite article.

90. Ibrahim, *Nasihat al-anam*, 97. The turli recipe calls for black eggplant, squash, beans, okra, and "quta"; but the same sentence listing the vegetables goes on to instruct the reader to "brown all of them except for the 'tamatim,'" then references only "tamatim" in the remainder of the recipe, never mentioning "quta" again. The phrasing implies that "tamatim" and "quta" are being used synonymously. Ibrahim also makes a handful of clear references to the African eggplant elsewhere, which he refers to as "green quta" (*quta khadra*), in the pickling section and with the compound term "al-badhinjan al-quta" in a stuffed vegetable recipe. Ibrahim, *Nasihat al-anam*, 52, 96. The reference to the use of "green quta" likely reflects an Ottoman Turkish technique for pickling still-green African eggplants, described in Işın, "Kavatanın Peşinde," 199–200.

91. Ibrahim, *Nasihat al-anam*, 42. In Cairene Arabic it is pronounced "TA-gin," with a hard "g" sound. The word is related to the Moroccan *tajin*, pronounced "ta-JEEN."

92. Mikha'il, *al-Tadbir al-manzili al-hadith*, 1:185. Here I reference the seventh edition of Mikha'il's text, published in 1933. For a discussion of his audience, see Russell, *Creating the New Egyptian Woman*, 146.

93. Mikha'il was a school director in Fayyum and author of numerous household management texts. For more on Mikha'il's work and audience, see Booth, "Girlhood Translated?" and Russell, *Creating the New Egyptian Woman*, 145–52.

94. Serry, "al-Tabkh al-manzili," 68.
95. Royal Agricultural Society, *al-Quta fi Misr*, 3.
96. Royal Agricultural Society, *al-Quta fi Misr*, 9.
97. Royal Agricultural Society, *al-Quta fi Misr*, 3.
98. Stowell, *Anglo-Egyptian Cookery*. The author notes that the book originated as a series of recipes she published in the *Egyptian Gazette* in 1922.
99. Stowell, *Anglo-Egyptian Cookery*, 169–70.
100. Booth, *Bayram al-Tunisi's Egypt*, 166–67.
101. In a parallel trend, Egyptian irrigation specialists gradually replaced British engineers during this period. Derr, *Lived Nile*, 63.
102. In 1939 over 98 percent of cultivated land was devoted to field crops. Ministry of Agriculture, "Agricultural Census of Egypt, 1939," 20–21.
103. Ministry of Agriculture, "Agricultural Census of Egypt, 1939," 50. The number of feddans on which tomatoes were grown in 1939 topped 30,000, compared to the following: watermelons 50,669; potatoes 17,127; and melons 12,490.
104. The average yield of tomatoes per feddan dropped slightly to 117 in 1939. For yield figures from 1910, see Bonaparte, "Vegetables," 583. For yield figures from 1929 and 1939, see Ministry of Agriculture, "Agricultural Census of Egypt, 1939," 50.
105. Bonaparte, *Egyptian Farm Crops*, 49; Linton, "Atmosphere and Climate," 15; Bonaparte, "Vegetables," 583. For seasonal breakdowns of crop cultivation, see Ministry of Agriculture, "Agricultural Census of Egypt, 1929," 54–57. Most crops were grown in just one season; a handful were grown in two, including millet, rice, potatoes, watermelons, and squash.
106. Ministry of Agriculture, "Agricultural Census of Egypt, 1929," 56–57. In the Nili, or flood season, yields were equal throughout Egypt. These yield figures are broken down only into the categories of Lower and Upper Egypt, not the governorate level.
107. Ministry of Agriculture, "Agricultural Census of Egypt, 1939," 54–55.
108. Mitchell, *Rule of Experts*, 20.
109. Ministry of Agriculture, *L'Egypte Agricole*, 79.
110. Hamdi, *Intaj al-tamatim*, 10. Exports from 1954 to 1956 ranged from 288 to 1,104 metric tons per year. Between 1960 and 2000 tomato exports never amounted to more than 1 percent of the total production figures for fresh tomatoes (by weight) in any given year. FAOSTAT, "Crops and Livestock Products."
111. ʿAli, ʿAbd al-Badiʿ, and Surur, *al-Khudrawat fi Misr*, 287.
112. ʿAli, ʿAbd al-Badiʿ, and Surur, *al-Khudrawat fi Misr*, 296–97.
113. ʿAli, ʿAbd al-Badiʿ, and Surur, *al-Khudrawat fi Misr*, 306.
114. ʿAli, ʿAbd al-Badiʿ, and Surur, *al-Khudrawat fi Misr*, 301.
115. ʿAli, ʿAbd al-Badiʿ, and Surur, *al-Khudrawat fi Misr*, 306–308. Jennifer Derr (*Lived Nile*, 76) notes that "while much of southern Egypt remained under basin irrigation through the middle of the twentieth century, select tracts of the region were perennially irrigated through private interests associated with the colonial capitalists who built the dam." These exceptions were for the benefit of the Egyptian Sugar Company.

116. Abu al-Sunun, *Murshid al-tabbakh al-hadith*; Amin and Saʿid, *Funun al-tahi al-hadith*.

117. Abu al-Sunun, *Murshid al-tabbakh al-hadith*, ḥaʾ.

118. Abu al-Sunun, *Murshid al-tabbakh al-hadith*, 110, 120, 163, 179. Examples of recipes labeled "Turkish" or "Eastern" with tomato include stuffed zucchini, green beans, spinach stew, and salad; Abu al-Sunun, *Murshid al-tabbakh al-hadith*, 120–22; 182.

119. Kamil, *Maljaʾ al-tabbakhin*, 11–17.

120. Amin and Saʿid, *Funun al-tahi al-hadith*, 143–45. The two recipes that "imply" tomatoes use the term "salsa" (sauce) without specifying what kind—which, absent any additional information and given the tomato-heavy content of the surrounding recipes, might be reasonably presumed to mean tomato sauce, as the next section of this chapter explains.

121. It is clear that the "quta" is being treated as a separate vegetable from the tomato because the two recipes that call for "quta" (*quta bi-l-lahm* and *quta dolma*, or quta with meat and stuffed quta) have exact equivalents in the same chapter calling for "tamatim" instead (*tamatim bi-l-lahm*, etc.).

122. Hamdi, *Intaj al-tamatim*, 5.

123. Hamdi, *Intaj al-tamatim*, 5.

124. Royal Agricultural Society, *al-Quta fi Misr*, 3.

125. *Scents and Flavors*; Nasrallah, trans., *Treasure Trove*, 315–22; Shah, *Sultan's Feast*, 77–78. The latter two cookbooks each have a chapter devoted to *sulusat* (singular *sals*), which translator Nawal Nasrallah (*Treasure Trove*, 315) describes as "a precursor of table sauce and pesto."

126. Rodinson, "Arabic Manuscripts," 154.

127. Gentilcore, *Pomodoro!*, 52.

128. Montagné, *New Larousse Gastronomique*, 807.

129. Amin and Saʿid, *Funun al-tahi al-hadith*, 53.

130. Amin and Saʿid, *Funun al-tahi al-hadith*, 145.

131. Amin and Saʿid, *Funun al-tahi al-hadith*, 166–67.

132. *Dictionary of Egyptian Arabic* (1986), under "ṣ-l-ṣ." The Hinds-Badawi dictionary attributes an Italian origin to the word.

133. Stowell, *Anglo-Egyptian Cookery*, 38–42.

134. ʿAli, ʿAbd al-Badiʿ, and Surur, *al-Khudrawat fi Misr*, 299.

135. Bonaparte, "Vegetables," 583. Bonaparte (*Egyptian Farm Crops*, 50) makes a similar comment in his earlier 1903 work but without mentioning use "in time of scarcity."

136. Mikhaʾil, *al-Tadbir al-manzili al-hadith*, 1:168; 1:185.

137. Mansur, *al-Maʾuna al-manziliyya*. My estimate of a 1930s publication date is based on the publication dates of other works by the same small and relatively obscure press.

138. Amin and Saʿid, *Funun al-tahi al-hadith*, 1105. They do not name a specific variety.

139. ʿAli, ʿAbd al-Badiʿ, and Surur, *al-Khudrawat fi Misr*, 287–88. This manual specifies that tomatoes for producing salsa "must be bright red ... full of pulp, have low water content and acidity, and be rich in sugars," then lists sixteen Italian and American varieties that conform to those specifications.

140. Gentilcore, *Pomodoro!*, 66–68; 86–87; 137. Gentilcore writes that Italian agronomists' interest was "as much technological and industrial as it was agricultural," *Pomodoro!*, 87.

141. Gentilcore, *Pomodoro!*, 79.

142. ʿAli, ʿAbd al-Badiʿ, and Surur, *al-Khudrawat fi Misr*, 287–88.

143. Gentilcore, *Pomodoro!*, 109–10; for processing industries in Argentina and the United States, see *Pomodoro!*, 115–16.

144. Derr, *Lived Nile*, 51; Tignor, "Economic Activities of Foreigners in Egypt," 421.

145. ʿAli, ʿAbd al-Badiʿ, and Surur, *al-Khudrawat fi Misr*, 288.

146. ʿAli, ʿAbd al-Badiʿ, and Surur, *al-Khudrawat fi Misr*, 288–90.

147. ʿAli, ʿAbd al-Badiʿ, and Surur, *al-Khudrawat fi Misr*, 288.

148. Ministry of Agriculture, "Rusum bayaniyyat ihsaʾiyya," 6. This infographic source does not provide precise figures but indicates that in 1930 approximately 800 metric tons of salsa were imported, falling to approximately 400 metric tons in 1931 and not exceeding 650 metric tons in the next three years.

149. Ministry of Agriculture, *L'Egypte Agricole*, 80.

150. Ministry of Agriculture, *Muntajat al-tamatim*, 2.

151. Gentilcore, *Pomodoro!*

152. Ministry of Agriculture, *Muntajat al-tamatim*, 1.

153. Ministry of Agriculture, *Muntajat al-tamatim*, 29.

154. Stewart, *Ordinary Affects*, 27.

155. Abul-Magd, *Imagined Empires*, 81.

156. Alderman, von Braun, and Sakr, *Egypt's Food Subsidy*, 50.

CHAPTER 3

1. Yusuf al-Qaʿid and Muhammad Bakr, "al-Tamatim laysat wahdaha al-majnuna! [It's not just tomatoes that are crazy!]," *al-Musawwar*, May 9, 1975. Some parts of this chapter have been adapted and revised from Gaul, "Revolutionary Landscapes and Kitchens of Refusal."

2. It is difficult to date this street cry definitively, but one memoir mentions tomatoes advertised in this way in Cairo in 1959. Fernea, *View of the Nile*, 34.

3. For a contemporary explanation of the origin of "crazy tomatoes," see Husam al-Fiqy, "Hamra ya quta ... sirr itlaq laqab ʿal-majnunaʾ ʿala al-tamatim," *Sada El-Balad*, March 10, 2020, www.elbalad.news/4208855.

4. E.g., Mitchell, "Limits of the State." Here, I approach a "food system" as the actors, institutions, and networks involved in producing, processing, distributing, and consuming food for a given population. See Braun et al., "Food Systems."

5. Barnes, *Staple Security*, 3.

6. For bread in Egypt, see Schewe, "Egypt's National Bread Loaf"; Barnes, *Staple Security*; Ramadan and El Nour, 'Aysh marahrah; Sha'lan, *al-Khubz*. For elsewhere in the Arab world, see Graf, *Food and Families*, chapter 5; Martínez, *States of Subsistence*.

7. Schewe, "Egypt's National Bread Loaf," 53–57.

8. Seikaly "Protest of the Poor," 138–39.

9. Seikaly "Protest of the Poor," 137.

10. Barnes, *Staple Security*.

11. Since the 1950s, the state has both periodically reduced the size of the subsidized loaf and increased its price, although not at the same time. Sara Seif Eddin, "Bread Subsidies: The History of a 'Red Line,'" *Mada Masr*, December 23, 2021, www.madamasr.com/en/2021/12/22/feature/politics/bread-subsidies-the-history-of-a-red-line/. See also Barnes, *Staple Security*, 65–70; and Gutner, "Political Economy of Food Subsidy Reform," 463.

12. Harrison, "Agricultural Processing," 244; Rowntree, "Marketing and Price Determination," 421. Horticultural crops, in contrast to field crops, generally include vegetables and fruits not grown on trees.

13. Barnes, *Staple Security*, 14–19.

14. Barnes, *Staple Security*, 26–31.

15. This is evident throughout the policy literature describing Egypt's food system. A report produced by the Nutrition Committee for the Middle East, convened under the auspices of the FAO and WHO in Cairo in 1958 with delegations from across the region, focuses largely on cereals and proteins; the authors point out that "statistical data on supplies of [fruits and vegetables] are grossly inadequate." FAO, "Report of the Nutrition Committee," 4. A government publication outlining the state's approach to food security (undated but likely produced in the late 1970s) focuses on cereals and to a lesser extent protein sources, mentioning horticultural crops only in passing. "Food Security in Egypt." An overview of the subsidy system published in the early 1980s focuses primarily on cereals, proteins, sugar, and oil. Alderman, von Braun, and Sakr, *Egypt's Food Subsidy*. For global context, see Shaw, *World Food Security*.

16. Ohnuki-Tierney, *Rice as Self*, 119.

17. FAOSTAT, "Crops and Livestock Products."

18. Funk and Dethier, "Language of Food"; Schewe, "Egypt's National Bread Loaf," 50; Barnes, *Staple Security*, 5–6.

19. Barnes, *Staple Security*.

20. Martínez, *States of Subsistence*, 196.

21. A significant factor in this dynamic was Egypt's dependence on imported fertilizers due to the expansion of perennial irrigation, which no longer provided nutrient-rich Nile silt to farmland. But the war cut off access to this crucial input; cereal production fell between 1939 and 1941, threatening famine and prompting demonstrations. Eric Schewe ("Egypt's National Bread Loaf," 54) explains that the British used "their monopoly control over imports into Egypt, especially the supply of fertilizer, to negotiate for British prerogatives in Egypt's agricultural policies." See also Richards, *Egypt's Agricultural Development*, 169; Mitchell, *Rule of Experts*, 20.

22. The Shell Company of Egypt, "Report on Cost of Living in Egypt—February 1942," 1942, FO 371/31572, BNA.
23. "Note by P. S. Palmer on Tour of Upper Egypt 25th January to 6th February," 1944, FO 922/11, BNA.
24. In Arabic, *al-ahkam al-'urfiyya*, often translated into English as "martial law." Schewe, "State of Siege," 73–74.
25. Schewe, "State of Siege," 74.
26. Schewe, "Egypt's National Bread Loaf," 59–60; Richards, *Egypt's Agricultural Development*, 169.
27. Schewe, "Egypt's National Bread Loaf," 50. For an in-depth study of these mechanisms, see Barnes, *Staple Security*.
28. Alderman, von Braun, and Sakr, *Egypt's Food Subsidy*, 13; Hassan-Wassef, "Food Habits of the Egyptians," 909–10.
29. Hassan-Wassef, "Food Habits of the Egyptians," 910. Hassan-Wassef notes that changes to the food system introduced new and more accessible forms of protein to low-income urban Egyptian populations.
30. Schewe, "Egypt's National Bread Loaf," 60; 50.
31. Hassan, "Nutritional Problems of Egypt," 8.
32. Hassan, "Nutritional Problems of Egypt," 8; Ministry of Agriculture, *Muntajat al-tamatim*, 2.
33. Hassan, "Nutritional Problems of Egypt," 9. See also Ministry of Education, "School Feeding in Egypt"; Rafat, *al-Taghdhiya al-madrasiyya*.
34. Hassan-Wassef, "Food Habits of the Egyptians," 902.
35. Ministry of Education, "School Feeding in Egypt," 12, 22, 26. The remaining 16 percent of meals were cooked meals consisting of meat, vegetables, rice, bread, and fruit; we can assume that these likely also often included tomatoes.
36. Official bread and tomato allocations were 600 and 240 grams, respectively. Tomatoes also formed a significant portion of the meals in schools attended by wealthier students, though in lower quantities. Ministry of Education, "School Feeding in Egypt," 26. In the educational system at this time "elementary schools" served most of the population; "primary and secondary schools" served a smaller number of elite students. Issawi, *Egypt at Mid-Century*, 67–68.
37. Rafat, *al-Taghdhiya al-madrasiyya*, 5; for reference, in 1947, Egypt's population was around 19 million. Issawi, *Egypt at Mid-Century*, 58.
38. Hassan, "Nutritional Problems of Egypt," 9.
39. Abul-Magd, *Militarizing the Nation*, 36.
40. Abul-Magd, *Militarizing the Nation*, 36.
41. Salem, *Anticolonial Afterlives in Egypt*, 164–66.
42. Sadowski, *Political Vegetables?*, 60. See also Richards, "Egypt's Agriculture in Trouble." Richards notes that the new cooperative system, state agencies assumed tasks once managed by landlords, including "input supply, marketing and organization of production."
43. Sadowski, *Political Vegetables?*, 63–64. Although various approaches to land reform were discussed, the form they ultimately took prioritized maintaining social

stability and expanding production, rather than a revolutionary redistribution of land and capital to the poorest farmers. The reforms largely benefitted farmers who already owned land or capital and transferred control over existing systems of production to the state. Abul-Magd, *Militarizing the Nation*, 55; Sadowski, *Political Vegetables?*, 56–61.

44. This system was not implemented all at once, but unfolded throughout the 1950s and 1960s. Sadowski, *Political Vegetables?*, 63–66. See also Nassar et al., "Crop Production Responses," 87–88.

45. Sadowski, *Political Vegetables?*, 68, 74; Dethier, *Trade, Exchange Rate*, 1:112.

46. Sadowski, *Political Vegetables?*, 73.

47. Harrison, "Agricultural Processing," 244. Harrison notes several other factors impacting horticultural production in the period before 1986, including "subsidized inputs, retail price controls, state export trading and processing monopolies."

48. Sadowski, *Political Vegetables?*, 75.

49. Sadowski, *Political Vegetables?*, 75.

50. Sadowski, *Political Vegetables?*, 66–67.

51. Sadowski, *Political Vegetables?*, 67.

52. Farraj, *Mazari' al-khudrawat*, np. Farraj was a professor in the Faculty of Agriculture at Cairo University.

53. FAO, "Horticulture in the Mediterranean," 131.

54. Tobgy, "Contemporary Egyptian Agriculture," 160.

55. Gharb, *Zira'at mahasil al-khudar*, np.

56. FAO, "Horticulture in the Mediterranean," 137.

57. Tobgy, "Contemporary Egyptian Agriculture," 160–1. FAO, "Horticulture in the Mediterranean," 130. Tomatoes far outranked other vegetables in both area and production in Egypt in 1952, 1956, 1960, and 1964.

58. Hamdi, *Intaj al-tamatim*, 5; Central Agency for Mobilisation and Statistics, "al-Kitab al-sanawi" (1973), 44.

59. FAO, "Horticulture in the Mediterranean," 138. Other sources attesting to static tomato yields during this period (at around approximately 15 metric tons per hectare) include Hamdi, *Intaj al-tamatim*, 5 (1939–56) and FAOSTAT (after 1960).

60. Hamdi, *Intaj al-tamatim*, 4.

61. Alderman, von Braun, and Sakr, *Egypt's Food Subsidy*, 13. For an overview of the state's "channels of public food provisioning" between the Nasser period and the late 1980s, see Gertel, "Contextualizing the Social Space," 16.

62. Rafat, *al-Taghdhiya al-madrasiyya*, 5. Muhammad Nasim Rafat (pp. 4–5) notes that the expansion of enrollment and other fiscal challenges put significant stress on the program as soon as 1952. It was funded with the help of US assistance starting in 1955–56 and was forced to shut down entirely in 1956 (presumably because of the Suez Crisis). His study recommended a shift from a universal program to a need-based one focused on schools with the poorest students (Rafat, *al-Taghdhiya al-madrasiyya*, 55–57). A later study indicates that the program was eventually restructured along these lines, operating with a combination of state funds and

international aid, though I have not found a comprehensive account of the program during the years between 1956 and 1967. Nasif, *al-Taghdhiya al-madrasiyya*, 99–100.

63. Agha, "Project Unsettled." This brought the total of Nubians displaced by dams since 1902 to an estimated 135,000. Mahmoud, "Dashing Nubians' Hopes."

64. Ayubi, "Government and the Infrastructure," 134–35.

65. Abaza, *Changing Consumer Cultures*, 90–95. Fahmy, *Some Aspects of Structural Changes*, 34–35. Fahmy notes the emphasis on producing consumer goods at the expense of capital goods in the 1950s. Their impact on how Egyptians cooked and ate tomatoes is addressed in chapters 4 and 5.

66. FAO, "Horticulture in the Mediterranean," 138. Egyptian Federation of Industry, "Annuaire, 1954–55," 69; Central Agency for Public Mobilisation and Statistics, "al-Kitab al-sanawi" (1973), 93.

67. Seremetakis, *Senses Still*, 1.

68. For a similar discussion, see Mann, "Food, Culture and Lifestyle," 157–58.

69. Interview with the author, November 18, 2016.

70. Rafik Baladi Oral History, UAOHC, AUC RBSCL.

71. Interview with the author, November 6, 2016.

72. Interview with the author, October 21, 2016.

73. Seikaly, "Protest of the Poor," 148; Waterbury, *Egypt of Nasser and Sadat*, 167; Salem, *Anticolonial Afterlives in Egypt*, 177; Mitchell, *Rule of Experts*, 211. For a discussion of rhetorical continuity between Nasser and Sadat, see Dessouki, "Policy Making in Egypt," 410.

74. Sadowski, *Political Vegetables?*, 53.

75. Gutner, "Political Economy of Food Subsidy Reform," 462. See also Sadowski, *Political Vegetables?*, 53–54; Kamal, *Half-Baked*, 17; Alderman, von Braun, and Sakr, *Egypt's Food Subsidy*, 9. The share of government expenditures on the food subsidy increased substantially in the 1970s not only because of the inclusion of additional subsidized items but because of the rising costs of food worldwide.

76. Abul-Magd, *Militarizing the Nation*, 55.

77. Springborg, *Family, Power, and Politics*, xiv.

78. Sadowski, *Political Vegetables?*, 32–33; Bush, "Crisis in Egypt," 15–37; Mitchell, "America's Egypt."

79. Richards, "Egypt's Agriculture in Trouble;" Dethier, *Trade, Exchange Rate*, 1:20.

80. Seikaly, "Protest of the Poor," 138.

81. Seif Eddin, "Bread Subsidies"; Gutner, "Political Economy of Food Subsidy Reform," 463.

82. FAOSTAT, "Crops and Livestock Products."

83. FAOSTAT, "Crops and Livestock Products"; World Bank, "World Bank Open Data."

84. Exports of fresh tomatoes between 1974 and 1981 averaged around 3,500 metric tons annually, with the highest year in that period 1978 (8,311 metric tons). By comparison, the average annual production of fresh tomatoes during that period

was more than 2.1 million metric tons. This was despite a series of government schemes for exporting tomatoes. As chapter 2 details, exports were around 2,300 metric tons in 1889, 1909, and 1929, when production was much lower. FAOSTAT, "Crops and Livestock Products."

85. Egypt's National Library, Dar al-Kutub, contains detailed agricultural census data from 1961 and 1981; I prioritized accessing data from significant tomato-producing governorates from those years.

86. The precise figure for 1961 is 19.95 percent. Ministry of Agriculture, "Agricultural Census of Egypt, 1929"; Ministry of Agriculture, "al-Taʿdad al-ziraʿi" (1961).

87. USDA, "Egypt: Major Constraints," 160. See also Tobgy, *Contemporary Egyptian Agriculture*, 163–64.

88. Beshai, "Systems of Agricultural Production," 273.

89. Censuses include data for fifteen categories of farm size, from less than 1 feddan to 100 feddans or more. I have aggregated this data into two categories: small farms of fewer than 5 feddans and large farms of 5 feddans or more. According to Mahmoud Abdel-Fadil's categorizations of farm sizes in 1961, 5 feddans is the minimum land plot for a farmer to qualify as a "rich peasant," meaning that his land is enough to support a family and generate extra capital. Abdel-Fadil, *Development*, 14; 44. The distinction marking 5 feddans as a "large farm" was also reflected in policy: for example, farmers with fewer than 5 feddans were not permitted to plant fruit trees. Richards, "Egypt's Agriculture in Trouble."

90. For comparison, the equivalent figures in Sharqiyya rose from 28 percent to 46 percent and in Qena from 54 percent to 59 percent.

91. Mabro, *Egyptian Economy*, 73, quoted in Sadowski, *Political Vegetables?*, 58. In 1952, before the reforms, small farms (fewer than 5 feddans) made up 35 percent of the total land area of Egypt's farms; in 1965, after the reforms, they accounted for 57 percent of the total area.

92. Abdel-Fadil, *Development*, 14; 44.

93. Sadowski, *Political Vegetables?*, 83.

94. FAOSTAT, "Crops and Livestock Products."

95. FAOSTAT, "Crops and Livestock Products." Yields continued to climb until they evened out around 38 metric tons per hectare around 2003/4.

96. Nassar et al., "Crop Production Responses," 93–94. Tobgy (*Contemporary Egyptian Agriculture*, 163) also notes that through the early 1970s there had been "little true breeding work on vegetable crops in Egypt" to develop varieties tailored for local conditions as had been done with field crops.

97. Nassar et al., "Crop Production Responses," 85–86.

98. Nassar et al, "Crop Production Responses," 93–94.

99. One example is the 1986 yellow leaf curl virus, which was "controlled through concerted efforts of the Ministry of Agriculture in cooperation with tomato growers." Harrison, "Agricultural Processing," 244.

100. Central Agency for Public Mobilisation and Statistics, "Statistical Yearbook" (1983), 98; (1986), 97; (1996), 124. Starting in the 1980s, these statistical year-

books present salsa production numbers in twelve-month periods, presumably fiscal years, split between two calendar years (e.g., 1991–92, 1992–93).

101. Rowntree, "Marketing and Price Determination," 437. Writing in 1993, Rowntree notes that "private-sector companies have not processed tomatoes over the past decade." Superbrands Brandsearch, "Heinz Egypt."

102. Fadila Khaled, "45 Years On: Remembering the Egyptian Bread Intifada," *Egyptian Streets*, January 18, 2022, https://egyptianstreets.com/2022/01/18/45-years-on-remembering-the-egyptian-bread-intifada/. My translation prioritizes the rhyme and cadence of the original. Khaled provides a more literal translation: "It's not enough for us to wear burlap, they are coming to take our loaf of bread."

103. Khaled, "45 Years On." Again, Khaled gives a more literal translation: "O thieves of the infitah, the people are hungry and uncomfortable."

104. Khaled, "45 Years On." Translation from original. A "geneih" is an Egyptian pound. Another version of this slogan names ʿAbd al-ʿAziz Hijazi, the official who issued the 1974 foreign investment law. Abul-Magd, *Militarizing the Nation*, 74–75.

105. Colla, "The People Want."

106. Thompson, "Moral Economy," 78.

107. Thompson, "Moral Economy," 79.

108. For a similar argument, see Barnes, *Staple Security*, 26–27.

109. Abdel-Malek, *Ashʿar Ahmad Fuʾad Najm*, 198.

110. ʿAmri, *al-Shaykh Imam*, 93.

111. ʿAmri, *al-Shaykh Imam*, 93. The Arab Socialist Union, a remnant of the Nasser era, was abolished in 1980.

112. For references to okra and squash as metaphors for corruption in the work of Bayram al-Tunisi from the 1920s, see Booth, *Bayram al-Tunisi's Egypt*, 595.

113. ʿAmri, *al-Shaykh Imam*, 93.

114. For estimates from 1976 and 1982 that specify a 50 percent spoilage rate for tomatoes, see USDA, "Egypt: Major Constraints," 147, and Sadowski, *Political Vegetables?*, 270. For a critical reassessment of what qualifies as "marketing losses" of produce, including tomatoes, see Heitkötter, "Market Reality," esp. 111–12.

115. Mikhaʾil, *al-Tadbir al-manzili al-hadith*, 1:185.

116. ʿAli, ʿAbd al-Badiʿ, and Surur, *al-Khudrawat fi Misr*, 288.

117. Although Richards ("Egypt's Agriculture in Trouble") and Heitkötter ("Market Reality") date the concentration of Cairo's wholesale vegetable trade at Rawd al-Farag to the 1940s, Bayram al-Tunisi's poetry from the 1920s also includes references to unscrupulous vegetable merchants operating in the area. Booth, *Bayram al-Tunisi's Egypt*, 142, 150.

118. Sadowski, *Political Vegetables?*, 172.

119. Naguib, *Kalimati*, 81.

120. Nourhan Mustafa, "Qissat wazir tamwin qadama istiqalatahu bi-sabab al-tamatim: 'Magnuna ya quta,'" *al-Masry al-Youm Lite*, December 1, 2016, https://lite.almasryalyoum.com/extra/122303/.

121. Dethier, *Trade, Exchange Rate*, 1:26.

122. Hamdi, *Intaj al-tamatim*, 11.
123. Hamdi, *Intaj al-tamatim*, 11.
124. Hamdi, *Intaj al-tamatim*, 12.
125. Dethier, *Trade, Exchange Rate*, 2:54.
126. Dethier, *Trade, Exchange Rate*, 1:26; Sadowski, *Political Vegetables?*, 169–70.
127. Sadowski, *Political Vegetables?*, 170.
128. Cuddihy ("Agricultural Price Management," iv) describes one effect of the agricultural price mechanisms under Nasser and Sadat "a long-run net tax on the [agricultural] sector estimated at 30% of value added."
129. Ahmad, "Taswiq al-zuruʿ."
130. Ahmad, "Taswiq al-zuruʿ," 34.
131. Ahmad, "Taswiq al-zuruʿ," 32–33.
132. Ahmad, "Taswiq al-zuruʿ," 33.
133. Ahmad, "Taswiq al-zuruʿ," 34.
134. Sadowski, *Political Vegetables?*, 174.
135. Sadowski, *Political Vegetables?*, 172.
136. al-Qaʿid and Bakr, "al-Tamatim laysat wahdaha al-majnuna!"
137. Quoted in Sadowski, *Political Vegetables?*, 172.
138. Sadowski, *Political Vegetables?*, 172–73.
139. Rowntree, "Marketing and Price Determination," 436.
140. Sadowski, *Political Vegetables?*, 169–70.
141. Sadowski, *Political Vegetables?*, 170, 176.
142. Hopkins, Mehanna, and Abdelmaksoud, "Farmers, Merchants," 51–55; Sadowski, *Political Vegetables?*, 179–81.
143. Abu Seif, *al-Futuwwa*. The film title is also sometimes translated as "The Bully."
144. See Schewe, "State of Siege," 6–8, for an overview of such narratives.
145. Fathy, "al-Futuwwa," 59.
146. Fathy, "al-Futuwwa," 59; Mejri, "Salah Abu Seif." For scholarship on the role of film and television in shaping conversations, social attitudes, and popular experience, see Elsaket, "Cinema-Going in Egypt"; Armbrust, *Mass Culture and Modernism*; and Abu-Lughod, *Dramas of Nationhood*.
147. For two examples of scholarship on forms of statist politics in Egypt, see Abdel Meguid and Faruqi, "Truncated Debate"; Posusney, *Labor and the State*.
148. Fathy, "al-Futuwwa," 61.
149. Jacob, *Working Out Egypt*, 229. On films, see Mejri, "Salah Abu Seif," 7; Schewe, "Egypt's National Bread Loaf," 59; Irwin, "'Futuwwa,'" 163.
150. Irwin, "'Futuwwa,'" 161.
151. Irwin, "'Futuwwa,'" 161–63. While the latter negative connotations are often associated with the modern period, Irwin (161) cites examples as early as the thirteenth century applying the term "futuwwa" to "turbulent" or "dangerous" men. For an extended analysis of the concept in modern Egypt, see Jacob, *Working Out Egypt*, 226–62.

152. Jacob, *Working Out Egypt*, 25.
153. Jacob, *Working Out Egypt*, 25; 230.
154. Selim, *Novel and the Rural Imaginary*, 1.
155. Selim, *Novel and the Rural Imaginary*, 4.
156. Selim, *Novel and the Rural Imaginary*, 1.
157. Selim, *Novel and the Rural Imaginary*, 2.
158. Ayman Khalil, "al-Futuwwa," *Majallat al-Nabd al-ibdaʿ al-ʿArabi* (blog), November 20, 2020, https://arabicreativity.wordpress.com/2020/11/20/%d8%a7%d9%84%d9%81%d8%aa%d9%88%d9%91%d8%a9-%d8%a8%d9%82%d9%84%d9%85-%d8%a3%d9%8a%d9%85%d9%86-%d8%ae%d9%84%d9%8a%d9%84/.
159. Selim, *Novel and the Rural Imaginary*, 3.
160. *Dictionary of Egyptian Arabic* (1986), under "ḥ-n-n." I have translated hinayyin as "dear" here, but more literal translations are kind, affectionate, or tender.
161. Khalil, "al-Futuwwa."
162. The corrupt merchant Abu Zayd also uses "tamatim," perhaps underscoring the fictional character's connection with the real-life Upper Egyptian families that controlled the Rawd al-Farag market.
163. Sadowski, *Political Vegetables?*, 177; Hopkins, Mehanna, and Abdelmaksoud, "Farmers, Merchants," 51–55.
164. Sharma, "Food Cries," 18.
165. Sharma, "Food Cries," 21.
166. Sharma references numerous street cries from Cairo including "may our morning be white" (milkman) and "how they did knead thee in the night, O cakes" (wheat-cakes). These share some common features with tomato street cries: "magnuna ya oota" literally means "crazy, o tomatoes," including a form of address like the wheat-cakes cry; an alternate cry for tomatoes is "Hamra ya oota," or "red, o tomato," invoking the food's color like the milkman's cry. Sharma, "Food Cries," 21–22.
167. Smith, *Acoustic World*, 43.
168. Martínez, *States of Subsistence*, 150.

CHAPTER 4

1. Letter from Aisha Farghali and Ensherah Al Rafii to Huda Shaʿrawi, March 11, 1937. HSC, AUC RBSCL.
2. Shaʿrawi, *Mudhakkirat*, 98.
3. Shaʿrawi, *Mudhakkirat*, 43. Powell, *Different Shade of Colonialism*, 181–84.
4. Shaʿrawi, *Mudhakkirat*, 35–37.
5. Baron, *Women's Awakening*, 155.
6. In the 1960s the Ministry of Education renamed "domestic science" (*al-tadbir al-manzili*) "home economics" (*al-iqtisad al-manzili*), reflecting a global shift in terminology.
7. Several state schools for girls operated in the nineteenth and early decades of the twentieth century, although they faced numerous challenges. They operated

alongside private foreign and mission schools. There were no state secondary schools for girls until the 1920s. Russell, *Creating the New Egyptian Woman*, 100–25; Badran, *Feminists, Islam, and Nation*, 142–48.

8. "Ihtifal jama'iyyat al-Ittihad al-Nisa'i al-Misri," *Fatat al-Sharq*, January 1934, 193–94. A delegation of Egyptian women students had also been sent to England in 1907. Russell, *Creating the New Egyptian Woman*, 122.

9. "Hadith taliba Misriyya," *al-Siyasa al-Usbu'iyya*, May 22, 1926, 9.

10. Layla, "Aswat al-nisa'," *al-Siyasa al-Usbu'iyya*, February 5, 1927, 26.

11. Qutb, "al-Kutub al-jadida: al-Ghidha' wa-l-matbakh wa-l-ma'ida," *al-Ahram*, May 31, 1934, 7.

12. Huda Sha'rawi, "Letter about 'Food, Kitchen and Table' by Basima Zaki Ibrahim," February 25, 1935, HSC, AUC RBSCL. Ibrahim does not appear to have studied in England.

13. Esmat Rushdi, "Domestic Science in Egypt," *Bulletin of the Egypt Education Bureau*, 1948, 9. For a history of the institute and many of its instructors, see 'Abd al-Mu'min and 'Abd al-Rahman, *Najmat wa-kawakib*.

14. 'Abd al-Mu'min and 'Abd al-Rahman, *Najmat wa-kawakib*, 142.

15. The phrase is borrowed from Sherene Seikaly (*Men of Capital*, 53); as we will see, "collectivity" in these books included the nation but was not strictly limited to it.

16. For discussions of the salience of the domestic sphere to articulations of anticolonial politics and social reform in Egypt prior to 1922, see Shakry, "Schooled Mothers"; Russell, *Creating the New Egyptian Woman*; Pollard, *Nurturing the Nation*; Badran, *Feminists, Islam, and Nation*; Booth, *May Her Likes*.

17. Hamdi, *Intaj al-tamatim*, 5.

18. This periodization is also reflected in a recent history of home economics education in Egypt, which covers 1937 through 1980. 'Abd al-Mu'min and 'Abd al-Rahman, *Najmat wa-kawakib*.

19. These markets have long been an important site for scholars interested in materials not collected by conventional repositories. As Lucie Ryzova (*Age of the Efendiyya*, 26–31) points out, the contents of used book markets reflect the ownership and use habits of the "social middle" from whose homes many of the books originate—rather than the criteria used to assemble formal libraries and archives.

20. Earlier Egyptian cookbooks tended to be written by men, including texts for professional chefs and household management manuals with chapters on cooking. Two exceptions by women authors include Munira Fransis's *al-Tabkh al-manzili* (1914) and Malaka Sa'd's *Rabbat al-dar* (1915). See Booth, "Girlhood Translated?"; Russell, *Creating the New Egyptian Woman*; and Serry, "'al-Tabkh al-manzili.'"

21. Mona Russell (*Creating the New Egyptian Woman*, 146) notes that one of these earlier texts, Mikha'il's *al-Tadbir al-manzili al-hadith*, included advice both for readers "with few or no servants" and for those "with a complete household staff." Beth Baron (*Women's Awakening*, 153–55) notes that advice on managing servants was a common feature of the women's press prior to the 1920s.

22. According to Nicola Humble (introduction, xiv), the English cookbook author Eliza Acton (1799–1859) was the first to divide her recipes this way. Willan

et al. (*Cookbook Library*, 8) date the regular appearance of divided recipes to the late nineteenth century.

23. For an argument that focuses on differences in Egyptian discourses of domesticity before and after 1952, see Bier, "Pleasures of Domesticity."

24. Malak Rouchdy ("Food Recipes," 121), for example, identifies a "new culinary fashion" whose roots she traces "to the end of the 1980s and the beginning of the 1990s," with a more global orientation and an emphasis on television.

25. Swain, *Economy, Family, and Society*, 68–75.

26. Katz, *Wives and Work*, 84–88.

27. Booth, "May Her Likes," 861. According to Booth, "the need to define how 'woman' and 'home' overlapped was crucial to (and necessitated by) the shift from a traditional patriarchy to a new public patriarchy inflected by nationalism, for the equation of women and the domestic could no longer be taken for granted in a milieu where women's duties were defined in terms of the nation's needs, which could not be fulfilled wholly in the home." Marion Katz (*Wives and Work*, 204) concurs, writing that although social expectations that wives should perform domestic work were not new, the way that gender was conceptualized in understandings of those expectations changed significantly starting in the nineteenth century. For an overview of debates about the domestic sphere in Egypt during this period, see Fay, "From Warrior-Grandees," 89–91.

28. The variant *al-tadbir al-manzili*, a noun-adjective phrase, was also common.

29. For an overview of the literature on medieval and early modern Cairene kitchens, see Lewicka, *Food and Foodways*, 90–96.

30. Bier ("Pleasures of Domesticity," 5) notes that modern kitchens became the reality for elite Egyptians "as more upper-middle-class families embraced single-family housing designs in the 1930s and 1940s."

31. Nicola and Osman, *Usul al-tahi*, 4. The word "mutawassit" might also be translated as "average."

32. Nicola and Osman, *Usul al-tahi*, 4. Electric blenders first appeared in cookbooks the late 1950s; e.g., Ibrahim, *Kitab al-sha'b* 1:11; Nicola, *Atbaq sari'a*, 11.

33. 'Abd al-Hamid, *Usul fann al-tahi*.

34. Sometimes synonyms *dar* or *manzil* are used instead of *bayt*.

35. Seikaly, *Men of Capital*, 53.

36. Seikaly, *Men of Capital*, 57.

37. While some of Ibrahim's earlier books include sections on managing servants, she eventually phased this mode of advice out of her texts, addressing instead how to manage the kitchen without any paid domestic labor. Examples of advice on managing staff: *Da'irat al-ma'arif*, 171; *al-Tabkh al-hadith*, 5. Ibrahim's volume *al-Fata'ir al-haditha* includes advice on managing a "home without servants" (p. 25). An advertisement in the back of *al-Tabkh al-hadith* identifies another title in her book series whose title references "a home without servants" (p. 272); and her two-part 1958 cookbook, *Ma'idat al-sha'b*, does not mention servants at all.

38. This is one way that the housewife bears similarities to the Egyptian male *efendi* subject. Ryzova, *Age of the Efendiyya*; Jacobs, *Working Out Egypt*.

39. Huda Sha'rawi, "Letter about 'Food, Kitchen and Table' by Basima Zaki Ibrahim," February 25, 1935, HSC, AUC RBSCL.

40. Nicola and Osman, *Usul al-tahi, kaf*. The adjective translated here as "refined" can carry connotations of advancement or progress as well as refinement or superiority.

41. Kaplan, "Manifest Domesticity," 184.

42. Russell, "Textbooks as a Source," 271.

43. Bier, "Pleasures of Domesticity," 7; 17.

44. Bier, "Pleasures of Domesticity," 7–8.

45. Barakat, "'Alaqat l-taghayyur al-tiknulujiyya," 111–12. As Bier ("Pleasures of Domesticity," 6) points out, there would have been even less access to appliances outside of major cities like Cairo.

46. Amin, *Madha hadatha li-l-Misriyyin?*, 107–108. Amin notes that while Egyptian migration to Gulf countries began in the 1960s, more working-class Egyptians began to migrate starting in the mid-1970s, increasing the number of Egyptians with access to goods previously associated with elite or upper middle-class lifestyles.

47. Bier, "Pleasures of Domesticity," 13–14.

48. Baron, *Women's Awakening*, 153.

49. Waterbury, *Egypt of Nasser and Sadat*, 209. Waterbury notes that this category of workers accounted for just 5 percent of urban income.

50. Ministry of Education, "Comparative Statistics of Education"; Waterbury, *Egypt of Nasser and Sadat*, 44.

51. Ibrahim, *Da'irat al-ma'arif*, 171. See also Bier, "Pleasures of Domesticity," 14.

52. Benedict Anderson (*Imagined Communities*, 172–77) describes how modern maps projected and even anticipated colonial, then national, forms of sovereignty in Asia and Africa.

53. Benton, *Search for Sovereignty*, 279.

54. Sami Zubaida ("Culinary History," 153) situates this dynamic in broad historical context, from the Ottomanized Egyptian elites of the nineteenth century through later manifestations of Egyptian taste that include "a pan-Arab or pan-Middle Eastern variety and flavor."

55. I use categories of "East" and "West" because cookbook authors did, not as an assertion of their coherence. I am more specific where possible (e.g., French sauces, British domestic science curricula).

56. Aydin, *Anti-Westernism in Asia*, 9; see also chapter 4.

57. Booth, "May Her Likes," 832.

58. Gershoni and Jankowski, *Redefining the Egyptian Nation*. Gershoni and Jankowski refer to this period as one of "supra-Egyptian" imaginings of the nation. For a critique of their work, see Smith, "Imagined Identities."

59. Gershoni and Jankowski, *Redefining the Egyptian Nation*, 141–42.

60. In this sense I disagree with Ryzova's assertion that "the efendi has no female counterpart" (*Age of the Efendiyya*, 15–16).

61. King, introduction, 3, 9.

62. Ibrahim, *al-Matbakh al-sharqi*, 4. The full title of the book is *al-Ghidha' wa-l-matbakh wa-l-ma'ida li-hayatina al-manziliyya: al-Matbakh al-sharqi*, or *Nourishment, Kitchen, and Table for Our Family Life: Eastern Cuisine*. While a review in *al-Ahram* dates Ibrahim's first book to 1934, subsequent books in the series (which all begin with the same title but have different subtitles) are undated. I cite and estimate a publication date of 1940 for all of them, but some of them might have been published as early as 1935, or later in the 1940s or even 1950s.

63. Ibrahim, *Ma'idat al-sha'b*, 1:3; 2:123.

64. Ibrahim, *al-Matbakh al-sharqi*, 4.

65. Ibrahim, *al-Matbakh al-sharqi*, 4–5.

66. Ibrahim, *Ma'idat al-sha'b*, 1:3, 49–50; 87; 2:123.

67. The introduction to 'Abd al-Latif's 1970 *Fann al-tahi al-hadith* includes a similar argument.

68. Taher, "Abla Nazira."

69. In total the book has 250 pages of Egyptian recipes and 60 pages of other "Eastern" recipes; 30 of those are recipes from Syria, Turkey and the Balkans, Greece, and the general category of "Arab" foods; 20 of the remaining pages are non-Arab Asian cuisines, from Iranian to Japanese. Only 10 pages are devoted to Moroccan, Algerian, Sudanese, and "other African dishes."

70. Examples of recipes with Shami variations for *mulukhiyya*, *mahshi*, and *kubayba* (kibbe), respectively, include Fahmy, *al-Ta'lim al-manzili: al-Tahi*, 162; Nicola and Osman, *Usul al-tahi*, 371–72; 'Abd al-Latif, *Fann al-tahi al-hadith*, 134. Although Fahmy's textbook was first published in 1931, I reference a 1939 edition here.

71. An exception from the genre, not discussed in this chapter, is a 1949 cookbook published in Egypt but addressing Sudanese housewives. Gaul, "Kitchen Arabic."

72. Claudia Roden belongs to one such family; for an account of their Egyptian cook learning her family's Syrian dishes, see Bardenstein, "Transmissions Interrupted," 354. The upwardly mobile Egyptian merchants in Naguib Mahfouz's Cairo Trilogy eat Levantine mezze when they are out at night and traditional Egyptian fare at home. Hafez, "Food as a Semiotic Code," 268.

73. Farraj, *al-Tamatim: al-Banadura*, 13.

74. Mikha'il, *al-Tadbir al-manzili al-hadith*, 1:168.

75. 'Abd al-Ra'uf, *al-Lali' al-durriyya*, 298. I cite a second edition of this book published in 1922; the first edition was published in 1912. For Ottoman recipes for "red stew" without tomatoes, see Kamil, *Malja' al-tabbakhin*, 11–12; Turabi Efendi, *Turkish Cookery Book*, 12.

76. 'Abd al-Ra'uf, *al-Lali' al-durriyya*, 303–304.

77. Examples of cultural references to the book include its depiction on a 1956 cover of *Ruz al-Yusuf* magazine, a scene in a popular play from the 1978 Faisal Nada

play *El Motazawegoon*, and a political joke I was told about Egypt's 2012 constitution. Gamal Kamil, "Lawhat al-usbu'," *Ruz al-Yusuf*, December 24, 1956, p. 26.

78. *Berridge House Recipe Book*; "Berridge House 'Who's Who, 1893–1957' by Helen M. Kelsall," LMA ACC/0900/257. This document lists five other Egyptian pupils who studied at Berridge House in the 1920s, including Fatima Fahmy.

79. For example, a specific set of white sauce variations appears in both: anchovy, brain, parsley, onion, and béchamel. Nicola and Osman, *Usul al-tahi*, 69–74; *Cookery: Berridge House Recipe Book*, 85–95.

80. Incidentally, the question of whether Egyptian fatta should be made with *dim'a* (tomato sauce) is a subject of fierce debate today.

81. Nicola and Osman, *Usul al-tahi*, 100; *Cookery: Berridge House Recipe Book*, 93–94. Although the two recipes are not identical, there are a number of common points: the use of carrot and onion in the base, the addition of cornflour as a thickening agent, the note to add red food coloring if needed, and the specified use of a "hair sieve," which Nicola and Osman translate literally as *munkhal sha'r*, a tool that does not appear in the book's list of kitchen tools.

82. Nicola and Osman, *Usul al-tahi*, 100.

83. It is possible that before the rise of tomatoes, "dim'a" referred to an onion-based sauce, though this question requires additional research. Klunzinger (*Upper Egypt*, 57; 60) describes "kabab bi déma" as meat with "a plain sauce" and references onion sauces as a typical accompaniment to meat in an account of his travels in Upper Egypt in the 1870s. Ahmad Taymur's (*al-Amthal al-'ammiyya*) collection of Egyptian proverbs includes one that addresses onions' propensity to produce dim'a, which literally means "tear." That said, a cookbook originally published in 1912 has three recipes for dim'a, all of which include tomatoes. 'Abd al-Ra'uf, *al-Lali' al-durriyya*, 31.

84. Nicola and Osman, *Usul al-tahi*, 101.

85. Gloucestershire Training College of Domestic Science, "Superior Household Cookery Demonstration," Spring Term 1927, D10118 8/1, GCA. A syllabus from one of the years she studied there presents the techniques in this order: boiling, steaming, stewing, roasting, grilling, and frying. *Fundamentals of Cooking* presents them as boiling, stewing, frying, grilling, roasting, and steaming.

86. Nicola and Osman, *Usul al-tahi*, 25–36.

87. Nicola and Osman, *Usul al-tahi*, 26. Their definition in this introductory section corresponds most directly to braising, which involves less liquid than stewing. However, the recipes that they include under the "tasbik" category in later chapters also include techniques best described as stews and casseroles, as I explain below.

88. Nicola and Osman, *Usul al-tahi*, 26–27.

89. Rushdi, "Domestic Science in Egypt," 10.

90. Nicola and Osman, *Usul al-tahi*, 260–62.

91. "Basliyya" is derived from the Arabic for "onion" (*basal*). One source lists a Levantine Arabic definition for basliyya as "an onion cooked with meat and the juice from tomatoes." Living Arabic Project, "basliyya," accessed January 4, 2025, www.livingarabic.com/en/search.

92. *Dictionary of Egyptian Arabic* (1986), under "makmur."
93. Nasrallah, "In the Beginning," 598.
94. For the history of musaqqaʿa, see Nasrallah, "In the Beginning"; for an account of yakhni that does not mention tomatoes in early nineteenth-century Cairo (even though they are mentioned in the context of mahshi in the same context), see Lane, *Manners and Customs*, 194; for a description of medieval Cairene cooking using tawajin, see Nasrallah, glossary, 607.
95. Nicola and Osman, *Usul al-tahi*, 261.
96. Enany, *Naguib Mahfouz*, 6–7.
97. Mahfouz, *Qasr al-shawq*, 36–37.
98. Mahfouz, *Bayn al-qasrayn*, 346–48. For an analysis of the role of sharkasiyya in the narrative, see Hafez, "Food as a Semiotic Code," 269–70. Hafez writes that the name of the dish "reverberates with echoes of upper-class life and its feminine form refers to the Circassian concubines in the Ottoman harems" (p. 269). The character who teaches the ʿAbd al-Jawad family to make sharkasiyya refers to her "Turkish" origins.
99. Nicola and Osman, *Usul al-tahi*, 356–74.
100. Nicola and Osman, *Usul al-tahi*, 356.
101. Today these are more typically referred to as "yalanji," the Turkish word for "liar."
102. *Dictionary of Egyptian Arabic* (1986), under "ʿ-ṣ-j"
103. Nicola and Osman, *Usul al-tahi*, 152.
104. For example, dimʿa is called for in the stuffed artichoke recipe. Nicola and Osman, *Usul al-tahi*, 364.
105. Nicola and Osman, *Usul al-tahi*, 371–72. It is made with meat, rice, onion, samna, lemon juice, salt and pepper, and uses a broth made from sheep's trotters.
106. Nicola and Osman, *Usul al-tahi*, 357.
107. Nicola and Osman, *Usul al-tahi*, 359.
108. Letter from Aisha Farghali and Ensherah Al Rafii to Huda Shaʿrawi, March 11, 1937. HSC, AUC RBSCL. The recipe calls for a kilo of either pepper or eggplant, "*hasab ma yurghab* [as desired]," using the formal passive voice typically used in printed recipes by the twentieth century.
109. Ibrahim, *al-Matbakh al-sharqi*, 4.
110. Ibrahim, *Maʾidat al-shaʿb*, 1:3.
111. ʿAbd al-Latif, *Fann al-tahi al-hadith*, waw to zaʾ.
112. Nicola, *Atbaq sariʿa*, 205.
113. Nicola, *Atbaq sariʿa*, 15. For more on the "working woman," see Bier, *Revolutionary Womanhood*.
114. Davidson and Hatcher, introduction, 18.
115. Seikaly, *Men of Capital*, 53; 55; 61.
116. Russell, "Textbooks as a Source," 285. See also Reynolds, *City Consumed*.
117. This is the same letter that commends Ibrahim's "good taste." Huda Shaʿrawi, "Letter about 'Food, Kitchen and Table' by Basima Zaki Ibrahim," February 25, 1935, HSC, AUC RBSCL.

118. Nicola and Osman, *Usul al-tahi*, kaf.
119. Ibrahim, *Maʾidat al-shaʿb*, 2:123.
120. Ministry of Education, "al-Maʿhad al-ʿali li-l-tadbir al-manzili."
121. Nicola, *Atbaq sariʿa*, 5.
122. Nicola, *Atbaq li-kul al-munasabat*, 5.
123. For example, Humble, introduction, xvi; Willan, Cherniavsky, and Claflin, *Cookbook Library*, 200.
124. For an example of this in the United States—specifically in the repackaging of the culinary knowledge of enslaved cooks for southern housewives—see Pellissier, "Knowledge Politics."
125. Naguib, *Nurturing Masculinities*, 1.

CHAPTER 5

1. Some parts of this chapter have been adapted and revised from Gaul, "Revolutionary Landscapes."
2. That said, "tasbika," with the "a" at the end (*taa marbuta*, in Arabic), is a colloquial Egyptian Arabic word. When the term "tasbika" does appear in written Arabic, for example in the titles of YouTube videos, it is typically spelled with a *taa marbuta* at the end.
3. "Tasbika" corresponds to the technique that Nicola and Osman termed "basliyya"; in other midcentury cookbooks it sometimes appears as "makmur."
4. Williams, *Marxism and Literature*, 132.
5. First remark from an audience member at a talk given at the American Research Center in Egypt on October 26, 2016; second from an oral history interview, October 5, 2016.
6. Naguib, *Nurturing Masculinities*, 1. See also Ghannam, "Gender and Food."
7. Naguib, *Nurturing Masculinities*, 111.
8. Khaled, "Making Mahshi."
9. Interview with the author, October 22, 2016.
10. As previous chapters demonstrate, tomatoes were increasingly available year-round, especially in Cairo and the Delta, including in processed form as salsa. The relationship of tomatoes to the other ingredients in tasbika has changed in more recent years, however, with the advent of supermarkets with frozen sections that carry okra and other out-of-season vegetables.
11. Interview with the author, November 18, 2016.
12. Naguib, *Nurturing Masculinities*, 111.
13. Naguib, *Nurturing Masculinities*, 108–10.
14. Stowell, *Anglo-Egyptian Cookery*, 169–70.
15. Stowell, *Anglo-Egyptian Cookery*, 169; 38–42. In her ethnography of food and masculinity in twenty-first century Cairo, Nefissa Naguib (*Nurturing Masculinities*, 76) also includes an assertion by one interlocutor that samna is "the one ingredient that signified Egyptian cooking." For an example of a very similar okra recipe to the

one described here but with oil rather than samna, attributed to a broad "Middle Eastern" rather than Egyptian origin, see Roden, *Middle Eastern Food*, 293.

16. Nicola and Osman, *Usul al-tahi*, 101.

17. Based on a sample of the following issues: April, June, and August 1946; December 1947; January and August 1948; May 1949; February and October 1950; January 1951; April and November 1953; June 1954; and November 1955. In these issues cauliflower appears from November through April, cucumber June through October, taro November through February, and spinach December through April. Tomatoes appear throughout the year.

18. Nicola, *Atbaq sari'a*, 205. She refers to this kind of food using the passive participle: "what we call *al-akl al-musabbak*."

19. I thank Malak Rouchdy for encouraging me to think in terms of descriptions of technique rather than lexicon as I began researching the history of tomato sauce in Egypt.

20. This is notable because in Egypt many foods and recipes do, in fact, date back centuries or more (although not always as frequently or as far back into antiquity as is popularly assumed). Medieval recipes for mulukhiyya, for instance, bear striking similarities to contemporary ones despite changes in kitchen technologies. For the premodern histories of some popular Egyptian foods, see Dorry, "Forbidden, Sprouted, Stewed"; Barakat, "We Are What We Eat." For medieval mulukhiyya recipes, see Nasrallah, trans., *Treasure Trove*, 115, 129, 153.

21. For a discussion of the vernacular as a mode of expression tied to a notion of community or belonging and not necessarily coterminous with colloquial language, see Booth, *Bayram al-Tunisi's Egypt*, 1–2, 10.

22. The nature of how tasbika is learned and transmitted as part of a "culinary vernacular" predisposes the technique to variation and adaptation, resisting the kind of standardization typical of the written recipe form. I am grateful to Antonio Tahhan for many conversations that enriched this line of thinking about food and recipes.

23. Seremetakis, *Senses Still*, 6–7.

24. Rivolta Femminile, "Manifesto," 229.

25. Berlant, *Cruel Optimism*, 18, 96.

26. This concept has been developed extensively in the field of anthropology, from which I borrow my understanding of it. See, for example, McGranahan, "Theorizing Refusal"; Ortner, "Resistance and the Problem"; Abu-Lughod, "Romance of Resistance."

27. McGranahan, "Theorizing Refusal," 3.

28. That said, the idea for distinguishing between the two concepts comes from Kyla Wazana Tompkins's work (*Racial Indigestion*, 191n7). I also draw on Sucharita Kanjilal's critique ("Beyond Bourdieu," 5) of Bourdieu's theory of taste.

29. These observations build on scholarship that contests the adoption of the paradigm of taste presented by Pierre Bourdieu (*Distinction*), who analyzed taste as a set of cultural preferences that signifies a person's social status and plays a key role in consolidating and upholding that status. Scholars critiquing Bourdieu's

framework of taste have highlighted the limitations of examples that draw from sociological data from France and reflect neither sensory ontologies nor epistemologies of culinary value and quality in other cultures. See also Kanjilal, "Beyond Bourdieu," 2; Stoller, *Taste of Ethnographic Things*; Leschziner and Dakin, "Theorizing Cuisine"; Watson, "Bourdieu's Food Space"; Fikry, "Today's Children, Tomorrow's Meals"; Highmore, "Taste after Bourdieu."

30. Williams, *Marxism and Literature*, 132.

31. Fikry, "Today's Children, Tomorrow's Meals," 87. For an account of the role that men in Cairo play in supplying their households with food, see Naguib, *Nurturing Masculinities*.

32. For discussions of the role of grandmothers and maternal culinary knowledge transmission in Palestine, see Kattan, "Ode to My Grandmothers," and Hobley, "House of Meat." For a critical take on "grandmothers' cooking," see Sejal Sukhadwala, "Why Do Indian Recipes Always Have to Come from Some Mythic Grandmother?," *The Guardian*, December 29, 2021, www.theguardian.com/commentisfree/2021/dec/29/indian-recipes-mythic-grandmother-burden-tradition.

33. For example, Katharina Graf describes how low-income cooks in Morocco gained access to new culinary technologies in ways that implicated them in new forms of dependence on market forces. Graf, "Cooking with(out) Others?" For a classic critique of the idea that advanced domestic technology has functioned to liberate women, see Cowan, *More Work for Mother*. For an argument about the promises that the home would become a place of "pleasure" for women in Nasser's Egypt, see Bier, "Pleasures of Domesticity."

34. Kaha advertisement, *al-Musawwar*, February 24, 1956, 51.

35. For a similar account from the 1990s see Mann, "Food, Culture and Lifestyle," 155–56.

36. Howeidy, "Cooking Taro."

37. Nor was this the case for every dish. Interview subjects used a *makhrata*, not a blender, to prepare mulukhiyya; one told me that it was better to cut onions with a knife, rather than preparing them in a blender. Interview with the author, November 6, 2016.

38. Interview with the author, November 18, 2016.

39. For a similar account of generational shifts in approaches to processing and preserving tomatoes at home, see Hobley, "House of Meat."

40. Interview with the author, November 6, 2016.

41. Yates-Doerr and Carney, "Demedicalizing Health"; see also Barnes and Taher, "Care and Conveyance."

42. For more on meat production in Egypt, see Fikry, "Today's Children, Tomorrow's Meals," 42–54.

43. The term "baladi" will be further explored in the conclusion of this book.

44. Interview with the author, October 5, 2016. For an account of a similar conversation, see Naguib, *Nurturing Masculinities*, 77.

45. Interview with the author, June 16, 2015.

46. Fahmy, *al-Taʿlim al-manzili*: al-Tahi, 14.
47. Nicola and Osman, *Usul al-tahi*, 67.
48. Nicola and Osman, *Usul al-tahi*, 67.
49. Pinkard, *Revolution in Taste*, 108–109. Such sauces were intended to "accent the natural characteristics of principal ingredients" rather than stand out on account of the flavors intrinsic to the sauces themselves.
50. Rachel Laudan (*Cuisine and Empire*, 288) notes that in the nineteenth and early twentieth centuries, béchamel became "by far the most useful sauce for making a dish appear French."
51. Shaʿrawi, *Mudhakkirat*, 237; ʿAbd al-Muʾmin and ʿAbd al-Rahman, *Najmat wa-kawakib*, 130.
52. Jones and Burnham, *al-Shuʾun al-manzili*, 286.
53. Many authors explicitly used labels invoking "modern cooking" in their book titles—e.g., Ibrahim, *al-Tabkh al-hadith*; ʿAbd al-Hamid, *Usul fann al-tahi: ʿala ahdath al-turuq*; ʿAbd al-Latif, *Fann al-tahi al-hadith*.
54. Williams, *Marxism and Literature*, 115–16.
55. Waines, "Cooking," 165.
56. Lewicka, *Food and Foodways*, 189–90.
57. Lewicka, *Food and Foodways*, 190.
58. Lane, *Manners and Customs*, 194–95. For an account of a similar stew in Upper Egypt in the 1870s, described as "roast-meat with onion sauce or made into a ragout," see Klunzinger, *Upper Egypt*, 60.
59. Klunzinger, *Upper Egypt*, 60. Although he mentions the tomato in a discussion of vegetables that are frequently stuffed, he does not name it among the ingredients added to stews.
60. One colleague relayed to me that in Syrian cooking, "tasbika" can refer to a similar approach to blending different flavors, regardless of whether tomatoes are used.
61. Pinkard, *Revolution in Taste*, 108.
62. Pinkard, *Revolution in Taste*. Rachel Laudan (*Cuisine and Empire*, 40) notes that similarly structured one-pot dishes, consisting of some combination of "grains, roots, greens, and a bit of meat" dominated humble cuisines for much of history in many parts of the world.
63. McGee, *Food and Cooking*, 164.
64. The point about nutrition is a parallel with the tomato's adoption in India. Kanjilal, "Beyond Bourdieu," 6. Hassan-Wassef, "Food Habits," 902.
65. Meneley, "Olive and Imaginaries," 69.
66. Hodder, *Entangled*, 94.
67. Hodder, *Entangled*, 135.
68. McGee, *Food and Cooking*, 271.
69. Zaouali, *Medieval Cuisine*, xix; see p. 47 for further comparisons between medieval and modern Arab stews.
70. Kanjilal, "Beyond Bourdieu," 7. For more on tomatoes as thickening agents, see McGee, *Food and Cooking*, 623–24.

71. Kamil, *Malja' al-tabbakhin*, 49; Ibrahim, *Nasihat al-anam*, 55. The former includes a recipe that combines tomatoes and sour grapes; the latter combines tomato and lemon juice.
72. Kamil, *Malja' al-tabbakhin*, 5.
73. McGee, *Food and Cooking*, 329.
74. Gentilcore, *Pomodoro!*, 63–64. The innkeeper in question, Luigi Bicchierai, lived near Florence but learned to cook from two friars from Naples, where the tomato had been familiar for longer.
75. Kamil, *Malja' al-tabbakhin*, 50–51.
76. *Arabic-English Lexicon*, under "s-b-k."
77. The former definition comes from the Hinds-Badawi dictionary; I am also grateful to Yasser Mongy for his input on the connotations of "tasbik/a." *Dictionary of Egyptian Arabic* (1986), under "s-b-k."
78. Interview with the author, October 22, 2016.
79. Interview with the author, October 21, 2016.
80. "Safha li-qalbak," *al-Musawwar*, February 20, 1959, 69.
81. Interview with the author, October 15, 2016.
82. For another account of a similar phenomenon, see Shahira Mehrez, "In the Lap of Luxury: Traces of a Bygone Era," *Rawi*, 2019, https://rawi-publishing.com/articles/luxury/.
83. Interview with the author, December 4, 2016.
84. Interview with the author, November 18, 2016. Of course some women did cook from cookbooks, as used copies and other interviews attest, but most women I spoke to tended to downplay their significance. Two exceptions include a woman who attended university overseas and had little other access to Egyptian culinary knowledge and another whose mother had trained to be a domestic science teacher, meaning that she used *Fundamentals of Cooking* as a foundational textbook and a professional guide, not only as a domestic cookbook.
85. Interview with the author, October 22, 2016.
86. Interview with the author, March 28, 2017.
87. Interview with the author, March 28, 2017.
88. King, introduction, 10.
89. Ray, "Foreword: Food in the Making and Unmaking of Asian Nationalisms," x.
90. Interview with the author, October 21, 2016.
91. Interview with the author, June 16, 2015.
92. An account of Egyptian nutritional trends between the mid-1950s and the mid-1990s identifies greater access to "sugars, oils and fats, and meat/poultry/fish" as one of the most prominent trends. Increases in rates of hypertension and diabetes have occurred over a similar timeline. Galal, "Nutrition Transition," 142–43; 145–46.
93. Interview with the author, November 1, 2016.
94. Rouchdy, "Food Recipes," 131. To some extent the shift can be read as part of a global low-fat diet trend that emerged in the 1960s and 1970s. La Berge, "Ideology of Low Fat."

95. Rouchdy, "Food Recipes," 130–34. The cookbook referenced is Magda El-Mehdawy's 2003 cookbook, published in translation as *My Egyptian Grandmother's Kitchen: Traditional Dishes Sweet and Savory*.

96. Meneley, "Olive and Imaginaries," 70–71.

CHAPTER 6

1. There is no definitive consensus on okra's point of origin (scholars have proposed West Africa, Ethiopia, and India), but its importance to a wide range of African and African diaspora cuisines is well-established. Mohammed, Amelework, and Shimelis, "Simple Sequence Repeat Markers," 1032.

2. Citing Ibn al-Baytar (1197–1248) and 'Abd al-Latif al-Baghdadi (1162–1231), Nawal Nasrallah (introduction, 9) writes that by the medieval period okra "was recognized as a vegetable indigenous to Egypt."

3. Nasrallah, introduction, 31; 250.

4. Nasrallah, introduction, 31. Similarly, Paulina Lewicka (*Food and Foodways*, 248) includes okra in a list of vegetables "which deserve special comment" because over time they "became the distinguishing marks of contemporary Egyptian/Cairene cookery."

5. The latter association may have stemmed from okra's possible historical diffusion from Ethiopia and other parts of Northeast Africa first through Upper Egypt then northward through the Nile Valley.

6. Nasrallah, trans., *Treasure Trove*, 135. See also Nasrallah, glossary, 492, 604; Nasrallah, appendix, 662. The recipe also appears in a fifteenth-century cookbook that replicates much of the anonymous cookbook cited here. Shah, *Sultan's Feast*, 34. As Nasrallah explains, this term for viscosity is derived from the word for saliva.

7. E.g., a recent book of global okra recipes includes a list of "slime-busting tips," including the addition of acid. Willis, *Okra*.

8. Shirbini, *Hazz al-quhuf*, 2:190–91.

9. Shirbini, *Hazz al-quhuf*, 2:190–91.

10. Lewicka, *Food and Foodways*, 250. The source quoted is the travelogue of Spanish priest Antonius Gonzales.

11. Lane, *Manners and Customs*, 194.

12. Klunzinger, *Upper Egypt*, 140–42; for okra in meals, see pp. 59; 160.

13. Foaden and Fletcher, *Egyptian Agriculture*, 2:379.

14. Interview with the author, October 11, 2023.

15. Williams, *Marxism and Literature*, 115–16.

16. Stowell, *Anglo-Egyptian Cookery*, 169.

17. Stowell, *Anglo-Egyptian Cookery*, 172.

18. Stowell, *Anglo-Egyptian Cookery*, preface.

19. The word Stowell uses is "Berberine," the English equivalent of the Arabic *barbari*. This term is a racial epithet that Egyptians use variously, and often indiscriminately, to refer to Nubians and Black Africans. On Berberine and "barbari"

meaning "Nubian," see Powell, *Different Shade of Colonialism*, 227n43. Due to the racialization of the domestic labor force in Cairo, it is impossible to know if Stowell's cook was from Nubia or elsewhere in the south, as is discussed below.

20. Stowell, *Anglo-Egyptian Cookery*, 2.
21. Stowell, *Anglo-Egyptian Cookery*, 275 (glossary); 293 (imperatives). For a brief discussion of "kitchen Arabic" in Egypt and Sudan, see Gaul, "Kitchen Arabic," 11–12.
22. Procida, "Feeding the Imperial Appetite"; Leong-Salobir, *Food Culture in Colonial Asia*; Walsh, *Domesticity in Colonial India*.
23. Stowell, *Anglo-Egyptian Cookery*, 2; Leong-Salobir, *Food Culture in Colonial Asia*, 60.
24. Stowell, *Anglo-Egyptian Cookery*, 2.
25. Smith, "Wretched Kush," 119; see pp. 114–24 for a full discussion of the evidence.
26. Zilfi, *Women and Slavery*, 131; 133.
27. Powell, *Different Shade of Colonialism*, 69.
28. Powell, *Different Shade of Colonialism*, chapter 5.
29. Powell, *Tell This In My Memory*, 129.
30. Beckett, "Nubia and the Berberine," 352–53.
31. ʿAli, *Taht khatt al-faqr*, 95, 125. Eve Troutt Powell (*Different Shade of Colonialism*, 22–23) writes that "constructions of race hardened after the middle of the [nineteenth] century" as "darker-skinned people of the south" were discussed interchangeably in Cairene contexts; Nefertiti Takla ("Barbaric Women," 392) traces how the "racialization of southern Egyptian migrant women" continued in the interwar period, as "the economic peripheralization of the Saʿid was reinforced by a racialized colonial discourse about southern Egyptians as primitive and inferior to northern Egyptians."
32. ʿAli, *Taht khatt al-faqr*, 43.
33. Moore, "Betraying Behita," 151.
34. Harris, *High on the Hog*; Twitty, *Cooking Gene*.
35. Harris, *High on the Hog*, 92.
36. Harris, *High on the Hog*, 1–2.
37. Kolb ("Okra," 6) states that Randolph's cookbook "gave some of the earliest published recipes for [okra's] use," and Corilyn Shropshire describes the book's second edition as "the first known cookbook to include a variety of tomato recipes." See Shropshire, "The History of Tomatoes in America," *Cook's Illustrated*, May 14, 2021, www.americastestkitchen.com/cooksillustrated/articles/3244-history-of-tomatoes-in-america.
38. Pellissier, "Knowledge Politics," 748.
39. Ryzova, *Age of the Efendiyya*; Jacob, *Working Out Egypt*.
40. Abu al-Sunun, *Murshid al-tabbakh al-hadith*, ḥaʾ.
41. For instance, the chapter includes a zucchini dish prepared au gratin (p. 120) and recipes for green beans that also reflect European cooking styles; one is labeled "English-style green beans" while another, "green beans in oil," is modeled on an

earlier artichoke recipe that involves a French mirepoix with carrots, celery, and onion, seasoned with bay leaf and garnished with parsley. Abu al-Sunun, *Murshid al-tabbakh al-hadith*, 114, 121.

42. Abu al-Sunun, *Murshid al-tabbakh al-hadith*, 120.
43. Abu al-Sunun, *Murshid al-tabbakh al-hadith*, 121.
44. Abu al-Sunun, *Murshid al-tabbakh al-hadith*, 121. All recipes in the book are titled in Arabic and French—e.g., *Bamias à l'Egyptienne/Bamiya ʿala al-tariqa al-Misriyya*. There are other instances of okra recipes in the cookbook, but they are clearly European in style. For example, one is for an okra soup in which "okra" is not even translated into Arabic but transliterated instead from English. See pp. 8, 122.
45. ʿAbd al-Hamid, *Usul fann al-tahi*, 28.
46. ʿAbd al-Hamid, *Usul fann al-tahi*, 28. Nawal Nasrallah notes that this category of dish was originally named after Buran, the wife of ʿAbbasid caliph al-Maʾmun (d. 833), and situates it in a genealogy of eggplant dishes that include modern *musaqqaʿa*. Nasrallah, "In the Beginning," 600–602.
47. Copper diqqiyyat make occasional appearances in collections of cooking items in nineteenth-century probate records.
48. Nicola, *Atbaq ladhidha*; Nicola, *Atbaq sariʿa*. Nicola wrote at least four books in this series, though I have only been able to access copies of three.
49. Nicola, *Atbaq ladhidha*, 87–88; Nicola, *Atbaq sariʿa*, 123–24.
50. Nicola, *Atbaq ladhidha*, 87.
51. Bonaparte, *Egyptian Farm Crops*, 38.
52. Interview with the author, October 21, 2016.
53. Darwiche, *Fi suhbat al-taʿam*, 147.
54. Interview with the author, October 22, 2016.
55. Interview with the author, November 18, 2016.
56. Interview with the author, October 11, 2023.
57. Ibn al-Baytar, *Kitab al-Jamiʿ*, 1:111. His invocation of "Misr" might be read as referring to Egypt as a whole or to Cairo.
58. Interview with the author, October 14, 2016.
59. Interview with the author, October 13, 2023.
60. Nasrallah, appendix, 662.
61. Lewicka, *Food and Foodways*, 250n582. The reference is to page 248 of Roden's *Middle Eastern Food*.
62. For more about Roden's background and work, see Kashdan, "Anglophone Cookbooks."
63. Roden, *Middle Eastern Food*, 248 ("Bamia Matbookha") and 293 ("Bamia bel Takleya").
64. Williams, *Marxism and Literature*, 111.
65. Talaat, "Weeka ya dunya weeka." I am grateful to Randa Abou-bakr, Magda Hasabelnaby, and Mounira Soliman, who shared this short story with me.
66. Talaat, "Weeka ya dunya weeka," 17.

67. White okra (bamiya bayda) is not a category I have seen in textual sources, but I often encountered it in speech and online (e.g., in YouTube cooking videos). That said, the usage is not universal.

68. Hassan-Wassef, "Food Habits of the Egyptians," 905; see p. 903 for a detailed chart of leafy greens and herbs consumed in Egypt.

69. Howeidy, "Cooking Taro."

70. Nicola and Osman, *Usul al-tahi*, 320–24.

71. Nicola and Osman, *Usul al-tahi*, 321.

72. Nicola and Osman, *Usul al-tahi*, 323–24.

73. Youssef, "Aesthetics of Difference," 75.

74. Youssef, "Aesthetics of Difference," 79. For an overview of discussions around Nubian literature in contemporary Egypt, see Hussein, "Identity Politics," 37–40.

75. Colla, "Translator's Afterword," 198–201.

76. Colla, "Translator's Afterword," 201–202.

77. Agha, "Nubia Still Exists," 1, 7, 8.

78. Scheer, "Are Emotions a Kind of Practice," 218, 204, 207.

79. Ray, "Culinary Difference."

80. Tunisi, *In Darfur*, 216–17.

81. Spelled here as "wayka."

82. Armanios, "Teta's Culinary Toolbox."

83. Shirbini, *Hazz al-quhuf*, 2:190–91.

84. Roden, *Middle Eastern Food*, 293.

85. Interview with the author, October 11, 2023.

86. Interview with the author, November 18, 2016.

87. Interview with the author, June 16, 2015.

88. Interview with the author, October 21, 2016.

89. Interview with the author, October 5, 2016.

90. Appadurai, "National Cuisine," 6.

91. Interview with the author, October 13, 2023.

92. Gupta and Ferguson, "Beyond 'Culture,'" 10.

93. Interview with the author, October 13, 2023.

94. Interview with the author, October 13, 2023.

95. Interview with the author, October 19, 2023.

96. Siddhartha Mitter, "Free Okra," *The Oxford American*, April 2005, https://siddharthamitter.com/2005/04/30/free-okra/.

97. The standing of okra in the United States is a complex subject that cannot be reduced to blanket rejection. For a nuanced account, see Shane Mitchell, "An Undeserved Gift," *The Bitter Southerner*, October 22, 2019, https://bittersoutherner.com/an-undeserved-gift-okra-shane-mitchell.

98. Harris, *High on the Hog*, 17.

99. Nasrallah, glossary, 584; Armanios, "Teta's Culinary Toolbox."

100. Nawaya, "The Mefraak: Cooking Okra with the Ancient Whisk," Google Arts & Culture, accessed June 10, 2024, https://artsandculture.google.com/story/the-mefraak-cooking-okra-with-the-ancient-whisk/tgWBKAg4zebl2w.

101. For an example of the two used as synonyms, see Armanios, "Teta's Culinary Toolbox." In a Sudanese restaurant in Cairo in 2024 I was served two different dishes, one made with fresh okra and presented to me as "bamiya mafruka," and another made with dried okra and presented as "weeka." While "weeka" appears in many written sources, I have not encountered "bamiya mafruka" in any of the cookbooks discussed here.

102. Interview with the author, October 13, 2023.

103. This is also the case with mulukhiyya, which some Egyptians reported making with tomato juice or grated tomato added to the broth; others serve it with a side of *dimʿa* (rich tomato sauce).

104. Kamal, "al-Matbakh al-Nubi."

105. Mannur, *Intimate Eating*, 5.

106. Mannur, *Intimate Eating*, 5.

CONCLUSION

1. Ibrahim, *al-Matbakh al-sharqi*, 161.
2. Yates-Doerr and Carney, "Demedicalizing Health."
3. Barnes, *Staple Security*, 5–7. Jessica Barnes invokes the framing of "becoming" to discuss the nature of wheat and bread in Egypt.
4. Gupta and Ferguson, "Beyond 'Culture,'" 9.
5. Messiri, *Ibn al-Balad*, 11.
6. For a contemporary example of this usage from Egypt, see Pozzi and El Sayed, "Baladi Food."
7. For example, G. Bonaparte ("Vegetables," 580) lists the two varieties of eggplant cultivated in Egypt in the early twentieth century as "the Roumi or Malti and the Baladi." Chapter 6 mentions Bonaparte's descriptions of baladi and rumi okra. "Rumi" sometimes connotes "Greek"; more generally, it is a reference to the lands and culture associated with the Byzantine Empire, including Anatolia. The Arabic word for turkey, an American bird, is *dik rumi* or "foreign rooster." *Dictionary of Egyptian Arabic* (1986), under "r-u-m."
8. Derr, *Lived Nile*, 77.
9. Ministry of Agriculture, *L'Egypte Agricole*, 79.
10. Ibrahim, *al-Matbakh al-sharqi*, 161.
11. Royal Agricultural Society, *al-Quta fi Misr*, n.p.
12. Royal Agricultural Society, *al-Quta fi Misr*, 39.
13. Ministry of Agriculture, *L'Egypte Agricole*, 79.
14. Bircher, *Gardens of the Hesperides*, 685.
15. Farraj, *Mazariʿ al-khudrawat*, 2.
16. Interview with the author, October 13, 2023.
17. Interview with the author, February 4, 2024.
18. For an account of the practices required to produce ethical home-reared meat and poultry in Egypt, see Fikry, "Today's Children, Tomorrow's Meals."

19. Armbrust, *Mass Culture and Modernism*, 26.
20. Armbrust, *Mass Culture and Modernism*, 26.
21. Nicola and Osman, *Usul al-tahi*, 57–58.
22. Armbrust, *Mass Culture and Modernism*, 25; Messiri, *Ibn al-Balad*, 1–2.
23. Booth, *Bayram al-Tunisi's Egypt*, 144.
24. Messiri, *Ibn al-Balad*, 1.
25. Naguib, *Nurturing Masculinities*, 109.
26. Naguib, *Nurturing Masculinities*, 112.
27. Naguib, *Nurturing Masculinities*, 113.
28. Barnes, *Staple Security*, 7–8.
29. Barnes, *Staple Security*, 13; Seif Eddin, "Bread Subsidies." Barnes points out that even though the most prominent usage of "baladi bread" refers to state-subsidized loaves, Egyptian bread made in homes can technically qualify as baladi bread too: "*Baladi* can also mean traditional, rural, or local and so can be used to describe any bread that is perceived as holding one of these characteristics" (Barnes, *Staple Security*, 12).
30. Barnes, *Staple Security*, 70–71. Katharina Graf (*Food and Families*, chapter 5) shows that this is not the case in Morocco, where urban women are attentive to the type and origin of the wheat they use for bread.
31. "The Six Hundred Seventy-Four Forms and a Dragon," 2023, www.yasmineelmeleegy.com/tomato, accessed January 12, 2025.
32. Layla Raik, "Future Farms: An Egyptian Artist's Fortune Telling of What's to Come," *Scene Eats*, June 29, 2024, https://sceneeats.com/InDepth/Future-Farms-An-Egyptian-Artist-s-Fortune-Telling-of-What-s-to-Come.
33. "Yasmine El Meleegy (Interview)," *Canvas: Art and Culture from the Middle East and Arab World*, February 2024, p. 159.
34. Lowe, *Intimacies of Four Continents*, 81.
35. Lowe, *Intimacies of Four Continents*, 83.
36. Nicola, *Atbaq sariʿa*, 5.
37. Fahmy, *All the Pasha's Men*, 24.
38. Rich, "Notes toward a Politics of Location," 214.

BIBLIOGRAPHY

ARCHIVES

American University in Cairo Rare Books and Special Collections Library (AUC RBSCL)
    University Archives Oral History Collection (UAOHC)
    Huda Shaarawi Collection (HSC)
British National Archives, London, UK (BNA)
Dar al-Watha'iq al-Qawmiyya (Egyptian National Archives), Cairo, Egypt (DWQ)
Gloucester County Archives, Gloucester, UK (GCA)
London Metropolitan Archives (LMA)

DATASETS

United Nations Food and Agriculture Organization (FAOSTAT). "Crops and Livestock Products." Accessed July 13, 2022. www.fao.org/faostat/en/#home.
World Bank. "World Bank Open Data." Accessed June 26, 2024. https://data.worldbank.org.

NEWSPAPERS AND PERIODICALS

al-Ahram
Bint al-Nil
Bulletin of the Egypt Education Bureau
Fatat al-Sharq
The Egyptian Gazette
al-Musawwar

Ruz al-Yusuf
al-Siyasa al-Usbuʿiyya

PRINT AND ELECTRONIC SOURCES

Abaza, Mona. *Changing Consumer Cultures of Modern Egypt: Cairo's Urban Reshaping.* Leiden: Brill, 2005.
ʿAbd al-Hamid, Samia. *Usul fann al-tahi: ʾAla ahdath al-turuq* [Fundamentals of the art of cooking: The most modern methods]. Daʾirat Maʿarif Manziliyya Kamila. Cairo: Matbaʿat Dar al-Taʾlif, 1953.
ʿAbd al-Latif, Samiha. *Fann al-tahi al-hadith* [The of art modern cooking]. Cairo: Maktabat al-Anglo al-Misriyya, 1970.
ʿAbd al-Muʾmin, ʿAli Rashad, and Manal ʿAbd al-Rahman. *Najmat wa-kawakib fi samaʾ al-iqtisad al-manzili: 1937–1980.* 5th edition. Cairo: Self-published, 2019.
ʿAbd al-Muʿti, Husam. *al-Maghariba fi Misr khilal al-qarn al-thamin ʿashar.* Alexandria: Biblioteca Alexandrina, 2015.
Abd al-Rahman, Abdel Rahim. "Morisco Settlement in Egypt through the Religious Court Documents of the Ottoman Age." In *L'expulsió dels moriscos: conseqüències en el món islàmic i el món cristià,* edited by Congres Internacional 380e Aniversari de L'Expulsio Dels Moriscos, Catalonia Departament de Cultura, 158–63. Barcelona: Generalitat de Catalunya, 1994.
ʿAbd al-Raʾuf, Ibrahim. *al-Laliʾ al-durriyya fi al-tadbir al-manzili wa-l-qawanin al-sihiyya* [Pearls that gleam: Managing the home and rules of hygiene]. 2nd edition. Cairo: Matbaʿat al-Maʿahid, 1922.
Abdel-Fadil, Mahmoud. *Development, Income Distribution, and Social Change in Rural Egypt (1952–1970).* Cambridge, UK: Cambridge University Press.
Abdel-Malek, Kamal Najib. *Ashʿar Ahmad Fuʾad Najm: Balaghat al-turath al-badil.* Cairo: National Center for Translation, 2016.
Abdel Meguid, Ahmed, and Daanish Faruqi. "The Truncated Debate: Egyptian Liberals, Islamists, and Ideological Statism." In *Egypt and the Contradictions of Liberalism: Illiberal Intelligentsia and the Future of Egyptian Democracy,* edited by Dalia Fahmy and Daanish Faruqi, 253–88. London: Oneworld Publications, 2017.
Abu-Lughod, Lila. *Dramas of Nationhood: The Politics of Television in Egypt.* Chicago: University of Chicago Press, 2005.
Abu-Lughod, Lila. "The Romance of Resistance: Tracing Transformations of Power through Bedouin Women." *American Ethnologist* 17, no. 1 (1990): 41–55.
Abu-Lughod, Lila, ed. *Remaking Women: Feminism and Modernity in the Middle East.* Princeton, NJ: Princeton University Press, 1998.
Abul-Magd, Zeinab. *Imagined Empires: A History of Revolt in Egypt.* Berkeley: University of California Press, 2013.
Abul-Magd, Zeinab. *Militarizing the Nation: The Army, Business, and Revolution in Egypt.* New York: Columbia University Press, 2017.

Abu Seif, Salah, dir. *al-Futuwwa* [The Thug]. Studio Misr, 1957.
Abu al-Sunun, Muhammad ʿAli. *Murshid al-tabbakh al-hadith* [Guide for the modern chef]. Cairo: Dar al-Kutub al-Misriyya, 1932.
Achaya, Konganda T. *A Historical Dictionary of Indian Food*. Oxford: Oxford University Press, 1998.
Addison, Lancelot. *West Barbary, or, A Short Narrative of the Revolutions of the Kingdoms of Fez and Morocco with an Account of the Present Customs, Sacred, Civil, and Domestick*. Oxford: John Wilmot, 1671; Ann Arbor, MI: Text Creation Partnership, 2001. https://quod.lib.umich.edu/e/eebo/A26378.0001.001.
Agha, Menna. "Nubia Still Exists: On the Utility of the Nostalgic Space." *Humanities* 8, no. 1 (March 2019): 1–12.
Agha, Menna. "Project Unsettled: Histories of Nubian Displacement." Accessed June 30, 2024. https://projectunsettled.com/un-resettlementshistory.html.
Ahmad, ʿIzz al-Din Humam. "Taswiq al-zuruʿ fi al-Jumhuriya al-ʿArabiyya al-Muttahida." Cairo: Maʿhad al-Takhtit al-Qawmi, April 1966.
Ahmed, Leila. *Women and Gender in Islam: Historical Roots of a Modern Debate*. New Haven, CT: Yale University Press, 1992.
Alderman, Harold, Joachim von Braun, and Sakr Ahmed Sakr. *Egypt's Food Subsidy and Rationing System: A Description*. Washington, DC: International Food Policy Research Institute, 1982.
ʿAli, Idris. *Taht khatt al-faqr* [Under the poverty line]. Cairo: Dar Merit, 2005.
ʿAli, Muhammad Bayumi, Muhammad ʿAbd al-Badiʿ, and Mustafa Surur. *al-Khudrawat fi Misr* [Vegetables in Egypt]. Cairo: Matbaʿat al-Muqtataf wa-l-Muqattam, 1930.
Allard, Jeanne. "El Tomate: Un Largo Trayecto Hasta La Mesa." *Historia Caribe* 2, no. 6 (2001): 45–54.
Amin, Abu Zayd, and Taghiyan Saʿid. *Kitab Funun al-tahi al-hadith* [The arts of modern cooking]. Cairo: Matbaʿat Muqtataf al-Muqattam, 1934.
Amin, Galal. *Madha hadatha li-l-Misriyyin?* Cairo: Dar El-Shorouk, 2013.
ʿAmri, Amir al-. *al-Shaykh Imam fi ʿasr al-thawra wa-l-ghadab*. Cairo: El Maraya, 2021.
Anderson, Benedict. *Imagined Communities: Reflections on the Origin and Spread of Nationalism*. Revised edition. London: Verso, 2016.
Anderson, Edgar. "Anatolian Mystery." *Landscape* (Spring 1958): 14–16.
Anderson, Edgar. "Foreword to 'The History of the Use of the Tomato: An Annotated Bibliography,' by George Allen McCue." *Annals of the Missouri Botanical Garden* 39, no. 4 (1952): 289–90.
Andrews, Jean. "Diffusion of Mesoamerican Food Complex to Southeastern Europe." *Geographical Review* 83, no. 2 (1993): 194–204.
Antaki, Dawud bin ʿUmar al-. *Tadkhirat uli al-albab al-jamiʿ li-l-ʿajab al-ʿujab*. Cairo: Maktabat al-Iman al-Mansura, 2006.
Appadurai, Arjun. "How to Make a National Cuisine: Cookbooks in Contemporary India." *Comparative Studies in Society and History* 30, no. 1 (January 1988): 3–24.

Armanios, Febe. "Teta's Culinary Toolbox: Memories of Mifrak and Okra Stew." *Egypt Migrations*, December 22, 2020. https://egyptmigrations.com/2020/12/22/tetas-culinary-toolbox/.

Armbrust, Walter. *Mass Culture and Modernism in Egypt*. Cambridge, UK: Cambridge University Press, 1996.

Artan, Tülay. "Aspects of the Ottoman Elite's Food Consumption: Looking for 'Staples,' 'Luxuries,' and 'Delicacies' in a Changing Century." In *Consumption Studies and the History of the Ottoman Empire, 1550–1922: An Introduction*, edited by Donald Quataert, 107–65. Albany: State University of New York Press, 2000.

Aydin, Cemil. *The Politics of Anti-Westernism in Asia: Visions of World Order in Pan-Islamic and Pan-Asian Thought*. New York: Columbia University Press, 2007.

Ayubi, N. N. "Government and the Infrastructure in Egyptian Agriculture." In *The Agriculture of Egypt*, edited by G. M. Craig, 128–45. Oxford: Oxford University Press, 1993.

Badawi, El-Said. *Mustawayat al-ʿArabiyya al-muʿasira fi Misr*. Cairo: Dar al-Maʿarif, 1973.

Badran, Margot. *Feminists, Islam, and Nation: Gender and the Making of Modern Egypt*. Princeton, NJ: Princeton University Press, 2001.

Barakat, Hala. "We Are What We Eat, We Were What We Ate." In *The Food Question in the Middle East*, edited by Iman Hamdi and Malak Rouchdy, 7–23. Cairo: American University in Cairo Press, 2017.

Barakat, Ruqayya. "ʿAlaqat al-taghayyur al-tiknulujiyya bi-dawr al-marʾa fi al-usra." MA thesis. Ain Shams University, 1969.

Bardenstein, Carol. "Transmissions Interrupted: Reconfiguring Food, Memory, and Gender in the Cookbook-Memoirs of Middle Eastern Exiles." *Signs* 28, no. 1 (2002): 353–87.

Barndt, Deborah. *Tangled Routes: Women, Work, and Globalization on the Tomato Trail*, 2nd edition. Lanham, MD: Rowman & Littlefield Publishers, 2008.

Barnes, Jessica. *Staple Security: Bread and Wheat in Egypt*. Durham, NC: Duke University Press, 2022.

Barnes, Jessica, and Mariam Taher. "Care and Conveyance: Buying Baladi Bread in Cairo." *Cultural Anthropology* 34, no. 3 (2019): 417–43.

Baron, Beth. *The Women's Awakening in Egypt: Culture, Society, and the Press*. New Haven, CT: Yale University Press, 1994.

Beckett, H. W. "Nubia and the Berberine." *Bulletin of the American Geographical Society* 44, no. 5 (1912): 351–54.

Bedevian, Armenag K. *Illustrated Polyglottic Dictionary of Plant Names*. 1935; reprint, Cairo: Madbouli, 1993.

Beinin, Joel, and Zachary Lockman. *Workers on the Nile: Nationalism, Communism, Islam, and the Egyptian Working Class, 1882–1954*. Cairo: American University in Cairo Press, 1998.

Ben Ismail, Youssef. "A History of the Ottoman Fez before Mahmud II (ca. 1600–1800)." *Muqarnas* 38 (2021): 155–83.

Benton, Lauren. *A Search for Sovereignty: Law and Geography in European Empires, 1400–1900*. Cambridge, UK: Cambridge University Press, 2009.

Berlant, Lauren. *Cruel Optimism*. Durham, NC: Duke University Press, 2011.

Berlant, Lauren. *The Female Complaint: The Unfinished Business of Sentimentality in American Culture*. Durham, NC: Duke University Press, 2008.

Beshai, A. A. "Systems of Agricultural Production in Middle and Upper Egypt." In *The Agriculture of Egypt*, edited by G. M. Craig, 265–77. Oxford: Oxford University Press, 1993.

Bhagat, Maya, Zachary Nowak, Adam Spitzig, and Kari Roynesdal. "(Re)Mapping the Columbian Exchange: Suggestions for an Updated Cartography." *Food and History* 20, no. 2 (2022): 59–86.

Bier, Laura. "The Pleasures of Domesticity: Household Appliances, Gender, and the Democratization of Well-Being in Nasser's Egypt." *Journal of Middle East Women's Studies* 19, no. 1 (2023): 1–25.

Bier, Laura. *Revolutionary Womanhood: Feminisms, Modernity, and the State in Nasser's Egypt*. Stanford, CA: Stanford University Press, 2011.

Bilgin, Arif. "From Artichoke to Corn: New Fruits and Vegetables in the Istanbul Market (Seventeenth to Nineteenth Centuries)." In *Living the Good Life*, edited by Elif Akçetin and Suraiya Faroqhi, 257–82. Leiden: Brill, 2017.

Bircher, Warda. *Gardens of the Hesperides: A Book on Old and New Plants for Egypt and Similar Climes*. Cairo: Anglo-Egyptian Bookshop, 1960.

Bonaparte, G. *A Manual of Egyptian Farm Crops and Vegetables*. Cairo: Printing Office J. Politis, 1903.

Bonaparte, G. "Vegetables." In *Text-Book of Egyptian Agriculture*, edited by George P. Foaden and F. Fletcher, vol. 2, 531–83. Cairo: National Printing Department, 1910.

Booth, Marilyn. *Bayram al-Tunisi's Egypt: Social Criticism and Narrative Strategies*. St. Antony's Middle East Monographs. Exeter: Published for the Middle East Centre, St. Antony's College; Oxford, UK: Ithaca Press, 1990.

Booth, Marilyn. "Before Qasim Amin: Writing Women's History in 1890s Egypt." In *The Long 1890s in Egypt: Colonial Quiescence, Subterranean Resistance*, edited by Marilyn Booth and Anthony Gorman, 365–98. Edinburgh: Edinburgh University Press, 2014.

Booth, Marilyn. "Girlhood Translated? Fénelon's Traité de l'éducation Des Filles (1687) as a Text of Egyptian Modernity (1901, 1909)." In *Migrating Texts: Translation and Circulation in the Late Ottoman Empire*, edited by Marilyn Booth, 266–99. Edinburgh: Edinburgh University Press, 2022.

Booth, Marilyn. *May Her Likes Be Multiplied: Biography and Gender Politics in Egypt*. Berkeley: University of California Press, 2001.

Booth, Marilyn. "'May Her Likes Be Multiplied': 'Famous Women' Biography and Gendered Prescription in Egypt, 1892–1935." *Signs* 22, no. 4 (1997): 827–90.

Booth, Marilyn. "Wayward Subjects and Negotiated Disciplines: Body Politics and the Boundaries of Egyptian Nationhood." *International Journal of Middle East Studies* 45, no. 2 (May 2013): 353–74.

Boulos, Loutfy. *Flora of Egypt*. 3 vols. Cairo: Al Hadara Publishing, 2002.
Bourdieu, Pierre. *Distinction: A Social Critique of the Judgement of Taste*. Translated by Richard Nice. Cambridge, MA: Harvard University Press, 1984.
Boyajian, James C. *Portuguese Trade in Asia under the Habsburgs, 1580–1640*. Baltimore, MD: Johns Hopkins University Press, 2010.
Braudel, Fernand. "Preface to the English Edition." In *The Mediterranean and the Mediterranean World in the Age of Philip II*, by Fernand Braudel, 2 vols. Translated by Siân Reynolds, vol. 1, 13–14. First California Paperback Printing. Oakland: University of California Press, 1995.
Braun, Joachim von, Kaosar Afsana, Louise O. Fresco, Mohamed Hassan, and Maximo Torero. "Food Systems—Definition, Concept and Application for the UN Food Systems Summit." Food Systems Summit Report, July 2021.
Buccini, Anthony F. "Western Mediterranean Vegetable Stews and the Integration of Culinary Exotica." In *Authenticity in the Kitchen: Proceedings of the Oxford Symposium on Food and Cookery*, edited by Richard Hosking, 132–45. Totnes, Devon: Prospect Books, 2005.
Burton, David. *The Raj at Table: A Culinary History of the British in India*. London: Faber and Faber, 1994.
Bush, Ray. "Crisis in Egypt: Structural Adjustment, Food Security and the Politics of USAID." *Capital & Class*, no. 53 (1994): 15–37.
Carney, Judith Ann, and Richard Nicholas Rosomoff. *In the Shadow of Slavery: Africa's Botanical Legacy in the Atlantic World*. Berkeley: University of California Press, 2011.
Casale, Giancarlo. "The Ethnic Composition of Ottoman Ship Crews and the 'Rumi Challenge' to Portuguese Identity." *Medieval Encounters* 13, no. 1 (2007): 122–44.
Central Agency for Public Mobilisation and Statistics [al-Jihaz al-markazi li-l-taʿbiʾa al-ʿamma wa-l-ihsaʾ]. "al-Kitab al-sanawi li-l-ihsaʾat al-ʿamma li-Jumhuriyat Misr al-ʿArabiyya, 1952–1972." Cairo, 1973.
Central Agency for Public Mobilisation and Statistics. "Statistical Yearbook, Arab Republic of Egypt." Cairo, 1983, 1986, 1996.
Clancy-Smith, Julia. *Mediterraneans: North Africa and Europe in an Age of Migration, c. 1800–1900*. Berkeley: University of California Press, 2011.
Clot, Antoine Barthélémy. *Aperçu général sur l'Égypte*. Brussels: Meline, Cans et Compagne, 1840.
Colla, Elliott. "The People Want." *Middle East Report*, Summer 2012. https://merip.org/2012/05/the-people-want/.
Colla, Elliott. "Translator's Afterword." In *Poor*, by Idris ʿAli, 197–203. Cairo: American University of Cairo Press, 2007.
Cookery: Berridge House Recipe Book. 10th edition. National Society's Training College of Domestic Subjects. London: Berridge House, 1952.
Counihan, Carole, and Susanne Højlund. Introduction to *Making Taste Public: Ethnographies of Food and the Senses*, edited by Carole Counihan and Susanne Højlund, 1–8. London: Bloomsbury, 2018.

Cowan, Ruth Schwartz. *More Work for Mother: The Ironies of Household Technology from the Open Hearth to the Microwave*. New York: Basic Books, 1983.

Crosby, Alfred W. *The Columbian Exchange: Biological and Cultural Consequences of 1492*. Westport, CT: Greenwood Press, 1972.

Cuddihy, William. "Agricultural Price Management in Egypt." World Bank Staff Working Paper. Washington, DC: World Bank, 1980.

Darwiche, Nawla. *Fi suhbat al-taʿam*. Cairo: Hunna li-l-Nashr wa-l-Tawziʿ, 2018.

Davidson, Cathy N., and Jessamyn Hatcher. Introduction to *No More Separate Spheres!: A Next Wave American Studies Reader*, edited by Cathy N. Davidson and Jessamyn Hatcher, 7–26. Durham, NC: Duke University Press, 2002.

Davies, Humphrey. Introduction to Yusuf al-Shirbini, *Hazz al-quhuf bi-sharh qasid Abi Shaduf*, xi–viii. New York: New York University Press, 2016.

Delile, Alire Raffeneau. "Florae Aegyptiacae illustratio." In *Description de l'Égypte, ou, Recueil des observations et des recherches qui ont été faites en Égypte pendant l'expédition de l'armée française: Histoire Naturelle*, edited by E. F. Jomard, vol. 2, 49–82. Recueil des observations et des recherches qui ont été faites en Égypte pendant l'expédition de l'armée française. Paris: Imprimerie impériale, 1813. www.biodiversitylibrary.org/bibliography/62506.

Derr, Jennifer. *The Lived Nile: Environment, Disease, and Material Colonial Economy in Egypt*. Stanford, CA: Stanford University Press, 2019.

Dessouki, Ali E. Hillal. "Policy Making in Egypt: A Case Study of the Open Door Economic Policy." *Social Problems* 28, no. 4 (1981): 410–16.

Dethier, Jean-Jacques. *Trade, Exchange Rate, and Agricultural Pricing Policies in Egypt*. World Bank Comparative Studies. 2 vols. Washington, DC: World Bank, 1989.

Dorry, Mennat-Allah El. "Food History in Egypt: State of Research." In *Food & Drink in Egypt & Sudan: Selected Studies in Archaeology, Culture, and History*, edited by Mennat-Allah El Dorry, 21–54. Cairo: Institut français d'archéologie orientale, 2023.

Dorry, Mennat-Allah El. "Forbidden, Sprouted, Stewed: An Archaeobotanical and Historical Overview of Fava Beans in Ancient Egypt." In *Food & Drink in Egypt & Sudan: Selected Studies in Archaeology, Culture, and History*, edited by Mennat-Allah El Dorry, 87–104. Cairo: Institut français d'archéologie orientale, 2023.

Dott, Brian R. *The Chile Pepper in China: A Cultural Biography*. New York: Columbia University Press, 2020.

Durmelat, Sylvie. "Can the Couscous Pot Speak?" *E-Phaïstos. Revue d'histoire Des Techniques / Journal of the History of Technology*, no. X-1 (2022).

Egyptian Federation of Industry [Federation Egyptienne de L'Industrie]. "Annuaire 1954–55." Cairo, 1955.

Elsaket, Ifdal. "Cinema-Going in Egypt in the Long-60s: Oral Histories of Pleasure and Leisure." In *Cinema in the Arab World: New Histories, New Approaches*, edited by Ifdal Elsaket, Daniel Biltereyst, and Philippe Meers, 150–74. London: Bloomsbury Academic, 2023.

Enany, Rasheed El-. *Naguib Mahfouz: The Pursuit of Meaning*. London: Routledge, 1993.

Enloe, Cynthia H. *Does Khaki Become You? The Militarisation of Women's Lives.* Boston: South End Press, 1983.

Estabrook, Barry. *Tomatoland: How Modern Industrial Agriculture Destroyed Our Most Alluring Fruit.* Kansas City, MO: Andrews McMeel Publishing, 2011.

Fahmy, Fatima. *al-Taʿlim al-manzili: al-Tahi* [Domestic education: Cooking]. Vol. 3 of 3 vols. Cairo: Wizarat al-Maʿarif al-ʿUmumiyya, 1939.

Fahmy, Fawzi R. *Some Aspects of Structural Changes in the Manufacturing Sector and Their Implications in Egypt, 1930–1970.* Cairo: Maʿhad al-Takhtit al-Qawmi, April 1968.

Fahmy, Khaled. *All the Pasha's Men: Mehmed Ali, His Army, and the Making of Modern Egypt.* Cambridge, UK: Cambridge University Press, 1997.

Fahmy, Khaled. *In Quest of Justice: Islamic Law and Forensic Medicine in Modern Egypt.* Berkeley: University of California Press, 2018.

Fahmy, Ziad. *Ordinary Egyptians Creating the Modern Nation through Popular Culture.* Stanford, CA: Stanford University Press, 2011.

Farmer, Tessa. "The Humble Tomato." *Middle East Report Online*, January 16, 2015. www.merip.org/humble-tomato.

Farraj, ʿIzz al-Din. *Mazariʿ al-khudrawat.* Cairo: Maktabat al-Anglo al-Misriyya, 1970.

Farraj, ʿIzz al-Din. *al-Tamatim: al-Banadura.* Cairo: Dar Misr li-l-Tibaʿa, 1972.

Fathy, Sameh. "al-Futuwwa (The Thug) (1957)." In *Classic Egyptian Movies: 101 Must-See Films.* Translated by Sarah Enany, 59–61. Cairo: American University in Cairo Press, 2018.

Fay, Mary Ann. "From Warrior-Grandees to Domesticated Bourgeoisie: The Transformation of the Elite Egyptian Household into a Western-Style Nuclear Family." In *Family History in the Middle East*, edited by Beshara Doumani, 77–97. SUNY Press, 2003.

Fenner, Sofia. *Shouting in a Cage: Political Life after Authoritarian Co-optation in North Africa.* New York: Columbia University Press, 2023.

Fernea, Elizabeth Warnock. *A View of the Nile: The Story of an American Family in Egypt.* New York: Doubleday, 1970.

Fikry, Noha. "Today's Children, Tomorrow's Meals: Rooftops as Spaces of Nurturance in Contemporary Egypt." *Gastronomica* 22, no. 2 (2022): 81–91.

Foaden, George P., and F. Fletcher, eds. *Kitab al-Ziraʿa al-Misriyya.* Cairo: al-Matbaʿa al-Amiriyya bi-Misr, 1911.

Foaden, George P., and F. Fletcher, eds. *Text-Book of Egyptian Agriculture.* 2 vols. Cairo: National Printing Department, 1908–10.

Food and Agriculture Organization of the United Nations (FAO). "Horticulture in the Mediterranean Area: Outlook for Production and Trade." Commodity Bulletin Series. 1968.

Food and Agriculture Organization of the United Nations (FAO). "Report of the Nutrition Committee for the Middle East, 18–26 November 1958." FAO Nutrition Meetings Report Series. Rome: FAO, 1959.

"Food Security in Egypt." Cairo: Ministry of Information State Information Services, 1977(?).

Foucault, Michel. "Nietzsche, Genealogy, History." In *Language, Counter-Memory, Practice: Selected Essays and Interviews*, edited by D. F. Bouchard, 139–64. Ithaca, NY: Cornell University Press, 1977.

Fransis, Munira. *al-Tabkh al-manzili* [Modern cooking]. Cairo: Matbaʿat al-Maʿarif al-ʿUmumiyya, 1914.

Frini, Mohamed. "Épices, Assaisonnement et Changement de La Saveur Dans La Gastronomie Tunisienne à l'époque Moderne." *Les Cahiers de Tunisie* 68, no. 218/219 (2018, 2014): 27–46.

Funk, Kathy, and Jean-Jacques Dethier. "The Language of Food." *Middle East Report*, April 1987. https://merip.org/1987/03/the-language-of-food/.

Galal, Osman M. "The Nutrition Transition in Egypt: Obesity, Undernutrition and the Food Consumption Context." *Public Health Nutrition* 5, no. 1a (2002): 141–48.

Gallagher, Nancy Elizabeth. *Egypt's Other Wars: Epidemics and the Politics of Public Health*. Syracuse, NY: Syracuse University Press, 1990.

Gaul, Anny. "Food, Happiness, and the Egyptian Kitchen (1900–1952)." In *Insatiable Appetite: Food as a Cultural Signifier*, edited by Kirill Dmitriev, Julia Hauser, and Bilal Orfali, 121–41. Leiden: Brill, 2019.

Gaul, Anny. "From Kitchen Arabic to Recipes for Good Taste: Nation, Empire, and Race in Egyptian Cookbooks." *Global Food History* 8, no. 1 (2022): 4–33.

Gaul, Anny. "Revolutionary Landscapes and Kitchens of Refusal: Tomato Sauce and Sovereignty in Egypt." *Gender & History* 34, no. 3 (2022): 789–809.

Gaul, Anny, and Graham Auman Pitts. "Introduction: Making Levantine Cuisine." In *Making Levantine Cuisine: Modern Foodways of the Eastern Mediterranean*, edited by Anny Gaul, Graham Auman Pitts, and Vicki Valosik, 1–20. Austin: University of Texas Press, 2021.

Gentilcore, David. *Pomodoro! A History of the Tomato in Italy*. New York: Columbia University Press, 2010.

Gershoni, Israel, and James P. Jankowski. *Redefining the Egyptian Nation, 1930–1945*. Cambridge, UK: Cambridge University Press, 1995.

Gertel, Jörg. "Contextualizing the Social Space of Urban Food Systems." In *The Metropolitan Food System of Cairo*, edited by Jörg Gertel, 11–24. Saarbrücken, Germany: Verlag für Entwicklungspolitik Saarbrücken, 1995.

Gertel, Jörg, and Said Samir. "The 'Search for Security': Informal Street Vendors in Matariya." In *The Metropolitan Food System of Cairo*, edited by Jörg Gertel, 87–102. Saarbrücken, Germany: Verlag für Entwicklungspolitik, 1995.

Ghannam, Farha. "Gender and Food in Everyday Life: An Ethnographic Study of a Neighborhood in Cairo." In *The Metropolitan Food System of Cairo*, edited by Jörg Gertel, 125–40. Saarbrücken, Germany: Verlag für Entwicklungspolitik, 1995.

Gharb, Ahmad ʿAtiyya. *Ziraʿat mahasil al-khudar*. Cairo: Dar al-Fikr al-ʿArabi, 1968.

Ghosh, Amitav. *In an Antique Land*. New York: Vintage, 1994.

Goldberg, Ellis. "Killing Them Softly: Dietary Deficiencies and Food Insecurity in Twentieth-Century Egypt." In *The Food Question in the Middle East*, edited by Malak Rouchdy and Iman Hamdy. Cairo Papers in Social Science 34. Cairo: American University in Cairo Press, 2017.

Graf, Katharina. "Cooking with(out) Others? Changing Kitchen Technologies and Family Values in Marrakech." *Journal of North African Studies* 29, no. 4 (2024): 575–600.

Graf, Katharina. *Food and Families in the Making: Knowledge Reproduction and Political Economy of Cooking in Morocco*. New York: Berghahn Books, 2024.

Grewe, Rudolf. "The Arrival of the Tomato in Spain and Italy: Early Recipes." *Journal of Gastronomy* 3, no. 2 (1987): 67–82.

Gupta, Aklil, and James Ferguson. "Beyond 'Culture': Space, Identity, and the Politics of Difference." *Cultural Anthropology* 7, no. 1 (1992): 6–23.

Gutner, Tamar. "The Political Economy of Food Subsidy Reform: The Case of Egypt." *Food Policy* 27, no. 5 (2002): 455–76.

Haeri, Niloofar. *Sacred Language, Ordinary People: Dilemmas of Culture and Politics in Egypt*. New York: Palgrave Macmillan, 2003.

Hafez, Sabry. "Food as a Semiotic Code in Arabic Literature." In *A Taste of Thyme: Culinary Cultures of the Middle East*, edited by Sami Zubaida and Richard Tapper, 257–80. London: Tauris Parke, 2000.

Hamdi, Saʿid. *Intaj al-tamatim*. Cairo: al-Lajna al-ʿUlya li-l-Wahadat al-Mujammaʿa wa-Matbaʿat Nasr, 1958.

Hamilton, Earl J. "What the New World Economy Gave the Old." In *First Images of America: The Impact of the New World on the Old*, edited by Fredi Chiappelli, Michael J. B. Allen, and Robert Louis Benson, vol. 2, 853–84. Berkeley: University of California Press, 1976.

Hampikian, Nairy. "Cairo: The Seen and the Unseen in the *Description de l'Égypte*." In *Napoleon in Egypt*, edited by Irene A. Bierman, 63–76. Reading, UK: Ithaca Press, 2003.

Hanna, Nelly. *Habiter au Caire: La maison moyenne et ses habitants aux XVIIe et XVIIIe siècles*. Cairo: Institut français d'archéologie orientale, 1991.

Harris, Jessica B. *High on the Hog: A Culinary Journey from Africa to America*. New York: Bloomsbury, 2011.

Harrison, Kelly M. "Agricultural Processing: Marketing and Trade in the Reform Era." In *Egypt's Agriculture in a Reform Era*, edited by Lehman B. Fletcher, 223–53. Ames: Iowa State University Press, 1996.

Hassan, ʿAli. "Nutritional Problems of Egypt." In *A Brief Review of Food and Nutrition in Five Countries: Five Lectures by Delegates to the United Nations Food Office*, by US Department of Agriculture, 6–10. Washington, DC: US Government Printing Office, 1944.

Hassan-Wassef, Habiba. "Food Habits of the Egyptians: Newly Emerging Trends." *La Revue de Santé de La Méditerranée Orientale* 10, no. 6 (2004): 898–915.

Hawkes, J. G., and J. Francisco-Ortega. "The Potato in Spain during the Late 16th Century." *Economic Botany* 46, no. 1 (1992): 86–97.

Heitkötter, Martina. "Market Reality and Food Security: How 'Marketing Losses' Can Feed the Hungry." In *The Metropolitan Food System of Cairo*, edited by Jörg Gertel, 104–21. Saarbrücken, Germany: Verlag für Entwicklungspolitik, 1995.

Herrera, Jorge Gil, and Luis F. Bernabé Pons. "The Moriscos Outside Spain: Routes and Financing." In *The Expulsion of the Moriscos from Spain: A Mediterranean Diaspora*, edited by Mercedes García-Arenal and Gerard A. Wiegers, 220–38. Leiden: Brill, 2014.

Highmore, Ben. "Taste after Bourdieu." *New Formations: A Journal of Culture/Theory/Politics* 87 (2016): 159–63.

Hill, Peter. "The First Arabic Translations of Enlightenment Literature: The Damietta Circle of the 1800s and 1810s." *Intellectual History Review* 25, no. 2 (2015): 209–33.

Hinds, Martin, and El-Said Badawi. *A Dictionary of Egyptian Arabic*. Beirut: Librairie du Liban, 1986.

Ho, Ping-ti. "The Introduction of American Food Plants into China." *American Anthropologist* 57, no. 2 (1955): 191–201.

Hobley, Rachel. "House of Meat." *Feminist Food Journal*, no. 2 (2022). www.feministfoodjournal.com/p/house-of-meat.

Hodder, Ian. *Entangled: An Archaeology of the Relationships between Humans and Things*. Chichester, UK: Wiley-Blackwell, 2012.

Hopkins, Nicholas, Sohair Mehanna, and Bahgat Abdelmaksoud. "Farmers, Merchants and Primary Agricultural Marketing in Egypt." In *The Metropolitan Food System of Cairo*, edited by Jörg Gertel, 43–67. Saarbrücken, Germany: Verlag für Entwicklungspolitik, 1995.

Howeidy, Amira. "Cooking Taro: Egypt's Famous Epiphany Dish." *Ahram Online*, January 19, 2021. https://english.ahram.org.eg/NewsContent/50/1208/399179/AlAhram-Weekly/Features/Cooking-taro-Egypts-famous-Epiphany-dish.aspx.

Humble, Nicola. Introduction to *Isabella Beeton, Mrs Beeton's Book of Household Management*, edited by Nicola Humble, vii–xxx. Oxford: Oxford University Press, 2000.

Hussein, Naglaa F Mahmoud. "Identity Politics of Color, Nation, and Land in the Literature of Nubian Egyptians, with Special Reference to Muhammad Khalil Qasim's al-Shamandoura." In *Who Defines Me: Negotiating Identity in Language and Literature*, edited by Yasser Fouad Selim and Eid Mohamed, 33–48. Newcastle upon Tyne: Cambridge Scholars Publishing, 2014.

Hyman, Clarissa. *Tomato: A Global History*. London: Reaktion Books, 2019.

Ibn Battuta, Abu ʿAbdallah Muhammad. *Tuhfat al-anzar fi gharaʾib al-amsar wa-ʿajaʾib al-asfar*. Al-Ihsan, 1904.

Ibn al-Baytar, ʿAbd Allah ibn Ahmad. *Kitab al-Jamiʿ li-mufradat al-adwiya wa-l-aghdhiya*. 2 vols. Beirut: Dar al-Kutub al-ʿIlmiyya, 1992.

Ibn al-Khuja, Muhammad. *Tarikh maʿalim al-tawhid fi al-qadim wa fi al-jadid*. Tunis, Tunisia: al-Matbaʿa al-Tunisiyya bi-Nahj Suq al-Balat, 1939.

Ibn al-Mujawir, Abu Bakr ibn Muhammad. *A Traveller in Thirteenth-Century Arabia: Ibn Al-Mujawir's Tarikh al-Mustabsir*. Translated by Gerald Rex Smith. London: Ashgate, 2008.

Ibrahim, Ahmad. *Kitab Nasihat al-anam fi husn al-taʿam* [Advice from mankind on the delectability of food]. 1st edition. Cairo: al-Matbaʿa al-ʿUmumiyya, 1893. https://digitalcollections.aucegypt.edu/digital/collection/p15795coll11/id/7501/rec/18.

Ibrahim, Basima Zaki. *Daʾirat al-maʿarif al-manziliyya al-haditha* [The modern domestic encyclopedia]. 4 vols. Cairo: Maktabat al-Nahda al-Misriyya, 1942.

Ibrahim, Basima Zaki. *al-Ghidhaʾ wa-l-matbakh wa-l-maʾida li-hayatina al-ʿaʾiliyya: al-Fataʾir al-haditha* [Nourishment, kitchen, and table for our family life: Modern pastry]. 2nd edition. Cairo: Wadiʿ Abu Fadil, 1940[?].

Ibrahim, Basima Zaki. *al-Ghidhaʾ wa-l-matbakh wa-l-maʾida li-hayatina al-ʿaʾiliyya: al-Matbakh al-sharqi* [Nourishment, kitchen, and table for our family life: Eastern cuisine]. Cairo: Wadiʿ Abu Fadil, 1940[?].

Ibrahim, Basima Zaki. *al-Ghidhaʾ wa-l-matbakh wa-l-maʾida li-hayatina al-ʿaʾiliyya: al-Tabkh al-hadith wa-l-alwan al-qawmiyya* [Nourishment, kitchen, and table for our family life: Modern cooking and national dishes]. Cairo: Wadiʿ Abu Fadil, 1940[?].

Ibrahim, Basima Zaki. *Maʾidat al-shaʿb* [The people's table]. 2 vols. Kitab al-shaʿb 12 & 13. Cairo: Matabiʿ al-Shaʿb, 1958.

Ichijo, Atsuko, Venetia Johannes, and Ronald Ranta, eds. Introduction to *The Emergence of National Food: The Dynamics of Food and Nationalism*, 1–14. London: Bloomsbury, 2019.

Ingram, Kevin. Introduction to *The Conversos and Moriscos in Late Medieval Spain and Beyond*, edited by Kevin Ingram, 1–21. Leiden: Brill, 2009.

Irwin, Robert. "'Tutuwwa': Chivalry and Gangsterism in Medieval Cairo." *Muqarnas* 21 (2004): 161–70.

Işın, Priscilla Mary. *Bountiful Empire: A History of Ottoman Cuisine*. London: Reaktion Books, 2018.

Işın, Priscilla Mary. "Kavatanın Peşinde." In *Yemekte Tarih Var: Yemek Kültürü ve Tarihçiliği*, edited by Ayşegül Avcı, Seda Erkoç, and Elvin Otman, 197–214. Istanbul: Tarih Vakfı Yurt Yayınları, 2012.

ʿIssa, Ahmed. *Dictionnaire Des Noms Des Plantes En Latin, Français, Anglais et Arabe*. Cairo: Imprimerie nationale, 1930.

Issawi, Charles. *Egypt at Mid-Century: An Economic Survey*. Revised edition. London: Oxford University Press, 1954.

Jacob, Wilson Chacko. *Working Out Egypt: Effendi Masculinity and Subject Formation in Colonial Modernity, 1870–1940*. Durham, NC: Duke University Press, 2011.

Jakes, Aaron. *Egypt's Occupation: Colonial Economism and the Crises of Capitalism*. Stanford, CA: Stanford University Press, 2020.

Jones, Evelyn G., and Helen A. Burnham. *al-Shuʾun al-manzili li-l-nashiʾat*. Translated by Isʿad Judah ʿAfifi. Cairo: Maktabat al-Nahda al-Misriyya, 1964.

Kamal, Mohamed. "al-Matbakh al-Nubi bayna al-dhakira wa-l-ibdaʿ." Interview by Salma Serry, March 17, 2023. Video. Matbakh Afikra. Accessed November 22, 2023. www.youtube.com/watch?v=unz7NLio_4c.

Kamal, Oday. *Half-Baked, the Other Side of Egypt's Baladi Bread Subsidy: A Study of the Market Intermediaries and Middlemen in the System.* Barcelona: CIDOB, Barcelona Centre for International Affairs, 2015.

Kamil, Mehmed. *Maljaʾ al-tabbakhin* [The refuge of chefs]. Translated by Muhammad Sidqi. Cairo: al-Matbaʿa al-ʿAmira al-Sharfiyya, 1915.

Kanjilal, Sucharita. "Beyond Bourdieu: What Tomatoes in Indian Recipes Tell Us about 'Taste.'" *Gastronomica* 21, no. 3 (2021): 1–12.

Kaplan, Amy. "Manifest Domesticity." In *No More Separate Spheres!: A Next Wave American Studies Reader*, edited by Cathy N. Davidson and Jessamyn Hatcher, 183–207. Durham, NC: Duke University Press, 2002.

Kashdan, Harry Eli. "Anglophone Cookbooks and the Making of the Mediterranean." *Food and Foodways* 25, no. 1 (2017): 1–19.

Kattan, Fadi. "Ode to My Grandmothers." Interview by Anastasia Miari, February 16, 2024. https://matriarcheats.substack.com/p/ode-to-my-grandmothers-interview.

Katz, Marion Holmes. *Wives and Work: Islamic Law and Ethics before Modernity.* New York: Columbia University Press, 2022.

Khaled, Sohila. "Making Mahshi." *ArabLit Quarterly* (Summer 2021): 41–48.

King, Michelle T. Introduction to *Culinary Nationalism in Asia*, edited by Michelle T. King, 1–20. London: Bloomsbury, 2019.

Klein, Lauren F. *An Archive of Taste: Race and Eating in the Early United States.* Baltimore, MD: Project Muse, 2020.

Klunzinger, C. B. *Upper Egypt: Its People and Its Products.* New York: Scribner, Armstrong, 1878.

Kolb, Carolyn. "Okra." In *The New Encyclopedia of Southern Culture: Foodways*, edited by John T. Edge, vol. 7, 206–7. Chapel Hill: University of North Carolina Press, 2007.

Konrad, Felix. "Global and Local Patterns of Communication at the Court of the Egyptian Khedives (1840–1880)." In *Court Cultures in the Muslim World: 7th to 19th Centuries*, edited by Albrecht Fuess and Jan-Peter Hartung, 235–58. New York: Routledge, 2011.

Kreklau, Claudia. "Neither Gendered nor a Room: The Kitchen in Central Europe and the Masculinization of Modernity, 1800–1900." *Global Food History* 7, no. 1 (2021): 5–35.

La Berge, Ann F. "How the Ideology of Low Fat Conquered America." *Journal of the History of Medicine and Allied Sciences* 63, no. 2 (2008): 139–77.

Lane, Edward William. *An Account of the Manners and Customs of the Modern Egyptians*, 3rd edition. London: Knight & Co, 1846.

Lane, Edward William, and Stanley Lane-Poole. *Arabic-English Lexicon.* Cambridge, UK: Islamic Texts Society, 1984.

Larkin, Brian. *Signal and Noise: Media, Infrastructure, and Urban Culture in Nigeria.* Durham, NC: Duke University Press, 2008.

Latham, John Derek. "Towards a Study of Andalusian Immigration and Its Place in Tunisian History." *Les Cahiers de Tunisie: Revue Des Sciences Humaines* 19–20 (1957): 203–49.

Laudan, Rachel. *Cuisine and Empire: Cooking in World History*. Berkeley: University of California Press, 2013.

Laudan, Rachel. "Slow Food: The French Terroir Strategy, and Culinary Modernism: An Essay Review." *Food, Culture & Society* 7, no. 2 (2004): 133–44.

Leong-Salobir, Cecilia. *Food Culture in Colonial Asia: A Taste of Empire*. London: Routledge, 2011.

Leschziner, Vanina, and Andrew Dakin. "Theorizing Cuisine from Medieval to Modern Times." *Collapse* 7 (2012): 347–77.

Lewicka, Paulina. *Food and Foodways of Medieval Cairenes: Aspects of Life in an Islamic Metropolis of the Eastern Mediterranean*. Leiden: Brill, 2011.

Linton, A. "Atmosphere and Climate in Relation to Agriculture." In *Text-Book of Egyptian Agriculture*, edited by George P. Foaden and F. Fletcher, vol. 1. Cairo: National Printing Department, 1908.

Long, Janet. "Tomatoes." In *Cambridge World History of Food*, edited by K. Kiple and K. Ornelas, 351–58. Cambridge, UK: Cambridge University Press, 2000.

Lott, Emmeline. *The English Governess in Egypt: Harem Life in Egypt and Constantinople*, 4th edition. London: Richard Bentley, 1867.

Lowe, Lisa. *The Intimacies of Four Continents*. Durham, NC: Duke University Press, 2015.

Mabro, Robert. *The Egyptian Economy, 1952–1972*. Oxford, UK: Clarendon Press, 1974.

MacDougall, Susan. "Embodying Levantine Cooking in East Amman, Jordan." In *Making Levantine Cuisine: Modern Foodways of the Eastern Mediterranean*, edited by Anny Gaul, Graham Auman Pitts, and Vicki Valosik, 153–69. Austin: University of Texas Press, 2021.

Mahfouz, Naguib. *Bayn al-qasrayn*. Cairo: Dar al-Shorouk, 2006.

Mahfouz, Naguib. *Qasr al-shawq*. Cairo: Dar al-Shorouk, 2006.

Mahmoud, Khaled. "Dashing Nubians' Hopes of Returning Home." *Sada*, August 13, 2018. https://carnegieendowment.org/sada/2018/08/dashing-nubians-hopes-of-returning-home?lang=en.

Mann, Bettina. "Food, Culture and Lifestyle: A View on Urban Middle Class Households." In *The Metropolitan Food System of Cairo*, edited by Jörg Gertel, 151–60. Saarbrücken, Germany: Verlag für Entwicklungspolitik, 1995.

Mannur, Anita. *Intimate Eating: Racialized Spaces and Radical Futures*. Durham, NC: Duke University Press, 2022.

Mansur, Hikmat. *al-Maʾuna al-manziliyya: Risala fi turuq takhzin wa-hifz al-mawadd al-ghidhaʾiyya*. Cairo: Matbaʿat al-Futuh, n.d.

Martínez, José Ciro. *States of Subsistence: The Politics of Bread in Contemporary Jordan*. Stanford, CA: Stanford University Press, 2022.

McCann, James. *Maize and Grace: Africa's Encounter with a New World Crop, 1500–2000*. Cambridge, MA: Harvard University Press, 2005.

McGee, Harold. *On Food and Cooking: The Science and Lore of the Kitchen*. New York: Scribner, 2004.

McGranahan, Carole. "Theorizing Refusal: An Introduction." *Cultural Anthropology* 31, no. 3 (2016): 319–25.

Mehdawy, Magda. *My Egyptian Grandmother's Kitchen: Traditional Dishes Sweet and Savory*. Cairo: American University in Cairo Press, 2010.

Mejri, Ouissal. "Salah Abu Seif and Arab Neorealism." *Wide Screen* 3, no. 1 (2011): 1–14.

Meneley, Anne. "The Olive and Imaginaries of the Mediterranean." *History and Anthropology* 31, no. 1 (2020): 66–83.

Messiri, Sawsan El-. *Ibn al-Balad: A Concept of Egyptian Identity*. Leiden: Brill, 1978.

Mikha'il, Fransis. *al-Tadbir al-manzili al-hadith* [Modern household management]. 7th edition. 2 vols. Cairo: Matbaʿat al-Maʿarif, 1933.

Ministry of Agriculture. "Agricultural Census of Egypt, 1929." Cairo: Government Press, 1934.

Ministry of Agriculture. "Agricultural Census of Egypt, 1939." Cairo: Government Press, 1946.

Ministry of Agriculture [Ministère de l'Agriculture]. *L'Egypte Agricole*. Cairo: Imprimerie nationale, 1937.

Ministry of Agriculture [Wizarat al-ziraʿa]. *Muntajat al-tamatim* [Tomato products]. Cairo: al-Matbaʿa al-Amiriyya, 1949.

Ministry of Agriculture [Wizarat al-ziraʿa]. *Nataʾij al-taʿdad al-ziraʿi ʿan al-sana al-ziraʿiyya 1981–82* [Results of the Agricultural Census of 1981–82]. Cairo: Wizarat al-Ziraʿa, 1993.

Ministry of Agriculture [Wizarat al-ziraʿa]. *Rusum bayaniyyat ihsaʾiyya ʿan al-sadir wa-l-warid min al-hasilat al-ziraʿiyya wa-l-hayawaniyya, 1930–34*. Cairo: al-Matbaʿa al-Amiriyya, 1936.

Ministry of Agriculture [Wizarat al-ziraʿa]. *al-Taʿdad al-ziraʿi al-rabiʿ 1961* [Agricultural census of 1961]. Vol. 1, part 2. Cairo: al-Jihaz al-Markazi li-l-Taʿbiʾa al-ʿAmma wa-li-l-Ihsaʾ, 1966.

Ministry of Education. "Comparative Statistics of Education, from 1953–54 to 1960–61." Cairo: Government Press, 1961.

Ministry of Education [Wizarat al-tarbiya wa-l-taʿlim]. "al-Maʿhad al-ʿali li-l-tadbir al-manzili bi-Halmiyyat al-Zaytun." United Arab Republic, 1959.

Ministry of Education, School Medical Service Department. "Report on School Feeding in Egypt." Cairo: Government Press, 1948.

Ministry of Interior [Nizarat al-dakhiliyya al-jalila]. "Mabadiʾ fima yataʿallaq bi-l-diyar al-Misriyya min al-ihsaʾ ʿam 1873—1874—1875—1876—1877." 1879.

Mitchell, Timothy. "America's Egypt." *Middle East Report*, no. 169 (April 1991). https://merip.org/1991/03/americas-egypt/.

Mitchell, Timothy. "The Limits of the State: Beyond Statist Approaches and Their Critics." *American Political Science Review* 85, no. 1 (1991): 77–96.

Mitchell, Timothy. *Rule of Experts: Egypt, Techno-Politics, Modernity.* Berkeley: University of California Press, 2002.

Mohammed, Wassu, Beyene Amelework, and Hussein Shimelis. "Simple Sequence Repeat Markers Revealed Genetic Divergence and Population Structure of Okra [Abelmoschus Esculentus] Collections of Diverse Geographic Origin." *Australian Journal of Crop Science* 7, no. 14 (2020): 1032–41.

Montagné, Prosper. *The New Larousse Gastronomique: The Encyclopedia of Food, Wine & Cookery.* Edited by Charlotte Turgeon. Translated by Marion Hunter. New York: Crown, 1977.

Moore, Taylor M. "Betraying Behita: Superstition and the Paralysis of Blackness in Out El Kouloub's *Zanouba*." *International Journal of Middle East Studies* 54, no. 1 (2022): 149–58.

Nabhan, Gary Paul. *Cumin, Camels, and Caravans: A Spice Odyssey.* Berkeley: University of California Press, 2014.

Naguib, Muhammad. *Kalimati li-l-tarikh.* Cairo: Dar al-Kutub al-Namudhaji, 1975.

Naguib, Nefissa. *Nurturing Masculinities: Men, Food, and Family in Contemporary Egypt.* Austin: University of Texas Press, 2015.

Nasif, Ihsan. *al-Taghdhiya al-madrasiyya khilal thalathin 'amman: 1952–1983.* Cairo: al-Markaz al-Qawmi li-l-Buhuth al-Tarbawiyya, 1984.

Nasrallah, Nawal. Appendix to *Treasure Trove of Benefits and Variety at the Table: A Fourteenth-Century Egyptian Cookbook.* Translated by Nawal Nasrallah, 647–74. Leiden: Brill, 2018.

Nasrallah, Nawal. Glossary to *Treasure Trove of Benefits and Variety at the Table: A Fourteenth-Century Egyptian Cookbook.* Translated by Nawal Nasrallah, 457–645. Leiden: Brill, 2018.

Nasrallah, Nawal. Introduction to *Treasure Trove of Benefits and Variety at the Table: A Fourteenth-Century Egyptian Cookbook.* Translated by Nawal Nasrallah, 1–57. Leiden: Brill, 2018.

Nasrallah, Nawal. "In the Beginning There Was No Musakka," *Food, Culture & Society* 13, no. 4 (2010): 595–606.

Nasrallah, Nawal, trans. *Treasure Trove of Benefits and Variety at the Table: A Fourteenth-Century Egyptian Cookbook.* Leiden: Brill, 2018.

Nassar, Saad, Fenton B. Sands, Mohamed A. Omran, and Ronald Krenz. "Crop Production Responses to the Agricultural Policy Reforms." In *Egypt's Agriculture in a Reform Era*, edited by Lehman B. Fletcher, 84–111. Ames: Iowa State University Press, 1996.

Nicola, Nazira. *Atbaq ladhidha wa-asnaf sari'a li-l-mar'a al-'amila* [Delicious dishes and quick recipes for the working woman]. Cairo: Dar al-Hilal, 1976[?].

Nicola, Nazira. *Atbaq li-kul al-munasabat* [Dishes for every occasion]. Cairo: Dar al-Hilal, 1974[?].

Nicola, Nazira. *Atbaq sari'a wa-iqtisadiyya wa-asnaf khassa bi-l-mar'a al-'amila wa marad al-sukkar* [Quick and economical dishes and recipes for the working woman and diabetics]. Cairo: Dar al-Hilal, 1977[?].

Nicola, Nazira. *Atbaq shahiya* [Appetizing dishes]. Cairo: Dar al-Hilal, 1975.

Nicola, Nazira, and Bahia Osman. *Usul al-tahi: al-nazari wa-l-'amali* [Fundamentals of cooking: Theory and practice]. Cairo: al-Matba'a al-Amiriyya, 1953.

Ohnuki-Tierney, Emiko. *Rice as Self: Japanese Identities through Time*. Princeton, NJ: Princeton University Press, 1995.

Ortner, Sherry. "Resistance and the Problem of Ethnographic Refusal." *Comparative Studies in Society and History* 37, no. 1 (1995): 173–93.

Pellissier, Marie. "Knowledge Politics, Historic Memory and the Virginia Housewife." *Gender & History* 34, no. 3 (2022): 747–51.

Petrovich, Maya. "How to Navigate the Oceans on a Tomato: Tracing the Ottoman Güveç." In *From Kebab to Ćevapčići: Foodways in (Post-)Ottoman Europe*, edited by Arkadiusz Blaszczyk and Stefan Rohdewald, 241–56. Wiesbaden, Germany: Harrassowitz Verlag, 2018.

Pickering, Charles. *The Races of Man; and Their Geographical Distribution*. London: H. G. Bohn, 1848.

Pinkard, Susan. *A Revolution in Taste: The Rise of French Cuisine, 1650–1800*. Cambridge, UK: Cambridge University Press, 2009.

Pollard, Lisa. *Nurturing the Nation: The Family Politics of Modernizing, Colonizing and Liberating Egypt, 1805–1923*. Berkeley: University of California Press, 2005.

Posusney, Marsha Pripstein. *Labor and the State in Egypt: Workers, Unions, and Economic Restructuring*. New York: Columbia University Press, 1997.

Powell, Eve Troutt. *A Different Shade of Colonialism: Egypt, Great Britain, and the Mastery of the Sudan*. Berkeley: University of California Press, 2003.

Powell, Eve Troutt. *Tell This in My Memory: Stories of Enslavement from Egypt, Sudan, and the Ottoman Empire*. Stanford, CA: Stanford University Press, 2012.

Pozzi, Sara, and Sara El Sayed. "Where Is Our Baladi Food?" In *The Food Question in the Middle East*, edited by Malak Rouchdy and Iman Hamdy, vol. 4. Cairo Papers in Social Science 34. Cairo: American University in Cairo Press, 2017.

Procida, Mary. "Feeding the Imperial Appetite: Imperial Knowledge and Anglo-Indian Domesticity." *Journal of Women's History* 15, no. 2 (2003): 123–49.

Rafat, Muhammad Nasim. *al-Taghdhiya al-madrasiyya wa-athar waqfha fi al-marhala al-ula*. Cairo: Wizarat al-Tarbiya wa-l-Ta'lim, 1957.

Ramadan, Mohamed, and Saker El Nour. *'Aysh marahrah: al-iqtisad al-siyasi li-l-siyada 'ala al-ghidha' fi Misr*. Cairo: Sifsafa, 2021.

Ray, Jonathan S. *After Expulsion: 1492 and the Making of Sephardic Jewry*. New York: New York University Press, 2013.

Ray, Krishnendu. "Culinary Difference: The Difference It Makes." *Graduate Association for Food Studies Notes on the Field*, December 11, 2018. https://gradfoodstudies.org/2018/12/11/culinary-difference/.

Ray, Krishnendu. "Domesticating Cuisine: Food and Aesthetics on American Television." *Gastronomica* 7, no. 1 (2007): 50–63.

Ray, Krishnendu. "Foreword: Food in the Making and Unmaking of Asian Nationalisms." In *Culinary Nationalism in Asia*, edited by Michelle T. King, x–xv. London: Bloomsbury, 2019.

Ray, Krishnendu. "Heritage-Making after the US Century." In *The Cultural Politics of Food, Taste, and Identity: A Global Perspective*, 254–60. London: Bloomsbury, 2021.

Ray, Krishnendu, Kathleen Burke, and Stephanie Jolly. "Food in the Indian Ocean World: Mobility, Materiality, and Cultural Exchange." *Verge: Studies in Global Asias* 9, no. 2 (2023): 2–36.

Raymond, André. "A Divided Sea: The Cairo Coffee Trade in the Red Sea Area during the Seventeenth and Eighteenth Centuries." In *Modernity and Culture from the Mediterranean to the Indian Ocean, 1890–1920*, edited by Leila Fawaz, C. A. Bayly, and Robert Ilbert, 46–57. New York: Columbia University Press, 2002.

Raymond, André. "Le commerce des épices au Caire, du xvie au xviiie siècle." In *Herbes, drogues et épices en Méditerranée: Histoire, anthropologie, économie du Moyen Âge à nos jours*, by Georges J. Aillaud et al., 115–24. Aix-en-Provence: Institut de recherches et d'études sur les mondes arabes et musulmans, 1988.

Raymond, André. "Tunisiens et Maghrébins au Caire au XVIIIe siècle." *Cahiers de Tunisie* 26–27 (1959): 336–71.

Reimer, Michael J. "Ottoman Alexandria: The Paradox of Decline and the Reconfiguration of Power in Eighteenth-Century Arab Provinces." *Journal of the Economic and Social History of the Orient* 37, no. 2 (1994): 107–46.

Reynolds, Nancy. *A City Consumed: Urban Commerce, the Cairo Fire, and the Politics of Decolonization in Egypt*. Stanford, CA: Stanford University Press, 2012.

Rich, Adrienne. "Notes toward a Politics of Location." In *Blood, Bread, and Poetry: Selected Prose, 1979–1985*, by Adrienne Rich, 210–31. New York: Norton, 1994.

Richards, Alan. "Egypt's Agriculture in Trouble." *Middle East Report* 84 (1980). https://merip.org/1980/01/egypts-agriculture-in-trouble/.

Richards, Alan. *Egypt's Agricultural Development, 1800–1980: Technical and Social Change*. London: Routledge, 1982.

Rivolta Femminile. "Manifesto: Female Revolt (Rivolta Femminile)." In *Feminist Manifestos: A Global Documentary Reader*, edited by Penny A. Weiss and Megan Brueske, 226–30. New York: New York University Press, 2018.

Robbins, Bruce. "Commodity Histories." *PMLA [Publications of the Modern Language Association]* 120, no. 2 (2005): 454–63.

Roden, Claudia. *The Book of Jewish Food: An Odyssey from Samarkand to New York*. New York: Knopf, 1996.

Roden, Claudia. *The New Book of Middle Eastern Food*. Revised edition. New York: Knopf, 2000.

Rodinson, Maxime. "Studies in Arabic Manuscripts Relating to Cookery." Translated by Barbara Inskip. In *Medieval Arab Cookery*, edited by Maxime Rodinson, A. J. Arberry, and Charles Perry, 92–163. London: Prospect Books, 2006.

Rogne, Erlend. "The Aim of Interpretation Is to Create Perplexity in the Face of the Real: Hayden White in Conversation with Erlend Rogne." *History and Theory* 48, no. 1 (2009): 63–75.

Roitman, Jessica Vance. "Sephardic Journeys: Travel, Place and Conceptions of Identity." *Jewish Culture and History* 11, no. 1–2 (2009): 208–28.

Rouchdy, Malak. "Food Recipes and Kitchen Space: Constructing Social Identities and New Frontiers." In *Cultural Dynamics in Contemporary Egypt*, edited by Maha Abdelrahman, Iman Hamdy, Malak Rouchdy, and Reem Saad, 121–42. Vol. 27. Cairo Papers in Social Science. Cairo: American University in Cairo Press, 2006.

Rowntree, J. "Marketing and Price Determination for Agricultural Commodities." In *The Agriculture of Egypt*, edited by G. M. Craig, 420–44. Oxford: Oxford University Press, 1993.

Royal Agricultural Society [al-Jamaʿiyya al-ziraʿiyya al-malakiyya]. *al-Jamaʿiyya al-ziraʿiyya al-malakiyya: al-ʿid al-dhahabi li-murur khamsin ʿaman ʿala taʾsisiha (1898–1948)*. Cairo: Matbaʿat Misr, 1948.

Royal Agricultural Society [al-Jamaʿiyya al-ziraʿiyya al-sultaniyya]. *al-Quta fi Misr* [The tomato in Egypt]. Cairo: Matbaʿat al-Shaʿb, 1922.

Royal Botanic Gardens, Kew. "Solanum aethiopicum." *Plants of the World Online*. Accessed December 31, 2024. http://powo.science.kew.org/taxon/urn:lsid:ipni.org:names:818158-1.

Russell, Mona L. *Creating the New Egyptian Woman: Consumerism, Education, and National Identity, 1863–1922*. New York: Palgrave Macmillan, 2004.

Russell, Mona L. "The Use of Textbooks as a Source of History for Women: The Case of Turn-of-the-Century Egypt." In *Beyond the Exotic: Women's Histories in Islamic Societies*, edited by Amira Sonbol, 270–94. Cairo: American University in Cairo Press, 2006.

Ryzova, Lucie. *The Age of the Efendiyya: Passages to Modernity in National-Colonial Egypt*. Oxford: Oxford University Press, 2014.

Saʿd, Malaka. *Rabbat al-dar* [The housewife]. Cairo: Matbaʿat al-Tawfiq, 1915.

Sadowski, Yahya M. *Political Vegetables? Businessman and Bureaucrat in the Development of Egyptian Agriculture*. Washington, DC: Brookings Institution, 1991.

Salem, Sara. *Anticolonial Afterlives in Egypt: The Politics of Hegemony*. Cambridge, UK: Cambridge University Press, 2020.

Samancı, Özge. "The Cuisine of Istanbul between East and West during the 19th Century." In *Earthly Delights: Economies and Cultures of Food in Ottoman and Danubian Europe, c. 1500–1900*, 77–98. Leiden: Brill, 2018.

Scents and Flavors: A Syrian Cookbook. Translated by Charles Perry. New York: New York University Press, 2017.

Scheer, Monique. "Are Emotions a Kind of Practice (and Is That What Makes Them Have a History)? A Bourdieuian Approach to Understanding Emotion." *History and Theory* 51, no. 2 (2012): 193–220.

Schewe, Eric. "How War Shaped Egypt's National Bread Loaf." *Comparative Studies of South Asia, Africa and the Middle East* 37, no. 1 (2017): 49–63.

Schewe, Eric. "State of Siege: The Development of the Security State in Egypt During the Second World War." PhD dissertation, University of Michigan, 2014.

Schielke, Samuli. "Living in the Future Tense: Aspiring for World and Class in Provincial Egypt." In *The Global Middle Classes: Theorizing through Ethnography*, edited by Rachel Heiman, Carla Freeman, and Mark Leichty, 31–57. Santa Fe, NM: School for Advanced Research Press.

Seikaly, Sherene. *Men of Capital: Scarcity and Economy in Mandate Palestine*. Stanford, CA: Stanford University Press, 2015.

Seikaly, Sherene. "A Protest of the Poor: On the Political Meaning of the People." In *The Aesthetics and Politics of Global Hunger*, edited by Anastasia Ulanowicz and Manisha Basu, 135–55. Cham, Switzerland: Palgrave Macmillan, 2017.

Selim, Samah. *The Novel and the Rural Imaginary in Egypt, 1880–1985*. London: Routledge, 2004.

Sen, Colleen Taylor. *Feasts and Fasts: A History of Food in India*. Foods and Nations. London: Reaktion Books, 2015.

Seremetakis, C. Nadia, ed. *The Senses Still: Perception and Memory as Material Culture in Modernity*. Chicago: University of Chicago Press, 1994.

Serry, Salma. "'al-Tabkh al-manzili' (1914) li-Munira Fransis: Bidayat taʿlim al-tahi li-l-binat fi Misr." *Alif: Journal of Comparative Poetics* 44 (2024): 62–85.

Shah, Ibn Mubarak. *The Sultan's Feast: A Fifteenth-Century Egyptian Cookbook*. Translated by Daniel L. Newman. London: Saqi, 2020.

Shakry, Omnia El. "Schooled Mothers and Structured Play: Child Rearing in Turn-of-the-Century Egypt." In *Remaking Women: Feminism and Modernity in the Middle East*, edited by Lila Abu-Lughod, 126–70. Princeton, NJ: Princeton University Press, 1998.

Shaʿlan, Samih ʿAbd al-Ghaffar. *al-Khubz fi al-maʾthurat al-shaʿbiyya*. Cairo: Ein for Human and Social Studies, 2002.

Shaʿrawi, Huda. *Mudhakkirat Huda Shaʿrawi*. Cairo: Dar al-Tanwir, 2013.

Sharma, Jayeeta. "Food Cries, Historical City Sounds, and the Twentieth Century Silencing of Street Vendors." *Food, Culture & Society* 24, no. 1 (2021): 16–30.

Shaw, D. John. *World Food Security: A History since 1945*. New York: Palgrave Macmillan, 2007.

Shaw, Thomas. *Travels, or, Observations Relating to Several Parts of Barbary and the Levant*. 3rd edition. 2 vols. Edinburgh: J. Ritchie, 1808. https://wellcomecollection.org/works/h9xhg8jf.

Shirbini, Yusuf al-. *Hazz al-quhuf bi-sharh qasid Abi Shaduf* [Brains confounded by the Ode of Abu Shaduf expounded]. 2 vols. New York: New York University Press, 2016.

Shohat, Ella. "The Sephardi-Moorish Atlantic: Between Orientalism and Occidentalism." In *Between the Middle East and the Americas: The Cultural Politics of Diaspora*, edited by Evelyn Alsultany and Ella Shohat, 42–62. Ann Arbor: University of Michigan Press, 2013.

Sienna, Noam. "Shakshuka for All Seasons: Tunisian Jewish Foodways at the Turn of the Twentieth Century." In *Making Levantine Cuisine: Modern Foodways of the Eastern Mediterranean*, edited by Anny Gaul, Graham Auman Pitts, and Vicki Valosik, 170–83. Austin: University of Texas Press, 2021.

Simon, Andrew. *Media of the Masses: Cassette Cultures in Modern Egypt*. Stanford, CA: Stanford University Press, 2022.

Smith, Bruce R. *The Acoustic World of Early Modern England: Attending to the O-Factor*. Chicago: University of Chicago Press, 1999.

Smith, Charles D. "Imagined Identities, Imagined Nationalisms: Print Culture and Egyptian Nationalism in Light of Recent Scholarship." *International Journal of Middle East Studies* 29 (1997): 607–22.

Smith, Stuart Tyson. *Wretched Kush: Ethnic Identities and Boundaries in Egypt's Nubian Empire*. London: Routledge, 2003.

Soghayar, Saad El. "Hamra Ya Qouta." High Quality, 2016. www.youtube.com/watch?v=3jjhcwO5I4A.

Springborg, Robert. *Family, Power, and Politics in Egypt: Sayed Bey Marei: His Clan, Clients, and Cohorts*. Philadelphia: University of Pennsylvania Press, 1982.

Stewart, Kathleen. *Ordinary Affects*. Durham, NC: Duke University Press, 2007.

Stoller, Paul. *The Taste of Ethnographic Things: The Senses in Anthropology*. Philadelphia: University of Pennsylvania Press, 1989.

Stowell, Thora. *The Anglo-Egyptian Cookery Book*. Alexandria, Egypt: Whitehead Morris, 1923.

Studnicki-Gizbert, Daviken. *A Nation upon the Ocean Sea: Portugal's Atlantic Diaspora and the Crisis of the Spanish Empire, 1492–1640*. Oxford: Oxford University Press, 2007.

Sturtevant, E. Lewis, and U. P. Hedrick. *Sturtevant's Notes on Edible Plants*. Albany: J.B. Lyon, 1919. Biodiversity Heritage Library, https://doi.org/10.5962/bhl.title.24577.

Subrahmanyam, Sanjay. *Across the Green Sea: Histories from the Western Indian Ocean, 1440–1640*. Austin: University of Texas Press, 2024.

Superbrands Brandsearch. "Heinz Egypt," n.d. Accessed July 16, 2024. www.brandsearch.superbrands.com/download/897/egypt-volume-1/68674/egypt-volume-1-heinz.pdf.

Swain, Simon. *Economy, Family, and Society from Rome to Islam: A Critical Edition, English Translation, and Study of Bryson's Management of the Estate*. Cambridge, UK: Cambridge University Press, 2013.

Tagliacozzo, Eric. "The Hajj by Sea." In *The Hajj: Pilgrimage in Islam*, edited by Shawkat M. Toorawa and Eric Tagliacozzo, 113–30. Cambridge, UK: Cambridge University Press, 2015.

Taher, Omar. "Abla Nazira: Sanayʿiyyat matbakh Misr." In *Sanayʿiyyat Misr: Mashahid min hayat baʿd bunat Misr fi al-ʿasr al-hadith*, 123–29. Cairo: Karma, 2017.

Takla, Nefertiti. "Barbaric Women: Race and the Colonization of Gender in Interwar Egypt." *International Journal of Middle East Studies* 53, no. 3 (2021): 387–405.

Talaat, Omnia. "Weeka ya dunya weeka." In *Tabikh al-wihda*, 13–20. Cairo: Dar Hawadeet, 2014.

Taymur, Ahmad. *al-Amthal al-'ammiyya: Mashruha wa-murattaba hasab al-harf al-awwal min al-mathal*. 4th edition. Cairo: Markaz al-Ahram li-l-Tarjama wa-l-Nashr, 1986.

Thompson, E. P. "The Moral Economy of the English Crowd in the Eighteenth Century." *Past & Present*, no. 50 (1971): 76–136.

Tignor, Robert. "The Economic Activities of Foreigners in Egypt, 1920–1950: From Millet to Haute Bourgeoisie." *Comparative Studies in Society and History* 22, no. 3 (1980): 416–49.

Tobgy, H. A., El. *Contemporary Egyptian Agriculture*. Beirut: Ford Foundation, 1974.

Tompkins, Kyla Wazana. *Racial Indigestion: Eating Bodies in the 19th Century*. New York: New York University Press, 2012.

Treasure Trove of Benefits and Variety at the Table: A Fourteenth-Century Egyptian Cookbook. Translated by Nawal Nasrallah. Leiden: Brill, 2018.

Trivellato, Francesca. *The Familiarity of Strangers: The Sephardic Diaspora, Livorno, and Cross-Cultural Trade in the Early Modern Period*. New Haven, CT: Yale University Press, 2009.

Tuchscherer, Michel. "Trade and Port Cities in the Red Sea–Gulf of Aden Region in the Sixteenth and Seventeenth Century." In *Modernity and Culture from the Mediterranean to the Indian Ocean, 1890–1920*, edited by Leila Fawaz, C. A. Bayly, and Robert Ilbert, 28–45. New York: Columbia University Press, 2002.

Tunisi, Muhammad ibn 'Umar al-. *In Darfur: An Account of the Sultanate and Its People*. Translated by Humphrey T. Davies. Paperback edition. New York: New York University Press, 2020.

Turabi Efendi. *Turkish Cookery Book: A Collection of Receipts*. London, 1864.

Twitty, Michael. *The Cooking Gene: A Journey through African-American Culinary History in the Old South*. New York: Amistad, 2017.

Um, Nancy. *The Merchant Houses of Mocha: Trade and Architecture in an Indian Ocean Port*. Seattle: University of Washington Press, 2009.

US Department of Agriculture (USDA). "Egypt: Major Constraints to Increasing Agricultural Productivity." Foreign Agricultural Economic Report. Washington, DC, June 1976.

van der Veen, Marijke. *Consumption, Trade and Innovation: Exploring the Botanical Remains from the Roman and Islamic Ports at Quseir al-Qadim, Egypt*. Frankfurt am Main, Germany: Africa Magna Verlag, 2011.

Villareal, Ruben L. *Tomatoes in the Tropics*. London: Routledge, 1980.

Villiers, Alan. *Sons of Sindbad*. New York: Charles Scribner, 1969.

Waines, David. "Cooking." In *Food Culture and Health in Pre-Modern Islamic Societies*, edited by David Waines, 164–68. Leiden: Brill, 2011.

Waines, David. "Ibn Battuta." In *Encyclopaedia of Islam Three*, edited by Kate Fleet et al. Accessed August 28, 2023. https://doi-org.proxy-um.researchport.umd.edu/10.1163/1573-3912_ei3_COM_30741.

Waines, David. *The Odyssey of Ibn Battuta: Uncommon Tales of a Medieval Adventurer*. Chicago: University of Chicago Press, 2010.

Walsh, Judith E. *Domesticity in Colonial India: What Women Learned When Men Gave Them Advice*. Lanham, MD: Rowman & Littlefield Publishers, 2004.

Warner, Michael. "Publics and Counterpublics." *Public Culture* 14, no. 1 (2002): 49.

Waterbury, John. *The Egypt of Nasser and Sadat: The Political Economy of Two Regimes*. Princeton, NJ: Princeton University Press, 2014.

Watson, Andrew. *Agricultural Innovation in the Early Islamic World: The Diffusion of Crops and Farming Techniques, 700–1100*. Cambridge, UK: Cambridge University Press, 2008.

Watson, Molly. "Bourdieu's Food Space." *Gastronomica*, June 18, 2012. https://gastronomica.org/2012/06/18/bourdieus-food-space/.

Wick, Alexis. *The Red Sea: In Search of Lost Space*. Berkeley: University of California Press, 2016.

Wilbour, Charles Edwin. *Travels in Egypt, December 1880 to May 1891. Letters of Charles Edwin Wilbour*, edited by Jean Capart. Brooklyn: Brooklyn Institute of Arts and Sciences, 1936.

Willan, Anne, Mark Cherniavsky, and Kyri Claflin. *The Cookbook Library: Four Centuries of the Cooks, Writers, and Recipes That Made the Modern Cookbook*. Berkeley: University of California Press, 2012.

Williams, Raymond. *Marxism and Literature*. Oxford, UK: Oxford University Press, 1977.

Willis, Virginia. *Okra: A Savor the South Cookbook*. Chapel Hill: University of North Carolina Press, 2014.

Yates-Doerr, Emily, and Megan A. Carney. "Demedicalizing Health: The Kitchen as a Site of Care." *Medical Anthropology* 35, no. 4 (2016): 305–21.

Youssef, Mary. "The Aesthetics of Difference: History and Representations of Otherness in 'al-Nubi' and 'Wahat al-Ghurub.'" *Alif: Journal of Comparative Poetics* 35 (2015): 75–99.

Zaouali, Lilia. *Medieval Cuisine of the Islamic World: A Concise History with 174 Recipes*. Translated by M. B. DeBevoise. American edition. Berkeley: University of California Press, 2007.

Zilfi, Madeline C. *Women and Slavery in the Late Ottoman Empire: The Design of Difference*. Cambridge Studies in Islamic Civilization. New York: Cambridge University Press, 2010.

Zubaida, Sami. "A Culinary History of 'National' Cuisine: Egypt and the Middle East." In *Cultural Dynamics in Contemporary Egypt*, edited by Maha Abdelrahman, Iman Hamdy, Malak Rouchdy, and Reem Saad, 143–55. Vol. 27. Cairo Papers in Social Science. Cairo: American University in Cairo Press, 2006.

Zubaida, Sami. "Hazz al-Quhuf: An Urban Satire on Peasant Life and Food from Seventeenth-Century Egypt." In *Food Between the Country and the City: Ethnographies of a Changing Global Foodscape*, edited by Nuno Domingos, José Manuel Sobral, and Harry G. West, 161–73. London: Bloomsbury, 2014.

Zubaida, Sami. "The Idea of 'Indian Food,' between the Colonial and the Global." *Food and History* 7, no. 1 (2009): 191–210.

INDEX

Figures are indicated by *fig.* and *map*, and notes are indicated by "n" followed by the note number.

'Abd al-Hamid, Sumayya, 162
'Abd al-Latif, Samiha, 64, 122
'Abd al-Ra'uf, Ibrahim, 114
Abdel-Fadil, Mahmoud, 86
Abdel-Malek, Kamal, 89
Abul-Magd, Zeinab, 79
Abu al-Sunun, Muhammad 'Ali, 64, 161–62
Abu Seif, Salah, 93, 94
Addison, Lancelot, 29
Advice from Mankind on the Delectability of Food (Ibrahim), 58–60, 169
aesthetics of difference, 170–72. *See also* culinary aesthetics of difference
affordances, of tomatoes, 144–45
afranji (Western foreignness), 183
Africa: cuisines, 113, 178; Egypt's place in, 24, 125, 155, 166, 180; Maghribi migration to Egypt, 30–31; Morisco resettlement in, 28–30; Nile Valley okra dishes, 167–68, 180; tomato's movement across, 30–35. *See also* African eggplant; Maghrib; slavery
African eggplant (Solanum aethiopicum), 48–51, 49*fig.*, 59, 65, 203nn5–6, 208n90
Agha, Menna, 171
agriculture: competing narratives around, 81–83; economic liberalization and, 83–84; land reform policies, 79–80;

213n43; tomato's increasing prominence and, 52–55; trends in tomato production, 84–88, 85*fig.*, 86*fig.*, 87*fig.*; twentieth-century cultivation data, 62–63, 63*fig. See also* integration and production; management and regulation
Alexandria: Egyptianization of shakshuka, 33–34; Maghribi migration to, 30–31; tomato's economic significance in, 55–56; trade routes, 31–32, 35, 56; use of "tamatim" in, 70; wholesale vegetable market in, 90, 91*fig.*, 92
'Ali, Idris, 159–60, 171
'Ali, Mehmed, 16, 54, 159, 194n72, 206n50
alienation, baladi as counterpoint to, 184–86
Anderson, Benedict, 7, 14
Andrews, Jean, 36–37, 200n84
Anglo-Egyptian Cookery Book (Stowell), 61, 129–30, 157–58
Appadurai, Arjun, 175
Arab socialism, 18, 79, 89, 217n111
Armanios, Febe, 173
Armbrust, Walter, 185
The Art of Modern Cooking ('Abd al-Latif), 64, 67
'assaj (cooking technique), 120, 121
Aswan High Dam, 18, 57–58, 63, 81, 82–83, 159. *See also* Nile dams

authority: kitchen sovereignty, 10, 106–10, 122–23, 131–33, 221n27; maternal knowledge, 126, 148–51; public commentary on, 95–96
Aztec people, 28, 38

badhinjaniyya (nightshade family), 4, 38, 48–52, 65, 202n114, 204n18
baladi ("of the country"): animal products, 138–39, 183, 186; bread, 173, 187, 236n29; characterized, 138–39, 182–83; contradictions of, 187, 188*fig.*; as counterpoint to alienation, 184–86; critique and, 189–90; dishes categorized as, 34, 184; as heirloom, 183–84; as self-identity, 186–87; tomatoes, 60–61, 61*fig.*, 183–84, 187–8, 188*fig.*; vegetables, 162, 182, 183, 235n7. See also afranji; samna
bamiya mafruka (okra dish), 179, 235n101. See also okra
banadura (term for tomato), 32, 60, 114
Barndt, Deborah, 4
Barnes, Jessica, 74, 75, 187, 236n29
Baron, Beth, 109
basliyya (cooking technique), 117–18, 224n91, 226n3
béchamel sauce, 115–116, 142, 147–48, 175, 224n79, 229n50. See also sauces
belonging: baladi concept and, 182, 184–86; culinary publics in understanding of, 6–9, 181; quta and tamatim as markers of, 47, 51–52, 69–71. See also difference
Benton, Lauren, 110
Berlant, Lauren, 132
Bier, Laura, 109
Bilad al-Sham (Levant): culinary category, 195n7, 205n34; defined, 24, 27*map*; links with Egypt, 31, 113, 166, 223n72; mulukhiyya in, 168; mung beans cultivated in, 36; reports of American foods in, 40; Shami recipes in cookbooks, 59, 105, 113, 116, 121, 223n70; term for tomato, 32, 60, 114
Bint al-Nil (Daughter of the Nile) magazine, 17–18, 130
bisara (fava bean dish), 34
The Black Market (al-Suq al-sawda') (1945), 95

The Book of Jewish Food (Roden), 6, 39–40
A Book of Middle Eastern Food (Roden), 5
Booth, Marilyn, 111, 186, 221n27
Bourdieu, Pierre, 227n29
Brains Confounded by the Ode of Abu Shaduf Expounded (al-Shirbini), 49–50, 156, 163, 173, 179
Braudel, Fernand, 28
bread, 74–77, 84, 88, 89, 187, 236n29
"bread-nurturing," 134, 140
British cookbooks: colonial, 61, 158; formatting of, 106, 112, 221n22
British occupation, 16–17, 24, 46, 55, 57–58
Buccini, Anthony, 29
Burke, Kathleen, 36

Cairene Arabic, 14, 47, 51, 69–70, 98, 99
Cairo: relationship with Egyptian state, 43, 47; represented in film, 93–96; usage of "quta" ("oota"), 47, 51–52, 69–70, 98; wholesale vegetable market in, 90, 92
capitalism, tomato cultivation and, 55–58
Carney, Judith, 31
Carney, Megan, 138
chile peppers: global diffusion of, 25, 37–8, 196n35; in harissa, 31; in koshari and similar dishes, 24, 42, 43; in other Egyptian dishes, 1; shatta, 169; weeka, 169, 173, 179, 180
Christianity, 28, 30, 32, 39, 59, 198n60. See also Coptic Christians
Clot, Antoine Barthélémy, 51, 52
coffee, northern trajectory, 41
Colla, Elliott, 88, 171
colonialism, 10, 102, 158–59, 190
commensality, 8, 76
community: baladi concept and, 183; commensality and, 8, 76; concept of terroir and, 5; extant scholarship, 15; language markers for belonging, 47, 51–52, 69–71
complaint, street cries as, 73, 98–100, 219n166. See also public protest
consumption, tomato: elite culinary cultures, 52–54, 72; expansion of cultiva-

tion practices and, 54–58; industry nationalization and, 81; by nonelites, 61–62, 195n12; reflected in cookbooks, 58–59; salsa production and, 66–69; twentieth-century increases in, 76, 76*fig.*, 80, 84. *See also* integration and production; management and regulation

cookbooks: domestic cookbooks as new genre, 105–6; domestic labor and public identity, 125; Eastern-Western paradigm in, 111–14; focus on urban elites, 49, 54, 60, 64; Ottoman Turkish recipes, 54; political importance of domestic labor, 121–24; "red okra" as Egyptian okra, 161–63; reflecting tomato's increasing prominence, 47, 58–59; sauces and stews in, 115–16; shifting norms around domestic labor, 102–5; stews for stovetop and oven, 116–20; stuffed vegetables and leaves, 120–21. *See also* Egyptian taste; *and specific cookbooks*

Coptic Christians, 59, 128, 137–38, 168, 173

corruption, 90, 92–96

cotton production, 54, 55, 57, 87

couscous, 23, 31, 33–34

"crazy tomatoes" street cry, 73, 98–100, 211n3

Crosby, Alfred, 25

culinary aesthetics of difference: characterized, 170–72; embodied practices, 176–80, 179*fig.*; exchanging difference, 174–76; narrating difference, 172–74

culinary care, 138

culinary nationalism, 5, 111, 151

culinary publics: author's approach, 15; baladi concept and, 182; capaciousness of, 180–81; centrality of home cooking to, 126, 131, 154; characterized, 6–9; culinary aesthetic of difference and, 170–72; political and economic influences on, 46–48; reflected in domestic manuals, 60; "separate spheres" paradigm, 7–8, 10–11, 122–23, 194n75; shifting norms around domestic labor, 102–5; state and society, 76–77, 100; street cries, 73, 98–100, 219n166. *See also* baladi; difference; Egyptian taste; geographic trajectories; home kitchens; integration and production; management and regulation

culture: alternative models for conceptualizing, 5–6; as both tradition and practice, 166; Eastern-Western paradigms, 110–13; as practice, 167–68, 171–72; as selective tradition, 157–61

dams. *See* Nile dams

Darwiche, Nawla, 164

Delile, A. R., 50

Derr, Jennifer, 58

dhawq (taste), 108, 121, 132–33

difference: beyond hegemonic narratives, 165–67; culinary aesthetic of, 170–72; culinary publics and, 6–9, 180–81; culture as practice, 167–68; culture as selective tradition, 157–61; embodied practices, 176–80, 179*fig.*; exchanging difference, 174–76; narrating difference, 172–74; normalizing "red okra," 163–65; okra across social class, 155–57; "red okra" as Egyptian okra, 161–63; reflected in language, 47, 51–52, 69–71; variations of okra preparation, 168–70

dimʿa (tomato sauce): Egyptian usage, 129; with fatta, 224n80; in *Fundamentals of Cooking*, 116, 118, 121, 225n104; with mulukhiyya, 22, 235n103; possible etymology and meaning, 224n83

Dimyat (Damietta): kitchen tools used in, 17, 33, 194n77; as major Ottoman city, 49, 204n10; recipes from, 59, 64, 112; Syrian traders in, 31; tomato harvests, 64; use of "banadura" in, 32

diqqiyya (small copper pot), 162-3

displacement, Nubian, 10, 17, 18, 48, 58, 71, 81, 171, 181

dolma (stuffed vegetables and leaves): Ottoman embrace of, 53; part of shared food culture, 52, 59, 105; recipe sent to Huda Shaʿrawi, 102, 121; supplanted by term "mahshi" in print, 114; as term in Arabic contexts, 59, 118, 120, 205n35, 210n121. *See also* mahshi; stuffed vegetables and leaves domestic labor: kitchen sovereignty, 10, 106–10, 122–23, 131–33, 221n27; political importance of, 121–24; public identity and, 125; "separate spheres" paradigm, 7–8, 10–11, 122–23, 194n75; shifts in norms around, 102–5; significance of enslaved cooks and, 158; sovereignty and, 9–11; time-saving technologies, 134–38, 136*fig*., 228n33

domestic science: Arabic translation of term, 107; curricula, 17, 103–4, 115, 123, 219n6; Higher Institute of Domestic Science (Cairo), 103–4, 123–24; influence on domestic cookbooks, 112, 115, 116–17, 141–43; training in British institutions, 103, 104, 115, 116, 117, 141; women's experience of, 126, 130, 143–44, 230n84. *See also* tadbir al-manzil

Dott, Brian R., 38

Eastern Cuisine (Ibrahim), 111–13
Eastern-Western paradigms, 110–13
"eating public," 8
economics: bread intifada (1977), 74, 84, 88; culinary publics and, 46–48; expansion of tomato cultivation, 55–58; liberalization policies, 18, 83–84; tomato as driver of growth, 87; tomato as economic indicator, 1–2; tomato pricing, 89–93, 91*fig*.; wartime price increases, 77–78. *See also* integration and production; management and regulation

education: culinary education at home, 126; school meal programs, 78, 81; for women and girls, expansions of, 17, 60, 102–4. *See also* domestic science; home kitchens

efendiyya, 13, 96, 111, 161, 193n55, 222n38
eggplant (Solanum melongena): baladi variety of, 183, 235n7; casseroles, 233n46; Egyptian cuisine and, 1, 4, 52, 208n90; introduction to Egypt, 50; stuffed, 1, 53, 121, 181, 225n108; tomato naming conventions and, 4, 50. *See also* African eggplant

Egypt: African context, 24, 125, 155, 166, 180; author's approach, 11–15; colonization of Nubia and Sudan, 159; culinary publics and, 6–9; earliest attestation of tomatoes in, 50; "Egyptian Arab nationalism," 111; Egyptian-ness as structure of feeling, 2–3, 127, 133, 151, 180; emergence of Egyptian culinary style, 58–62, 61*fig*.; hegemonic understandings of, 165–66; Maghribi migration to, 30–31; medieval okra consumption, 155–56; nation-state and kitchen history, 15–18, 194n77; provincialization of Upper Egypt, 54–55; "red okra" as Egyptian okra, 161–63; relocating tomato history, 3–6; shifting relationship with Cairo, 43, 47, 69–70; sovereignty and the domestic, 9–11; spelling and terminology herein, 20–21; text outline, 19–20; tomatoes and sovereignty, 62–65; tomato's current ubiquity in, 1–2. *See also* baladi; difference; Egyptian taste; geographic trajectories; home kitchens; integration and production; management and regulation

Egyptian Feminist Union, 103
Egyptian taste: domestic realm and public identity, 125; kitchen sovereignty and, 106–10; midcentury domestic cookbooks, 105–6; political importance of domestic labor, 121–24; sauces and stews, 115–16; shifting norms around domestic labor, 102–5; stews for stovetop and oven, 116–20; stuffed vegetables and leaves, 120–21; tomatoes as vehicle for, 114; Western knowledge and Eastern taste, 110–14

El Meleegy, Yasmine, 187, 188*fig*.
embodied practices, 176–80, 179*fig*.
embodied qualia, 144
environmental degradation, 82
Escoffier, Auguste, 141
Estabrook, Barry, 4

Fahmy, Fatima, 141–42, 169
Fahmy, Khaled, 15
fat, 140–43, 150–52. *See also* samna
Fatih, Samih, 95
fava beans, 22, 34, 168
fawazir (riddles), 89
fellahin (peasants): contrasted with middle classes and elites, 108, 50, 204n13; foods

represented in cookbooks, 59–60; forced labor of, 54–55; and representations of Egypt, 96–97; "tamatim" term usage, 70; tomato consumption, 63, 151
feminist perspectives: on historical methodology, 11; on publics, 7–8; women-authored cookbooks and, 102–3
fertilizers, 57–58, 79–81, 82, 87, 187, 212n21
Fikry, Noha, 134
film, tomatoes in, 93–98
flavor vs. taste, 132–33, 227n29
food: conceptualizing culinary cultures, 2–3, 5–6, 8, 127, 151, 181; decline in quality, 82–83; dissent and, 88–89; Eastern-Western paradigm in, 110–13; economic liberalization and, 83–84; Egyptian state and, 74–77; flavor vs. taste, 132–33, 227n29; memory and, 13–14, 176–77; as mode of critique, 181, 189–90; past-present boundaries, 151; politics of, 9–11; post-1952 food policy, 79–81; sensory and affective qualities, 131, 132–33, 136–39, 150; World War II impacts, 77–78
foreign aid, 79, 83, 84
free-market policies, 79, 83–84
Free Officers' coup (1952), 18, 79, 106
French aesthetics, 141–43, 229n49
ful mudammas (slow-cooked fava beans), 22, 168
Fundamentals of Cooking (Nicola and Osman): distinction from previous cookbooks, 105–6; Egyptian regional specialties, 112; on kitchen equipment, 107–8; koshari recipes, 42–43; on Maghribi and Mediterranean connections, 33; okra recipes, 162–63, 169–70, 173–74; as public duty, 123; on sauces, 115–16, 141; soup recipes, 185; on stuffed vegetables, 120–21; on tasbik technique, 116–20, 130; as too complex, 150, 230n84
Fundamentals of the Art of Cooking ('Abd al-Hamid), 162
Future Farms (Organic) (art installation), 187, 188*fig*.
futuwwa ("youthful masculinity"): film genre and, 95–96; genealogy of term, 96, 218n151; modern connotations of, 95–96, 97

garlic and cumin (flavor combination), 1, 42, 59, 117, 180, 208n86
gender: masculinity, futuwwa film genre and, 95–96; "separate spheres" paradigm, 7–8, 10–11, 122–23, 194n75; shifting norms around domestic labor, 102–5. *See also* efendiyya; futuwwa; housewife; women
generational difference, 70, 176
Gentilcore, David, 4, 56, 145–46
geographical difference, 51, 69–70
geographic trajectories: amid violence and expulsion, 44–45; eastward to Egypt, 30–35; embracing nonlinear narratives, 24–26; global connections, 22–24; Morisco resettlement in North Africa, 28–30; Portuguese and Spanish trade networks, 36–40; Spanish cultivation in Mexico, 28; trade routes via Suez, 35–36, 40–43
Ghosh, Amitav, 43
Graf, Katharina, 228n33
"green" Egyptian dishes, 168–70
Grewe, Rudolf, 28
Guide for the Modern Chef (al-Sunun), 64, 161–62

Hallegua, Queenie, 39
Hamdi, Sa'id, 90–91
Hanna, Nelly, 16
Harris, Jessica B., 160, 178
Hassan, 'Ali, 78
Hassan-Wassef, Habiba, 78, 168
Hawwa' magazine, 115
health concerns, 121–22, 138–40, 152
Hijaz region, 16, 31, 35, 40–42
history, culinary: author's methodology, 11–15; culinary public as framework, 6–9; embracing nonlinear narratives, 24–26; gaps in Middle Eastern record, 25; kitchen history in Egypt, 15–18, 194n77; "non-perishable traces" in, 11, 131; relocating tomato history, 3–6; Western biases in, 3–6, 24, 25, 43
Hodder, Ian, 144

home economics. *See* domestic science
home kitchens: continuity in historical narratives of, 147–48; early stews, 143–44; equipment, 18–19, 80, 107–9; fat in sauces, 140–43; kitchen sovereignty in practice, 131–33; maternal knowledge, 126, 148–51, 230n84; reformist approaches, 152–53; as sites of meaning-making, 126–28, 153–54; sourcing and processing ingredients, 133–40, 135*fig.*; tasbika, characterized, 128–29; tomato chemistry, 144–46; in understanding history, 129–31
Ho Ping-ti, 25
hormone use, 82
hot peppers. *See* chile peppers
housewife: Arabic terms for, 108, 221n34; contradictions of, 104, 109, 124, 189; kitchen items necessary for, 17–18; non-Egyptian, 129, 160, 226n124; as reading audience, 104, 106, 108–9, 122, 124, 133. *See also* domestic labor; home kitchens; kitchen sovereignty
Howeidy, Amira, 168

Iberian imperialism, 28–30, 32, 44–45
"ibn al-balad" ("son of the country"), 183, 186–87
Ibn al-Baytar, 165
Ibn Battuta, 35
Ibrahim, Ahmad, 58–60, 66, 114, 169, 208n90
Ibrahim, Basima Zaki: on baladi tomato, 182, 184; culinary critiques, 122; on Egyptian identity and Western cuisines, 111–13; professional cohort, 104; recipes without tomatoes, 169; Huda Sha'rawi's endorsement of, 103, 108, 123
identity: baladi as self-identity, 186–87; domestic labor and public identity, 125; Egyptian identity and material culture, 15; Egyptian-ness as structure of feeling, 2–3, 127, 133, 151, 180; emergence of Egyptian culinary style, 58–62; Western knowledge and Eastern taste, 110–14. *See also* difference; Egyptian taste; nationalism; social class
India, 22, 24, 35–43, 145, 175

Indian Ocean trade routes, 35–43
industrialization, 5, 18, 68, 81, 134, 185–87, 188*fig.*
inequality: in access to resources, 57–58, 71, 109–10; normalization of, 47–48. *See also* marginalization
infitah (economic liberalization), 18, 83–84, 88
integration and production: belonging and difference, 69–71; Egyptian sovereignty and, 62–65, 63*fig.*; elite culinary cultures, 52–54; emergence of Egyptian culinary style, 58–62, 61*fig.*, 71–72; expansion of cultivation practices, 54–58; post-1960 production trends, 84–88, 85*fig.*, 86*fig.*, 87*fig.*; "quta" term usage, 48–52, 49*fig.*; salsa consumption and production, 66–69; socio-political influences, 46–48; tomato as baladi and, 187–89
Intimate Eating (Mannur), 6
irrigation: competing narratives around, 82–83; impact on farmland, 212n21; nineteenth-century expansions, 54–55, 57–58; Nubian displacement and, 10, 17, 18, 48, 58, 71, 81; twentieth-century advancements, 63. *See also* Nile dams
Irwin, Robert, 218n151
Işın, Priscilla Mary, 51, 203n5, 204n19, 205n22
Isma'il, Khedive, 16, 54, 57, 58
Italy: African eggplants cultivated in, 207n63; historical narratives about tomatoes in, 4, 39; cultural influences, 24, 66–69, 210n132; Huda Sha'rawi's travels in, 102; ties to Tunisia, 30, 32; tomato in early culinary literature, 28; tomato's increasing popularity in, 56, 145; trade partner with Egypt, 32, 56, 67–8

al-Jabarti, 'Abd al-Rahman ibn Hasan, 183
Jacob, Wilson Chacko, 96
Jakes, Aaron, 57
Japan, 110–11, 223n69
Jews: expulsion from Iberia, 32, 44, 198n58; food culture, 6, 32–3, 39–40, 42, 59;

trading networks, 32, 39–40, 198n60, 201n107
Jolly, Stephanie, 36

Kamal, Mohamed, 180
Kamil, Mehmed, 54
kamuniyya (stew), 34
Kanjilal, Sucharita, 48, 145
Kaplan, Amy, 10, 109
Kashdan, Harry, 192n24, 233n62
Katz, Marion, 221n27
kebab, 54, 145, 172
Kennedy, Alicia, 9
Khalil, Ayman, 97
khichri: Arabic spellings of, 35, 42, 199n74–5; connections to Egyptian koshari, 22, 24, 35–36, 200n79; presence on the Red Sea, 42. *See also* koshari
King, Michelle, 5, 111, 151
kitchen history, 15–18, 194n77
kitchen sovereignty, 10, 106–10, 122–23, 131–33, 221n27
Klein, Lauren, 11
Klunzinger, C. B., 52, 53–54
knowledge: of Aztec people, 28; of domestic laborers, 158–60, 165–66, 189; embodied, 14, 127, 141, 150, 176–80; exchange across regional boundaries, 174–76; facilitating tomato's integration, 23; limitations of, 125; maternal transmission of, 126, 148–51, 163–64; Western knowledge and Eastern taste, 110–14. *See also* cookbooks; geographic trajectories; home kitchens
koshari: connections to South Asian khichri, 22, 24, 35–36, 200n79; described, 1, 22, 24; early printed recipes, 42–43, 64, 112, 203n133; media coverage, 195n8; possible introduction to Egypt, 24, 35–36, 42. *See also* khichri

land reform, 79–80, 86–87, 213n43
Lane, Edward, 53, 143, 156
language. *See* vernacular expression
lateral agency, 132
Latham, John Derek, 196n35
Laudan, Rachel, 5, 9
Leong-Salobir, Cecilia, 158

Levant (Bilad al-Sham): defined, 24, 27*map*; Levantine as culinary category, 195n7, 205n34; links with Egypt, 31, 113, 166, 223n72; mulukhiyya in, 168; mung beans cultivated in, 36; reports of American foods in, 40; Shami recipes in cookbooks, 59, 105, 113, 116, 121, 223n70; term for tomato, 32, 60, 114
Lewicka, Paulina, 143
liberalization, economic, 18, 83–84, 88
literal/palatal taste, 133
local foods. *See* baladi
Lott, Emmeline, 53

Maghrib: Egyptian identity and, 24, 125; influences on Egyptian cuisine, 23, 33–34; Maghribi migration to Egypt, 30–31; Morisco resettlement in, 28–30; shakshuka's association with Tunisia, 23, 29, 198n66. *See also* North Africa
"magnuna ya oota" ("crazy tomatoes"), 73, 98–100, 211n3, 219n166
Mahfouz, Naguib, 119–20
mahshi (stuffed vegetables and leaves): as baladi food, 185; category in *Fundamentals of Cooking,* 118, 120–21; common use of tomato, 114; as complex recipe, 175; flexibility in recipes for, 121, 125; as "mahshuwwat," 120; part of shared food culture, 52–53, 59, 125, 223n70; supplanting term "dolma" in print, 114; and tasbika, 128. *See also* dolma; stuffed vegetables and leaves
management and regulation: competing narratives, 81–83; competing priorities, 73–74; contestation through film, 93–96; economic liberalization, 83–84; food and dissent, 88–89; food and the state, 74–77, 212n15; post-1952 food policy, 79–81; pricing tomatoes, 89–93, 91*fig.*; state and society, 100; street cry as complaint, 98–100; trends in tomato production, 84–88, 85*fig.*, 86*fig.*, 87*fig.*; urban-rural divides, 96–98; World War II influences, 77–78
Mannur, Anita, 6, 8, 180–81
Marei, Sayed, 84, 88–89

marginalization: displacement, 10, 17, 18, 48, 57–58, 71, 81, 171, 181; normalization of, 47–48; reflected in language, 70–71; of subaltern knowledge, 158–61, 165–66, 189
Martínez, José Ciro, 99–100
masculinity, futuwwa film genre and, 95–96, 218n151. *See also* efendiyya
Mashriq (eastern Arab region), 105, 113–14, 116, 125, 162, 166, 180
material culture: Egyptian identity and, 15; industry nationalization, 18, 81. *See also* integration and production
maternal knowledge, 126, 148–51, 163–64
matmur/makmur (cooking technique), 117–18, 162, 226n3
McCann, James, 26, 37
McGee, Harold, 143–44, 145
meaning-making, in home kitchens, 126–28, 153–54
medieval period, 143, 145, 155–56, 162, 227n20
Mediterranean region: culinary influences, 24; dispersion of foods eastward across, 30–35; in historical scholarship, 25–26, 196n22; Jewish expulsion from Iberia, 32, 44, 198n58; Morisco expulsion from Iberia, 28–30, 44, 196n35; increase in tomato's popularity, 53, 56
Mejri, Ouissal, 95
memory, 13–14, 82–83, 130–131, 151, 176–77
Meneley, Anne, 154
menemen (Turkish dish), 29
El-Messiri, Sawsan, 183, 186
Mexico, 28, 37–40
middling cuisine, 9, 13
mifrak (wooden tool), 178–79, 179*fig.*
Mikha'il, Fransis, 60, 67, 114
Mitter, Siddhartha, 177–78
mobility, in conceptualizing culinary cultures, 5–6
Moore, Taylor, 160
Moriscos (Iberian Muslim converts), 28–30, 196n35
Morocco, 29–30, 59, 228n33, 236n30
moussaka. *See* musaqqa'a
Mubarak, Hosni, 84, 88

mulukhiyya (leafy green), 22, 34, 51, 107, 156, 158, 164, 168, 227n20
musaqqa'a: as cooking technique, 117–18; as dish, 122, 225n94
al-Musawwar magazine, 149
Muslims: expulsion from Iberia, 28–30, 44, 196n35; Islamic significance of Hijaz region, 40–41; Maghribi influences on Egyptian cuisine, 23, 33–34; Maghribi migration to Egypt, 30–31; Morisco resettlement in North Africa, 28–30
Mustafa, 'Abd al-Fattah, 97

Naguib, Muhammad, 90
Naguib, Nefissa, 13, 127, 186
Nahuatl language, 46, 50
Nasrallah, Nawal, 118, 155
Nasser, Gamal 'Abdel, 18, 79, 81, 83
"national cuisines," critiques of, 4–5
nationalism: baladi concept and, 186–87; belonging and difference, 47, 51–52, 69–71; centrality of domestic labor in, 121–24; conceptualizing food beyond, 2–3, 5–6, 8, 127, 151, 181; consumer culture in study of, 15; Eastern-Western paradigms in, 110–11; emergence of Egyptian culinary style, 58–62, 61*fig.*; expansion of tomato cultivation and, 55–58; idealized versions of domesticity and, 108–9, 125; state sovereignty and the domestic, 9–11, 221n27; tomatoes and Egyptian sovereignty, 62–65, 63*fig.*
nation-state: critiques of, 93–96, 98–100, 189–90; domestic realm and, 9–11; economic liberalization, 83–84; Egyptian, chronology of, 15–18; food and state intervention, 74–77, 212n15; post-1952 food policy, 79–81; tomato pricing controls, 91–93; WWII subsidy programs, 77–78. *See also* management and regulation
nayy f-nayy (meatless tasbika), 152
Negm, Ahmed Fouad, 74, 89
"new Arab home," 122
Nicola, Nazira: béchamel sauce recipes, 142; British education of, 116, 224n85; cookbook series for the "working woman," 122, 162–63; critique of tasbika, 130; as

educator, 104; developmentalist rhetoric, 124; known as "Abla Nazira," 115; on Maghribi and Mediterranean connections, 33; as radio personality, 115; on writing *Fundamentals of Cooking*, 112, 123. See also *Fundamentals of Cooking*
nightshade family (badhinjaniyya), 4, 38, 48–52, 65, 202n114, 204n18
Nile dams: Aswan High Dam, 18, 57–58, 63, 81, 82–83, 159; Aswan Low Dam (constructed under British occupation), 17, 57; perennial irrigation, 48, 57–58; raising of Aswan Low Dam, 17, 63; transformation of Egyptian landscape, 10. *See also* displacement, Nubian
Nile River, 10, 17, 48, 54–55, 57–58
"non-perishable traces" in history, 11, 131
North Africa: Egypt's place in, 24, 125; Maghribi migration to Egypt, 30–31; Morisco resettlement in, 28–30; tomato's movement across, 30–35. *See also* Maghrib
Nubia: displacement from, 10, 17, 18, 48, 58, 71, 81, 171, 181; domestic workers from, 158–60; okra preparation, 180

Ohnuki-Tierney, Emiko, 8, 75–76
oil industry, 18
okra (bamiya): beyond hegemonic narratives, 165–67; culinary aesthetic of difference and, 170–72; embodied practices in preparation of, 176–80, 179*fig.*; embodying capaciousness, 180–81; exchanging difference through, 174–76; green and white dishes, 168–70; marginalized culinary knowledge, 158–61; narrating difference through, 172–74; non-tomato-based ("white okra"), 167–68; normalizing "red okra," 163–65; popularity across social class, 51, 143, 155–57; "red okra" as Egyptian okra, 161–63; in tasbika, 128, 129; tomato-based ("red okra"), 157
open-door policy. *See* infitah
Osman, Bahia: as Berridge House graduate, 115; as educator, 104; as magazine columnist, 115; on Maghribi and Mediterranean connections, 33; on writing

Fundamentals of Cooking, 123. *See also Fundamentals of Cooking*
Ottoman Empire: culinary influence in Egypt, 52–53, 59, 65–66, 105, 112–14, 120; elite food cultures, 40, 52–54; formation of Egyptian nation-state, 43; imprecise ethnic categorizations, 200n84; incorporation of Egypt, 16, 41; in kitchen history, 16; in Mediterranean context, 27*map*, 28; "quta/kavata" in, 49, 51; response to Portuguese incursions, 41; tomato's global spread and, 36, 39; tomato's introduction to Egypt, 23

Pact of Steel (1939), 69
palatal/literal taste, 133
pasta, Mediterranean influences and, 24
peasants. *See* fellahin
Pellissier, Marie, 160
The People's Table (Ibrahim), 123, 169
pesticides, 79, 81, 82–83, 87
Petrovich, Maya, 39, 43
Philippines, 38, 201n96
pistos (Castilian dish), 29
poetic world-making, 7
Portugal, 36–39, 41
Powell, Eve Troutt, 159, 232n31
privatization, economic, 83–84
production and consumption. *See* integration and production; management and regulation
profiteering, 90, 92–96
public good, tomatoes as, 75
public protest: bread intifada (1977), 74, 84, 88, 89; through film, 93–96; slogans, 88; state and society, 76–77, 100; street cries as complaint, 73, 98–100, 219n166; vegetables and other foods invoked in, 88–89
publics. *See* culinary publics

quality, decline in, 82–83
qulqas (taro), 168–69
quta: definition and pronunciation, 46, 203n1; latest references to, 65; origin and usage, 48–52, 49*fig.*, 203n4; in Ottoman Turkish cookbooks, 54; reflecting belonging and difference, 47, 51–52, 69–71, 98

racialization, 160, 232n31
racketeering, 90, 92–96
Randolph, Mary, 160
Rawd al-Farag market, 90, 92, 93–96, 217n117
Ray, Krishnendu, 5, 11, 13, 26, 36, 172
Red Sea: in historical scholarship, 25–26, 196n22; "paradox" of, 202n117; trade routes to Egypt via, 35–36, 40–43. *See also* Suez Canal
The Refuge of Chefs (Kamil, trans. Sidqi), 54, 59, 65
refusal, in making tasbika, 132, 140, 141
Reimer, Michael, 31
religion, trade and, 40
Reynolds, Nancy, 15
Rich, Adrienne, 190
Rivolta Femminile (collective), 11, 131
Roden, Claudia, 5–6, 39–40, 166, 173
Rodinson, Maxime, 66
Roitman, Jessica Vance, 39
Rosomoff, Richard, 31
Rouchdy, Malak, 152, 221n24
Royal Agricultural Society, 57, 58, 60, 66
Rushdi, Esmat, 117
Russell, Mona, 123
Ryzova, Lucie, 12–13

Sadat, Anwar, 18, 83–84, 89
Sadowski, Yahya, 80, 83, 90, 92
salsa: canned, availability of, 135–36, 135*fig.*, 153*fig.*; Egyptian production of, 68–69, 81; defined, 46, 66; as preservation technique, 67–69; production increases, 81, 88; as shorthand for tomato sauce, 66–67, 115
samna (clarified butter): as feature of Egyptian cooking, 116, 118, 121–22, 125, 129–30, 150, 169; health concerns around, 121–22, 138–41; importance to tasbika, 118, 128, 140–41, 146; samna baladi, 138–9, 150, 163, 185
sauces: béchamel and other white sauces, 115–116, 118, 142, 147–48, 175, 224n79, 229n50; in cookbooks, 66, 115–16, 140–43, 210n125; fat in, 140–43; French approach to, 66, 112, 115–16, 141–43, 229n49. *See also* dimʻa; tasbika; tomato sauces
Saʻid (Upper Egypt): association with okra, 155–56, 166, 173; association with weeka, 173, 175–76; kishk Saʻidi, 112; provincialization of, 54–55; transmission of southern food culture to northern cities, 147, 151, 163, 173, 174–77
Scheer, Monique, 171–72
Seikaly, Sherene, 74, 108, 122
selective tradition, 142, 157
Selim, Samah, 96–97
"separate spheres" paradigm, 7–8, 10–11, 122–23, 194n75
Sephardic Jews, 5–6, 32, 39–40, 198n60, 201n105
Seremetakis, Nadia, 14, 131
Serry, Salma, 60
shakshuka: association with Tunisian Arabic, 198n66; described, 22; Egyptianization of, 33–34; in Judeo-Arabic cookbooks, 32–33, 197n41; origin of, 23; similarities with other Mediterranean dishes, 29
al-Sharif, Mahmud, 97
sharkasiyya (chicken dish), 102, 105, 116, 119–20, 225n98
Sharma, Jayeeta, 98–99, 219n166
shatta. *See* chile peppers
Shaw, Thomas, 29, 31
Shawqi, Farid, 94
Shaʻrawi, Huda, 102–5, 108, 116, 121, 123
al-Shirbini, Yusuf, 49–50, 156, 163, 173, 179
Shohat, Ella, 44
Sidqi, Muhammad, 54
Sienna, Noam, 29, 32, 198n66
slavery: and dispersal of American foods, 31; and domestic labor, 16, 102, 156, 158–60; erasure and marginalization of knowledge, 160, 226n124; slave trade in Sudan, 159
slime. *See* zaflata
slippery texture (zaflata), 164–65, 169, 177–79, 179*fig.*
social class: author's methodology and, 12–13; elite culinary cultures, 52–54; kitchen sovereignty and, 107–10; nonelite tomato consumption, 61–62,

195n12; norms around domestic labor and, 102–5; okra consumption and, 51, 155–57, 162–63; reflected in language, 69–71; reformist approaches signifying, 152; subaltern knowledge, marginalization of, 158–60, 165–66, 189. *See also* inequality
social difference. *See* difference; inequality; marginalization
social imaginaries, 7
Solanum aethiopicum (African eggplant), 48–51, 49*fig.*, 59, 65, 203nn5–6, 208n90
Solanum melongena (eggplant): baladi variety of, 183, 235n7; in casseroles, 233n46; Egyptian cuisine and, 1, 4, 52, 208n90; introduction to Egypt, 50; stuffed, 53, 121, 225n108; tomato naming conventions and, 4, 50. *See also* African eggplant
sourness, 26, 66, 143, 145
sovereignty: domestic realm and, 9–11; kitchen sovereignty, 10, 106–10, 122–23, 131–33, 221n27; tomatoes and, 62–65, 63*fig.*
Spain, 28–30, 38, 39, 44
spices, trade in, 30, 35, 40–41, 199n72
Springborg, Robert, 84
staple-status, of foods, 75–76
stews: Aztec, 28; in cookbooks, 54, 60, 61, 66, 114, 115–18, 145; health concerns around, 121–22; kamuniyya, 1, 34; medieval, 22, 143–44, 145; nineteenth-century, 143–44, 145, 156; in Ottoman cuisine, 52–54; for stovetop and oven, 116–20; turli, 54, 59, 66–67, 114, 118, 208n90; as typical lunch, 22; Western Mediterranean category of, 29–30; yakhni, 54, 65, 114, 118, 225n94. *See also* okra; tasbika
Stowell, Thora, 61, 67, 129–30, 157–58
street cries, 73, 98–100, 219n166
structural adjustment programs, 88
structures of feeling, 3, 127
Studnicki-Gizbert, Daviken, 37–38
stuffed vegetables and leaves: as baladi food, 185; as Levantine food, 205n34; in cookbooks, 19, 120–21, 161, 210n118, 210n121, 225n104; eggplant, 1, 53, 121,

181, 225n108; part of shared food culture, 52–54, 181, 205n35, 206n38, 208n90, 210n118; and tomatoes, 53–54, 229n59. *See also* dolma; mahshi
subsidy programs, 74–79, 81, 83–84, 87, 88, 214n62
Sudan, 159, 172–73, 179–80
Suez, trade routes via Red Sea, 35–36, 40–43
Suez Canal: British occupation, 55–58; British political interference and, 17; construction of, 10, 16; nationalization of, 18; Suez Crisis, 91, 214n62

tadbir al-manzil (household management), 106–7, 219n6, 221nn27–28. *See also* domestic science
Taher, Omar, 112
Takla, Nefertiti, 232n31
Talaat, Omnia, 167, 172, 174, 178
tamatim: defined, 46; reflecting belonging and difference, 47, 51–52, 69–71, 98; supplanting of "quta" term, 51, 64, 65
Tangled Roots (Barndt), 4
taqmiʿ (okra preparation technique), 162, 164–65
tasbika: characterized, 118, 128–29; Egyptian taste and, 116–20; embodying kitchen sovereignty, 131–33; etymology of, 146; low-fat approaches, 152–53, 153*fig.*; maternal lines of transmission, 126, 148–51; narrated through historical continuities, 147–48; precursors to, 143–44; as quintessentially Egyptian, 127, 131, 153–54; sourcing and processing ingredients, 133–40, 135*fig.*, 153*fig.*, 226n10; in textual and oral histories, 129–31; tomato chemistry and, 144–46; as traditional, 140–43, 150–51
taste vs. flavor, 132–33, 227n29
tawajin (casseroles), 59, 114, 117, 119, 208n91, 225n94
terroir, concept of, 5
Thompson, E. P., 88
The Thug (al-Futuwwa) (1956), 93–98, 186
tomatoes: author's approach, 11–15; chemical properties of, 66, 144–46; culinary

tomatoes *(continued)*
publics and, 6–9; current ubiquity of, 1–2; domestication, 23; earliest attestation in Egypt, 50, 52; Egyptian sovereignty and, 62–65, 63*fig.*; in everyday lives, 2–3; kitchen history in Egypt, 15–18, 194n77; as nonelite item, 61–62, 195n12; relocating tomato history, 3–6; reluctant adoption of, 24–25, 196n31; sovereignty and the domestic, 9–11; spelling and terminology herein, 20–21; text outline, 19–20. *See also* baladi; difference; Egyptian taste; geographic trajectories; home kitchens; integration and production; management and regulation

The Tomato in Egypt (Royal Agricultural Society), 57, 60, 66, 114, 184

Tomatoland (Estabrook), 4

tomato sauces: in cookbooks, 60, 61, 66–67, 114–16, 130; European, 56, 66, 68, 145–46; global history of, 39; in humble cuisines, 61–62, 145–46; rising popularity in Egypt, 52–54, 130. *See also* dimʿa; salsa; tasbika

Tompkins, Kyla Wazana, 3, 5, 227n28

trade: nineteenth-century expansion, 56; Ottoman-European routes, 31; Portuguese networks, 36–39; via Suez, 35–36, 40–43

tradition: critical attitudes toward, 121–22, 152; cultural activity as both practice and, 166; narrating tasbika as, 122, 148–51; normalizing "red okra" as, 163–65; "red okra" as modern and traditional, 161–63

Tripartite Aggression (1956), 91, 214n62

Trivellato, Francesca, 32

al-Tunisi, Bayram, 61–62, 217n112, 217n117

al-Tunisi, Muhammad, 172–73

Tunisia, 29–30, 31, 32–33, 61–62, 172–73, 196n35, 197n41, 198n66

Turkey: contemporary tomato production, 4; culinary connections to shakshuka, 29; Morisco resettlement in, 29; rising popularity of tomato in, 53, 56; trade partner with Egypt, 56; transmission of African eggplant to, 50–51. *See also* Ottoman Empire

turli (stew), 54, 59, 66–67, 114, 118, 208n90

Twitty, Michael, 160

"two 1492s," 44–45

umami, 144, 145–46

Under the Poverty Line (ʿAli), 159–60, 171

United States: Egypt's foreign policy and, 18, 83; enslaved peoples, culinary knowledge of, 160; okra as divisive in, 177–78; tomato exports to, 68

Upper Egypt. *See* Saʿid

ʿUrabi, Ahmed, 55

urban-rural dynamics: depicted in film, 96–98; in satire, 49–50; tomato's popularity in urban areas, 52–54, 72, 76*fig.*

vernacular expression: cartoons, 1, 149, 203n2; "crazy tomatoes" street cry, 98–100; film, 34, 93–98; Levantine term for tomatoes, 31–32, 60, 114; as mode of inquiry, 14; protest slogans, 88; quta, origin and usage, 48–52; reflecting belonging and difference, 47, 51–52, 69–71, 98; salsa as shorthand for tomato, 66–67; satirical verses, 89; songs, 2, 34, 97–98; tasbika as vernacular technique, 127, 130–31, 227n22; taste vs. flavor, 132–33

The Virginia House-wife (Randolph), 160

Waines, David, 35, 143

Wali, Youssef, 93

Warner, Michael, 7

weeka (okra dish), 167, 169–70, 172–76, 177, 179–80, 235n101

wholesale profiteering, 90, 92–96

Wick, Alexis, 25–26, 202n117

Wilbour, Charles Edwin, 54

Williams, Raymond, 3, 142, 166

women: adoption of new technologies, 135–38, 135*fig.*, 228n33; author's methodology and, 12; kitchen sovereignty and, 10, 106–10, 131–33, 221n27; knowledge exchange, 174–76; maternal knowledge transmission, 126, 148–51, 163–64; okra dishes for "working women," 162–63;

political importance of domestic labor, 121–24; "separate spheres" paradigm, 7–8, 10–11, 122–23, 194n75; shifting norms around domestic labor, 102–5. *See also* Egyptian taste; home kitchens

World War I, 17

World War II: British interference in Egypt, 17; impact on food system, 77–78; increased production following, 65, 69; state sovereignty and food provision, 10

yakhni (stew), 54, 65, 114, 118, 225n94
yay (wooden tool), 178–79, 179*fig*.
Yates-Doerr, Emily, 138
Youssef, Mary, 170–71

zaflata (okra's slippery texture), 164–65, 169, 177–79, 179*fig*.
Zaouali, Lilia, 145
zooq (taste), 132. *See also* dhawq
Zubaida, Sami, 24, 42, 52, 195n8, 199n78, 222n54

CALIFORNIA STUDIES IN FOOD AND CULTURE

Darra Goldstein, Editor

1. *Dangerous Tastes: The Story of Spices*, by Andrew Dalby
2. *Eating Right in the Renaissance*, by Ken Albala
3. *Food Politics: How the Food Industry Influences Nutrition and Health*, by Marion Nestle
4. *Camembert: A National Myth*, by Pierre Boisard
5. *Safe Food: The Politics of Food Safety*, by Marion Nestle
6. *Eating Apes*, by Dale Peterson
7. *Revolution at the Table: The Transformation of the American Diet*, by Harvey Levenstein
8. *Paradox of Plenty: A Social History of Eating in Modern America*, by Harvey Levenstein
9. *Encarnación's Kitchen: Mexican Recipes from Nineteenth-Century California: Selections from Encarnación Pinedo's* El cocinero español, by Encarnación Pinedo, edited and translated by Dan Strehl, with an essay by Victor Valle
10. *Zinfandel: A History of a Grape and Its Wine*, by Charles L. Sullivan, with a foreword by Paul Draper
11. *Tsukiji: The Fish Market at the Center of the World*, by Theodore C. Bestor
12. *Born Again Bodies: Flesh and Spirit in American Christianity*, by R. Marie Griffith
13. *Our Overweight Children: What Parents, Schools, and Communities Can Do to Control the Fatness Epidemic*, by Sharron Dalton
14. *The Art of Cooking: The First Modern Cookery Book*, by the Eminent Maestro Martino of Como, edited and with an introduction by Luigi Ballerini, translated and annotated by Jeremy Parzen, and with fifty modernized recipes by Stefania Barzini
15. *The Queen of Fats: Why Omega-3s Were Removed from the Western Diet and What We Can Do to Replace Them*, by Susan Allport
16. *Meals to Come: A History of the Future of Food*, by Warren Belasco
17. *The Spice Route: A History*, by John Keay

18. *Medieval Cuisine of the Islamic World: A Concise History with 174 Recipes,* by Lilia Zaouali, translated by M. B. DeBevoise, with a foreword by Charles Perry
19. *Arranging the Meal: A History of Table Service in France,* by Jean-Louis Flandrin, translated by Julie E. Johnson, with Sylvie and Antonio Roder; with a foreword to the English-language edition by Beatrice Fink
20. *The Taste of Place: A Cultural Journey into Terroir,* by Amy B. Trubek
21. *Food: The History of Taste,* edited by Paul Freedman
22. *M. F. K. Fisher among the Pots and Pans: Celebrating Her Kitchens,* by Joan Reardon, with a foreword by Amanda Hesser
23. *Cooking: The Quintessential Art,* by Hervé This and Pierre Gagnaire, translated by M. B. DeBevoise
24. *Perfection Salad: Women and Cooking at the Turn of the Century,* by Laura Shapiro
25. *Of Sugar and Snow: A History of Ice Cream Making,* by Jeri Quinzio
26. *Encyclopedia of Pasta,* by Oretta Zanini De Vita, translated by Maureen B. Fant, with a foreword by Carol Field
27. *Tastes and Temptations: Food and Art in Renaissance Italy,* by John Varriano
28. *Free for All: Fixing School Food in America,* by Janet Poppendieck
29. *Breaking Bread: Recipes and Stories from Immigrant Kitchens,* by Lynne Christy Anderson, with a foreword by Corby Kummer
30. *Culinary Ephemera: An Illustrated History,* by William Woys Weaver
31. *Eating Mud Crabs in Kandahar: Stories of Food during Wartime by the World's Leading Correspondents,* edited by Matt McAllester
32. *Weighing In: Obesity, Food Justice, and the Limits of Capitalism,* by Julie Guthman
33. *Why Calories Count: From Science to Politics,* by Marion Nestle and Malden Nesheim
34. *Curried Cultures: Globalization, Food, and South Asia,* edited by Krishnendu Ray and Tulasi Srinivas

35. *The Cookbook Library: Four Centuries of the Cooks, Writers, and Recipes That Made the Modern Cookbook*, by Anne Willan, with Mark Cherniavsky and Kyri Claflin

36. *Coffee Life in Japan*, by Merry White

37. *American Tuna: The Rise and Fall of an Improbable Food*, by Andrew F. Smith

38. *A Feast of Weeds: A Literary Guide to Foraging and Cooking Wild Edible Plants*, by Luigi Ballerini, translated by Gianpiero W. Doebler, with recipes by Ada De Santis and illustrations by Giuliano Della Casa

39. *The Philosophy of Food*, by David M. Kaplan

40. *Beyond Hummus and Falafel: Social and Political Aspects of Palestinian Food in Israel*, by Liora Gvion, translated by David Wesley and Elana Wesley

41. *The Life of Cheese: Crafting Food and Value in America*, by Heather Paxson

42. *Popes, Peasants, and Shepherds: Recipes and Lore from Rome and Lazio*, by Oretta Zanini De Vita, translated by Maureen B. Fant, foreword by Ernesto Di Renzo

43. *Cuisine and Empire: Cooking in World History*, by Rachel Laudan

44. *Inside the California Food Revolution: Thirty Years That Changed Our Culinary Consciousness*, by Joyce Goldstein, with Dore Brown

45. *Cumin, Camels, and Caravans: A Spice Odyssey*, by Gary Paul Nabhan

46. *Balancing on a Planet: The Future of Food and Agriculture*, by David A. Cleveland

47. *The Darjeeling Distinction: Labor and Justice on Fair-Trade Tea Plantations in India*, by Sarah Besky

48. *How the Other Half Ate: A History of Working-Class Meals at the Turn of the Century*, by Katherine Leonard Turner

49. *The Untold History of Ramen: How Political Crisis in Japan Spawned a Global Food Craze*, by George Solt

50. *Word of Mouth: What We Talk About When We Talk About Food*, by Priscilla Parkhurst Ferguson

51. *Inventing Baby Food: Taste, Health, and the Industrialization of the American Diet*, by Amy Bentley

52. *Secrets from the Greek Kitchen: Cooking, Skill, and Everyday Life on an Aegean Island*, by David E. Sutton
53. *Breadlines Knee-Deep in Wheat: Food Assistance in the Great Depression*, by Janet Poppendieck
54. *Tasting French Terroir: The History of an Idea*, by Thomas Parker
55. *Becoming Salmon: Aquaculture and the Domestication of a Fish*, by Marianne Elisabeth Lien
56. *Divided Spirits: Tequila, Mezcal, and the Politics of Production*, by Sarah Bowen
57. *The Weight of Obesity: Hunger and Global Health in Postwar Guatemala*, by Emily Yates-Doerr
58. *Dangerous Digestion: The Politics of American Dietary Advice*, by E. Melanie DuPuis
59. *A Taste of Power: Food and American Identities*, by Katharina Vester
60. *More Than Just Food: Food Justice and Community Change*, by Garrett M. Broad
61. *Hoptopia: A World of Agriculture and Beer in Oregon's Willamette Valley*, by Peter A. Kopp
62. *A Geography of Digestion: Biotechnology and the Kellogg Cereal Enterprise*, by Nicholas Bauch
63. *Bitter and Sweet: Food, Meaning, and Modernity in Rural China*, by Ellen Oxfeld
64. *A History of Cookbooks: From Kitchen to Page over Seven Centuries*, by Henry Notaker
65. *Reinventing the Wheel: Milk, Microbes, and the Fight for Real Cheese*, by Bronwen Percival and Francis Percival
66. *Making Modern Meals: How Americans Cook Today*, by Amy B. Trubek
67. *Food and Power: A Culinary Ethnography of Israel*, by Nir Avieli
68. *Canned: The Rise and Fall of Consumer Confidence in the American Food Industry*, by Anna Zeide
69. *Meat Planet: Artificial Flesh and the Future of Food*, by Benjamin Aldes Wurgaft
70. *The Labor of Lunch: Why We Need Real Food and Real Jobs in American Public Schools*, by Jennifer E. Gaddis

71. *Feeding the Crisis: Care and Abandonment in America's Food Safety Net*, by Maggie Dickinson
72. *Sameness in Diversity: Food and Globalization in Modern America*, by Laresh Jayasanker
73. *The Fruits of Empire: Art, Food, and the Politics of Race in the Age of American Expansion*, by Shana Klein
74. *Let's Ask Marion: What You Need to Know about the Politics of Food, Nutrition, and Health*, by Marion Nestle, in conversation with Kerry Trueman
75. *The Scarcity Slot: Excavating Histories of Food Security in Ghana*, by Amanda L. Logan
76. *Gastropolitics and the Specter of Race: Stories of Capital, Culture, and Coloniality in Peru*, by María Elena García
77. *The Kingdom of Rye: A Brief History of Russian Food*, by Darra Goldstein
78. *Slow Cooked: An Unexpected Life in Food Politics*, by Marion Nestle
79. *Yerba Mate: The Drink That Shaped a Nation*, by Julia J. S. Sarreal
80. *Wonder Foods: The Science and Commerce of Nutrition*, by Lisa Haushofer
81. *Ways of Eating: Exploring Food through History and Culture*, by Benjamin A. Wurgaft and Merry I. White
82. *From Label to Table: Regulating Food in America in the Information Age*, by Xaq Frohlich
83. *Intoxicating Pleasures: The Reinvention of Wine, Beer, and Whiskey after Prohibition*, by Lisa Jacobson
84. *The Quinoa Bust: The Making and Unmaking of an Andean Miracle Crop*, by Emma McDonell
85. *On Hunger: Violence and Craving in America, from Starvation to Ozempic*, by Dana Simmons
86. *The Pierogi Problem: Cosmopolitan Appetites and the Reinvention of Polish Food*, by Fabio Parasecoli, Agata Bachórz, and Mateusz Halawa
87. *Nile Nightshade: Tomato, A Kitchen History of Modern Egypt*, by Anny Gaul

Founded in 1893,
UNIVERSITY OF CALIFORNIA PRESS
publishes bold, progressive books and journals
on topics in the arts, humanities, social sciences,
and natural sciences—with a focus on social
justice issues—that inspire thought and action
among readers worldwide.

The UC PRESS FOUNDATION
raises funds to uphold the press's vital role
as an independent, nonprofit publisher, and
receives philanthropic support from a wide
range of individuals and institutions—and from
committed readers like you. To learn more, visit
ucpress.edu/supportus.